D1634174

WITHDRAWN

LIVERPOOL JMU LIBRARY

3 1111 01369 0001

MURDER, MEDICINE AND MOTHERHOOD

Since the early 1990s, unexplained infant death has been reformulated as a criminal justice problem within many Western societies. This shift has produced wrongful convictions in more than one jurisdiction. This book uses a detailed case study of the murder trial and appeals of Kathleen Folbigg to examine the pragmatics of proof beyond a reasonable doubt. It explores how legal processes, medical knowledge and expectations of motherhood work together when mothers are charged with killing infants who have died in mysterious circumstances. The author argues that Folbigg, who remains in prison, was wrongly convicted.

The book also employs Folbigg's trial and appeals to consider what lessons courts have learned from prior wrongful convictions, such as those of Sally Clark and Angela Cannings. The author's research demonstrates that the *Folbigg* court was misled about the state of medical knowledge regarding infant death, and the case proceeded on the incorrect assumption that behavioural and scientific evidence provide independent proofs of guilt. Individual chapters critically assess the relationships between medical research and expert testimony; unexamined cultural assumptions about good mothering; and the manner in which contested cases are reported by the press.

Murder, Medicine and Motherhood

EMMA CUNLIFFE

·HART·
PUBLISHING
OXFORD AND PORTLAND, OREGON
2011

Published in the United Kingdom by
Hart Publishing Ltd
16C Worcester Place
Oxford
OX1 2JW
Tel: +44 (0)1865 517530
Fax: +44 (0)1865 510710
Email: mail@hartpub.co.uk
http://www.hartpub.co.uk

Published in North America (US and Canada) by
Hart Publishing
c/o International Specialized Book Services
920 NE 58th Avenue, Suite 300
Portland, OR
97213-3786
USA
Tel: +1-503-287-3093 or toll-free: 1-800-944-6190
Fax: +1-503-280-8832
Email: orders@isbs.com
http://www.isbs.com

© Emma Cunliffe 2011

Emma Cunliffe has asserted her right under the Copyright, Designs and Patents Act 1988,
to be identified as the author of this work.

All rights reserved. No part of this publication may be reproduced, stored in a retrieval system,
or transmitted, in any form or by any means, without the prior permission of Hart Publishing,
or as expressly permitted by law or under the terms agreed with the appropriate reprographic
rights organisation. Enquiries concerning reproduction which may not be covered by the above
should be addressed to Hart Publishing Ltd at the address above.

British Library Cataloguing in Publication Data
Data Available

ISBN: 978-1-84946-157-3

Typeset by Hope Services Ltd, Abingdon
Printed and bound in Great Britain by
TJ International Ltd, Padstow, Cornwall

ACKNOWLEDGEMENTS

This book is based on my PhD dissertation, which was completed at the University of British Columbia Faculty of Law. Financial assistance from the UBC Hampton Fund allowed me to complete my research. My PhD supervisor, Susan Boyd, and my other committee members – Christine Boyle, Dorothy Chunn and Wesley Pue – helped me in every conceivable way. My research assistants, Christina Cabulea, Elspeth Kaiser-Derrick, Yun Li and Ashleigh Keall modelled diligence, good humour and persistence throughout the project. Their work was supported by financial assistance from the UBC Faculty of Law. The staff members at the Court Registry of the Supreme Court of New South Wales were tremendously helpful while I was conducting my court record research. I also gratefully acknowledge the expert guidance provided by the editorial and production team at Hart, particularly the deft touch of their fabulous copyeditor, Lisa Gourd.

Thank you to my family, who have supported me throughout my research, even when it took me half a world away from them. Thank you to Ian, who wisely didn't believe me when I said I was almost done but helped me to get on with it anyway.

This book is dedicated to my father, who taught me my first and best lessons about law and justice.

TABLE OF CONTENTS

TABLE OF CASES

TABLE OF LEGISLATION

LIST OF ILLUSTRATIONS

1

Introduction

That life is complicated is a fact of great analytic importance. Law too often seeks to avoid this truth by making up its own breed of narrower, simpler, but hypnotically powerful rhetorical truths. Acknowledging, challenging, playing with these *as* rhetorical gestures is, it seems to me, necessary for any conception of justice.

PJ Williams, *The Alchemy of Race and Rights*[1]

WHEN KATHLEEN FOLBIGG was convicted in the New South Wales (NSW) Supreme Court of killing her four infants,[2] most commentators characterised the case as simple – even if her motives seemed incomprehensible. She is evil, suggested the popular Sydney newspaper the *Daily Telegraph*.[3] She is incapable of love, confirmed the rival broadsheet newspaper, the *Sydney Morning Herald*.[4] Both newspapers reported that Kathleen Folbigg's father had killed her mother when Folbigg was a little girl, as if that explained something important about the case.[5]

Trial and appellate judges who sat on the case were satisfied with the jury's verdict. The Trial Judge characterised the case as one in which there was 'no question about the offender's responsibility for killing her children'.[6] The Appeal Court agreed that the evidence against Folbigg was 'overwhelming'.[7] Sully J held that the possibility that the Folbigg infants died of natural causes was 'a debating point' and not a reasonable basis for doubt.[8] The High Court of Australia dismissed Folbigg's applications to argue the case further, pointing to the strength of the adverse inferences that could be drawn from the accused's diary entries.[9] A further appeal that was predicated on jury irregularities was also dismissed.[10]

---

[1] (Cambridge, Harvard University Press, 1991) 10.

[2] *R v Folbigg* [2003] NSWSC 895 (24 October 2003).

[3] Editorial, 'The Depths of Sadness, Seeds of Evil, a Quiet Peace' *Daily Telegraph* (Sydney, 22 May 2003) 30.

[4] L Glendinning, 'Incapable of Love, Compelled to Kill: The Diaries of a Tortured Mother' *Sydney Morning Herald* (25–26 October 2003) 1.

[5] L Knowles, 'This Pretty Little Girl Grew Up to Be a Killer' *Daily Telegraph* (Sydney, 24 May 2003) 22; L Glendinning, 'Dead by Their Mother's Hand' *Sydney Morning Herald* (22 May 2003) 1.

[6] *R v Folbigg* (above n 2) sentencing decision, para 59 (Barr J).

[7] *R v KF* (2005) 152 A Crim R 35, [2005] NSWCCA 23 (17 February 2005).

[8] Ibid (conviction and sentencing appeal), para 143.

[9] *Folbigg v The Queen* [2005] HCA Trans 657.

[10] *Kathleen Folbigg v R* [2007] NSWCCA 371 (21 December 2007).

Within law's categories and within the flattened morality of the daily press, the *Folbigg* case was fairly easily disposed of. Yet Folbigg continues to insist upon her innocence:

> I'm simply waiting for the truth to be seen or uncovered or proven etc. That day I shall not gloat, or say, 'I told you so' I'll simply cry and keep crying all the tears that are due to me.[11]

A convicted offender who continues to proclaim her innocence is not extraordinary. Still, *Folbigg* is an important case. Folbigg's conviction stands after other convictions very like hers have been overturned. Folbigg's case is also identifiably different from those that were overturned, as successive appeal court judges have emphasised.

In this book, I suggest that Folbigg has been wrongly convicted of killing her children. However, I cannot say how the Folbigg children died. Given the passage of time and uncertainties within the evidence, I do not venture that I have uncovered the truth that Folbigg waits for. To write this story as one of factual innocence vindicated would oversimplify it as much as the narratives of guilt that are most often constructed around Folbigg. Instead, I ask what constituted proof beyond a reasonable doubt in Folbigg's case and position that proof within the social and medical context from which it arose. Ultimately, I question the sufficiency of that proof. Folbigg lived a complicated emotional life. Her guilt was ascertained through a web of medical and social knowledges about motherhood and infant death. This is not a case that accurately lends itself to easy answers. For that reason, the story of Folbigg's prosecution helps to illuminate some of the most difficult questions about the place and function of criminal responsibility in contemporary neoliberal society.

Academic commentary on child homicide often remarks that it is difficult to persuade sceptical judges and jurors that a mother has killed her children.[12] Seemingly contradicting this assertion, a number of recent wrongful convictions of mothers suggests that prosecutors and courts may, for a period of time, have been too ready to accept allegations of homicide.[13] Throughout this book, I seek to make sense of the dissonance between widely asserted difficulties of proving child homicide and these wrongful convictions. Clear cases of child homicide

---

[11] Kathleen Folbigg, letter quoted in R Jackson, *Inside Their Minds: Australian Criminals* (Sydney, Allen & Unwin, 2008) 153. In this extract, as elsewhere, Kathleen Folbigg's text is reproduced exactly as it appeared in the original document. In particular, unconventional spelling, grammar and usage are not marked by 'sic'.

[12] See, eg, MA Prentice, 'Prosecuting Mothers who Maim and Kill: The Profile of Munchausen Syndrome by Proxy Litigation in the Late 1990's' (2001) 28(3) *American Journal of Criminal Law* 373; A Wilczynski, *Child Homicide* (London, Greenwich Medical Media, 1997) 33–34; K Polk and C Alder, *Child Victims of Homicide* (Cambridge, Cambridge University Press, 2001) 5–9; AW Craft and DMB Hall, 'Munchausen Syndrome by Proxy and Sudden Infant Death' (2004) 328 *British Medical Journal* 1309; J Stanton and A Simpson, 'Murder Misdiagnosed as SIDS: A Perpetrator's Perspective' (2001) 85 *Archives of Disease in Childhood* 454.

[13] In addition to the cases discussed in this chapter, see S Goudge, *Report of the Inquiry into Pediatric Forensic Pathology Services in Ontario* (Toronto, Queen's Printer, 2008).

plainly arise. Folbigg's trial, however, is not one of them. In such a case as hers, how does the prosecution prove that a mother has committed murder in the absence of conclusive medical evidence? This book investigates the ways in which medical science and normative conceptions of motherhood inform fact determination and are re-inscribed by the terms on which a murder case is argued when a child's death is at stake.

As I describe further in chapter two, the case against Folbigg was predicated on the argument that four infants born to Kathleen and Craig Folbigg, who died successively over the course of a decade, were killed by smothering. As primary caregiver, Kathleen was the only person who had the opportunity to kill the infants. Each child's death was investigated at the time of death, and each of the first three deaths was ascribed to natural causes. In two cases, an autopsy attributed sudden infant death syndrome (SIDS) as the cause of death. One death was ascribed to complications from epilepsy. The fourth and final death was ruled 'undetermined' by the investigating pathologist, with a note that myocarditis, a natural heart disease, was a possible cause of death.

The case for convicting Folbigg accordingly depended to a considerable extent on the capacity of medical science to distinguish between natural causes and smothering in a given infant's death. In chapters three and four, I assess whether this distinction can be reliably drawn, given the current state of knowledge within pathology and cognate fields. While research into SIDS has progressed considerably since the 1950s, and autopsy protocols have also improved, the most rigorous research demonstrates that it is not possible to distinguish between smothering and natural causes of death, including SIDS, in very young infants unless there are positive physical signs of smothering. No such signs were found on any Folbigg infant. This indistinguishability persists in a case in which multiple children have died within a single family. Expert evidence to this effect has been accepted in a number of Australian and English courts, in judgments discussed later in this chapter. In chapter five, I demonstrate that experts offered competing interpretations of the Folbigg children's deaths, but the medical research on infant death was not adequately reflected within the expert testimony at Folbigg's trial.

Despite the work done by the prosecution to exclude alternative causes of death, there was real expert disagreement at trial about cause of death in each of the Folbigg children. Accordingly, the case against Folbigg also depended to a marked extent on the argument that Folbigg was a demonstrably unfit mother. Normative conceptions of motherhood provided a means by which to resolve any residual uncertainty. The logic adopted (consciously or not) in *Folbigg* and in similar cases was that a mother who is identifiably inadequate is more likely to kill her children. There was no evidence that any of the Folbigg children were physically abused during their lives or that they were malnourished or neglected. No medical doctor, nurse or friend saw any sign of abuse, neglect or aversion in the children. However, Folbigg's husband testified that Folbigg was frequently impatient and occasionally physically rough with the children. This testimony was supported to some extent by evidence given by Folbigg's foster sister. In chapter six I explore the effect of this testimony and its relationship with normative expectations of motherhood. Chapter seven considers the manner in which the prosecution made use of diaries kept by Folbigg during her children's lives. I suggest that the defence faced a challenging task in explaining nuanced distinctions between self-blame and criminal guilt, emotion and action, to counter prosecution submissions about the meaning of these diaries.

I regard *Folbigg* as a 'telling instance' in the contemporary criminalisation of mothers. Peter Fitzpatrick explains:

> The telling instance is a text or situation embedding a reiterative concern of the modern period. It manifests not only a persistent irresolution but also a constant demand for resolution, and indeed it can be most telling when what is offered is an anfractuous[14] resolution. . . [T]he telling instance is the symptom of an obsession. All of which places texts dealt with like this in a somewhat ambiguous position. They are at one and the same time evidence and authority. As cogent evidence, the telling text has to be one which has achieved a significant purchase, a palpable authority. . .[15]

In some ways, the *Folbigg* case has the potential to tell us far more about our cultural expectations of motherhood and the faith we place in the twinned institutions of criminal trials and forensic science than about Folbigg herself.[16] The case symbolises an obsession with the need to understand how and why infants die, a persistent sense that malevolent mothering is at the heart of the problem of unexplained infant death, and a cultural faith in the criminal justice system's truthfinding capability. Throughout Folbigg's trial, both parties resisted the possibility that some questions have no clear answers. The circuitous resolution apparent within the eventual judgments was to construct a monstrously guilty mother, whose manifest consciousness of her own wrongful actions removed any residual doubt about the medical experts' capacity to identify how her children died.

I document the process of constructing Folbigg's guilt in order to understand how an overwhelming criminal case was established and maintained in a time of medical controversy and despite concerns about wrongful convictions in other, similar cases. This introduction describes several cases in which mothers have been wrongly convicted and/or wrongly accused of murdering infants and identifies the legal principles emerging from these cases.

---

[14] The *Oxford English Dictionary* defines 'anfractuous' as 'winding, sinuous, involved; roundabout, circuitous; spiral': 2nd edn (Oxford, Oxford University Press, 1989), www.oed.com.

[15] P Fitzpatrick, *Modernism and the Grounds of Law* (Cambridge, Cambridge University Press, 2001) 4.

[16] Wesley Pue argues that we often learn more about present collective identity from our shared stories than we do about the people those stories concern. WW Pue, 'In Pursuit of Better Myth: Lawyers' Histories and Histories of Lawyers' (1995) 33 *Alberta Law Review* 730–67.

I. The Immediate Legal Context of *Folbigg*

Chapters three and four of this book describe the shifting scientific understanding of unexpected infant death between 1950 and 2008. These chapters demonstrate that Folbigg was prosecuted at a moment when many paediatric forensic pathologists adhered to the belief that multiple unexplained infant deaths within a single family constituted proof, without additional evidence, of homicide. This belief was always contested within its field and has now largely abated. Folbigg's case was not, however, the only one prosecuted during the period when a punitive interpretation of multiple unexplained infant deaths was ascendant within medical science. In this section, I describe five other cases prosecuted against mothers between 1998 and 2008 in which the fact of multiple unexplained infant deaths was an element of the prosecution, and in which there was no confession or direct physical evidence of harm caused by parent to child. In each of these cases, the court ultimately concluded that expert evidence offered in support of the prosecution was predicated on an empirically unsupported belief that recurrent infant deaths within a single family were ipso facto homicides.

Read together, the five cases *Phillips, Matthey, Clark, Cannings* and *Anthony*[17] sound a warning against permitting expert evidence that is predicated on an erroneous assumption about what evidence might constitute proof beyond a reasonable doubt.[18] In *Clark*, the evidence was put in terms of the 'odds against' two natural deaths occurring in a single family. In *Matthey, Cannings* and *Anthony*, the impugned logic was not expressed in terms of statistics but nonetheless permeated the prosecution case. In *Phillips, Clark, Matthey* and *Anthony*, some direct evidence of improper maternal conduct was deemed insufficiently cogent to overcome the expert disagreement. In *Phillips, Matthey, Clark* and *Cannings*, the prosecution sought to rely on coincidence evidence that was excluded (in some cases on appeal) as being no more than a collection of mundane incidences of family life or contemporary motherhood.

Other Australian Cases

Folbigg was bracketed by two Australian cases, *Phillips* and *Matthey*, neither of which proceeded to verdict. In 1998, Tracey Louise Phillips was charged with murdering her son Benjamin. Benjamin died aged eight months, after Phillips found him lying on his stomach and having difficulty breathing. An autopsy failed

---

[17] *R v Phillips* [1999] NSWSC 1175 (17 December 1999) Bell J; *R v Matthey* [2007] VSC 398; *R v Clark* [2003] EWCA Crim 1020; *R v Cannings* [2004] EWCA Crim 1; and *R v Anthony* [2005] EWCA Crim 952.

[18] On the eroding presumption of innocence within criminal procedure, see generally R Ericson, 'The Decline of Innocence' (1994) 24 *University of British Columbia Law Review* 367; R Ericson and K Haggerty, *Policing the Risk Society* (Toronto, University of Toronto Press, 1997) 322–30.

to discern the cause of death but found that Benjamin was well nourished and apparently healthy immediately before his death. Benjamin had two surviving siblings and two siblings who had died in infancy, at ages two and a half years, and eight months. These two deaths were respectively attributed to aspiration pneumonia and SIDS. The Phillips children had suffered several life-threatening episodes (ALTEs).[19]

The prosecution sought to introduce evidence of the two uncharged deaths and several ALTEs in support of its case that Phillips had killed Benjamin. Specifically, the prosecution alleged that because of the improbability of these episodes occurring coincidentally, Phillips must have caused Benjamin's death by induced asphyxia. Under section 98 of the Evidence Act 1995 (NSW), such evidence may be introduced if the events are substantially and relevantly similar, and the circumstances in which they occurred are substantially similar. The similarities on which the prosecution relied were that:

(i)   each event occurred with respect to a natural child of the accused;
(ii)   in each case the accused located the child at a time when the child was not breathing or was experiencing breathing difficulties;
(iii)   the accused arranged in each case to take the child to hospital;
(iv)   the accused's de facto husband was 'unavailable' in the context of a background of domestic friction.[20]

The defence resisted the application to introduce coincidence evidence, on the basis that these similarities were too generic to satisfy the test in section 98, and also argued that similarities (ii) and (iv) were not established by the evidence. Virginia Bell J reviewed the uncharged events in some detail in her judgment and criticised the prosecution's approach to the question of whether the events were related:

> It is to be borne in mind that the fact in issue is the cause of death of Benjamin. A vice to be avoided is to proceed upon an assumption that Benjamin's death was the result of induced asphyxia in order to strengthen the inference to be drawn from the other material as tending to the view that the various medical emergencies were all the result of the mother's deliberate acts.[21]

Bell J excluded the evidence of uncharged events entirely. Subsequently, the prosecution discontinued the case against Phillips.

On the day that counsel in Folbigg's case presented their oral submissions as to sentencing, a Melbourne newspaper reported that it had identified a family who had experienced four infant deaths, but no charges had been laid.[22] The plain implication of the report was that these children had been murdered. In 2004, Carol Louise Matthey, the mother of the children, was charged with four counts

---

[19] 'ALTE' is variously decoded within the medical scientific literature as 'acute life-threatening episode' or 'apparent life-threatening episode'. The distinction seems to reflect a writer's position on whether it is possible that the episode in question was induced or fabricated by a child's carer.

[20] *R v Phillips* (above n 17) 21.

[21] Ibid, paras 75–76.

[22] 'Authorities were Told of Child Deaths' *The Age* (29 August 2003) 1.

of murder. The case reached the Victorian Supreme Court in October 2007, after an extended committal hearing in the Melbourne Magistrates' Court. During preliminary argument, the defence applied to exclude much of the prosecution's medical evidence as well as some circumstantial evidence offered in support of Matthey's guilt.

Coldrey J's decision on the admissibility of prosecution evidence contains a detailed description of the deaths of and death investigation for each of the Matthey children, as well as quite a lot of information about the circumstantial evidence. He focused particularly on the evidence offered by three prosecution experts who also participated in the *Folbigg* case – Allan Cala, Susan Mitchell Beal, and Janice Ophoven. Coldrey J adopted the detailed test for admitting expert evidence described by Heydon JA in the 2001 NSW Court of Appeal decision *Makita (Australia) Pty Ltd v Sprowles*.[23] This test requires the party seeking admissibility to demonstrate that the opinion emanates from a field of specialised knowledge in which the witness is demonstrably expert. The opinion must be 'wholly or substantially' based on expert knowledge, and the facts which found that opinion must be proved by admissible evidence. Furthermore,

> . . . an attempt to make the basis of the opinion explicit may reveal that it is not based on specialised expert knowledge, but, to use Gleeson CJ's characterisation of the evidence in *HG v The Queen*, on 'a combination of speculation, inference, personal and second-hand views as to the credibility of the complainant, and a process of reasoning which went well beyond the field of expertise'.[24]

If this is the case, the opinion must be excluded.

Coldrey J applied the admissibility test to the expert opinions offered in *Matthey* and identified a number of areas in which the experts over-reached their expertise. For example, the fact that each child was alone with Matthey at the time of death was 'almost inevitabl[e]' in light of her status as primary caregiver; and Matthey's decision not to use an apnoea monitor on her children while they were outside the home 'cannot be regarded as suspicious'.[25] Coldrey J quoted with approval an expert report prepared by the Director of the Victorian Institute of Forensic Medicine:

> In my view, it is wrong on the forensic pathology evidence available in this case to conclude that one or more of the Matthey children are the victims of a homicide. There is no merit in forcing certainty where uncertainty exists. The very existence of the enigma of SIDS demonstrates how little we know about why some babies die. It is not for a pathologist to conclude that a number of infant or childhood deaths, with no significant pathological findings at all, are homicides on the basis of controversial circumstantial grounds. If this case is to result in a prosecution, I want to clearly state there is no pathological basis for concluding homicide. The findings are perfectly compatible with natural causes.[26]

[23] *Makita (Australia) Pty Ltd v Sprowles* (2001) 52 NSWLR 705, quoted in *R v Matthey* (above n 17).
[24] *Makita*, quoted in *Matthey* (above n 17), citations omitted.
[25] *Matthey* (above n 17).
[26] Stephen Cordner, expert report, quoted ibid, para 140.

LIVERPOOL JOHN MOORES UNIVERSIT
LEARNING SERVICES

The pathologist referred to other medically reported cases in which families had experienced multiple unexplained deaths which were presumed to have been natural.

In his judgment on the admissibility of the evidence against Matthey, Coldrey J directed the prosecution to reassess its medical evidence in accordance with the principles established in *Makita*.[27] He also excluded much of the circumstantial evidence on which the prosecution sought to rely, including evidence of a fire in the Matthey house and evidence that suggested Matthey's relationship with her children was marked by 'unwanted and unplanned pregnancies, mediocre parenting, and indifference to their deaths'.[28] Shortly after Coldrey J issued this decision, the prosecution announced that it would discontinue the case against Matthey.

English Cases

Between *Phillips* and *Matthey*, the England and Wales Court of Appeal (Criminal Division) (ECCA) heard appeals in three cases involving mothers convicted of murdering multiple children. These cases, especially *R v Clark*[29] and *R v Cannings*,[30] are more widely known than their Australian counterparts. *Clark* was decided in January 2003, but the judgment was not delivered until 11 April 2003, during Folbigg's trial. *Cannings* followed in January 2004. A third mother, Donna Anthony, was exonerated in 2005.[31] Additionally, in June 2003, Trupti Patel was acquitted by a Crown Court jury of killing three children.[32] Because Patel's case did not result in any published judicial decision, I will not discuss it further but will focus on the ECCA judgments in *Clark*, *Cannings* and *Anthony*.

Clark was the first and most notorious of the English cases. Clark was convicted in 1999 of murdering her sons Harry and Christopher. At her trial, prosecution experts testified that the infants' deaths were consistent with suffocation and that there was some evidence of physical harm to both children. The prosecution case was that Clark was coping badly with motherhood and became particularly stressed when her husband was travelling or unavailable. Sir Roy Meadow, a paediatrician who had become a leading figure in the field of unnatural infant death, testified that the odds of two children from a family with Clark's socioeconomic characteristics dying of SIDS were approximately '1 in 73 million'. He further explained that this was something that would occur 'about once every hundred years' in England and Wales.[33] An appeal from Clark's conviction was unsuccess-

---

[27] *Makita* (above n 23).
[28] *Matthey* (above n 17) para 203.
[29] Above n 17.
[30] Above n 17.
[31] *R v Anthony* (above n 17).
[32] J Vasagar and R Allison, 'How Cot Deaths Shattered Mother's Dreams' *The Guardian* (12 June 2003), www.guardian.co.uk/society/2003/jun/12/medicineandhealth.lifeandhealth1.
[33] *Clark* (above n 17) paras 96–97.

ful. Subsequently, it emerged that a pathologist who had autopsied both children had failed to disclose the results of Harry's toxicology tests, and the case was referred back to the ECCA.

In its second appeal judgment, the ECCA held that the new evidence supported the possibility that Harry died of natural causes. Furthermore, 'it follows that no safe conclusion could be reached that Christopher was killed unnaturally.'[34] The Court criticised the expert witness who had failed to disclose Harry's toxicology results. It also roundly criticised Meadow for the graphic terms in which he described the 'odds against' two natural infant deaths occurring in the Clark family. Kay LJ accepted that Meadow's evidence 'grossly overstates the chance of two sudden deaths within the same family from unexplained but natural causes'. In particular, the evidence assumed without demonstrating that the two deaths must be entirely independent events, and that other unmeasured risk factors could be excluded. Meadow's evidence also improperly focused the jurors' minds on the improbability of two events occurring simultaneously, when their task was to deliver two single verdicts. Since *Clark* was delivered, statistical evidence of this sort has been routinely excluded from similar cases, including *Folbigg*.

Cannings was decided in January 2004. Angela Cannings was convicted of murdering two children after a trial at which the prosecution introduced evidence that three children in the Cannings family had died and that the children had experienced multiple ALTEs. (Only two charges were laid.) The prosecution proceeded on the basis that the sheer number of deaths and unexplained ALTEs in this family warranted the conclusion that Cannings had killed her children. The ECCA explained 'there was no direct evidence and very little indirect evidence to suggest that' the deaths were unnatural.[35] In particular, the evidence about Cannings was that she was 'a woman of good character, described as a loving mother, apparently free of personality disorder or psychiatric condition'.[36]

No statistical evidence about the unlikelihood of repeated unexplained infant deaths was introduced at Cannings' trial. Nonetheless, the ECCA concluded that the prosecution case 'depended on specialist evidence about the conclusions to be drawn from the history of three infant deaths and further ALTEs in the same family'.[37] In particular, Meadow's evidence in this trial was that while three deaths in the same family were not in themselves conclusive of homicide, 'the pattern revealed by the history as a whole was compelling.'[38] In answer, the ECCA referred to 'a substantial body of research, not before the jury, and received by us in evidence, suggesting that such deaths can and do occur naturally, even when they are unexplained'. This research is discussed in chapter four. The judgment also mentions the improbability that three children could be smothered with no physical signs of injury on any of them.[39] Alluding to *Clark* and *Patel*, the judgment concludes:

[34] Ibid, para 153.
[35] *Cannings* (above n 17) para 14.
[36] Ibid, para 4.
[37] Ibid, para 129.
[38] Ibid, para 137.
[39] Ibid, para 160.

[T]he occurrence of three sudden and unexpected infant deaths in the same family is very rare, or very rare indeed, and therefore demands an investigation into their causes. Nevertheless the fact that such deaths have occurred does not identify, let alone prescribe, the deliberate infliction of harm as the cause of death. Throughout the process great care must be taken not to allow the rarity of these sad events, standing on their own, to be subsumed into an assumption or virtual assumption that the dead infants were deliberately killed, or consciously or unconsciously to regard the inability of the defendant to produce some convincing explanation for these deaths as providing a measure of support for the Prosecution's case. If on examination of all the evidence every possible known cause has been excluded, the cause remains unknown.[40]

The Court recommended that as a matter of prosecutorial practice,

. . . where a full investigation into two or more sudden unexplained infant deaths in the same family is followed by a serious disagreement between reputable experts about the cause of death, and a body of such expert opinion concludes that natural causes, whether explained or unexplained, cannot be excluded as a reasonable (and not a fanciful) possibility, the prosecution of a parent or parents for murder should not be started, or continued, unless there is additional cogent evidence, extraneous to the expert evidence.[41]

This reasoning formed one of the bases on which Folbigg appealed her conviction to the NSW Court of Criminal Appeal. This ground was dismissed by the Court. While accepting *Cannings'* basic premise, Justice Scully distinguished the English decision on several bases. In doing so he appeared to narrow the ratio decidendi in *Cannings* to the circumstances in which the particular prosecution expert had become the subject of judicial criticism in another case.[42] Even on this very narrow reading of *Cannings*, the scientific evidence led by the prosecution in *Folbigg* should now be questioned in light of Coldrey J's decision in *R v Matthey*.[43] I return to this point in chapter five.

Anthony[44] followed from the holdings in *Clark* and *Cannings*. Donna Anthony was convicted of murdering two children. At trial, there was reasonably substantial evidence indicating that Anthony had given false and contradictory accounts of her children's medical histories, possibly fabricating histories of apnoea. Some of Anthony's friends testified that she had seemed relieved after her first child's death. Meadow testified that the circumstances of the children's lives and deaths 'did not demonstrate that [they were] likely to have died from natural causes'.[45] He also told the jury that there were 'incredibly long odds' against two children dying of natural unexplained causes in the same family.[46] Despite some evidence of 'deliberate interference' with the Anthony children, the ECCA found that the rarity of two infant deaths underpinned and informed the prosecution experts' evidence 'and must inevitably have permeated the way in which the jury would

---

[40] Ibid, para 177.
[41] Ibid, para 178.
[42] *R v KF* (above n 7) paras 134–38.
[43] *Matthey* (above n 17).
[44] *Anthony* (above n 17).
[45] Ibid, paras 64 and 68.
[46] Ibid, para 69.

have approached this evidence'.[47] The Court accepted that the verdict depended substantially on the coincidence of two unexplained deaths occurring in a single family. While Judge LJ was concerned about aspects of Anthony's behaviour and account of her children's deaths, he concluded that the expert evidence could not exclude the possibility that her children died naturally. Accordingly, Anthony's conviction was quashed. Judge LJ expressed that this was a case in which a new trial should perhaps ideally have been ordered, but given the passage of time and the death of a significant witness, the ECCA decided not to make any such order.

The judicial reasoning in these five cases is predicated on two associated conceptions of the place of medical evidence in the criminal process. First, the test for admitting expert evidence presumes that it is possible to distinguish between a medical opinion – ie, one founded on distinctively scientific or clinical reasoning and expertise – and the lay reasoning that remains the exclusive preserve of the jury. Second, the judgments are unanimous that when medical knowledge is unable to provide certain answers about cause of death, the benefit of doubt must go to the accused unless other evidence compensates for that uncertainty. They are similarly critical of attempts to rely on ambiguous behavioural or coincidence evidence to supplement an uncertain expert case. In this book, I unpack these founding principles and consider how they played out within the *Folbigg* case.

II. The Core Concerns of This Book

The manner in which infant deaths are investigated and categorised has changed dramatically over the course of the past twenty years. During the 1970s, 1980s and early 1990s, medical professionals, coroners and investigating police officers mostly treated families who experienced medically unexplained infant death with considerable sympathy.[48] This treatment reflected a prevailing public discourse that constructed unexplained infant death as a tragedy for which no one could be

---

[47] Ibid, para 85.

[48] Of course, this attitude was always contested, but for examples of the sympathetic treatment of families who experience medically unexplained infant death, see MP Johnson and K Hufbauer, 'SIDS as a Medical Research Problem Since 1945' (1982) 30 *Social Problems* 65–81; and JS Wigglesworth, 'Pathological Investigations in Cases of Sudden Infant Death' (1987) *Journal of Clinical Pathology* 1481– 83. The manifestations of this trend within medical science are explained below in ch 4. During Folbigg's trial, it was suggested that police who investigated the Folbigg children's deaths were less rigorous than they might have been because of Folbigg's evident distress and their sympathy for the bereaved mother. See the *Folbigg* trial transcript, which is contained in the *Folbigg* case files, held by the New South Wales Court of Criminal Appeal registry under file numbers 60496 of 2002, 2002/70046, 60279 of 2004 and 2004/1814. For example, *Folbigg* trial transcript, 576 per former police officer Stephen Charles Saunders; and L Knowles, 'Police Upset by Mum's Anguish: No Interview at Baby's Death' *Daily Telegraph* (Sydney, 12 April 2003) 16. For more extensive twentieth-century histories of the treatment of mothers who are suspected of murdering their children, see, eg, KJ Kramar, *Unwilling Mothers, Unwanted Babies: Infanticide in Canada* (Vancouver, University of British Columbia Press, 2005) Introduction; and MG Spinelli, 'Infanticide: Contrasting Views' (2005) 8 *Archives of Women's Health* 15–24.

held responsible, although medical science was working to understand and reduce its incidence.[49]

By the late 1990s, a significant shift had occurred. From the moment a child died, the mother was scrutinised as a potential murderer. Medical journals, statistical analyses of infant homicide and public discourse about infant death pressed the idea that a diagnosis of sudden infant death syndrome could sometimes, or perhaps often, mask murder.[50] Relatedly, the construction of child homicide as a morally heinous crime that deserves the harshest punishment the criminal justice system can mete out was gaining ground in the public consciousness. For example, in a book that considered notorious Australian cases, including the Port Arthur massacre (in which 35 people were killed and 25 injured) and the backpacker murders (of at least seven hitchhikers), Rochelle Jackson wrote about Folbigg: 'The idea of a mother killing her children is abhorrent and seems the worst crime that could be committed.'[51] This belief has historically been balanced by a sense that a mother who kills her infant commits a crime that, while morally wrong, deserves a degree of sympathy and understanding.[52]

Folbigg was prosecuted at a time when there was a particularly punitive stance towards sudden unexplained infant death. The belief that motivated this stance appears to be that, because of the historical shortcomings of medical knowledge about the causes and pathology of sudden infant death, some mothers were literally getting away with murder. The inadequacy of homicide detection was held to create an immediate danger for the surviving and future children of mothers who have murdered infants, and a broader (but no less serious) risk to the administration of justice. Despite genuine professional medical disagreement about the incidence and indications of infant homicide, there was a growing public perception in the United Kingdom and Australia that penalties for child-killing were unrea-

---

[49] This discourse was significantly influenced by the rise of groups such as SIDS and Kids Australia (a federated group of organisations that claims its roots in parents' and doctors' groups started in the early 1970s). These groups were successful in attracting public, political and medical attention to the problem of medically unexplained infant death. See Johnson and Hufbauer (ibid). MJ Thearle and H Gregory, 'Evolution of Bereavement Counselling in Sudden Infant Death Syndrome, Neonatal Death, and Stillbirth' (1992) 28 *Journal of Paediatrics and Child Health* 204–9 provides an account of the growing attention paid to the needs of bereaved parents in Australia during the 1970s and 1980s.

[50] See, eg, RD Krugman, 'Landmarks in Child Abuse and Neglect: Three Flowers in the Desert' (1998) 102 *Pediatrics* 254–56; R Meadow, 'Unnatural Sudden Infant Death' (1999) 80 *Archives of Disease in Childhood* 7–14; American Academy of Pediatrics, 'Distinguishing Sudden Infant Death Syndrome from Child Abuse Fatalities' (2001) 107 *Pediatrics* 437–41 [2001 AAP Policy Statement]; J Stanton and A Simpson, 'Murder Misdiagnosed as SIDS: A Perpetrator's Perspective' (2001) 85 *Archives of Disease in Childhood* 454–59; A Wilczynski, *Child Homicide* (London, Greenwich Medical Media Ltd, 1997) 36; Canadian Centre for Justice Statistics, *Family Violence in Canada: A Statistical Profile* (Ottawa, Statistics Canada, 1998–2005), www.statcan.ca/english/freepub/85-224-XIE/free.htm; C Alder and K Polk, *Child Victims of Homicide* (Cambridge, Cambridge University Press, 2001); A Havill, *While Innocents Slept: A Story of Revenge, Murder, and SIDS* (New York, St Martins True Crime, 2002); J Cooke, 'Expert Calls for Child Murder Law Reform' *Sydney Morning Herald* (5 September 1997) 11; and M Downey, 'British Claim Cot Death Diagnosis can Mask Child Murder' *Sydney Morning Herald* (8 January 1999) 4.

[51] R Jackson, *Inside their Minds: Australian Criminals* (Sydney, Allen & Unwin, 2008) 179.

[52] Kramar (above n 48) discusses the historical Canadian debate over the moral blameworthiness of mothers who commit infanticide, and identifies a similar trend.

sonably low, and significant prosecution resources therefore began to be devoted to investigating and prosecuting marginal cases. I demonstrate that the resulting environment of suspicion affected the investigation and prosecution of the *Folbigg* case and the manner in which medical evidence was presented in the *Folbigg* trial.

Chapter two provides an introduction to the *Folbigg* trial, sentencing and appeals. Chapters three and four provide an overview of the developing research field of sudden unexplained infant death, particularly the shifting understandings of the relationship between SIDS and homicide. Chapter five moves into a close analysis of the scientific evidence in *Folbigg*, comparing that evidence with the research from which it ostensibly emerged. In chapters six and seven, I reintroduce the question of gender and normative expectations of mothering. The role of these expectations is rarely explicitly considered within critical analyses of the medical evidence that led to a rash of wrongful convictions,[53] but I consider them to be crucial to a full understanding of the paediatric forensic pathology cases. I suggest in chapter six that the prosecution relied upon the Folbigg family arrangements and on normative conceptions of motherhood to render Folbigg an identifiably inadequate mother, and the defence was only somewhat able to resist this categorisation. In chapter seven, I explore the crucial diary evidence and consider how Folbigg's own experience of mothering was or was not reflected in her trial. Finally, in chapter eight, I analyse how the *Folbigg* trial was reported by the major Sydney newspapers and consider what that reportage might have allowed the public to understand about Folbigg's case in particular and unexpected infant death more generally.

---

[53] Throughout this book, I use the phrase 'wrongful conviction' to refer to a conviction that is unsound: because it did not proceed according to applicable legal and evidentiary principles; because fresh evidence has emerged to cast doubt on the original verdict; or because the accused is demonstrably factually innocent. The phrase is often used as if its content is self-evident, and its usage is frequently narrowed to encompass only the conviction of a demonstrably factually innocent person. See, eg, RA Leo, 'Rethinking the Study of Miscarriages of Justice: Developing a Criminology of Wrongful Conviction' (2005) 21 *Journal of Contemporary Criminal Justice* 201 and the studies surveyed therein.

2

The *Folbigg* Case

THIS CHAPTER PROVIDES a general sketch of the case against Kathleen Folbigg and the judicial decisions generated by her case. While the *Folbigg* case was closely reported in the Australian print media, it received little academic attention. Uniquely, Sharmila Betts and Jane Goodman-Delahunty have expressed concern that the expert testimony may have been influenced by biases that pushed experts towards overestimating the likelihood of a suspicious cause of death for each infant.[1] Lee FitzRoy has criticised the popular tendency to rely on Folbigg's family history as confirmatory indicia of her guilt, although FitzRoy did not question the fact of that guilt.[2] Belinda Morrissey has pointed to the prosecution's tendency to conflate Kathleen Folbigg's subjectivity with the diary she kept during her last pregnancy and afterwards,[3] a point that I have also made in a slightly different form from Morrissey's and to which I return in chapter seven.[4]

I. The Case against Folbigg

Kathleen Megan Folbigg was convicted on 21 May 2003 of three counts of murder, one of manslaughter and one of inflicting grievous bodily harm. Her trial was conducted before a judge and jury in the New South Wales Supreme Court. The prosecution case was that Folbigg had smothered each of her children in separate incidents between 1989 and 1999, and that she had assaulted her son Patrick before his death. The children were aged between 19 days and 19 months when they died. Each child's death was investigated at the time of death, and in no instance did the investigator identify physical signs of foul play. In the appendix, I set out the dates of birth and death for the Folbigg children, together with the originally ascribed causes of death.

[1] S Betts and J Goodman-Delahunty, 'The Case of Kathleen Folbigg: How Did Justice and Medicine Fare?'(2007) 39 *Australian Journal of Forensic Sciences* 11.

[2] L FitzRoy, '"Violent Women"? An Exploratory Study of Women's Use of Violence' (PhD dissertation, Royal Melbourne Institute of Technology, 2005) 21.

[3] B Morrissey, 'Monstrous Semantics: The Case of the Criminal Diary' unpublished manuscript on record with the author.

[4] E Cunliffe, '(This is Not a) Story: Using Court Records to Explore Judicial Narratives in *R v Kathleen Folbigg*' (2007) 27 *Australian Feminist Law Journal* 71.

Caleb was born to Kathleen and Craig Folbigg in 1989 and died when he was 19 days old.[5] He was a healthy baby, although his parents were concerned about his tendency to gasp when feeding. Caleb was diagnosed by his paediatrician as suffering from a 'floppy larynx'. Kathleen initially tried to breastfeed Caleb, but she switched to bottle feeding almost immediately after his birth. Caleb's death was attributed to sudden infant death syndrome (SIDS) after an autopsy performed by a local pathologist. At trial, a day-planner in which Kathleen recorded Caleb's sleep and eating patterns, as well as appointments with medical staff, was entered into evidence.

Patrick was born in 1990, and Craig took several months off work after he arrived. Soon after Craig returned to work, when Patrick was four months old, Kathleen found Patrick 'moribund', or close to death, in his crib one night while Craig was sleeping. Patrick was pale and gasping for breath. Ambulance officers rushed Patrick to hospital, where he was eventually diagnosed with viral encephalitis. While he was still in hospital, Patrick suffered a seizure as he was being held by Craig. Subsequently, he was diagnosed with epilepsy and blindness (presumed consequent to the viral infection) and placed on medication. When Patrick was about eight months old, Kathleen found him dead in his crib one day while Craig was at work. Efforts to resuscitate the boy were unsuccessful, and a hospital autopsy concluded that he had asphyxiated consequent to an epileptic fit.

Sarah was born in 1992 and lived for approximately ten and a half months. Although she was a healthy child, she suffered from mild sleep apnoea, and the apnoea monitoring alarm that the Folbiggs used persistently sounded false alarms. Kathleen found Sarah dead in her bed one night, and she could not be revived by Craig, who performed rudimentary CPR, or by the ambulance officers who attended within minutes of being called. An autopsy conducted by the senior pathologist at the NSW forensic pathology laboratory concluded that Sarah had died of SIDS. There was no sign of any maltreatment or harm to Sarah (or to any of the children) on autopsy.

The Folbiggs waited some time after Sarah died before trying to have another child. Kathleen eventually broached the possibility of becoming pregnant with Craig, explaining that she felt that a family was incomplete without children. Craig testified at Kathleen's trial that he was 'shocked' at the suggestion. He ultimately agreed on condition that they discuss the proposal with specialists in infant death and follow any suggestions those specialists made about how to safeguard the child from the risk of death. Laura was born soon after, in 1997.

When Laura died, she was 19 months old. Kathleen and Craig had been arguing that day, although the subject and extent of that argument were variously described during the investigation and at trial. Laura had a cold, which she had been suffering from for about a week. Kathleen told police that after she had

---

[5] The facts set out in this section are taken from a variety of documents contained in the *Folbigg* case files. Except where specifically noted, these facts were uncontested at trial. The *Folbigg* case files are held by the NSW Court of Criminal Appeal registry under file numbers 60496 of 2002, 2002/70046, 60279 of 2004 and 2004/1814.

shared morning tea with Craig and Laura at Craig's work, Laura had fallen asleep in the car. Sometime later, after Kathleen put Laura to sleep in her bed, she heard the little girl cough. A few minutes later, Kathleen checked on Laura to find her unresponsive and seemingly not breathing. Kathleen called the emergency services and attempted CPR, but Laura could not be revived. When the ambulance officers attended Laura, she had electrical signals in her heart, which suggested that she had only very recently died.

When Laura died, her autopsy was conducted by Dr Allan Cala at the central mortuary in Sydney. Cala reported:

> The death of Laura Folbigg cannot be regarded as 'another SIDS' (Sudden Infant Death Syndrome). The family history of no living children following four live births is highly unusual . . .
>
> The possibility of multiple homicides in this family has not been excluded. If homicidal acts have been committed, it is most likely that these acts have been in the form of deliberate smothering. Smothering, whether deliberately or accidentally inflicted, may leave no trace. There are no specific post-mortem findings for smothering. It is usually performed by one person, in the absence of any witnesses. It is relatively easy for an adult to smother an infant or small child with a hand, pillow, soft toy or other similar object.[6]

Many pathologists believe that an infant younger than about a year old may be suffocated without leaving physical signs.[7]

Soon after Laura's death, Kathleen Folbigg moved out of the Folbigg family home. She told Craig that she no longer wished to continue their marriage of 16 years. At around this time, Craig asked Kathleen what he should do with her personal effects, and Kathleen allegedly told Craig to throw them away.[8] In the meantime, Detective Bernie Ryan of the NSW Police visited Craig at work, inviting him to share any suspicions he might have about Kathleen's role in the children's deaths.

Craig initially rebuffed Ryan's suggestions but changed his mind when he found a diary Kathleen had written after Sarah's death. Craig testified at Kathleen's eventual trial that what he read in the diary 'made me want to vomit'.[9] The diary contained a number of entries in which Kathleen appeared to accept direct responsibility for her children's deaths. Craig called Detective Ryan and gave the diary to him. In a long police interview, Folbigg denied the accusations that she had killed her children or harmed Patrick, and she explained several of the most damaging entries. Police subsequently found another diary, which spanned the time in which Kathleen was pregnant with Laura, and after Laura was born. This

---

[6] AD Cala, 'Coroners Act 1950 Autopsy Report re Laura Elizabeth Folbigg' (1 March 1999) contained in *Folbigg* case files (ibid).

[7] See below chs 3 and 4 for detailed discussion of the state of medical knowledge about unexpected infant death and its relationship with homicide.

[8] Trial transcript of *R v Kathleen Megan Folbigg*, New South Wales Supreme Court, 1 Apr–21 May 2003, Grahame Barr J presiding [*Folbigg* trial transcript] 180. The trial transcript is contained in the *Folbigg* case files (above n 5).

[9] *Folbigg* trial transcript (ibid) 180.

diary contained statements that were even more disturbing than the first diary. The case file does not disclose why Kathleen had left her diaries behind when she moved out, although the Prosecution hinted at trial that she would have destroyed the diaries if she was aware of their continued existence.[10] Kathleen had told police that she had destroyed her diaries on the Mothers' Day after Laura died. Craig testified that Kathleen did not seem to hide her diaries from him or others.[11] Kathleen did not testify at trial, and therefore the diaries, her police interview and other witnesses' testimony provide the total sum of information that was before the jury about Kathleen's experience of mothering and her qualities as a mother.

Craig gave inconsistent accounts of Kathleen's behaviour and mothering capacity. In an intercepted telephone conversation with his sister, Craig said that he was feeling 'pretty bad' after Kathleen left him and that police had 'planted horrible things in my head' and twisted his words to make Kathleen seem guilty.[12] At Kathleen's trial he sought and received a certificate to protect him from prosecution for lying to police, testifying that he had lied because he wanted to protect Kathleen.[13] As I describe in chapter six, Craig's evidence at trial was considerably more condemning of Kathleen than his previous statements to police and friends had been.

Kathleen Folbigg was charged in April 2001 with killing her four children and remanded in custody until May, when she was released on strict bail conditions. After a very brief committal hearing in May 2002, she was indicted to stand trial in the NSW Supreme Court. Folbigg's trial lasted nine weeks in April and May 2003. The trial judge characterised the case as one in which there were 'relatively few issues of fact'.[14] Beyond the obvious question of how the children died, those facts that were in issue mainly related to five incidents during which Folbigg allegedly lost her temper with a child. Nonetheless, the defence vigorously contested all four aspects of the prosecution's case. In particular, the defence argued that the medical scientific evidence was inconclusive; the 'coincidences' and behavioural tendencies to which the prosecution pointed were variously nonexistent or benign; and the behavioural evidence and diaries were ambiguous. Each of these strands is described further in subsequent chapters. The jury deliberated for a day and a half before finding the accused guilty of three counts of murder (of Patrick, Sarah and Laura), one count of causing grievous bodily harm (Patrick's life-threatening episode, or ALTE[15]) and one count of manslaughter (in relation to Caleb).

---

[10] Police 'located another diary, this time from the period 1997 to 1998, in a secluded spot where she could easily have missed it': *Folbigg* trial transcript (above n 8) 47.

[11] Ibid, 433–34.

[12] Ibid, 309. Similar conversations with other friends are also recounted in the transcript: ibid, 304–15.

[13] Ibid, 95–98 and 360–61.

[14] Justice Graham Barr, summing-up, *Folbigg* case files (above n 5) 79.

[15] 'ALTE' stands variously for 'acute life-threatening episode' or 'apparent life-threatening episode'. See above ch 1, n 19.

II. Judicial Decision-Making in *Folbigg*

After being convicted, Folbigg was sentenced to a cumulative term of 40 years' imprisonment, with a non-parole period of 30 years. This sentence was later reduced on appeal to 30 years maximum, with a non-parole period of 25 years. Folbigg was convicted by a jury, and therefore we can only speculate about why she was found guilty. Seventeen written judicial decisions arose from her case, however, and these judgments constitute the most authoritative 'legal' accounts of Folbigg's trial and subsequent appeals.[16]

Interlocutory Judgments

The sheer number of judicial decisions issued in *Folbigg* reflects the extent to which this was a hard-fought case. Before the trial began, the defence applied to sever the counts against Folbigg on the basis that the prosecution could not establish any distinctive similarities between the four deaths except by relying on an impermissible reversal of the onus of criminal proof. This application was rejected by a judge of the NSW Supreme Court[17] and then by the NSW Court of Criminal Appeal.[18] An application for special leave to appeal to the High Court of Australia was unsuccessful.[19] Two other pre-trial motions were subject to a non-publication order, which appears not to have been lifted.

During the trial, Grahame Barr J issued seven written judgments. On 1 April 2003, the day the trial began, the prosecution applied to open on a statement written by prosecution pathologist Allan Cala, in which Cala expressed an opinion about Laura's state of health before her death. Cala had reached this opinion after viewing a video of Laura taken the day before she died. The defence had not previously seen the statement, and Barr J denied the prosecution application on this basis.[20] Two

---

[16] The judicial decisions and High Court of Australia transcripts, in chronological order, are as follows: *R v Folbigg* [2002] NSWSC 1127 (29 November 2002) [*Folbigg* pre-trial decision]; *R v Kathleen Megan Folbigg* [2003] NSWCCA 17 (13 February 2003) [*Folbigg* pre-trial appeal]; *Folbigg v The Queen* S59/2003 (19 February 2003) [*Folbigg* pre-trial HCA appeal]; *R v Kathleen Megan Folbigg* 21 February 2003 (Unrept, NSWSC, Wood J); *R v Kathleen Megan Folbigg* 7 March 2003 (Unrept, NSWSC, Barr J); *R v Kathleen Megan Folbigg* 1 April 2003 (Unrept, NSWSC, Barr J); *R v Kathleen Megan Folbigg* 3 April 2003 (Unrept, NSWSC, Barr J); *R v Kathleen Megan Folbigg* 14 April 2003 (Unrept, NSWSC, Barr J); *R v Kathleen Megan Folbigg* 15 April 2003 (Unrept, NSWSC, Barr J); *R v Kathleen Megan Folbigg* 16 April 2003 (Unrept, NSWSC, Barr J); *R v Kathleen Megan Folbigg* 24 April 2003 (Unrept, NSWSC, Barr J); *R v Kathleen Megan Folbigg* 7 May 2003 (Unrept, NSWSC, Barr J); *R v Folbigg* [2003] NSWSC 895 (24 October 2003) Barr J [*Folbigg* sentencing decision]; *R v KF* (2005) 152 A Crim R 35, [2005] NSWCCA 23 (17 February 2005) [*Folbigg* conviction and sentencing appeal]; *Folbigg v The Queen* [2005] HCA Trans 657; *Kathleen Folbigg v R* [2007] NSWCCA 128 (16 May 2007) [*Folbigg* procedural appeal]; *Kathleen Folbigg v R* [2007] NSWCCA 371 (21 December 2007) [*Folbigg* jury appeal].

[17] *R v Folbigg* [2002] NSWSC 1127 (29 November 2002).

[18] *R v Folbigg* [2003] NSWCCA 17 (13 February 2003).

[19] *Folbigg v The Queen* S59/2003 (High Court of Australia 19 February 2003).

[20] *R v Folbigg*, 1 April 2003 (Unrept, NSWSC, Barr J).

days later, Barr J ruled that the jury could see this video, which showed Laura playing in her backyard pool, over the defence objections that the video would cause
the jury to judge the case on emotion rather than reason.[21] On 14 April, Barr J gave
the prosecution permission to cross-examine its witness John Napier Hilton on the
cause of Sarah's death.[22] Hilton attributed that death to SIDS, and the prosecution
submitted that this attribution was improper in light of the professional standards
established by the American Academy of Pediatrics (AAP) in respect of multiple
unexplained infant deaths.

On day 10 of the trial, Barr J allowed Cala to give his opinion on Laura's health
before her death, based on the video that had been shown several days earlier.[23]
The following day, Barr J excluded two prosecution questions that would elicit
evidence from Cala that the existence of multiple unexplained infant deaths
within a family made it more likely that those deaths were murder. Barr J characterised that reasoning as predicated on 'common sense' rather than expertise and
therefore excluded it from the body of expert opinion that could properly form
the subject of expert evidence.[24]

About a week after Barr J excluded the prosecution's evidence about multiple
infant deaths, he allowed the prosecution to ask its witnesses whether the medical
literature reported any cases in which a family had suffered three or more SIDS
deaths. Barr J distinguished this evidence from that which he had previously
excluded:

> It seems to me to be permissible for Dr Berry to give evidence that the sudden death of
> four infants in the same family who were previously well due to natural disease is
> unprecedented, and he can make that statement of opinion from his own experience.
> He can also say that he knows of no substantiated examples from the literature.
>
> So long as he deals with the cases individually and does not rely on the kind of coin-
> cidence reasoning against which I ruled in considering Dr Cala's evidence, it seems to
> me also that Dr Berry is entitled to say that he is unable to rule out that Caleb, Patrick,
> Sarah and possibly Laura were suffocated.[25]

Subsequently, Barr J also prohibited the prosecution from asking defence expert
Roger Byard about his opinion of the most likely single cause of multiple unexplained infant deaths.[26]

I explore the implications of these decisions by Barr J in greater detail in chapter five. In addition to the written judgments Barr J delivered, he gave several oral
decisions about the admissibility of particular evidence. I likewise return to these
decisions as they become relevant.

---

[21] Ibid, 3 April 2003 (Unrept, NSWSC, Barr J).
[22] Ibid, 14 April 2003 (Unrept, NSWSC, Barr J).
[23] Ibid, 15 April 2003 (Unrept, NSWSC, Barr J).
[24] Ibid, 16 April 2003 (Unrept, NSWSC, Barr J).
[25] *R v Folbigg*, 24 April 2003 (Unrept, NSWSC, Barr J), paras 5–6.
[26] *R v Folbigg*, 7 May 2003 (Unrept, NSWSC, Barr J).

Sentencing Judgment

The first substantial judicial discussion of the facts of the *Folbigg* case was the sentencing judgment delivered by Barr J in October 2003.[27] The trial judge sentenced Folbigg to a minimum term of 30 years' imprisonment, with a maximum term of 40 years. In this judgment, Barr J set out the history of Folbigg's life and the circumstances of each child's birth and life. In accordance with the prosecution theory, which had presumably been accepted by the jury, Barr J attributed each of the deaths to smothering. Barr J explained that the evidence for inflicted deaths was relatively strong:

> No such [expert] witness was prepared to say that the signs pointed only to smothering but the medical evidence generally was that the result of each event was consistent with having been caused by acute asphyxiation. The jury accepted that evidence . . .
> The arguments in favour of natural explanations for the deaths and Patrick's ALTE were unimpressive in the light of the whole of the evidence.[28]

Given that the prosecution had its case that the infants were smothered, Barr J considered what factors had led Folbigg to kill her children. He attributed Folbigg's tendency to lose her temper and harm her children to her early childhood experiences of deprivation, physical and possibly sexual abuse:

> I accept that by the age of eighteen months the offender was a seriously disturbed and regressed little girl. . .
> It is well established that children who are neglected and suffer serious physical and sexual trauma may suffer a profound disturbance of personality development. The evidence for such a disturbance in the offender is strong, as her diaries reveal.[29]

Reproducing many of the most incriminating diary entries, Barr J concluded that Folbigg was not psychotic but that her early childhood 'explained her adult state of mind and suggests a reason why she killed her children'.[30]

The acts of killing her children were attributed in the sentencing judgment to momentary lapses of self control, which were otherwise out of character for Folbigg:

> The offender was not by inclination a cruel mother. She did not systematically abuse her children. She generally looked after them well, fed and clothed them and had them appropriately attended to by medical practitioners. Her condition[31] and her anxiety about it left her unable to shrug off the irritations of unwell, wilful and disobedient children. She was not fully equipped to cope.[32]

---

[27] *R v Folbigg* [2003] NSWSC 895 (24 October 2003) Barr J.
[28] Ibid, paras 31 and 32.
[29] Ibid, para 52.
[30] Ibid, para 57.
[31] This 'condition' is somewhat vaguely described elsewhere in the judgment as a severe personality disorder, a tendency to depression and resultant difficulty controlling her emotions: ibid, para 91.
[32] Ibid, para 95.

Nonetheless, Barr J held that her actions 'constituted a serious breach of the trust the children placed in the offender'.[33] Concluding that Folbigg would 'always be a danger if given the responsibility of caring for a child', Barr J crafted a sentence that was designed in part to ensure that this would 'never happen'.[34] Furthermore, Barr J found that if the offender ever admitted the offences to anyone except herself, she would be at significant risk of committing suicide.[35]

This sentencing judgment, which was influenced by the pre-sentencing psychiatric reports, crafts a disturbing narrative of Folbigg as a mother whose incapacity to cope with motherhood was irrevocably established from her own infancy. The judgment begs the question why, if Folbigg would inevitably pose a danger to children in her care, it took so long for anyone to notice how poorly she was coping.

Appeals from Conviction and Sentence

Folbigg appealed both conviction and sentence. The NSW Court of Criminal Appeal dismissed the appeal from her conviction but reduced her sentence, finding that the sentence fixed by the trial judge was 'so crushingly discouraging as to put at risk any incentive that she might have to apply herself to her rehabilitation'.[36] The High Court of Australia again denied special leave to appeal.

The NSW Court of Criminal Appeal decision confirming Folbigg's conviction typifies the appellate treatment of the factual foundation for conviction. The Court understood the prosecution's case at trial to include the proposition that it was not a reasonable possibility that any child died of an identifiable natural cause. In the absence of such a cause, the Court characterised the prosecution case to be:

> [6] That it was not a reasonable possibility that there was, in any individual case, some other natural cause of death;
>
> [7] That, absent a natural cause of death in any one of four successive infant deaths in a single family, the only inference rationally available was that the deaths had been caused in some unnatural way;
>
> [8] That the only rational inference as to the nature of the unnatural cause was that each of the children had been suffocated by somebody; and
>
> [9] That the only person to whom the evidence pointed in that connection was, in each case, the appellant.[37]

The Court of Appeal's discussion of the possibility that any Folbigg child's death could properly be ascribed to SIDS is somewhat unclear, but I infer that the

---

[33] Ibid, para 82.
[34] Ibid, para 97.
[35] Ibid, para 98.
[36] *R v KF* (2005) 152 A Crim R 35, [2005] NSWCCA 23 (17 February 2005) para 186.
[37] Ibid, para 80.

reference in subparagraph 6 to 'some other natural cause' included SIDS.[38] If I am correct, the Court's reasoning obscures a confusion at trial about the nature of SIDS diagnosis and the conditions that must be present in order to diagnose SIDS. SIDS is a challenging concept, which is explained in chapter three. The confusion that arose at trial about the nature of SIDS is described in detail in chapter five. Reducing this complex area to a set of straightforward propositions about reasonable possibilities and rational inferences, the Court's judgment arguably reflects the prosecution's efforts to (over)simplify SIDS at trial. I argue in chapter five that simplifying SIDS allowed the prosecution to conceal the extent of medical uncertainty about infant death from the trial judge and jury.

Deciding whether to ascribe criminal responsibility to a mother in the context of multiple infant deaths is a task that is fraught with moral and factual difficulty, making the temptation to shop for expert answers particularly strong. The NSW Court of Appeal decision in the first *Folbigg* appeal hints at the reassurance provided by medical evidence. Writing for the Court, Sully JA held in this regard:

> In the present case there was, in my opinion, ample evidence at trial to justify these findings, reached beyond a reasonable doubt:
>
> 1. None of the four deaths, or Patrick's ALTE, was caused by an identified natural cause.
> 2. It was possible that each of the five events had been caused by an unidentified natural cause, but only in the sense of a debating point possibility and not in the sense of a reasonable possibility. The evidence of the appellant's episodes of temper and ill-treatment, coupled with the very powerful evidence provided by the diary entries, was overwhelmingly to the contrary of any reasonable possibility of unidentified natural causes. So were the striking similarities of the four deaths.
> 3. There remained reasonably open, therefore, only the conclusion that somebody had killed the children, and that smothering was the obvious method.
> 4. In that event, the evidence pointed to nobody other than the appellant as being the person who had killed the children; and who, by reasonable parity of reasoning, had caused Patrick's ALTE by the same method.[39]

If it is not fairly possible on the current state of medical knowledge to exclude natural causes of death, whether identified or unidentified, this conclusion becomes far less secure. The medical evidence was surveyed first in the judgment, before the Court of Appeal turned to the other supporting evidence provided by the prosecution. Arguably, the prosecution's reasoning on the medical evidence underpinned the Court's conclusion that the behavioural, diary and coincidence

---

[38] Alternatively, it is possible that the Court accepted that it was not rationally possible that four children in a single family died of SIDS. This latter reasoning would directly conflict with the ECCA decision in *R v Cannings* [2004] EWCA 1, but the Court did not express an intention to depart from *Cannings*. Accordingly, I prefer the interpretation that SIDS is referred to, albeit obliquely, in subparagraph 6. For discussion of *R v Cannings*, see above ch 1.

[39] *R v KF* (2005) 152 A Crim R 35, [2005] NSWCCA 23 (17 February 2005) para 143. See also para 128, where Sully JA expressed a personal view about the strength of the medical evidence excluding identified natural causes of death.

evidence supported a finding of guilt. Notably, the behavioural, diary and coincidence evidence are used in the Court of Appeal judgment in a manner that implies that this evidence is independent of the medical conclusions about cause of death. I demonstrate in chapter four that pathologists regularly draw upon each of these types of evidence in ascertaining cause of death. A risk of 'double counting' adverse behavioural evidence arises when a court treats behavioural evidence and medical evidence as if they provide independent validation of one another.

Some time after the first appeal was dismissed, the NSW Court of Criminal Appeal heard a second appeal from conviction, on the basis that two jury irregularities had arisen during Folbigg's trial. This appeal became possible because the court registry had not entered the results of the first appeal into the court file.[40] These jury irregularities were conceded by the prosecution, although their materiality to Folbigg's convictions was vigorously contested. One juror had researched Folbigg on the internet and learned her family history from pre-trial reports. A second juror had asked a friend, who was a nurse, how long it would take a child's body to cool after death. I return to the second irregularity in chapter six. The NSW Court of Criminal Appeal dismissed this further appeal, finding that 'although the irregularities should not have occurred . . . they were not material and did not give rise to a miscarriage of justice'.[41]

According to the judicial accounts therefore, Folbigg stands properly convicted of killing her children and of assaulting Patrick before his death. The efforts repeatedly made by Folbigg's counsel to challenge her conviction, as well as Folbigg's protestations of innocence, have not displaced the judges' assurance that this conviction is sound – indeed, that the evidence for conviction remains overwhelming. Accordingly, I am interested in what makes this case different from those in which convictions have been overturned or charges dismissed.

Given the legal, scientific and cultural context, I am interested in how the prosecution constructed its case against Kathleen Folbigg and how Folbigg and her lawyers contested that case. This book considers the extent to which the prosecution relied on the types of reasoning that have been elsewhere disapproved. It explores how the defence deployed cases in which mothers were exonerated and other tactics used to contest the prosecution case. A central theme is the relationship between the medical evidence in *Folbigg* and the debates that were and are taking place within forensic paediatric pathology about unexpected infant death and murder. I also consider how the case was framed and given moral ordering within the Australian press reporting.

It is not possible to obtain a nuanced sense of these dynamics from judgments alone. Accordingly, I turned to the textual record of the *Folbigg* case; the scientific literature from which expert evidence about the causes of infant death emerged; and the press reporting. I hoped that these sources would provide me with a nuanced understanding of how unexpected infant death was legally and socially

---

[40] *Kathleen Folbigg v R* [2007] NSWCCA 128 (16 May 2007).
[41] *Kathleen Folbigg v R* [2007] NSWCCA 371 (21 December 2007) para 62.

redefined as indicating a significant risk of covert homicide, as well as provide me with an empirical basis from which to explore how broader social trends played out in *Folbigg*. In the ensuing chapters, I convey the key findings of that empirical research and apply what I have learned to the *Folbigg* court record.

3

Unexplained Infant Death: A Shifting Theory of Maternal Culpability

W ITHIN CONTEMPORARY WESTERN societies, infant death is a problem that warrants significant research and intervention.[1] For centuries, unexplained infant mortality has elicited suspicion about the mother's possible role in causing a child's death.[2] The prevailing understanding of infant mortality has, however, changed over time – with attendant realignments of research emphasis and of the nature and extent of intervention in families who experience infant death. In this chapter and the next, I trace the shifting nature of scientific knowledge about the relationship between sudden infant death and murder since the mid-twentieth century. I illustrate that these shifts are partly informed by cultural and legal events, as well as by varying understandings of when the criminal justice system should become involved in a suspicious death.

Paediatric forensic pathologists and other experts engage dynamically and reciprocally (though not always uniformly) with legal and popular knowledges to co-produce hegemonic understandings of infant death.[3] In this chapter, having provided a history of mid- to late twentieth-century research into sudden unexpected infant death, I identify the uneven rise of one such hegemony – the belief that a mother who experiences multiple unexplained infant deaths must have murdered her children. In chapter four, I look more closely at the relationship between smothering and unexpected infant death as it has been variously understood within the scientific literature over the same time period. In order to put this discussion into its context within the *Folbigg* case, I begin by explaining how the relationship between unexpected infant death and murder became relevant to Folbigg's trial.[4]

---

[1] This is expressly noted by the Australian Bureau of Statistics in its published research into infant death. See, eg, Australian Bureau of Statistics, *Causes of Infant and Child Deaths* (Canberra, Australian Government Publishing Service, 1998) 3.

[2] See the essays collected in M Jackson (ed), *Infanticide: Historical Perspectives on Child Murder and Concealment, 1550–2000* (Aldershot, Ashgate, 2002); and R Firstman and J Talan, 'SIDS and Infanticide' in RW Byard and HF Krous (eds), *Sudden Infant Death Syndrome: Problems, Progress & Possibilities* (New York, Oxford University Press, 2001) 291–300.

[3] See S Jasanoff, *Science at the Bar: Law, Science and Technology in America* (Cambridge, Harvard University Press, 1995) 8.

[4] The *Folbigg* case files are held by the NSW Court of Criminal Appeal registry under file numbers 60496 of 2002, 2002/70046, 60279 of 2004 and 2004/1814. For an outline and general discussion of the case, see above chs 1 and 2.

I. The Folbigg Children's Deaths

The Folbigg children's deaths were investigated at the time of each death, and an autopsy was performed on each child. Only Laura's death was immediately flagged as suspicious; the remaining children had various natural causes of death ascribed after initial investigation. The children's deaths do not fit uniformly into any single statistical category by age or ascribed cause.[5] Caleb was 19 days old when he died, while the other Folbigg children were between 8 months and 19 months old at their time of death. The appendix sets out the dates of birth and death for all four children, the date of Patrick's ALTE[6] and the initially ascribed cause of death for each child. Each child's autopsy report recorded some positive physiological abnormality: Caleb suffered from a 'floppy larynx'; Patrick was diagnosed as suffering from epilepsy after his ALTE; Sarah had narrowed upper airways; and there was evidence of myocarditis (inflammation) in Laura's heart muscles.

Caleb's and Sarah's deaths were initially diagnosed as SIDS, while no cause was attributed for Laura's death. Patrick's death was ascribed to asphyxia resulting from the epilepsy he developed after his ALTE, though this diagnosis was expressed in tentative and variable terms on the documents generated after his death.[7] The relative lack of information about Patrick's death presented a challenge to both parties at Folbigg's trial. This was particularly acute because the investigating physician and other specialists gave evidence that contradicted the opinions they recorded contemporaneously to Patrick's ALTE and death. It proved difficult to untangle the extent to which these shifting opinions could be attributed to: the greater experience of the relevant doctors at the time they testified compared with when they treated Patrick; the shifting medical understanding of infant death; and the subsequent infant deaths within the Folbigg family.

At Folbigg's trial, the Crown argued that all four children had been smothered by their mother. There was almost no positive physical evidence of smothering, except a suggestion (resisted by the autopsying pathologist) that two unphotographed 'pinpoint abrasions' on Sarah's upper lip could have occurred when the child's mouth and nose were covered. The Crown had to demonstrate beyond a reasonable doubt that the deaths were unnatural, which required it to disprove two alternative possibilities. First, it had to demonstrate in relation to each child that positive findings of malformation or illness could not reasonably have caused that child's death, and that Patrick's ALTE was not caused by a virus or other

---

[5] The Australian Bureau of Statistics categories are reflected in Australian Bureau of Statistics, 'Mortality and Morbidity: Infant Mortality' (4102.0 Australian Social Trends, 2002), www.abs.gov.au/Ausstats.

[6] 'ALTE' stands variously for 'acute life-threatening episode' or 'apparent life-threatening episode'. See above ch 1, n 19.

[7] Asphyxia is a contested diagnostic term. It means that a person has died from lack of oxygen but does not define the cause of that lack of oxygen. The unqualified use of this term to describe cause of death in criminal proceedings is criticised in ST Goudge, *Inquiry into Pediatric Forensic Pathology in Ontario Report* (Toronto, Queen's Printer for Ontario, 2008) 148–52.

natural cause. Second, the Crown needed to prove beyond a reasonable doubt that the deaths did not fit the criteria for a natural but unexplained death.

Natural but unexplained infant death was compendiously referred to by lawyers and experts throughout the case as sudden infant death syndrome (SIDS). In claiming that the deaths were not SIDS, the Crown relied in part on expert evidence that the medical literature had never reported a case in which a family experienced three or more SIDS deaths. In response to the Crown's arguments, the defence suggested that reasonable alternative causes of death existed for each of the children and also that it would be unsafe to convict Folbigg without positive physical evidence of smothering. These submissions drew the jury into the heart of one of the more contentious debates taking place within paediatric forensic pathology and cognate disciplines.

Crown expert Janice Ophoven (on whose report the Crown relied at pre-trial but who did not testify at trial) framed her understanding of the four deaths in terms of the rarity of repeat SIDS, reasoning that the only realistic possibility was that the deaths were deliberately caused. Grahame Barr J ruled during the trial that the expert witnesses could not testify directly about the cumulative improbability of recurrent infant deaths but must confine their opinions to the cause of death of each individual child.[8] This ruling may well have prompted the Crown to decide that it would not call Ophoven to testify. Nonetheless, Ophoven's opinion affected both the trial itself and the public account of the trial. In an expert report that was quoted in the Sydney newspapers before and after Folbigg's trial[9] and on which the NSW Court of Criminal Appeal relied in its pre-trial appeal judgment,[10] Ophoven wrote:

> None of the deaths in the Folbigg case can be attributed to SIDS. It is well recognised that the SIDS process is not a hereditary problem and the statistical probability that 4 children in one sibship could die from SIDS is infinitesimally small. If you calculate the risk of this event occurring 4 times in one family, using routine statistical probability for a random event occurring 4 times in one family (with an occurrence <1/1,000 live births) it would be less than 1 in 1 trillion.[11]

This form of statistical reasoning was highly controversial within the medical research community and was excluded from the criminal justice process by the England and Wales Court of Appeal (Criminal Division) (ECCA) in *R v Clark*.[12]

Australian pathologist Allan Cala, who became a key witness for the Crown, was initially more circumspect than Ophoven. Like all the experts (including defence expert Roger W Byard), Cala was concerned at the familial pattern of

---

[8] *R v Folbigg* (unreported judgment of Barr J on 16 April 2003). This ruling and its effects are closely analysed below in ch 5.

[9] E Connolly, 'Sudden Deaths of Four Siblings One-in-a-Trillion Chance, Court Told' *Sydney Morning Herald* (24 April 2001) 3; F O'Shea, 'Accused Mother cannot Say "I Do"' *Daily Telegraph* (Sydney, 24 April 2001) 7; and L Glendinning, 'Dark Secrets of the Mother who Killed Her Babies' *Sydney Morning Herald* (22 May 2003) 6.

[10] *R v Kathleen Megan Folbigg* [2003] NSWCCA 17 (13 February 2003) [*Folbigg* pre-trial appeal].

[11] Janice Ophoven, 'Expert Report' contained in *Folbigg* case files (above n 4).

[12] *R v Clark* [2003] EWCA Crim 1020. See discussion of this case above in ch 1.

deaths: 'the death of Laura Folbigg cannot be regarded as "another SIDS" . . . The family history of no living children after four live births is highly unusual.'[13] Cala's opinion that the Folbigg children had been murdered became more firm as the case progressed.

Susan Beal, an eminent paediatrician and SIDS researcher who was called by the Crown at trial, wrote in her expert paediatric and epidemiological report:

> As far as I am aware there has never been three or more deaths from SIDS in the one family anywhere in the world, although some families, later proven to have murdered their infants, had infants who were initially classified as SIDS.[14]

Beal's assertion, together with similar information from Cala, formed the basis for the Crown's argument at trial.

Forensic pathologist Byard, who was called by the defence, suggested in his witness statement and at trial that it was inappropriate to generalise about the likelihood of repeat deaths in the Folbigg family. He therefore contested the probative value of evidence that suggested that medical literature had never reliably reported three SIDS deaths in one family. In particular, Byard pointed to the various positive findings on each Folbigg autopsy and the possibility of alternative, natural causes of death in each child.[15] Nonetheless, Byard also testified that recurrent SIDS deaths were rare and that, to his knowledge, no triple SIDS had been reliably reported within the literature.

As I explain in chapter five, in the Crown's language SIDS eventually became a metonym for all natural causes of infant death – including, for example, the epilepsy that was originally ascribed as the cause of Patrick's death. The defence preferred a stricter interpretation. Peter Zahra SC, acting for Folbigg, adhered to Byard's opinion that the possibility of multiple deaths from unrelated natural causes should neither be excluded from consideration nor subjected to statistical analysis based on the unlikelihood of repeated SIDS deaths. This chapter and the next explore the reasons and justifications for those alternative conceptions of the best way to understand the pattern of infant death within the Folbigg family, while chapter five traces the controversy at trial in greater detail. Before exploring the relationship between SIDS and murder, I provide an introduction to the elusive concept of SIDS.

II. Sudden Infant Death Syndrome (SIDS)

SIDS is often described as a diagnosis of exclusion – a cause of death without a known physiological trigger. The term has been used as a 'convenient diagnostic

[13] Allan Cala, 'Autopsy Report to Coroner', *Folbigg* case files (above n 4).
[14] Susan Mitchell Beal, 'Expert Report', *Folbigg* case files (above n 4).
[15] Roger Byard, 'Expert Report', *Folbigg* case files (above n 4).

dustbin'[16] or 'wastebasket'[17] in which to place all manner of infant deaths since the late 1960s. The definition has changed over time, and these changes speak to the ways in which medical attitudes to SIDS have also changed.[18] Historically, sudden unexpected infant death was closely associated with 'death by overlying' (where an infant is suffocated by a sleeping, sometimes intoxicated, parent) and other forms of accidental and, arguably, even non-accidental suffocation.[19] In the 1940s and 1950s, some pathologists suggested that sudden unexpected infant death was identifiably different from asphyxiation, but their 1949 proposal for a medical research agenda fell by the wayside for a number of years.[20]

Michael Johnson and Karl Hufbauer suggest that sudden infant death emerged as a coherent medical problem in the late 1960s within the United States.[21] In 1969, at the second international congress into sudden infant death, J Bruce Beckwith proposed a definition for sudden infant death syndrome: 'the sudden death of any infant or young child, which is unexpected by history, and in which a thorough post-mortem examination fails to demonstrate an adequate cause of death'.[22] Beckwith's definition became the standard within infant death research and clinical pathology for many years. The 1969 conference ushered in a period of intensive research into the causes and prevention of infant death. Johnson and Hufbauer credit bereaved parents' groups, researchers and government officials with working together to transform SIDS 'from an obscure medical mystery into an important medical research problem' over the course of the 1970s.[23]

During the 1970s and 1980s, the predominant attitude within the research community was that sudden unexplained infant deaths resulted from natural causes, and researchers competed to identify those causes. Perhaps due in part to their willingness to fund research directly and to lobby government for research grants, parents became the research community's natural allies: '[a]ffected parents need to know the cause of their baby's death, and they look to the pathologist

---

[16] JL Emery, 'Infanticide, Filicide, and Cot Death' (1985) 60 *Archives of Disease in Childhood* 505, 505.

[17] VJ DiMaio, 'Repeat Sudden Unexpected Infant Death' (2005) 365 *The Lancet* 1137–38, 1137.

[18] I am here drawing upon Wittgenstein's notion that the meaning of words and phrases is contingent upon their use in language, and this meaning shifts with time and context: L Wittgenstein, *Philosophical Investigations* (Oxford, Blackwell, 1958). It follows that by tracing shifts in language usage, we can understand something of the changes that have taken place within the communities that use that language. The utility of using Wittgenstein's insights to help understand scientific knowledge is discussed in M Erickson, *Science, Culture and Society: Understanding Science in the Twenty-First Century* (Cambridge, Polity, 2005) 64–67.

[19] MP Johnson and K Hufbauer, 'Sudden Infant Death Syndrome as a Medical Research Problem Since 1945' (1982) 30 *Social Problems* 65–81, 67–69; and Firstman and Talan, 'SIDS and Infanticide' (above n 2).

[20] Johnson and Hufbauer (ibid) 67–68. In the Australian context, the asphyxiation theory was challenged by Melbourne pathologist Keith Bowden in an article that is widely cited within the medical literature as an early example of SIDS research: K Bowden, 'Sudden Death or Alleged Accidental Suffocation in Babies' (1950) 1 *Medical Journal of Australia* 65–72.

[21] Johnson and Hufbauer (above n 19).

[22] JB Beckwith, 'Discussion of Terminology and Definition in the Sudden Infant Death Syndrome' in AB Bergman, JB Beckwith and CG Ray (eds), *Sudden Infant Death Syndrome: Proceedings of the Second International Conference on the Sudden Causes of Death in Infants* (Seattle, University of Washington Press, 1970) 14–22, 18.

[23] Johnson and Hufbauer (above n 19) 65.

for the answer.'[24] SIDS researchers and bereaved parents' groups were hailed for overcoming ignorance and apathy in their quest to understand and to prevent SIDS.[25]

In 1972, Alfred Steinschneider published an article in which he suggested that 'prolonged apnoea' may form part of the mechanism by which SIDS deaths occur.[26] Prolonged apnoea is an extended moment in which an infant stops breathing during sleep – Steinschneider defined it as any period longer than two seconds, although many would require fifteen seconds.[27] Steinschneider reported his observations of five infants from three families. All of these infants experienced prolonged apnoea, and two (from the same family) subsequently died. Their deaths were attributed to SIDS after full autopsies. Steinschneider noted that this family had experienced three previous infant deaths, and suggested the possibility that vulnerability to SIDS might run in families. Eleven years after Steinschneider published this study, Gregory described the Steinschneider article as initiating a scientific revolution or paradigm shift within the medical profession with regard to infant death.[28]

In so describing Steinschneider's article, Gregory was drawing upon Thomas Kuhn's articulation of scientific revolutions and their role within science research. Kuhn defined a scientific revolution as:

> the community's rejection of one time-honored scientific theory in favour of another incompatible with it. [This variation] produced a consequent shift in the problems available for scientific scrutiny and in the standards by which the profession determined what should count as an admissible problem or as a legitimate problem-solution.[29]

According to Kuhn, these shifts do not occur in a vacuum of 'pure research' but must be understood with reference to broader social, economic and institutional context. Gregory explains that after Steinschneider's article was published, a scientific revolution occurred within SIDS research. Most research scientists worked from the apnoea hypothesis, and sleep monitoring was universally recommended to parents, particularly parents of high-risk infants (such as those who'd had a sibling die of SIDS).[30] Gregory's quantitative analysis of the literature published between 1972 and 1982 supports his proposition that SIDS research underwent a profound shift.[31] In Kuhn's terms, the range of problems available for scientific

[24] M Valdes-Dapena, 'The Pathologist and the Sudden Infant Death Syndrome' (1982) 106 *American Journal of Pathology* 118–31, 119. See also GJ Gregory, 'Citation Study of a Scientific Revolution: Sudden Infant Death Syndrome' (1983) 5 *Scientometrics* 313–27, 314; and Johnson and Hufbauer (above n 19).

[25] Gregory, 'Citation Study' (ibid); and Johnson and Hufbauer (above n 19).

[26] A Steinschneider, 'Prolonged Apnea and the Sudden Infant Death Syndrome: Clinical and Laboratory Observations' (1972) 50 *Pediatrics* 646.

[27] See DC Shannon and DH Kelly, 'SIDS and Near-SIDS' (1982) 306 *New England Journal of Medicine* 1022–28.

[28] Gregory, 'Citation Study' (above n 24) 315.

[29] TS Kuhn, *The Structure of Scientific Revolutions*, 3rd edn (Chicago, University of Chicago Press, 1996) 7.

[30] Gregory, 'Citation Study' (above n 24) 315.

[31] Ibid. See also M Valdes-Dapena, 'Sudden Infant Death Syndrome: A Review of the Medical Literature 1974–1979' (1980) 66 *Pediatrics* 597–614.

scrutiny was constrained by the orthodoxy that SIDS was somehow related to apnoea. Even those research scientists who disagreed with Steinschneider's theory framed their research in terms of that disagreement.

Steinschneider's hypothesis was attractive for many reasons. For parents, the possibility of preventing SIDS through apnoea monitoring provided hope and reassurance.[32] For researchers, the idea that SIDS had a set mechanism that could be identified in particular infants before they died gave them a problem they could actually solve.[33] According to Kuhn, the possibility of solution is a key ingredient in a professional community's decision to build consensus around a new paradigm.[34]

Somewhat unexpectedly, the prolonged apnoea hypothesis proved difficult to conclusively verify or refute.[35] After years of study there was no strong evidence that infant apnoea monitors averted infant death except in premature infants.[36] By the late 1980s, researchers variously felt that more fertile fields lay within neuroscience and respiratory regulation, cardiology and genetics, or in the possibility of a 'multifactoral' cause.[37] Whatever the SIDS mechanism, most researchers within paediatric pathology adhered to an idiopathic explanation – that is, they believed that the cause of sudden infant death was a subtle abnormality within the infant rather than coming, for example, exclusively from environmental factors.[38]

At the same time, epidemiologists were uncovering evidence of certain patterns within SIDS deaths. A correlation between prone (face-down) sleep position and infant death had long been postulated by Australian paediatricians, including Susan Beal, who later was a prosecution expert in the *Folbigg* case.[39] For some time, the expert community was cautious about whether the statistical correlation was sufficiently firm, and knowledge of alternative risks sufficiently good, to form the basis of a public health campaign.[40] Australian SIDS researchers eventually

---

[32] Gregory, 'Citation Study' (above n 24) 323–24. See also RS Raring, *Crib Death: Scourge of Infants, Shame of Society* (Hicksville, Exposition Press, 1975).

[33] Gregory, 'Citation Study' (above n 24) 324.

[34] Kuhn (above n 29) 153–55.

[35] AB Bergman, 'Wrong Turns in Sudden Infant Death Syndrome Research' (1997) 99 *Pediatrics* 119.

[36] American Academy of Pediatrics, 'Prolonged Infantile Apnoea' (1985) 76 *Pediatrics* 129–31; and Bergman (ibid).

[37] CE Hunt and RT Brouilette, 'Sudden Infant Death Syndrome: 1987 Perspective' (1987) 110 *Journal of Pediatrics* 669–78. See also the essays collected in PJ Schwarz, DP Southall and M Valdes-Dapena (eds), 'The Sudden Infant Death Syndrome: Cardiac and Respiratory Mechanisms and Interventions' (1988) 533 *Annals of the New York Academy of Science*.

[38] G Gregory, 'Influence of the Public on a Scientific Revolution: The Case of Sudden Infant Death Syndrome' (1990) 11 *Science Communication* 248, 253–55.

[39] SM Beal and H Blundell, 'Sudden Infant Death Syndrome Related to Position in the Cot' (1978) 2 *Medical Journal of Australia* 217–18; S Beal, 'Sleeping Position and Sudden Infant Death Syndrome (Letter)' (1988) 149 *Medical Journal of Australia* 562. Dutch researchers independently came up with the same theory in the late 1980s: GA Jonge and AC Engelberts, 'Cot Deaths and Sleeping Position (Letter)' (1989) ii *Lancet* 1149–50.

[40] See generally vol 27, issue 6 of the *Journal of Paediatric and Child Health*. An overview of the pros and cons is provided in FJ Stanley and RW Byard, 'The Association between Prone Sleeping Position and Sudden Infant Death Syndrome (SIDS): An Editorial Overview' (1991) 27 *Journal of Paediatric and Child Health* 325–28.

met in July 1991 to consider whether to encourage caregivers to lay infants to sleep on their backs. They unanimously agreed to proceed with this recommendation.[41] Many SIDS researchers acknowledge that the public health campaign successfully reduced the incidence of SIDS without necessarily casting much light on the causes of sudden infant death.

In 1989, the year of Caleb Folbigg's birth and death, the SIDS rate in New South Wales was 2.06 per 1,000.[42] In 1993, the year of Sarah Folbigg's death, the rate had declined to 0.89 per 1,000.[43] By 1999, when Laura Folbigg died, the rate was 0.62 SIDS deaths per 1,000 infants.[44] In urban areas that were not capital cities (such as Newcastle and Singleton, where the Folbiggs lived) these rates were consistently higher. For example, in 1993 the urban rate in non-capital cities was 1.23 SIDS deaths per 1,000 live births. Most experts attributed the decline in SIDS deaths between 1989 and 1999 to the 'back to sleep campaign', which encouraged parents to lay their babies to sleep on their backs rather than prone or on their sides.[45] All four Folbigg children were lying on their backs when they were found dead, and this became a feature in the prosecution case that SIDS was an unlikely cause of death for any of the children.[46]

While the incidence of SIDS was declining over the course of the 1990s, autopsy protocols and child death investigations were also becoming more thorough. This is an early glimmer of a problem that became increasingly acute within the field of SIDS research: many researchers believed that infant deaths were under-investigated and that it was a lack of appropriate death investigation procedures rather than a lack of medical knowledge that explained a significant proportion of SIDS deaths.[47] By the 1990s, Beckwith's original definition of SIDS was felt by many paediatricians and paediatric pathologists (including Beckwith)[48] to be too vague – both in terms of what constitutes a 'thorough post-mortem

---

[41] SM Beal et al, 'A Scientific Review of the Association between Prone Sleeping Position and Sudden Infant Death Syndrome' (1991) 27 *Journal of Paediatrics and Child Health* 323–24. An international conference was convened in the US in 1994 to consider whether to adopt this recommendation. See M Willinger, HJ Hoffman and RB Hartford, 'Infant Sleep Position and Risk for Sudden Infant Death Syndrome: Report of Meeting Held January 13 and 14, 1994, National Institute of Health, Bethesda, MD' (1994) 93 *Pediatrics* 814–19.

[42] Australian Bureau of Statistics, 'SIDS in Australia 1981–2000: A Statistical Overview' 11, available at www.sidsandkids.org/research/.

[43] Ibid.

[44] Ibid.

[45] See, eg, RW Byard and SM Beal, 'Has Changing Diagnostic Preference been Responsible for the Recent Fall in Incidence of Sudden Infant Death Syndrome in South Australia?' (1995) 31 *Journal of Paediatrics and Child Health* 197–199, 199.

[46] However, SIDS is far from unknown among babies who sleep on their backs. See, eg, SM Beal, P Baghurst and G Antoniou, 'Sudden Infant Death Syndrome (SIDS) in South Australia 1968–97, Part 2: The Epidemiology of Non-prone and Non-covered SIDS Infants' (2000) 36 *Journal of Paediatrics and Child Health* 548–51.

[47] P Fleming et al, *Sudden Unexpected Deaths in Infancy: The CESDI SUDI Studies 1993–1996* (London, The Stationery Office, 2000). See also Byard and Beal, 'Has Changing Diagnostic Preference Been Responsible?' (above n 45); M Bass et al, 'Death Scene Investigation in Sudden Infant Death' (1986) 315 *New England Journal of Medicine* 100–5.

[48] JB Beckwith, 'Foreword' in Byard and Krous (eds) (above n 2) ix–x.

investigation'[49] and because it did not set a limit on the age of a child whose death may be attributed to SIDS.[50] A number of alternative definitions were proposed[51] and rejected.[52]

In 1992, Australian pathologists developed a national SIDS autopsy protocol in an effort to prevent mis-categorisation of infant deaths.[53] At that time, medical researchers still did not know what actually caused SIDS deaths, nor whether there were multiple causes collected within a single category.[54] (This uncertainty continues to the present day, raising the question of why some scientific truth claims have come to be embraced over others.) Following the national protocol, Australian pathologists and paediatricians began to distinguish more systematically between 'pure SIDS deaths' (in which no significant findings emerge from autopsy, post-mortem tests, medical history or investigation), 'borderline SIDS' (in which some findings emerge, though insufficient to constitute a cause of death) and infant deaths attributable to known causes.[55] According to the Australian Bureau of Statistics, reclassification accounts for at least some of the apparent decline in SIDS between the early 1990s and 1999.[56]

By the late 1990s, pathologists were increasingly prone to using the 'undetermined' cause of death diagnosis that Cala ascribed to Laura Folbigg's death.[57] This diagnosis was variously described during Folbigg's trial; it is used differently by different pathologists but most often correlates with borderline SIDS. That is, it

---

[49] C Rambaud, C Guilleminault and P Campbell, 'Definition of Sudden Infant Death Syndrome' (1994) 308 *British Medical Journal* 1439, 1439 reporting the proceedings of the second International Conference on Sudden Infant Death Syndrome (conducted in 1992); HJ Krous et al, 'Sudden Infant Death Syndrome and Unclassified Sudden Infant Deaths: A Definitional and Diagnostic Approach' (2004) 114 *Pediatrics* 234–38, 234. For arguments against change, see EA Mitchell et al, 'Definition of Sudden Infant Death Syndrome: Keep Current Definition' (1994) 309 *British Medical Journal* 607. The shortcomings in Beckwith's definition of SIDS were explicitly foreshadowed in 1969 in Beckwith, 'Discussion of Terminology and Definition' (above n 22).

[50] Krous et al (ibid).

[51] Eg: M Willinger, LS James and C Catz, 'Defining the Sudden Infant Death Syndrome (SIDS): Deliberations of an Expert Panel Convened by the National Institute of Child Health and Human Development' (1991) 11 *Pediatric Pathology* 677–84.

[52] Rambaud, Guilleminault and Campbell (above n 49); and Mitchell et al (above n 49).

[53] See RW Byard, 'Inaccurate Classification of Infant Deaths in Australia: A Persistent and Pervasive Problem' (2001) 175 *Medical Journal of Australia* 5–7.

[54] PW Goldwater, 'Sudden Infant Death Syndrome: A Critical Review of Approaches to Research' (2003) 88 *Archives of Disease in Childhood* 1095–100.

[55] See, eg, RW Byard, J MacKenzie and SM Beal, 'Formal Retrospective Case Review and Sudden Infant Death' (1997) 86 *Acta Paediatrics* 1011–12; M Arnestad, Å Vege and TO Rognum, 'Evaluation of Diagnostic Tools Applied in the Examination of Sudden Unexpected Deaths in Infancy and Early Childhood' (2002) 125 *Forensic Science International* 262–68.

[56] Australian Bureau of Statistics, 'SIDS in Australia 1981–2000' (above n 42) 2. A similar phenomenon was observed in the US: MH Malloy and M MacDorman, 'Changes in the Classification of Sudden Unexplained Infant Deaths: United States, 1992–2001' (2005) 115 *Pediatrics* 1247–53. But see Byard and Beal, 'Has Changing Diagnostic Preference Been Responsible?' (above n 45) (dealing with the decline in infant deaths between 1984 and 1992).

[57] Byard, MacKenzie and Beal (above n 55) 1011. See CJ Bacon, 'Standard System for Postmortem Examination and Certification Needs to be Agreed' (2000) 320 *British Medical Journal* 310–11 for the relevant English statistics between 1996 and 1998. English pathologists use 'unascertained' rather than 'undetermined', but its meaning seems to be the same.

generally describes an infant death in which some findings emerge, though they are considered insufficient to constitute a cause of death. In 2001, the American Academy of Pediatrics (AAP) published a policy statement in which it recommended that the 'undetermined' label should apply instead of SIDS when investigations 'reveal substantial and reasonable uncertainty regarding the cause or manner of death'.[58] This policy statement became central to Kathleen Folbigg's trial. While paediatric pathologists debated the merits of these shifts, a different potential explanation for some SIDS deaths emerged.

III. The Emergence of Murder

Michel Foucault described *entstehung*, or emergence, as a moment within an ongoing struggle between forces in the production of truth.[59] Relevantly, emergence is the moment in which a discourse that has previously been marginalised takes a more authoritative role. 'Emergence is thus the entry of forces; it is their eruption, the leap from the wings to centre stage, each in its youthful strength.'[60] Emergence provides a useful metaphor for the shift that took place within SIDS research in the mid-1990s, because it focuses on a human process of reconfigured emphasis rather than advancing the notion that new ideas appear spontaneously or naturally from scientific enquiry to further science's progressive march. The shift that interests me is the growing concern among paediatric forensic pathologists during the 1990s that some sudden infant deaths, previously considered natural, might in fact be disguised homicides. While this shift had numerous antecedents, much can be understood from the curious fortunes of Steinschneider's 1972 article on prolonged apnoea.

The medical community's response to Steinschneider's article was never as uniformly positive as Gregory suggested when he praised the paradigm shift in SIDS research.[61] In 1973, John Hick wrote to the medical journal *Pediatrics*, suggesting that Steinschneider had described a pattern of child abuse and murder in the family that experienced five infant deaths, rather than a pattern of natural illness and death.[62] Steinschneider's reply to this letter warned against identifying child abuse as an easy explanation for a seemingly intractable research problem:

> The possibility of child abuse should be considered in every case of sudden infant death. However, extreme restraint must be exercised that this diagnosis not become one of exclusion. *Failure to define the cause* of a sudden infant death can never be used as sup-

[58] American Academy of Pediatrics, 'Distinguishing Sudden Infant Death Syndrome from Child Abuse Fatalities' (2001) 107 *Pediatrics* 437–41, 438.

[59] M Foucault, 'Nietzsche, Genealogy, History' in DF Bouchard (ed), *Language, Counter-Memory, Practice* (Ithaca, Cornell University Press, 1977) 139–64.

[60] Ibid, 149–50.

[61] Gregory, 'Citation Study' (above n 24).

[62] JF Hick, 'Sudden Infant Death Syndrome and Child Abuse' (1973) 52 *Pediatrics* 147.

port for the diagnosis of child abuse. Humanity as well as logic dictates the need for positive evidence as well as extreme sensitivity in the collection of such information.[63]

In this statement Steinschneider imports the law's logic – parents must be treated as being innocent of child abuse, and other possibilities should be explored, until there is positive evidence that they have harmed their children. The editor applauded Steinschneider for his approach to the matter.[64] Hick's letter appears to have been mostly ignored within the research community, although others later raised the same concern.[65]

Hick's suspicions were seemingly vindicated in 1995 when Waneta Hoyt, whose infants' deaths Steinschneider reported, was convicted of murdering her five children.[66] The district attorney who prosecuted the case became aware of the Hoyt family after reading Steinschneider's paper and connecting the salient facts with government death records. *Pediatrics* published an erratum to Steinschneider's article, with an editor's note: 'This is an incredible story. The whole apnoea home monitoring to prevent SIDS movement began with Steinschneider's original paper.'[67]

Waneta Hoyt confessed to the murders during a long police interview conducted in 1994. She later recanted, claiming that the confession had made under duress.[68] Steinschneider's role in lending scientific legitimacy to Hoyt's claim that her infants had died of natural causes became the subject of close scrutiny within the popular press.[69] Journalists speculated about how many other mothers might have murdered their children without detection.[70] The leading journal *Science* framed the *Hoyt* case as a trial for SIDS research and SIDS researchers, as much as for the accused.[71] In a flurry of articles, commentaries and letters published in *Pediatrics* after Hoyt's conviction, the paediatric community sought to come to terms with the meaning and consequences of Hoyt's conviction.[72] One

---

[63] A Steinschneider, 'Reply to John F Hick' (1973) 52 *Pediatrics* 147.

[64] Ibid.

[65] See, eg, V DiMaio, 'SIDS or Murder' (1988) 81 *Pediatrics* 747; and E Krongrad, 'Infants at High Risk for Sudden Infant Death Syndrome??? Have They been Identified??? A Commentary' (1991) 88 *Pediatrics* 1274.

[66] JF Hick, 'Very Important Erratum? Twenty Years Later' (1994) 93 *Pediatrics* 944; R Firstman and J Talan, *The Death of Innocents: A True Story of Murder, Medicine, and High-Stakes Science* (New York, Bantam Books, 1997); and G Pinholster, 'Multiple "SIDS" Case Ruled Murder' (1995) 268 *Science* 494.

[67] See editor's note to Hick, 'Very Important Erratum?' (ibid).

[68] G Judson, 'Mother Guilty in the Killings of 5 Babies' *New York Times* (22 April 1995), available at www.nytimes.com; E Nieves, 'In Prison: A Mother Proclaims Innocence in Babies' Deaths' *New York Times* (19 May 1995), available at www.nytimes.com; and G Pinholster, 'SIDS Paper Triggers a Murder Charge' (1994) 264 *Science* 197–98.

[69] Eg: Firstman and Talan, *The Death of Innocents* (above n 66); Judson (ibid); and S Begley and A Underwood, 'The Nursery's Littlest Victims' *Newsweek* (22 September 1997) 72–73.

[70] Begley and Underwood (ibid); and A Toufexis, 'When is Crib Death a Cover for Murder?' *Time* (11 April 1994), available at www.time.com.

[71] Pinholster, 'SIDS Paper Triggers a Murder Charge' (above n 68); and Pinholster, 'Multiple "SIDS" Case Ruled Murder' (above n 66).

[72] Eg: GA Little and JG Brooks, 'Accepting the Unthinkable' (1994) 94 *Pediatrics* 748–49; JFL, 'A Housewife is Convicted of Murdering Her Five Children' (1995) 95 *Pediatrics* A32; MP Samuels and DA Southall, 'Child Abuse and Apparent Life Threatening Events' (1995) 96 *Pediatrics* 167–68;

concern expressed in those pages was how to deal with the fact that this new development had emerged from 'legal and not scientific inquiry'.[73] The editor of *Pediatrics* who had originally published Steinschneider's article, Jerold Lucey, was quoted by *Newsweek* as saying, 'We should never have published this article . . . [S]ome physicians still believe SIDS runs in families. It doesn't – murder does.'[74]

The questions that had been asked about Steinschneider's research in 1973 were receiving very different answers by 1995. Even before Hoyt was found guilty, many paediatric pathologists seemed to redefine Steinschneider's article at best as being an embarrassingly naïve study and at worst as rendering him, morally, an accessory to murder. This shifting response is partly attributable to the emergence of positive evidence against Hoyt and to the inconclusive nature of scientists' attempts to prove or disprove Steinschneider's hypothesis. It is also, however, reflective of a change within the broader cultural context in which paediatric pathologists were working.

David Garland has described how the dominant discourses regarding criminality were profoundly transformed between the early 1970s and the mid-1990s. Broadly speaking, during the post-WWII period, criminality was perceived in Britain and America as 'a problem of defective or poorly adapted individuals and families, or else as a symptom of need, social injustice, and the inevitable clash of cultural norms'.[75] Criminals could accordingly be identified in part through their lack of fit with other social norms. By the 1990s, however, a 'culture of control' had become more pervasive and criminality correspondingly less distinct – 'a normal, routine, commonplace aspect of modern society, committed by individuals who are, to all intents and purposes, perfectly normal'.[76] Ian Hacking has traced how this shift manifested within the cultural and medical approach to child abuse during this period.[77] Kirsten Kramar has similarly demonstrated that by the late twentieth century, infanticide had been reconstructed within the Canadian public imagination as an extreme form of child abuse, warranting more severe punishment than was previously accepted within that society.[78] Paediatric forensic pathologists were on the front lines of these shifts, because they are the ones who medically investigate individual children's deaths, and because their conclusions are important to deciding whether to lay criminal charges.

V DiMaio, 'Letter' (1995) 96 *Pediatrics* 168; GA Little and JG Brooks, 'Reply to DiMaio and Samuels and Southall' (1995) 96 *Pediatrics* 168; and JFL, 'Mothers Who Murder Their Children' (1996) 98 *Pediatrics* A38.

[73] Little and Brooks, 'Accepting the Unthinkable' (ibid) 748.

[74] Begley and Underwood (above n 69).

[75] D Garland, *The Culture of Control: Crime and Social Order in Contemporary Society* (Oxford, Oxford University Press, 2001) 15. For an account of shifts within Australian criminology, see D Brown, ''Losing My Religion': Reflections on Critical Criminology in Australia' in K Carrington and R Hogg (eds), *Critical Criminology: Issues, Debates, Challenges* (Cullompton, Willan Publishing, 2002) 73–113.

[76] Garland (ibid).

[77] I Hacking, *The Social Construction of What?* (Cambridge, Harvard University Press, 1999) ch 5.

[78] KJ Kramar, *Unwilling Mothers, Unwanted Babies: Infanticide in Canada* (Vancouver, University of British Columbia Press, 2005) ch 1.

The generalised trend towards criminalisation was tied specifically to a mistrust of mothers in the context of unexplained infant death. At its simplest level, this connection can be explained by the fact that mothers still tend to be the primary caregivers in contemporary Western society. Within a dyadic heterosexual parenting arrangement, the mother is therefore the parent most likely to have the opportunity to kill a child and also most likely to find a child dead. (In many cases, including *Folbigg*, finding the child later becomes a marker of suspicion.) Fiona Raitt and Suzanne Zeedyk, however, have identified another reason why mothers have been the primary suspects in many cases. They suggest that the absence of conclusive evidence about cause of death creates a need 'to look for additional means of explaining the events under investigation'.[79] Discourses about proper mothering came to work as a circuit breaker for science, transferring public focus away from the inability of forensic pathology to explain a set of infant deaths. A longstanding gap in science could thereby be written off as never having been a gap at all.

By the time Hoyt was charged, the possibility that a mother might murder her children yet appear well-adjusted and loving to a somewhat expert observer had become more real. Ironically, as Kathleen Daly has pointed out, late twentieth-century struggles for formal gender equality had some negative consequences for women, as overly simple statistical analyses were used to argue that women were leniently treated in the criminal justice system.[80] The spectre of covert homicide haunted the criminological and scientific literature of the mid- to late 1990s. The amount of 'positive evidence' required to raise suspicion in a pathologist's mind may correspondingly have declined. Even so, the socioeconomic markers of potential criminality were not irrelevant. For example, news articles regarding Hoyt's murder trial invariably referred to the facts that she had left school early to have her first child and that she resided in a trailer park during the time when she is alleged to have killed her children.[81]

Picking up on these cultural shifts and especially on Hoyt's conviction, many paediatric pathologists were embarrassed by Steinschneider's apparent naivety, and they hurried to distance themselves from his research. After Hoyt's conviction, the desire to give mothers the benefit of the doubt in the absence of positive evidence was marginalised within the medical literature almost (but never completely) to the point of disappearing. In place of the previous caution about labelling parents, the (pre-existing) notion that pathologists could identify homicide via a familial pattern of infant deaths leapt into centre stage. In the process, the distinction between medical research and criminal investigation – upon which Steinschneider insisted – was reconfigured.

---

[79] F Raitt and MS Zeedyk, 'Mothers on Trial: Discourses of Cot Death and Munchausen's Syndrome by Proxy' (2004) 12 *Feminist Legal Studies* 257, 264.

[80] K Daly, 'Gender and Punishment Disparity' in GS Bridges and MA Myers (eds), *Inequality, Crime and Social Control* (Boulder, Westview Press, 1994) 117.

[81] Eg, G Judson, 'Mother Guilty in the Killings of 5 Babies' *New York Times* (22 April 1995), available at www.nytimes.com.

4

Distinguishing Homicide from SIDS

R V FOLBIGG, like its companion cases *Clark, Cannings, Anthony, Phillips* and *Matthey*,[1] engaged one of the most uncertain aspects of paediatric forensic pathology: distinguishing sudden infant death syndrome (SIDS) from smothering. SIDS and imposed asphyxiation have coexisted within both popular and medical consciousness since the term 'sudden infant death syndrome' was first framed:

> These two inscrutable entities of sudden infant death and infanticide – one an aberration of the undeveloped body, the other a riddle of the contorted mind – have lived parallel lives through the ages, shadowing each other, occasionally intersecting . . . [I]t has become clear that any broad discussion of SIDS must include the infanticide factor – in spite of how vague it is, but more important, *because* of how vague it is.[2]

In part, this coexistence is a hangover from the prevalent mid-twentieth-century understanding of sudden infant death as being due to asphyxiation, whether accidental or deliberate.[3] Many pathologists believe that there are no conclusive physical signs by which it is possible to distinguish SIDS from smothering in a very young child. In this chapter, I explain the work that has been done within medical research to identify markers that will distinguish these causes and identify some ways in which gendered expectations inform this research. First, however, I explain that some criminologists and legal commentators have attempted to overcome the difficulties of identifying smothering deaths by estimating the 'true incidence' of infant homicide, particularly homicides committed by mothers.

---

[1] *R v Clark* [2003] EWCA Crim 1020 (Court of Appeal); *R v Cannings* [2004] EWCA Crim 1 (Court of Appeal); *R v Anthony* [2005] EWCA Crim 952 (Court of Appeal); *R v Phillips* [1999] NSWSC 1175 (17 December 1999) (Supreme Court of New South Wales); and *R v Matthey* [2007] VSC 398 (Supreme Court of Victoria). For an overview of these cases, as well the *Folbigg* case, see above chs 1 and 2.

[2] R Firstman and J Talan, 'SIDS and Infanticide' in RW Byard and HF Krous (eds), *Sudden Infant Death Syndrome: Problems, Progress and Possibilities* (New York, Oxford University Press, 2001) 292.

[3] See K Bowden, 'Sudden Death or Alleged Accidental Suffocation in Babies' (1950) 1 *Medical Journal of Australia* 65–72; and SM Beal, 'The Rise and Fall of Several Theories' in Byard and Krous (eds) (ibid) 236–38.

I. The 'True Incidence' of Child Homicide

The difficulties pathologists experience when seeking to distinguish natural from unnatural infant deaths have given rise to a slew of research that is directed towards identifying the 'true incidence' of child homicide.[4] Government statistical reports regarding child homicide frequently state that the statistics under-report the true incidence of homicide.[5] This true incidence is most often understood as the sum of: identified, prosecuted homicides; identified but unprosecuted homicides; and unidentified homicides.

The term 'covert homicide' and its correlates have various uses within the legal and medical literature. For example, Ania Wilczynski defines her 'dark figure' of infant homicide to include all unprosecuted deaths from abuse and neglect, deaths in which violence was a contributing factor although not the cause, as well as all deaths that pathologists consider may be deliberate smothering.[6] Fiona Brookman and Jane Nolan include cases in which the defendants are acquitted and those in which pathologists believe the infants may have been smothered in their estimate of the 'true incidence' of infanticide.[7] Mary Overpeck draws on deaths through unintentional injury, deaths from unknown causes, and SIDS deaths in her discussion of the epidemiology of infanticide.[8] Some medical scientists use the phrase 'covert homicide' to refer specifically to smothering deaths and other deliberately inflicted deaths that are not identified during autopsy.[9] Others use the phrase 'gentle battering' to describe smothering deaths that may not be identifiable on autopsy but are diagnosed through the post-mortem investigation.[10] The degree of

---

[4] Dorothy Chunn has pointed out that although the image of huge amounts of undetected crime pervades mainstream criminological literature, homicide statistics are usually considered to be reasonably accurate: because bodies are hard to hide and because 'science' can provide unequivocal evidence of homicide. Reducing the 'dark figure' of homicide is thus often perceived as a matter of improved methods of detection (personal correspondence with author, November 2008). Despite this widely held presumption, the boundaries of homicide are contested – eg, some scholars criticise the exclusion of deaths caused by industrial accident from homicide statistics. See I Grant, D Chunn and C Boyle, *The Law of Homicide* (Scarborough, Carswell, 1994) ch 1.

[5] Eg, H Strang, *Children as Victims of Homicide* (Canberra, Australian Institute of Criminology, 1996) 2.

[6] A Wilczynski, *Child Homicide* (London, Greenwich Medical Media, 1997) 34–36.

[7] The term 'infanticide' is used here in its general sense, not in its technical legal sense. See F Brookman and J Nolan, 'The Dark Figure of Infanticide in England and Wales' (2006) 21 *Journal of Interpersonal Violence* 869.

[8] Again, in its general sense. M Overpeck, 'Epidemiology of Infanticide' in MG Spinelli (ed), *Infanticide: Psychosocial and Legal Perspectives on Mothers Who Kill* (Washington, DC, American Psychiatric Publishing, 2003) 19.

[9] C Bacon, 'How Common is Repeat Sudden Infant Death Syndrome?' (2008) 93 *Archives of Disease in Childhood* 323; S Levene and CJ Bacon, 'Sudden Unexpected Death and Covert Homicide in Infancy' (2004) 89 *Archives of Disease in Childhood* 443; and HA Pollack, 'Changes in the Timing of SIDS Deaths in 1989 and 1999: Indirect Evidence of Low Homicide Prevalence among Reported Cases' (2006) 20 *Pediatric and Perinatal Epidemiology* 2.

[10] JL Emery and EM Taylor, 'Investigation of SIDS' (1986) 315 *New England Journal of Medicine* 1676.

certainty required about cause of death before it will be attributed to homicide varies from author to author.

A slippage arises within the literature, with some authors using conviction rates for unlawful homicide (which must, of course, be proven beyond a reasonable doubt) to assert that many child killers go unprosecuted and unpunished in circumstances where conviction is appropriate. These accounts do not acknowledge the possibility that the evidence might not establish cause of death to the criminal standard, or that a defence may apply, or that the author's ascribed cause of death might simply be wrong. The possibility of an innocent explanation remains unidentified even when the author disagrees with the cause of death originally ascribed by the autopsying pathologist. Perhaps the most apposite example of this phenomenon is provided by the New South Wales Child Death Review Team (CDRT). In 2002 (before Kathleen Folbigg was convicted but after she was charged), CDRT published a report entitled *Fatal Assault of Children and Young People.*[11] The report includes a table headed 'Fatal Non-Accidental Injury: Prior Violence', which lists the death of an 18-month-old female. The method of death is listed as 'suffocation', with the note 'three previous sibling deaths in the family'.[12] If, as seems highly probable from the broader context, this is a reference to Laura Folbigg's death, it is startlingly incomplete. CDRT did not cast Laura's method of death in tentative terms, flag that criminal charges were pending in respect of this death or note that a different cause of death had been listed on her autopsy report.[13]

A second child, whose death is listed in the same table as being due to 'induced asphyxia', contains a similar note: 'two prior sibling deaths in the family'.[14] This and other information supplied in the report fits with Benjamin Phillips, whose death gave rise to *R v Phillips.*[15] Notably, however, the charges against Tracey Louise Phillips, which are discussed above in chapter one, did not proceed after Bell J excluded the prosecution's coincidence reasoning. In her judgment, Bell J noted that while the investigating pathologist was unable to determine the cause of Benjamin Phillips' death, the autopsy report concluded that it was consistent with either SIDS or induced asphyxia.[16] The prosecution discontinued proceedings against Phillips before the 2002 CDRT report was published. Again, this legal context is suppressed within the CDRT report, which includes a selective case history of 'Joe', an eight-and-a-half-month-old child who appears to be Benjamin Phillips.[17]

Elsewhere in its 2002 report, CDRT reinforces the facticity of its attributed causes of death despite the possible absence of legal proof and condemns the

---

[11] New South Wales Child Death Review Team (CDRT), *Fatal Assault of Children and Young People* (Sydney, NSW Commission for Children and Young People, 2002).

[12] Ibid, 52.

[13] See the outline of the *Folbigg* case above in ch 2.

[14] New South Wales CDRT (above n 11).

[15] *R v Phillips* (above n 1).

[16] Ibid, paras 6–8.

[17] NSW CDRT (above n 11).

inadequacy of the criminal justice system's response to fatal child assault: 'Of the 19 children who died from non-accidental injury, only five of the perpetrators have received criminal convictions to date.'[18] At the time, neither autopsying pathologists nor criminal courts had concluded that Laura Folbigg's death or Benjamin Phillip's death was a homicide. Moreover, the proceeding arising from Benjamin Phillip's death had been discontinued. Nonetheless, the possibility that pathologists and/or criminal courts might legitimately conclude that these deaths were not proven homicide is nowhere entertained.

The case studies and statistics reported in the CDRT 2002 report *objectified* knowledge about the causes of infant death in Dorothy Smith's pejorative sense of the term.[19] The CDRT institutional processes transformed these contested and uncertain deaths into undisputed homicides. The decision CDRT made to classify these deaths as homicides was elided by the factual prose style adopted in the report. Its choices became more difficult to identify because confidentiality prompted CDRT to adopt pseudonyms and limit the amount of detail about any individual death. Nonetheless, the CDRT fatal assault reports have become authoritative sources of quantitative information about fatal child abuse in New South Wales and have provided a model for other jurisdictions.[20]

The terms 'covert homicide', 'infanticide' (in its general, non-technical sense) and 'child homicide' can each be used in a way that emphasises the probable or even suspected mode of death to the exclusion of the legal question of whether a particular person should be convicted of a crime in respect of a given death. In his discussion of the television programme *CSI*, Nolan has pointed out that prosecutors and court proceedings are absent from the show because 'the conviction is in the science'.[21] The tendency to regard scientific belief in an unnatural cause of death as conclusive for both social and legal purposes also pervades the criminological literature on unexplained infant death. At times, as in the CDRT report quoted above, this scientific belief becomes a warrant to criticise the criminal justice system for inaction or even for obstructing truth-finding. This outcome may be inevitable in light of the co-construction of legal and medical understandings about infant death. Nonetheless, it leaves the impression that there exists a substantial number of parents, particularly mothers, who murder their infants without being convicted of any crime. Secondarily, it reinforces the sense that

---

[18] Ibid, xiv.

[19] DE Smith, *Texts, Facts and Femininity: Exploring the Relations of Ruling* (London, Routledge, 1990) 214. See also M Campbell, 'Dorothy Smith and Knowing the World We Live In' (2003) 30 *Journal of Sociology* 3, 8; and E Cunliffe and A Cameron, 'Writing the Circle: Judicially Convened Sentencing Circles and the Textual Organisation of Criminal Justice' (2007) 19 *Canadian Journal of Women and the Law* 1.

[20] See, eg, M Irenyi, K Kovacs and N Richardson, 'Fatal Child Abuse' (Melbourne, Australian Institute of Family Studies, 2008); N Axford and R Bullock, *Child Death and Significant Case Reviews: International Approaches* (Edinburgh, Scottish Executive, 2005); and R Lawrence, 'Understanding Fatal Assault of Children: A Typology and Explanatory Theory' (2004) 26 *Children and Youth Services Review* 837.

[21] T Nolan, 'Depiction of the "CSI Effect" in Popular Culture: Portrait in Domination and Effective Affectation' (2007) 41 *New England Law Review* 575, 588.

identifying these murders is largely a question of improving scientific investigation and criminal enforcement, rather than illuminating the assumptions that underpin the medicine itself. This prevailing analysis obscures the fact that the medical and criminological categorisation of cause of death is, at least partly, a human and political process.

In the ensuing discussion and throughout this book, I distinguish between:

1. **Category one deaths,** which are identified on autopsy alone as probable deliberately inflicted deaths (for example, through anatomical, histological or toxicological findings);
2. **Category two deaths,** which forensic pathologists, coroners or police identify as probable deliberate smothering deaths, based on the death investigation or 'psychosocial' information about the infant's family, perhaps in combination with findings on autopsy; and
3. **Category three deaths,** which are deliberately inflicted but not identified as such through autopsy, death investigation or otherwise, either because a thorough investigation is not performed or because the death is indistinguishable from a death by natural causes.

None of these categories equate to the legal verdict of guilty of murder or manslaughter, because none of them speak conclusively to the requirements of proof within the criminal law. For example, a 'probable' cause and mode of death will not constitute proof of the *actus reus* to the criminal standard without additional evidence, and no category addresses the need to demonstrate *mens rea*. Recent re-examinations of cases in which parents were wrongly convicted demonstrate that categories one and two may include some deaths that are not deliberately inflicted, as well as some cases in which the presumed cause of death cannot be proven to the criminal standard.[22] In short, the investigation into cause of death is only a partial aspect of any homicide prosecution, and pathologists can occasionally be wrong.

My proposed taxonomy is different from those that others use. For example, infant homicides categorised under the Australasian SIDS autopsy protocol as 'known causes' would be category one or two deaths. 'Borderline SIDS deaths' would be category two if homicide was identified on investigation as a probable cause. 'Pure SIDS deaths' may still harbour some category three deaths.[23] A different taxonomy is warranted because of two conflations within the criminological literature. First, there is a conflation between suspected cause of death and the evidence that is sufficient to justify a criminal conviction. Second, some commentators conflate detectable but undetected infant homicides with those homicides

---

[22] For the clearest example of cases in which the forensic pathologists' conclusions are now believed to be factually wrong, see ST Goudge, *Inquiry into Pediatric Forensic Pathology in Ontario Report* (Toronto, Queen's Printer for Ontario, 2008). The English and Australian cases described above in ch 1 include some in which a pathologist identified concerns about cause of death, but the evidence was inadequate to justify a murder conviction. See also *R v Clark* (above n 1); *R v Cannings* (above n 1); *R v Anthony* (above n 1); *R v Phillips* (above n 1); and *R v Matthey* (above n 1).

[23] See RW Byard, J MacKenzie and SM Beal, 'Formal Retrospective Case Review and Sudden Infant Death' (1997) 86 *Acta Paediatrics* 1011.

that could not be detected according to current best practice. These conflations have enabled a discourse that suggests that the criminal justice system fails to respond adequately to the problem of infant homicide. If one takes seriously the proposition that criminal guilt must be proven beyond a reasonable doubt, it is useful to adopt a taxonomy that accounts for the possibility of undetected homicide while resisting both of the conflations I have identified.

Categories one and two provide a basis from which it is possible to study how many *probable* inflicted deaths result in charges and convictions, while bearing in mind that 'probable' here refers solely to the view of death investigation specialists on physical cause of death. It is inappropriate for such studies to proceed on the basis that inclusion within category one or two should always, or even usually, result in charges being laid or convictions recorded, as CDRT arguably presumes in its report.[24] Category three is by definition not susceptible to any numeric estimation (indeed, it is not possible to know whether such deaths exist). Since the phrase 'battered child syndrome' was first coined in 1962,[25] a great deal of effort has gone into reducing the number of category three deaths by enhancing the quantity and quality of autopsies and post-mortem investigations.[26]

In the context of the *Folbigg* case, the four infants showed no physical signs of inflicted death on autopsy. This was especially significant in respect of Laura, because her age placed her outside the range of sudden infant deaths that is most often considered at risk of being indistinguishable from smothering on autopsy.[27] If one accepts the prosecution theory that Folbigg killed her children, then Caleb, Patrick and Sarah's deaths were initially category three deaths. After Laura died, all four deaths were ascribed by police and some pathologists to category two. Of course, the defence contested the proposition that any of the infants were smothered. Separating infant deaths into these categories, while recalling that none of them equates to criminal proof of murder, provides a helpful aid to understanding much of the research that has been done to increase pathologists' capacity to identify infant homicides. The criminal justice system presumes that, absent a confession or eyewitness, forensic pathologists are the only ones who can identify the mode and cause of death. I explore the limits of this field of expert knowledge, describing the research that has been undertaken to distinguish natural yet unexpected infant deaths from homicide.

[24] See also P Fleming et al, *Sudden Unexpected Deaths in Infancy: The CESDI SUDI Studies, 1993–1996* (London, Stationery Office, 2000) 128.

[25] CH Kempe et al, 'The Battered-Child Syndrome' (1962) 181 *Journal of the American Medical Association* 105.

[26] See, eg, HF Krous and RW Byard, 'International Standardized Autopsy Protocol' in Byard and Krous (eds) (above n 2) 319; American Academy of Pediatrics, 'Distinguishing Sudden Infant Death Syndrome from Child Abuse Fatalities' (2001) 107 *Pediatrics* 437–41 [2001 AAP Policy Statement]; and American Academy of Pediatrics, 'The Changing Concept of Sudden Infant Death Syndrome: Diagnostic Coding Shifts, Controversies Regarding the Sleeping Environment, and New Variables to Consider in Reducing Risk' (2005) 116 *Pediatrics* 1245 [2005 AAP Policy Statement].

[27] P Betz, R Hausmann and W Eisenmenger, 'A Contribution to a Possible Differentiation between SIDS and Asphyxiation' (1998) 91 *Forensic Science International* 147; and S Banaschak, P Schmidt and B Madea, 'Smothering of Children Older than One Year of Age: Diagnostic Significance of Morphological Findings' (2003) 134 *Forensic Science International* 163.

II. The Difficulty with Smothering

In 1968, SS Asch suggested on the basis of Freudian theory rather than empirical study that a large percentage of crib deaths were infants who had been smothered by postnatally depressed mothers.[28] In 1977, Walter Kukull and Donald Peterson analysed US infant death and homicide statistics in order to test the hypothesis that SIDS conceals the true incidence of infant homicide. They concluded that the rate of unlawful infant homicides had not materially altered after sudden infant death syndrome and its correlate term crib death became medically acknowledged 'causes' of death. In consequence, they found no statistical support for the proposition that SIDS had created a means of reclassifying filicides as natural deaths.[29] In the course of their analysis, Kukull and Peterson asserted that 'a post-mortem examination could distinguish most cases of infanticide from SIDS.'[30] They cited J Bruce Beckwith's research in support of their belief that medical science could distinguish between smothering and SIDS.[31]

In 1988, Beckwith reiterated his view that most smothering deaths are distinguishable from SIDS, provided careful autopsies are performed.[32] In 1998, P Betz and colleagues reported that they could distinguish between asphyxiation and SIDS deaths based on a study of smothered infants less than two years old.[33] In a 2003 article reporting the deaths of seven children (aged 1–7 years) from smothering, S Banaschak and colleagues drew a similar conclusion for deaths in that age range.[34]

In relation to infants less than one year old, Beckwith represents a minority opinion among paediatric pathologists, albeit a respectable one.[35] Pathologists generally agree that certain gross pathological findings, such as the presence of blood in the nose or on the face of an infant, are more indicative of smothering than of SIDS.[36] Other signs of smothering include pressure marks or bruising on

[28] SS Asch, 'Crib Deaths: Their Possible Relationship to Post-partum Depression and Infanticide' (1968) 35 *Mt Sinai Hospital Journal of Medicine* 214.

[29] WA Kukull and DR Peterson, 'Sudden Infant Death and Infanticide' (1977) 106 *American Journal of Epidemiology* 485.

[30] Ibid, 486.

[31] JB Beckwith, 'Observations on the Pathological Anatomy of Sudden Infant Death Syndrome' in AB Bergman, JB Beckwith and CG Ray (eds), *Proceedings of the Second International Conference on the Causes of Sudden Death in Infants* (Seattle, University of Washington Press, 1970). For additional discussion of Beckwith's work, see above ch 3, s II.

[32] JB Beckwith, 'Intrathoracic Petechial Hemmorhages: A Clue to the Mechanism of Death in Sudden Infant Death Syndrome?' (1988) 533 *Annals of New York Academy of Sciences* 35.

[33] Betz, Hausmann and Eisenmenger (above n 27). These infants were identified through perpetrator confessions.

[34] Banaschak, Schmidt and Madea (above n 27).

[35] M Valdes-Dapena, 'The Sudden Infant Death Syndrome: Pathologic Findings' (1992) 19 *Clinics in Perinatolology* 701; RW Byard and HF Krous, 'Suffocation, Shaking or Sudden Infant Death Syndrome: Can We Tell the Difference?' (1999) 35 *Journal of Paediatrics and Child Health* 432; and 2001 AAP Policy Statement (above n 26).

[36] MA Green, 'A Practical Approach to Suspicious Death in Infancy: A Personal View' (1999) 51 *Journal of Clinical Pathology* 561; Byard and Krous (ibid); and M Bohnert, M Grosse Perdekamp and S Pollak, 'Three Subsequent Infanticides Covered Up as SIDS' (2004) 119 *International Journal of Legal Medicine* 31.

the lower face and torn skin inside the mouth. The specificity of certain signs, such as haemorrhages in the eyes, is more disputed. None of the Folbigg infants had blood in their noses or on their faces when attended by emergency services personnel. Other tell-tale physical signs of smothering were also absent in every child. Even so, the literature on this subject widely endorses the proposition that for an infant of less than 12 months, 'it is difficult if not impossible to distinguish at autopsy between SIDS and accidental or deliberate suffocation with a soft object.'[37] This proposition engages the prospect that the SIDS diagnosis harbours some category two and three deaths.

In 1978, John Emery published an article in which he suggested that SIDS was indistinguishable on autopsy from deliberate smothering, which he termed 'gentle battering'.[38] He suggested that the wide acceptance of SIDS as a natural cause of death had resulted in a loss of discrimination about the causes of infant death with the result that 'it will not be possible for the "gently battered" deaths to be sufficiently isolated as to stand up in court' until the quality of medical research improved.[39] Nonetheless, Emery plainly contemplated that it is possible to identify probable smothering deaths from careful investigations into the scene of death, the clinical history and the consistency or otherwise of parents' accounts. In other words, smothering deaths could not invariably become category one deaths based on current medical knowledge, but appropriate death investigation could place these deaths within category two. This subsequently formed a theme throughout Emery's work.[40] According to Emery, the most significant challenge was to encourage universal, high-quality investigations into infant death. Emery became the eminent pathologist in this field, publishing regularly on the relationship between SIDS and smothering between the late 1970s and his death in 2000.[41]

In 1982, Elizabeth Taylor co-authored an article with Emery in which they reported that three of 65 SIDS and unexpected infant deaths they reviewed were probably due to non-accidental smothering.[42] Taylor and Emery proposed that there were benefits to keeping smothering deaths within the rubric of SIDS, as this would allow paediatricians to work with and support parents to care for subsequent siblings.[43] The 1982 article drew a strong response from one paediatrician, who suggested that Taylor and Emery's paper 'contains serious allegations against

---

[37] American Academy of Pediatrics, 'Distinguishing Sudden Infant Death Syndrome from Child Abuse Fatalities' (2006) 118 *Pediatrics* 421 [2006 AAP Policy Statement].

[38] JL Emery, 'The Deprived and Starved Child' (1978) 18 *Medicine, Science and the Law* 138.

[39] Ibid, 138.

[40] See especially Emery and Taylor (above n 10).

[41] Emery's stature is evidenced by a controversy that arose after his death, when his name was attached posthumously by former colleagues to a letter about the appropriate way to treat repeated infant deaths within a family. RG Carpenter et al, 'Repeat Sudden Unexpected and Unexplained Infant Deaths: Natural or Unnatural?' (2005) 365 *The Lancet* 29; C Bacon, 'Repeat Sudden Unexpected Infant Deaths' (2005) 365 *The Lancet* 1137; and J Gornall, 'Was Message of Sudden Infant Death Study Misleading?' (2006) 333 *British Medical Journal* 1165.

[42] EM Taylor and JL Emery, 'Two-Year Study of the Causes of Postperinatal Deaths Classified in Terms of Preventability' (1982) 57 *Archives of Disease in Childhood* 668, 671.

[43] Ibid, 673.

parents . . . without scientific evidence and which are at variance with the majority of epidemiological research'.[44]

In their 1982 article and in those they subsequently published, Taylor and Emery did not fully explain how they identified smothering deaths nor explicitly suggest a set of indicia for distinguishing smothering from natural causes of death.[45] The closest that the authors came to establishing such criteria was in a 1990 article in which they described the characteristics of families who experienced various forms of infant death, including filicide by smothering. In eight probable filicides identified in that article, several 'adverse background factors' were identified.[46] The most relevant factors are reproduced in Table 4.1.

Table 4.1 Taylor and Emery: Adverse Background Factors for Eight Probable Filicides*

Adverse Factor	Number (Total n = 8)
Mother's Upbringing and Home Background	6
Domestic Financial Situation	6
Parents' Health[†]	8
Mother's Competence	6
Bonding	7
Crisis at Time of Infant's Death	7
Mean Number (Range) of Adverse Factors	6.6 (3–11)

* This table reproduces only those factors reported as being most prevalent within probable filicides.
[†] In context, this seems to include mental health.

In their discussion, Taylor and Emery explain that these probable filicides 'came from as wide a cross-section of society' as the general population in class terms.[47] They described these deaths as presenting initially as natural, 'and it was only later in the confidential inquiry that the evidence fell into place'.[48] The authors also explain that a death was only classified as a probable filicide with the agreement of all the 'professional workers' who took part in a confidential case discussion into the death.[49]

This discussion is the most comprehensive explanation of Emery and colleagues' methods that I have found. It provides some insight into the process by which the authors identified filicides and especially their reasons for suspecting that this evidence would not sustain criminal convictions. Taylor and Emery appear to have

[44] DP Southall, 'Two-Year Study of the Causes of Postperinatal Deaths Classified in Terms of Preventability' (1983) 58 *Archives of Disease in Childhood* 75.

[45] This literature does not use the language of 'risk', although Emery and colleagues' work became an exercise in risk assessment. See RV Ericson and KD Haggerty, *Policing the Risk Society* (Toronto, University of Toronto Press, 1997).

[46] EM Taylor and JL Emery, 'Categories of Preventable Infant Deaths' (1990) 65 *Archives of Disease in Childhood* 535, 537.

[47] Ibid.

[48] Ibid.

[49] Ibid, 537 and 539.

identified likely filicides by a combination of factors, particularly the psychiatric health of one or both parents and 'degrees of stress' within the family.[50] As they noted, this is a subjective process,[51] involving value judgements about such culturally relative questions as 'the quality of competent mothering'.[52] Their insistence on seeking a consensus within the case conferences lent the appearance of rigour to the probable diagnoses. It does, however, seem that some factors are too ambivalent to sustain proof of homicide without further evidence (for example, the existence of financial stress within the family), and others may be as likely to form a relevant defence as they are to constitute evidence of homicide (dependent upon the nature of a psychiatric condition experienced by the alleged smothering parent). Emery continued to advocate a child protection and parent-helping model for responding to these deaths, rather than criminal sanction.[53]

In 1982, Ian Wilkey and colleagues published a ten-year 'total population study' of infant murders in Brisbane, Australia. In two cases, a mother had admitted smothering an infant but was not charged. Wilkey et al explained:

> As it can be impossible for the pathologist to distinguish between death due to smothering and death due to the sudden infant death syndrome and as it is possible that a mother distressed by a sudden infant death may admit to having caused the death; deaths of this type can cause a pathological and forensic problem which cannot at present be resolved.[54]

Like Taylor and Emery, Wilkey et al regarded the pathologist's posited inability to distinguish between smothering and SIDS as a bar to criminal proceedings. Wilkey et al seemed to endorse the prosecutorial decision not to proceed against mothers who confess to smothering *because* the pathological findings cannot support or refute the confession, which may well be false.[55] Notably, neither Wilkey et al nor Emery and Taylor suggested that the lack of criminal sanction is particular cause for concern – rather, they identified the need for more research and support for parents at high risk. Wilkey et al's report is in keeping with Wilczynski's findings that the NSW Director of Public Prosecution almost never proceeded against parents without conclusive pathological evidence *and* a confession during her study period (1989–93).[56]

---

[50] Ibid.

[51] Ibid, 538.

[52] See the chapters collected in M Albertson Fineman and I Karpin (eds), *Mothers in Law: Feminist Theory and the Legal Regulation of Motherhood* (New York, Columbia University Press, 1995); AR Appell, 'Protecting Children or Punishing Mothers: Gender, Race, and Class in the Child Protection System' (1997) 48 *South Carolina Law Review* 577; and KJ Swift, *Manufacturing 'Bad Mothers': A Critical Perspective on Child Neglect* (Toronto, University of Toronto Press, 1995).

[53] JL Emery, 'Infanticide, Filicide, and Cot Death' (1985) 60 *Archives of Disease in Childhood* 505, 506; Taylor and Emery, 'Two-Year Study' (above n 42) 673; and JL Emery, 'Families in which Two or More Cot Deaths have Occurred' (1986) 1 *The Lancet* 313.

[54] I Wilkey et al, 'Infanticide and Neonaticide' (1982) 22 *Medicine Science and the Law* 31, 32–33.

[55] See also Emery, 'Infanticide, Filicide, and Cot Death' (above n 53) 506; and S Leadbetter and B Knight, 'SIDS and Suffocation' (1989) 299 *British Medical Journal* 455. Compare R Meadow, 'SIDS and Suffocation: Author's Reply' (1989) 299 *British Medical Journal* 455.

[56] Wilczynski (above n 6) 29–30.

Emery's estimates (in sole and co-authored publications) of the proportion of gentle battering within SIDS deaths varied from publication to publication, as did the terms in which he expressed the likelihood that the relevant deaths were in fact due to smothering. Table 4.2 sets out these estimates and the relevant language in which Emery and colleagues expressed their conclusions.

Table 4.2 provides some interesting insights into the assertion that some homicides are misclassified as natural unexpected infant deaths. First, the 10–20 per cent figure provided within the 1993 article,[57] which was not supported by any reference to empirical studies, became the most widely cited among Emery's estimates of the proportion of SIDS deaths that are covert homicides. For example, Wilczynski used the 1993 article when estimating her 'dark figure' of child homicide.[58] Four other substantial publications between 2001 and 2007 also refer to the 20 per cent estimate.[59] The second most cited estimate is Emery's 1985 figure of 2–10 per cent, which was based on a textual review of cases and represented those cases in which 'the question of unnatural death was raised' rather than those in which homicide was the most probable explanation. In the reports of Emery and his colleagues regarding their own death investigations, the estimate of probable smotherings varied from 4.6–7.0 per cent in respect of all infant deaths (including deaths that were never ascribed to SIDS), except when there were recurrent infant deaths within single families. Recurrent deaths are specifically considered below.

Emery's early estimates were couched in guarded terms. For example, his 1985 estimate of cases in which 'the question . . . was raised' on a documentary review was further qualified by his warning that '[t]hese are not court proved cases, simply deaths that required further study.'[60] Nonetheless, many authors have used the estimates as if they represent the true incidence of unprosecuted homicides. The upper range of the 1985 estimate (10 per cent) became a firm figure drawn from 'detailed psychosocial investigations' according to Susan Creighton[61] and were referred to as SIDS deaths that 'are actually' child abuse and neglect deaths by Phillip McClain et al.[62] Similarly, the lower end of Emery's 1993 estimate of 'deaths attributed to SIDS that may be unnatural'[63] (again, 10 per cent) became the proportion of the average number of cot deaths that fell within the 'true

---

[57] JL Emery, 'Child Abuse, Sudden Infant Death Syndrome, and Unexpected Infant Death' (1993) 147 *American Journal of Diseases of Children* 1097.

[58] Wilczynski (above n 6) 29–30. See also J Stanton and A Simpson, 'Filicide: A Review' (2002) 25 *International Journal of Law and Psychiatry* 1; AW Craft and DMB Hall, 'Munchausen Syndrome by Proxy and Sudden Infant Death' (2004) 328 *British Medical Journal* 1309; and Brookman and Nolan (above n 7).

[59] Overpeck (above n 8) 27; C Alder and K Polk, *Child Victims of Homicide* (Cambridge, Cambridge University Press, 2001) 21–22; N Sesardic, 'Sudden Infant Death or Murder? A Royal Confusion about Probabilities' (2007) 58 *British Journal for the Philosophy of Science* 299, 305–6; and Levene and Bacon (above n 9) 443.

[60] Emery, 'Infanticide, Filicide and Cot Death' (above n 53) 506.

[61] SJ Creighton, 'Fatal Child Abuse: How Preventable is It?' (1995) 4 *Child Abuse Review* 318, 320.

[62] PW McClain et al, 'Estimates of Fatal Child Abuse and Neglect, United States, 1979 through 1988' (1993) 91 *Pediatrics* 338, 342.

[63] Emery, 'Child Abuse, SIDS and Unexpected Infant Death' (above n 57) 1099.

Table 4.2 Emery and Colleagues' Estimates of the Proportion of SIDS Deaths Attributable to Smothering

Year	Authors	Number of Deaths†	Number Smothered	%	Notable Terms Used
1982	Taylor & Emery	65*	3	4.6	'high degree of suspicion'
1983	Taylor, Emery & Carpenter	Not given (Figure displays proportionate distribution)	Not given		'possibility'
1985	Emery	50	5	10	'question of unnatural death was raised . . . not court proved cases, simply deaths that require further study'
		120	2	1.7	
1986	Emery	27 (12 families)*	12 (5 families)	44 (42)	'possible cause', 'likely differential diagnosis', 'definite question mark', 'Almost certain in two [families] and . . . most likely in three'. (Two mothers confessed.)
1986	Taylor & Emery	401*	24	6.0	'the possibility of active intervention', 'possible filicide'.
1988	Emery, Gilbert & Zugibe	3*	3	100	One perpetrator convicted in US court, described as 'probable infanticide' and as exceptional because jury convicted despite SIDS diagnosis. Estimates that 1 in 10 deaths diagnosed as SIDS 'were in fact suffocated' (citing 1982 and 1985 studies).
1990	Taylor & Emery	115*	8	7.0	'probable filicide'
1993	Emery	Not given	Not given	10–20	'Perhaps one in five or 10 deaths in children currently attributed to SIDS may be an unnatural death.' (No citation for this figure.)
1993	Wolkind et al	57 (27 families)*	31	55	'These enquiries are not designed to produce legal evidence for use in court.'
2000	Emery & Waite	Not given	Not given	10	'In the early 1980s, when we publicly gave the figure of 10%, our findings were fiercely contested, but they were confirmed recently.'

† Based on the date ranges supplied within these articles, some deaths are reported more than once.

* indicates that the reviewed deaths include undetermined or unascertained infant deaths as well as deaths ascribed to SIDS.

incidence of child homicide' in Wilczynski's published work.[64] Sara Levene and Christopher Bacon have relied in part on Emery to suggest that if there are 1,000 sudden unexpected deaths in infancy per year in England and Wales, this would include 100 to 200 covert homicides (ultimately settling on around 10 per cent as the right figure).[65]

Each of these authors overlooks Emery and colleagues' assertions that the deaths they report are *identifiable* homicides, provided that a detailed death investigation is conducted. Instead, these authors use Emery and colleagues' work to suggest that the relevant percentage of unexpected infant deaths is hidden from official view. These snippets from broader discussions by those who use Emery and colleagues' work do not convey the full import of their original context, in which Emery's figures are almost invariably treated as strong proof of an associated number of unprosecuted and unidentified homicides.

The tendency to forget Emery's methodology and caveats has occasionally been contested within the medical community. In an article that sparked a flurry of criticism, Roy Meadow reported in 1989, 'Between 2 and 10% of babies currently labelled as dying from the sudden infant death syndrome have probably been smothered by their mothers.'[66] Although Meadow did not cite Emery's 1985 study, this appears to have been his primary source for the figure given in that sentence.[67] John Napier Hilton, who later autopsied Sarah Folbigg and testified in support of the possibility of natural causes of death for the Folbigg infants, typified the responses published in the *British Medical Journal* to that assertion:

> Somehow [Emery's] statement has become transmogrified into something quite different and has acquired a certain statistical sanctity. What Emery may be saying is that a small number of children whose deaths are sudden and unexpected require unusually detailed investigation before being labelled as sudden infant death syndrome, not that they are victims of homicide perpetrated by their mothers or anyone else.
>
> I find it difficult to react to a distortion of this nature, and the potentially catastrophic consequences to parents arising therefrom, with anything other than horror.[68]

In light of subsequent events, Hilton's warning seems prescient. Some paediatricians and pathologists continued to question both Emery's findings and the misuse of his numbers by other researchers; and to raise concerns about the damaging impact of asserting that homicides had occurred when those allegations were unproven.[69] Emery and Alison Waite echoed these concerns, while confirming a preference for greater parental support rather than criminal sanctions: 'We do not need to create a pool of parents to whom a label of unproved homicide is

[64] Wilczynski (above n 6) 36.

[65] Levene and Bacon (above n 9).

[66] R Meadow, 'ABC of Child Abuse: Suffocation' (1989) 298 *British Medical Journal* 1572, 1572.

[67] Meadow, 'SIDS and Suffocation: Author's Reply' (above n 55).

[68] JMN Hilton, 'Smothering and Sudden Infant Death Syndrome' (1989) 299 *British Medical Journal* 178, 179.

[69] Eg, DP Southall, MP Samuels and VA Stebbens, 'Smothering and Sudden Infant Death Syndrome' (1989) 299 *British Medical Journal* 178; Leadbetter and Knight (above n 55); and PJ Fleming et al, 'Categories of Preventable Infant Death' (1991) 66 *Archives of Disease in Childhood* 170.

publicly attached.'[70] However, others adopted Emery and colleagues' findings and used them in their own research, often without giving due consideration to the caveats Emery expressed within his work. I have not identified a similar challenge to the tendency to misuse Emery's work within the criminological or legal literature, where Emery's figures seem to have been used, and are still being used, less carefully.

Although the tendency to misuse Emery's work has occasionally been challenged within the medical community, the criminological and legal literature that deals with unexpected infant death remains rife with less careful uses of Emery's figures.[71] While Emery and colleagues have observed in three articles that the legal system may not convict these parents of homicide,[72] it is not accurate to classify the probable unnatural deaths Emery and colleagues study as either category three deaths or covert homicides. By definition, these deaths have been identified as being suspicious and investigated as such before being ascribed to category one or two on my taxonomy. Therefore, they do not advance the question of whether some mothers kill their infants without detection, after a thorough autopsy, death scene investigation and case conference. Nor do Emery and colleagues explain how and when parents were criminally charged in respect of the infant deaths they described.[73]

It is not possible to extrapolate from the work of Emery and colleagues that any proportion of unexpected infant deaths that are thoroughly investigated at the time of death are wrongly attributed to natural causes such as SIDS. Although Emery and colleagues have occasionally commented on the difficulties of legal proof, it is also improper to conclude from this published research that they believe the criminal justice system fails to convict parents in appropriate circumstances. Rather, Emery and colleagues have worked towards improving systems of child death investigation and enhancing the support offered to new parents (especially mothers) who are at high risk of becoming overwhelmed. In this regard, they have utilised a welfarist discourse rather than the now predominant neoliberal understanding of appropriate state responses to potentially criminal events. The work of Emery and colleagues is nonetheless routinely employed within criminological and legal literature to support the proposition that infant homicides are under-detected and is regularly invoked in favour of a call to make it easier to convict parents whom pathologists believe to have killed a child.[74]

---

[70] JL Emery and AJ Waite, 'These Deaths Must be Prevented without Victimising Parents' (2000) 320 *British Medical Journal* 310, 310.

[71] See, eg, Wilczynski (above n 6); Brookman and Nolan (above n 7); Overpeck, (above n 8); CDRT (above n 11); Alder and Polk (above n 59); and Creighton (above n 61).

[72] Taylor and Emery, 'Two-Year Study' (above n 42); Emery, 'Infanticide, Filicide and Cot Death' (above n 53); Emery and Taylor (above n 10).

[73] With the notable exception of JL Emery, EF Gilbert and F Zugibe, 'Three Crib Deaths, a Babyminder and Probable Infanticide' (1988) 28 *Medicine Science and the Law* 205. In this case, the authors report that the caregiver was prosecuted and convicted.

[74] Eg, Wilczynski (above n 6); Brookman and Nolan (above n 7); and J Stanton and A Simpson, 'Murder Misdiagnosed as SIDS: A Perpetrator's Perspective' (2001) 85 *Archives of Disease in Childhood* 454.

III. Identifying Homicide

The work of Emery and colleagues is aimed towards developing a process for infant death investigation that would distinguish probable smothering from SIDS deaths. This distinction would shift unexplained deaths along a scale of uncertainty, largely to help doctors and health workers identify when it is appropriate to teach parenting skills and offer support to families. This approach has not, however, been the only route taken by those interested in the problem of how best to distinguish SIDS from unnatural infant deaths. Others have focused on a correlation between child abuse and unexpected infant death, postulating that this correlation (if present) may allow infant death specialists to identify infant deaths that warrant close investigation.

The research that considers whether some SIDS deaths were really unidentified child abuse was motivated to a significant extent by C Henry Kempe and colleagues' landmark paper 'The Battered-Child Syndrome'.[75] In this 1962 article, the authors reported that they had identified 302 cases of what we would now call physical child abuse, including 33 deaths, from a survey of American hospitals.[76] They cautioned paediatricians and pathologists to be more alert to the possibility that broken bones and other injuries in very young children might be caused by abusive parents. In 1989, Dominick DiMaio and Vincent DiMaio wrote that '[p]rior to 1962, the battered baby syndrome was unrecognized . . . It was left to Kempe et al . . . to give widespread recognition to this syndrome.'[77] In the wake of Kempe et al's article, x-rays became a standard part of autopsy procedure for infants and young children.

Expressly linking child abuse and SIDS, Jacqueline Roberts and colleagues considered whether factors predictive of child abuse[78] also predict SIDS. They concluded that individual factors were not predictive of SIDS, except a public health nurse's concern over feeding. The authors suggest that elevated concerns about feeding might be an early warning sign of 'abnormal responses in the baby' that subsequently dies of SIDS.[79] Ronald O'Halloran and colleagues reported that there was no statistically significant difference between the reporting rates for child abuse in families that had experienced SIDS compared with control families in a US county.[80] On balance, the statistical research did not strongly support a correlation between child abuse and SIDS.

[75] Kempe et al, 'The Battered-Child Syndrome' (1962); and JM Cameron, HRM Johnson and FE Camps, 'The Battered Child Syndrome' (1966) 6 *Medicine, Science and the Law* 2.

[76] Kempe et al (ibid) 105.

[77] D DiMaio and V DiMaio, *Forensic Pathology*, 1st edn (New York, Elsevier, 1989) 307.

[78] Such as emotional disturbance in the mother, referral to social worker or concern over parenting capacity to perform tasks such as breastfeeding.

[79] J Roberts et al, 'Is There a Link between Cot Death and Child Abuse?' (1984) 289 *British Medical Journal* 789.

[80] RL O'Halloran et al, 'Child Abuse Reports in Families with Sudden Infant Death Syndrome' (1998) 19 *American Journal of Forensic Medicine and Pathology* 57.

In 1979, David Berger reported two cases in which a mother simulated prolonged apnoea (or 'near-miss SIDS' as it was then widely described)[81] in a living child by covering the child's nose and mouth. In one case, the mother had experienced two previous unexpected infant deaths, which had been attributed to SIDS. Berger suggested that the risk factors for SIDS correlated with those for child abuse and that this overlap made it difficult to distinguish between the two phenomena. He suggested that a thorough post-mortem or pre-diagnostic investigation and careful questioning would help to identify those parents who may have harmed their children.[82] In 1981, AMB Minford reported a similar case to Berger's in the *British Medical Journal*.[83] There was no suggestion in that report of infant deaths in the family, and the abused infant also survived. During the 1980s, other authors occasionally published small-scale case studies providing similar reports,[84] although they rarely mentioned deaths in either the abused child or siblings.[85]

Munchausen Syndrome by Proxy and 'Meadow's Law'

In 1977, Roy Meadow published his landmark article 'Munchausen Syndrome by Proxy: The Hinterland of Child Abuse'.[86] In this article, Meadow reported two cases in which a mother fabricated illness in a child. He suggested that these cases were particularly difficult because the mothers presented as caring and attentive. Meadow suggested that the phenomenon of a parent fabricating illness in a child should be termed 'Munchausen Syndrome by Proxy' (MSbP). Neither case involved smothering or induced apnoea of the sort described by Berger, Minford and Rosen, and in neither case did the child die. In 1982, Meadow published a further report of 19 children from 17 families. Two of these children died, although neither appears to have been smothered. In each case, the illness was fabricated by the child's mother, but in none of these cases was the mechanism induced suffocation.[87]

---

[81] See DC Shannon and DH Kelly, 'SIDS and Near-SIDS' (1982) 306 *New England Journal of Medicine* 1022–28.

[82] D Berger, 'Child Abuse Simulating "Near-Miss" Sudden Infant Death Syndrome' (1979) *Journal of Pediatrics* 554.

[83] AMB Minford, 'Child Abuse Presenting as Apparent "Near-Miss" Sudden Death Syndrome' (1981) 282 *British Medical Journal* 521.

[84] CL Rosen et al, 'Two Siblings with Recurrent Cardiorespiratory Arrest: Munchausen Syndrome by Proxy or Child Abuse?' (1983) 71 *Pediatrics* 715; DP Southall et al, 'Apnoeic Episodes Induced by Smothering: Two Cases Identified by Covert Video Surveillance' (1987) 294 *British Medical Journal* 1637; and DP Southall, 'Role of Apnea in the Sudden Infant Death Syndrome: A Personal View' (1988) 81 *Pediatrics* 73.

[85] But see CL Rosen, JD Frost and DG Glaze, 'Child Abuse and Recurrent Infant Apnea' (1986) 109 *Journal of Pediatrics* 1065; and DA Rosenberg, 'Web of Deceit: A Literature Review of Munchausen Syndrome by Proxy' (1987) 11 *International Journal of Child Abuse and Neglect* 547 (which is a reanalysis of published work and should not be counted as a new report).

[86] R Meadow, 'Munchausen Syndrome by Proxy: The Hinterland of Child Abuse' (1977) 2 *The Lancet* 343.

[87] R Meadow, 'Munchausen Syndrome by Proxy' (1982) 57 *Archives of Disease in Childhood* 92.

In 1984, Meadow described 32 cases of fictitious epilepsy caused by mothers whom he diagnosed as suffering from MSbP, including seven children in whom seizures followed partial suffocation. Suffocation appears to have been identified from 'forensic photographs' that revealed pressure marks on the face or neck.[88] Two thirds of the children did not experience any seizures, and Meadow suggests that their symptoms were wholly fabricated by the mothers. Seven children had died of cot death from the total pool of siblings to this research group (of 32 index infants and 33 siblings).[89] Meadow suggested that the 1984 study presents 'an important association with sudden unexplained death in infancy (cot death)'.[90] In the discussion, he described the incidence of cot deaths as 'a particular worry' and argues, citing Taylor and Emery,[91] that '[i]nfanticide has been a feature of human behaviour for a very long time and we have to accept that it occurs.'[92] Meadow did not indicate whether the cot deaths were particularly clustered within the families where actual suffocation had been identified, nor does he seem to have reviewed the relevant death investigation files.

In 1989, DiMaio and DiMaio described the most common forms of infant homicide, citing Munchausen Syndrome by Proxy, induced apnoea and unidentified physical abuse as factors that increase the likelihood of smothering. Providing several examples, DiMaio and DiMaio suggested that US prosecutors were unwilling to pursue charges against mothers who smothered their children.[93] DiMaio and DiMaio explained:

> It is the general policy of the authors to ascribe the first death in a family presenting as SIDS as SIDS. The second death by the same mother is labeled as undetermined and a more intensive investigation of the circumstances surrounding the death are [sic] conducted. The police are usually asked to interview the family, though in a discreet fashion. A third such death in the family is felt by the authors to be homicide, unless proven otherwise.[94]

This appears to be the first time that this formulation, which was subsequently attributed to Meadow,[95] appeared in print. DiMaio and DiMaio cited almost none of the literature that then existed on recurrence rates in support of their preferred approach to multiple SIDS deaths.

Meadow published again on cot death and smothering in 1989. In this article, published as part of a series on child abuse, Meadow made his controversial assertion that '[b]etween 2 and 10% of babies currently labelled as dying from the sudden

---

[88] R Meadow, 'Fictitious Epilepsy' (1984) 2 *The Lancet* 25, 26. The reliability of diagnoses drawn from photographs of purported bruising would probably be questioned today.

[89] It is unclear from the text whether there was any overlap between the 32 'index children' and the 33 'siblings'. It does seem that none of the index children died. Ibid, 25.

[90] Ibid.

[91] Taylor and Emery, 'Two-Year Study' (above n 42).

[92] Ibid, 27.

[93] DiMaio and DiMaio, 1st edn (above n 77) 318–19.

[94] Ibid, 290.

[95] Eg, L Glendinning, 'Dark Secrets of the Mother who Killed Her Babies' *Sydney Morning Herald* (22 May 2003) 6; and R Hill, 'Multiple Sudden Infant Deaths: Coincidence or Beyond Coincidence?' (2004) 18 *Paediatric and Perinatal Epidemiology* 320, 320 (but see 326).

infant death syndrome have probably been smothered by their mothers.'[96] Meadow also suggested that a history of apnoea in a SIDS victim, the death of an infant at more than six months of age and previous unexplained deaths within the same family should all be regarded as risk factors for smothering.[97]

Meadow's piece arguably obscured more than it revealed: how much certainty is needed to call a death a 'probable' smothering? And can we know whether any of these deaths were in fact smotherings? He did not cite any research in support of his propositions. I have already mentioned Hilton's horrified response to Meadow's 1989 article.[98] Others were similarly sceptical. David Southall, Martin Samuels and Valerie Stebbens wrote:

> Most researchers in this subject will accept that a very small proportion of cot deaths is due to undetected infanticide (including smothering), but they would not attempt to estimate the proportion involved without substantial data . . .
>
> In over 350 patients presenting to our hospital with cyanotic episodes, in only seven patients were the episodes due to smothering. Although a proportion of these episodes resulted in a loss of consciousness, no infants died . . .
>
> Epidemiological studies have shown that only 8% of infants suffering cot deaths have experienced preceding cyanotic episodes . . . [W]e must conclude that these data do not support the hypothesis that smothering is a major cause of cot death.[99]

Meadow defended his view that a significant proportion of SIDS cases were smothering perpetrated by mothers. In an author's reply letter, he raised his personal experience with induced cyanotic episodes and explained that '[f]rom my own experience of over 25 proved cases of suffocation, it was always the mother.'[100] Notably, however, his letter did not explain what constituted proven suffocation. The difficulties that pathologists experience in distinguishing SIDS from suffocation, coupled with the postulated but largely unproven correlation between SIDS and child abuse, enabled an emergent discourse that blamed mothers for causing a significant minority of unexplained infant deaths.

In 1990, Meadow published a more detailed explanation of his research into the relationship between SIDS and suffocation. His criterion for concluding 'certain or near-certain suffocation' was that the case filled at least one of three indicia: reliable observation of the smothering behaviour; a confession supported by circumstantial evidence; or a finding of criminal guilt. Of the 27 cases Meadow reported, eleven fulfilled all three criteria and twelve fulfilled two. Nine children died, presumably as a result of the abuse (although this is not explicitly stated). 18 out of 33 siblings born in these families had died, and Meadow mentions that the ascribed cause of death for most of these siblings was SIDS. 13 of these deceased siblings had experienced recurrent apnoea. Many of the children had other unexplained disorders.[101]

---

[96] Meadow, 'ABC of Child Abuse' (above n 66) 1572.
[97] Ibid.
[98] Above, text to n 68.
[99] Southall, Samuels and Stebbens (above n 69).
[100] Meadow, 'SIDS and Suffocation: Author's Reply' (above n 55) 179.
[101] R Meadow, 'Suffocation, Recurrent Apnea and Sudden Infant Death' (1990) 117 *Journal of Pediatrics* 351.

A picture of abusive mothering was by this time emerging from Meadow's work, and in its extreme form, the risk of infant homicide seemed very real. If one accepts Meadow's data and the underlying theory of MSbP,[102] all of these mothers persistently sought out medical attention for their infants, and some went to the extent of harming their children in order to secure that medical care. Other research has confirmed Meadow's suggestion that some mothers repeatedly harm their children in order to secure medical attention for the children. For example, Southall described 30 cases of smothering confirmed via covert video surveillance. 12 siblings from nine families in the total set of 39 patients had previously died unexpectedly. The vast majority of the abusing parents had diagnosed personality disorders and histories of fabricating their own illnesses.[103] Southall did not identify what proportion of abusive parents were mothers, but it appears from the case discussions to have been a significant majority.

The prospect that recurrent infant deaths might raise suspicions of murder gained strength from Meadow's and others' findings that a disproportionate number of infant deaths were concentrated within MSbP families. By 2001, DiMaio and DiMaio had become more confident in their belief that multiple SIDS deaths necessarily connote homicide. In the second edition to their text, they reprinted their 1989 language and added:

> It is the authors' opinion that, while a second SIDS death with one mother is improbable, it is remotely possible and she should be given the benefit of the doubt under most, but not all, circumstances. A third case, in our opinion, is not possible and is a case of homicide.[104]

Others were still uncomfortable with this line of reasoning. For example, Marianne Arnestad and colleagues suggested that findings considered by Meadow to be consistent with smothering were also indicative of SIDS; they described the identification of smothering based on these signs as 'dangerous.'[105]

Despite these warnings, a further conflation occurred when Emery's research into sudden infant death and smothering coalesced with Meadow's research into MSbP, to produce a theory of recurrent unexplained infant death as *necessarily*

---

[102] Both have been criticised on many grounds. See, eg, DB Allison and M Roberts, *Disordered Mother or Disordered Diagnosis? Munchausen by Proxy Syndrome* (London, Analytic Press, 1998); F Raitt and MS Zeedyck, 'Mothers on Trial: Discourses of Cot Death and Munchausen's Syndrome by Proxy' (2004) 12 *Feminist Legal Studies* 257; and L Wrennall, 'Munchausen Syndrome by Proxy/ Fabricated and Induced Illness: Does the Diagnosis Serve Economic Vested Interests, Rather Than the Interests of Children?' (2007) 68 *Medical Hypotheses* 960.

[103] DP Southall et al, 'Covert Video Recordings of Life-Threatening Child Abuse: Lessons for Child Protection' (1997) 100 *Pediatrics* 735. See also CN Bools, BA Neale and R Meadow 'Co-morbidity Associated with Fabricated Illness Munchausen Syndrome by Proxy' (1992) 67 *Archives of Disease in Childhood* 72; MP Samuels et al, 'Fourteen Cases of Imposed Upper Airway Obstruction' (1992) 67 *Archives of Disease in Childhood* 162; and RW Byard and SM Beal, 'Munchausen Syndrome by Proxy: Repetitive Infantile Apnoea and Homicide' (1993) 29 *Journal of Pediatrics and Child Health* 77.

[104] VJ DiMaio and D DiMaio, *Forensic Pathology*, 2nd edn (Boca Raton, CRC Press, 2001) 327.

[105] M Arnestad, Å Vege and TO Rognum, 'Evaluation of Diagnostic Tools Applied in the Examination of Sudden Unexpected Deaths in Infancy and Early Childhood' (2002) 125 *Forensic Science International* 262.

unnatural. This is most starkly evident in DiMaio and DiMaio's formula for multiple sudden infant death. Mapping this shift onto the categories I proposed earlier in this chapter, recurrent unexplained infant deaths were now reclassified as category two deaths by some experts. These experts believed that recurrent deaths that had in the past been treated as natural were in fact unnaturally inflicted through smothering. The theory was detached both from Emery's insistence on a thorough death investigation and from Meadow's original research context of mothers who were proven to repeatedly harm or fabricate illness in their children. In the final section of this chapter, I describe the changing understanding of recurrent sudden infant death within individual families.

IV. Exploring the Correlation between Recurrence and Homicide

By 2001, the American Academy of Pediatrics (AAP) Committee on Child Abuse and Neglect felt sufficiently comfortable with emerging research into the correlation between recurrent infant death and homicide to list 'the prior death of a sibling' as a factor that 'should indicate the possibility of intentional suffocation' in any infant death that otherwise resembles SIDS.[106] Yet by April 2003, while Folbigg's trial was in progress, a shift was underway: most clearly signalled when the English Court of Appeal issued its judgment in *R v Clark*.[107] In that judgment, the Court criticised Meadow's evidence that the likelihood of a family such as Clark's experiencing two natural SIDS was approximately 1 in 73 million. Kay LJ held that the figure very likely 'grossly overstates the chance of two sudden deaths within the same family from unexplained but natural causes'[108] and that 'we are quite sure that the evidence should never have been before the jury in the way that it was when they considered their verdicts.'[109]

In 2005, the AAP Taskforce on Sudden Infant Death Syndrome concluded:

> [T]he vast majority of either initial or second sudden unexpected infant deaths within a family seem to be natural rather than attributable to abuse, neglect, or homicide. However, the task force maintains that a complete autopsy, examination of the death scene, and review of the clinical history are necessary to obtain the most accurate diagnosis.[110]

The AAP Committee on Child Abuse and Neglect, although softening its earlier language, still considered that recurrence could constitute a suspicious circumstance:

[106] 2001 AAP Policy Statement (above n 26) 438.
[107] Above n 1.
[108] Ibid, 178.
[109] Ibid, 177.
[110] 2005 AAP Policy Statement (above n 26) 1251, citations omitted.

Controversy exists in the medical literature regarding the likelihood of a repetition of SIDS within a sibship. When an infant's sudden and unexpected death has been thoroughly evaluated and alternate genetic, environmental, accidental, or inflicted causes of death have been carefully excluded, parents should be informed that the risk of SIDS in subsequent children is not likely increased. Although repetitive sudden and unexpected infant deaths occurring within the same family should compel investigators to consider the possibility of serial homicide, it is important to remember that serial infant deaths within a sibship can also be explained by a fatal, inheritable disorder, 2 separate and unrelated natural disease processes, or an unrecognized environmental hazard.[111]

The question of how best to understand recurrent unexpected infant deaths continues to confound forensic paediatric pathologists.[112] In what follows, I describe some of the debates that have arisen and continue to simmer regarding recurrence.

A review of the literature on recurrence reveals no discernible common thread between the various studies that might otherwise provide a core understanding of recurrent unexpected infant death and reflect a consensus within the expert communities. The studies are so varied in research methodology, scope and definition, founding assumptions and intended purpose, that very few useful generalisations can be made about them. Instead, in this section I describe the variation between these studies and delineate the state of knowledge about recurrent unexpected infant death before and after Folbigg was convicted. I am particularly attentive to both the threshold at which given authors are prepared to attribute an infant death to inflicted causes, and to the extent to which authors suggest that their findings can be generalised to other families who experience recurrent unexpected infant death. While many reanalyses and commentaries have been published, the following discussion focuses on those studies that report original empirical research.

Early Studies of Recurrence

Early studies into recurrent unexpected death were conducted in the 1980s with an eye to establishing whether SIDS possessed a genetic component. In 1972, Alfred Steinschneider had postulated a genetic aspect to prolonged apnoea,[113] in light of the fact that the Hoyts had experienced five infant deaths. Initial epidemiological

---

[111] 2006 AAP Policy Statement (above n 37), citations omitted.

[112] PS Blair and PJ Fleming, 'Recurrence Risk of Sudden Infant Death Syndrome' (2008) 93 *Archives of Disease in Childhood* 269; Bacon, 'How Common is Repeat Sudden Infant Death Syndrome?' (above n 9); MJ Campbell et al, 'Recurrence Rates for Sudden Infant Death Syndrome (SIDS): the Importance of Risk Stratification' (2008) 93 *Archives of Disease in Childhood* 936; and C Bacon, 'Recurrence of Sudden Infant Death Syndrome' (2008) 122 *Pediatrics* 869.

[113] A Steinschneider, 'Prolonged Apnea and the Sudden Infant Death Syndrome: Clinical and Laboratory Observations' (1972) 50 *Pediatrics* 646–54.

research into the rate of recurrence drew from birth and death certificates[114] or self-reports from parents who were enrolled in SIDS support programmes.[115] These studies found that the rate of recurrence was elevated when compared with the general population risk, but the degree of elevation was not large enough to support a wholly genetic explanation.[116] These authors did not expressly consider the possibility that their estimated recurrence rates might include a proportion of covert homicides, and these early studies have been criticised on that basis.

Other researchers encountered recurrence in the course of more intervention-ist efforts to identify and reduce the risks of SIDS among particular infants. Emery pioneered this work in England, and his co-authored 1986 and 1993 publications estimated that the risk of repeat SIDS was three times the general population risk.[117] Emery concluded on the basis of his confidential investigations that recur-rent unexpected infant death raised the possibility of homicide, although he also emphasised the likelihood of natural explanations. In 1986, he reported that of 12 examples of repeat unexpected infant death, five were 'almost certain' or 'most likely' homicides. Three families had genetic disorders, in two families both dead infants showed evidence of mild infection, and in two families both deaths remained completely unexplained.

In 1993, Emery's group identified a disparity in the incidence of filicide between, on one hand, families who had been referred to a study of recurrent infant death (61 per cent) and, on the other hand, those enrolled in a support programme, who formed the primary data set for the study (42 per cent). They suggested that physicians may have been more likely to refer suspicious cases to the authors.[118] In another publication, which did not report directly on his empir-ical research, Emery estimated the rate of homicide among recurrent infant death as approximately one third, compared with a 10 per cent rate of suspicion for single deaths.[119] Emery and colleagues continued to insist upon a distinction between the information that formed the basis of their conclusions and the evi-dence that would be needed to prove homicide beyond a reasonable doubt in a courtroom.[120]

Susan Beal and HK Blundell found in 1987 that when the risk of recurrence was carefully assessed, there existed two groups of SIDS families. In one group,

[114] LM Irgens, R Skjaerven and DR Peterson, 'Prospective Assessment of Recurrence Risk in Sudden Infant Death Syndrome Siblings' (1984) *Journal of Pediatrics* 349; DR Peterson et al, 'Infant Mortality among Subsequent Siblings of Infants Who Died of Sudden Infant Death Syndrome' (1986) 108 *Journal of Pediatrics* 911; and WG Gunteroth, R Lohmann and PS Spiers, 'Risk of Sudden Infant Death Syndrome in Subsequent Siblings' (1990) 116 *Journal of Pediatrics* 520.

[115] DR Peterson et al, 'The Sudden Infant Death Syndrome: Repetitions in Families' (1980) 97 *Journal of Pediatrics* 265.

[116] Eg, Gunteroth, Lohmann and Spiers (above n 114) 524.

[117] Emery, 'Families in which Two or More Cot Deaths have Occurred' (above n 53); and S Wolkind et al, 'Recurrence of Unexpected Infant Death' (1993) 82 *Acta Paediatrics* 873. See also Emery, 'Child Abuse, SIDS, and Unexpected Infant Death' (above n 57).

[118] Wolkind et al (ibid).

[119] JL Emery, 'Cot Death and Child Abuse' (1993) 1 *Bailliere's Clinical Paediatrics* 235.

[120] Eg, S Wolkind, 'Recurrence of Unexpected Infant Death' (1993) *Acta Paediatrics* 876.

constituting 92 per cent of SIDS families, the risk of recurrence was less than twice the general risk. These families:

> had their first infant death from SIDS between 2 weeks and 12 months of age, were not severely socially deprived, had no family history of sudden unexpected unexplained deaths in children or young adults, and no bronchomalacia at necropsy.[121]

In the remaining 8 per cent of families, the risk of recurrence was 'significantly increased'. Beal and Blundell adopted a similar research methodology to Emery's, relying on home visits, questions to parents, autopsy records, as well as clinical, family and obstetric histories. Beal and Blundell did not identify any homicides among this research population. The journal in which this study was published later printed a letter from Meadow, suggesting that Beal and Blundell should have 'acknowledge[d] that some of these deaths will have been caused directly by the mothers'.[122]

Large Population Studies of Recurrence

Joseph Oren et al reported in 1987 that they had experienced two cases of triple SIDS and two cases of quadruple SIDS in their apnoea monitoring programme, which enrolled with 1,341 infants between 1973 and 1986. The researchers liaised directly with families, reviewed autopsy results and clinical histories, and stated that they explicitly considered and excluded the possibility of child abuse in every instance. However, in two instances, dead infants from families with recurrent infant death were not autopsied.[123] Vincent DiMaio suggested that Oren et al were describing cases of homicide in this report,[124] a suggestion that was vigorously resisted by the authors.[125] No retraction or correction was published to this study. Seeking to learn whether DiMaio's allegation was ever substantiated in a courtroom, I conducted careful research into the medical literature and *Boston Globe* newspaper archives. It seems that no parent to infants who died during this study was ever charged with a criminal offence arising out of the deaths.[126]

In 1998, Alison Waite and colleagues published the first major report for the Care of Next Infant (CONI) programme conducted in England by the Foundation for Sudden Infant Death. Emery was a member of the steering committee for this

---

[121] SM Beal and HK Blundell, 'Recurrence Incidence of Sudden Infant Death Syndrome' (1988) 63 *Archives of Disease in Childhood* 924, 30.

[122] R Meadow, 'Recurrent Cot Death and Suffocation' (1989) 64 *Archives of Disease in Childhood* 179.

[123] J Oren, DH Kelly and DC Shannon, 'Familial Occurrence of Sudden Infant Death Syndrome' (1987) 80 *Pediatrics* 355.

[124] V DiMaio, 'SIDS or Murder' (1988) 81 *Pediatrics* 747.

[125] D Kelly, 'SIDS or Murder? Reply to Vincent DiMaio' (1988) 81 *Pediatrics* 747.

[126] See RA Knox, 'Suffolk DA May Revisit Infant Deaths to Seek Evidence of Homicide' *Boston Globe* (10 September 1997) A01 (Factiva). Firstman and Talan suggest that Daniel Shannon ignored strong circumstantial evidence of Munchausen Syndrome by Proxy in some cases, although they do not link that allegation to the cases described in the 1987 publication: R Firstman and J Talan, *The Death of Innocents: A True Story of Murder, Medicine, and High-Stakes Science* (New York, Bantam Books, 1997) 589–605.

programme.[127] CONI assisted bereaved parents in caring for subsequent children after losing an infant to SIDS. The authors reported that of the first 5,000 babies enrolled in CONI, 44 babies died, and 35 of these deaths were unexpected. Among the unexpected infant deaths that occurred while the infants were enrolled in the CONI programme, eight were attributed to SIDS. Parents were convicted of homicide in relation to a total of five unexpected deaths (arising from four families); two deaths were attributed to non-accidental injury, although no conviction ensued; and in two cases the pathologist suspected non-accidental injury, but this was not the coroner's attributed cause of death.[128] In their reanalysis of these suspicious deaths, Robert Carpenter et al concluded that 'there are circumstances in the histories that cause concern, but our full enquiries were unable to determine a cause, or even a probable cause of death.'[129] In one case, filicide 'could not be excluded, but insufficient evidence' existed to pursue the possibility. Four deaths were due to overlying (when a sleeping adult accidentally rolls onto a co-sleeping infant). In seven instances, a mother declined further investigation, and in two cases the necropsy was inadequate to reach a conclusion about cause of death. The remaining deaths (n=20) were classified in this report as natural, explained deaths.[130] The total study population was 4182 families.

The CONI report also set out the attributed causes of death for infant deaths that occurred prior to enrolling in the CONI programme. The enrolled families had experienced an additional 112 infant deaths before the deaths that led to them entering the CONI programme.[131] 104 families had experienced two infant deaths at the time of enrolment. Of these families, 62 had experienced two SIDS deaths and 20 had experienced one SIDS death and one death from known causes. Eight had experienced one SIDS death and one death for which the cause was not recorded. Five families had two deaths from other known causes, and nine families had two deaths for which the cause was not recorded. Four families had experienced three infant deaths including the enrolled death. One family had experienced three SIDS deaths; one family had two SIDS and one death from known causes; one family had one SIDS and two deaths from known causes; and one family had three deaths from known causes.[132]

What such data reveals is that there was a significant disparity between the causes attributed to infant deaths experienced prior to enrolment in CONI and those experienced while enrolled in the programme: 72 per cent of prior deaths were attributed to SIDS, compared with 23 per cent of unexpected CONI deaths. Presumably, this reflects the greater care with which CONI infant deaths were

---

[127] A Waite et al, *Report on 5000 Babies Using the CONI (Care of Next Infant) Programme* (Sheffield, University of Sheffield, 1998).

[128] Ibid, Appendix 2. See also Levene and Bacon (above n 9) 445.

[129] RG Carpenter (Personal correspondence with the author, 6 November 2008).

[130] Waite et al (above n 127) App 2. Carpenter and colleagues subsequently changed some of the classifications used in this report. These changes are identified and defended in Carpenter et al, 'Natural or Unnatural?' (above n 41); and in personal correspondence (ibid).

[131] Waite et al (above n 127) 20.

[132] Ibid, 6.

investigated and the growing understanding about causes of infant deaths over the study period (1988–98).

Meadow's Studies of Recurrent Death and Subsequent Research Directions

In 1999, Meadow published his first study of recurrent infant death. This study was based on medical records, transcripts of police interviews and Meadow's meeting with one or both parents in most of the families he documented. Unlike previous studies, Meadow focused on cases in which the criminal justice system and/or family court had concluded that a parent had killed one or more infants. He identified 24 families who had experienced recurrent infant death. 18 families experienced two deaths; five families had three deaths; and one family had four infant deaths. The mother was judged responsible for harming the children in 86 per cent of the cases Meadow reported. Meadow has stated:

> The likelihood that the court verdicts about parental responsibility for the death were correct is very high indeed. . . [A]ll experts, particularly the judge, are aware of the dire implications of the verdict. . .[133]

Throughout this article, Meadow appeals to the independent validation of scientific work that is provided by the putatively rigorous judicial process of assessing expert evidence. This reliance on the legal system's independence presents interesting challenges, because Meadow testified as an expert witness in these cases – and therefore helped to secure the legal verdicts on which he relies for validation of his theories.

The stated aim of Meadow's 1999 article was '[t]o identify features to help paediatricians differentiate between natural and unnatural infant deaths'.[134] In that article, Meadow provided some risk factors for recurrent homicide, including the low socioeconomic status of families, maternal smoking throughout pregnancy, problematic pregnancies and unusual medical histories of recurrent apnoea and/or seizures in infants. Meadow noted, 'Nearly all the perpetrators were the child's mother.'[135] In his discussion, Meadow suggested that courts are 'impressed by evidence' about the statistical improbability of multiple infant deaths in a given family.[136]

However, Meadow's presumption that SIDS could be estimated on a randomised basis has been criticised by Stephen Watkins, who suggests that this approach 'seriously misunderstands probability theory'.[137] In particular, Watkins has explained that Meadow's assumption that SIDS is an entirely random event

---

[133] R Meadow, 'Unnatural Sudden Infant Death' (1999) 80 *Archives of Disease in Childhood* 7, 10.
[134] Ibid.
[135] Ibid.
[136] Ibid, 11.
[137] SJ Watkins, 'Conviction by Mathematical Error?' (2000) 320 *British Medical Journal* 2.

denies studies that demonstrate an increased risk of recurrence within families. In addition, Meadow erred when he extrapolated from families' epidemiological characteristics to estimate the particular risk of recurrence for that family.[138] Watkins' concerns were echoed by the President of the Royal Statistical Society in a letter to the Lord Chancellor.[139]

After Meadow published the 1999 article, the Court of Appeal of England and Wales rejected Meadow's evidence in several cases, including *Clark*, *Cannings* and *Anthony*.[140] In *Clark* and *Anthony*, Meadow was criticised for providing incorrect and grossly misleading statistical evidence.[141] In *Cannings*, Judge LJ suggested that Meadow maintained an overly dogmatic approach to investigating multiple infant deaths.[142] These criminal convictions, which presumably constituted three of the 19 reported by Meadow in his 1999 article, were overturned.[143]

A large-scale population-based study of infant death emerged from English research in 2000, after Peter Fleming and colleagues concluded their confidential inquiries into sudden death in infancy (the CESDI SUDI study).[144] Between 1993 and 1996, the multidisciplinary research team investigated all sudden and unexpected infant deaths (of infants aged one week to one year) in five counties. They did not interview families in cases where a family member was subject to police investigation, although they collected other data about these births and deaths.[145] In total, the review identified 363 SIDS cases during the study period and 93 explained infant deaths. Four of the SIDS families became subject to police investigation, as did ten of the families who experienced unexpected, explained infant death.

During the CESDI SUDI study, 13 families experienced more than one infant death. In two families, a first infant death was attributed to SIDS, and a second 'was attributed to non-accidental injury', although the authors do not set out the basis on which this attribution was made.[146] The study is unusual in its use of multiple child death review teams, a feature which led to the possibility of comparing decision-making practices. When discussing the possibility of maltreatment, the authors identify:

---

[138] Ibid.

[139] R Nobles and D Schiff, 'Misleading Statistics within Criminal Trials: The Sally Clark Case' (2005) 2 *Significance* 17.

[140] Above n 1.

[141] *Clark* (above n 1) paras 100–3. Similar criticisms were made in *Anthony* (above n 1) paras 91–92.

[142] *Cannings* (above n 1) paras 175–78.

[143] Meadow was eventually disciplined by the General Medical Council for his role in *Clark*. The General Medical Council's decision was reversed by the English High Court of Justice, which found that 'it was difficult to think that the giving of honest albeit mistaken evidence could save in an exceptional case properly lead to a finding of serious professional misconduct': *Meadow v General Medical Council* [2006] EWHC 146 (Admin) (16 February 2006).

[144] The full title of the study was 'Confidential Enquiry into Stillbirths and Deaths in Infancy: Sudden Unexpected Death in Infancy'. See Fleming et al, *The CESDI SUDI Studies* (above n 24).

[145] Ibid.

[146] Ibid, 29.

[T]here were sometimes inconsistencies between different panels in assessing the same cases. Some panels appeared to be harsher in their judgments than others, particularly with regard to the behaviour of carers.[147]

The observation that some teams judged carers more harshly than others provides a comparatively rare glimpse of the fact that categorising the cause of infant death as natural or unnatural depends in significant part on a team's assessment of the caregiving capabilities of an infant's primary caregiver, usually the mother.

While the caregiving assessment is arguably an inescapable feature of infant death review,[148] it seems to be systematically denied within or omitted from the expert evidence given by prosecution pathologists in criminal trials that involve infant death.[149] This denial lends an aura of scientific objectivity to pathologists' determination of cause of death, reinforcing the presumption that this determination arises from the disinterested process of observation and classification, rather than from a contingent process in which normative expectations of child-rearing play a significant role. As a result, a mother whose caregiving skills do not meet prevalent cultural expectations may be doubly penalised within the criminal process – first by a pathologist who draws on this information in ascribing cause of death and later by a trier of fact who uses evidence about her behaviour to validate the scientific evidence. Arguably, this was the reasoning process employed by the NSW Court of Criminal Appeal when it concluded that Folbigg's diary 'lent terrible credibility and persuasion'[150] to expert evidence, which was itself informed by the contents of that diary.

The CESDI SUDI authors concluded that the risk of SIDS is greatly affected by factors such as the presence of smokers in a household, the presence of at least one wage earner in the household and maternal age.[151] They relied on similar logic to that criticised in *Clark* to suggest that it is possible to estimate the risk of recurrence by squaring a family's base risk of SIDS.[152] The report notes, however, that this approach does not take into account the possibility of unidentified risks. In relation to recurrent infant death, the authors concluded:

> When a second SIDS death occurs in the same family, in addition to a careful search for an inherited disorder there must always be a very thorough investigation of the circumstances – although it would be inappropriate to assume that maltreatment was always the cause.[153]

---

[147] Ibid, 113.
[148] See ST Cordner, *Paediatric Forensic Pathology: Limits and Controversies* (Report commissioned by the Inquiry into Pediatric Forensic Pathology in Ontario, 2008) 99–100, available at www.goudgeinquiry. ca. See also S Jasanoff, *Science at the Bar: Law, Science and Technology in America* (Cambridge, Harvard University Press, 1995); and P Roberts, 'Science in the Criminal Process' (1994) 14 *Oxford Journal of Legal Studies* 469.
[149] Eg, *Cannings* (above n 1); *Matthey* (above n 1); and Goudge (above n 22).
[150] *R v KF* (2005) 152 A Crim R 35, [2005] NSWCCA 23 (17 February 2005) 143 [*Folbigg* conviction and sentencing appeal] para 132.
[151] Fleming et al, *The CESDI SUDI Studies* (above n 24) 92.
[152] See above ch 1, text accompanying nn 33–34; and above, text accompanying nn 134–43.
[153] Ibid.

The authors do not consider the prospect of three or more such deaths.

In 2000, Beal published an updated analysis of recurrent infant death in South Australia. She noted the difficulty of producing statistically significant recurrence analyses in light of the falling SIDS rates.[154] Beal concluded that of 20 families who experienced recurrent infant death between 1970 and 2001, two were proven filicides and a further four were suspected filicides.[155] Beal suggested that the following factors provided 'clues to filicide': abuse of other children and infants; recurrent acute or apparent life-threatening episodes (ALTEs);[156] Munchausen syndrome in the mother (or perpetrator); reluctance to be involved with or occasionally obsessive involvement with the SIDS association; family suspicion; and conflicting statements about the circumstances of infant death.[157] She did not cite empirical or published research or describe the methodology she used to generate this list.

In 2003, Dolores Stanton reported that she had studied three families who each experienced two unexpected infant deaths.[158] Stanton identified 'maltreatment issues' in two of these families. She provided some detail about these cases, and it appears that the suspicious feature in both maltreatment cases was a pattern of ALTEs that occurred only while the infants were in their mothers' care.[159] Seemingly misunderstanding both the statistical data and the basis on which the state might institute child apprehension proceedings, Stanton concluded that a filicide rate of 55 per cent 'exceeds the balance of probabilities and would justify judicial care proceedings in all such cases'.[160] Stanton's article was published in August 2003, just after Folbigg's trial.

The Second 'Care of Next Infant' (CONI) Report

In 2005, prompted in part by the decisions in *Clark* and *Cannings*, Carpenter et al published a close analysis of recurrent death among CONI infants. The research population overlapped in part with that described in Waite's 1998 paper. Carpenter and colleagues' analysis was based on 'detailed enquiries into the previous death and the CONI death, including a family interview, a review of autopsies, and case discussions'.[161] They reported that of 46 unexpected deaths in families that had already experienced one SIDS, six were probable homicides.

---

[154] SM Beal, 'Recurrence of Sudden Unexpected Infant Death in a Family' in Byard and Krous (eds) (above n 2) 281.

[155] Ibid, 285.

[156] For discussion of ALTEs, see above ch 1, esp n 19.

[157] Ibid, 286.

[158] AN Stanton, 'Sudden Unexpected Death in Infancy Associated with Maltreatment: Evidence from Long-Term Follow-Up of Siblings' (2003) 88 *Archives of Disease in Childhood* 699.

[159] Ibid, 700.

[160] Ibid, 699. This reasoning is as inappropriate as Meadow's statistical analysis, not least because it presumes that Wolkind et al had 100% confidence that 55% of recurrent infant deaths were caused by homicide. It is obvious from the text of the original article that this is not so. See Wolkind et al (above n 117).

[161] Carpenter et al, 'Natural or Unnatural?' (above n 41) 29.

Two of these probable homicides occurred in families that had already experienced two fully unexplained infant deaths. Four homicides were 'overt', meaning that the infant had obvious non-accidental injuries. Two were 'covert', although in both cases the CONI infant had several fractured ribs. One father was convicted in criminal court, and one father was held responsible in family court. One homicide was committed by a babysitter. In three cases, no prosecution ensued. Among the remaining families, three sets of deaths were fully explained; six families experienced one SIDS and one explained deaths; 18 families experienced double SIDS; and 13 families were not fully investigated.[162]

Two families who were enrolled in CONI experienced triple infant deaths (ie, the death of an infant, which led to enrolment, plus two subsequent deaths). One of these was a triple homicide, and one was triple SIDS. Historical data revealed a total of ten registered families with triple infant deaths. Carpenter et al were unable to fully investigate the remaining eight families, but they noted that in a total of four cases, the family seemed to have experienced triple SIDS.[163] The authors concluded:

> From the best available data, we believe that the occurrence of a second or third sudden unexpected death in infancy within a family, although relatively rare, is in most cases from natural causes. For a host of reasons, not the least of which is the protection of parents from false accusations, it is essential that all sudden unexpected infant deaths are submitted to a detailed, expert investigation like this study, which includes a full family history, clinical history, and paediatric autopsy. Also, adequate post-mortem material must be retained from every unexplained infant death for re-examination in the event of recurrence.[164]

Despite the relatively modest suggestion that detailed expert investigations are called for in all cases of sudden unexpected infant death, Carpenter et al's analysis proved controversial. The authors were criticised for classifying deaths as either natural or unnatural, without a middle category such as unascertained.[165] While acknowledging the 'problems of interpretation' that arose when working with these cases, Carpenter et al denied that they should have used a third category: 'To introduce a grey category would be to go beyond the data.'[166]

Bacon criticised Carpenter et al for taking 'the benign view that a death should be classified as natural unless there was compelling evidence to the contrary – an approach that is appropriate in the courts but not in scientific debate'.[167] Jonathan Gornall echoed Bacon's criticism: 'This would be the correct approach in a criminal court, where guilt must be proven beyond a reasonable doubt.'[168] Gornall also suggested that the Carpenter et al paper should not have played a part in the deci-

---

[162] Ibid, 31–32.
[163] Ibid, 33.
[164] Ibid, 34.
[165] Bacon, 'Repeat Sudden Unexpected Infant Deaths' (above n 41).
[166] RG Carpenter et al, 'Authors' Reply' (2005) *The Lancet* 1138.
[167] Bacon, 'Repeat Sudden Unexpected Infant Deaths' (above n 41) 1137.
[168] Gornall (above n 41).

sions of the Court of Appeal of England and Wales to quash Cannings' and Anthony's convictions because it had not been peer reviewed at the time when the courts relied upon it.[169] An inconsistency arises between Gornall's argument that Carpenter et al improperly used a higher than normal forensic standard of certainty in ascribing cause of death and Gornall's suggestion that it was inappropriate for a court to rely on the fact that the paper before it had been published in a peer-reviewed journal. Arguably, this inconsistency reflects a broader uncertainty about the extent to which scientific experts can or should adjust their logic and reasoning to meet legal standards of proof.[170]

Carpenter and colleagues' analysis, which was lauded by some,[171] appears to be the largest study of recurrent infant death reported in the literature. It has the benefit of being based on a study population that is, after the initial death, randomised instead of referral-based.[172] It is also based on a careful, even exhaustive, review of every second and subsequent infant death, while aspiring to a similar review for all unexpected infant deaths. This approach has numerous advantages for a case that becomes a criminal or child welfare prosecution: it enables defence experts to review the original findings; the original process is transparent to lawyers, judges and juries, which helps to guard against the possibility that a review team engages in reasoning or makes assumptions that would be impermissible in a courtroom; and it enables the original investigators to recall and justify decision-making that may have happened years earlier by the time a case comes to court.

When brought into the criminal context, the Carpenter et al study provides enough detail to enable courts to consider the analogies and differences between their reported cases and a pattern of infant death within a particular family. Perhaps most significantly, Carpenter et al approached the task of ascribing cause of death with a robust sense of the limits of contemporary knowledge about the causes of infant death. Correspondingly, they identified the need to proceed carefully before attributing an infant death to category one or two, given the possibility that a finding of criminal guilt will result from such an attribution. The context in which Carpenter and colleagues described their preferred approach includes the CESDI SUDI observation that review teams vary in their willingness to identify maltreatment as a cause of death.

V. Conclusion

In this chapter, I have traced the collapsing and reconstituted distinctions between smothering and natural unexpected infant death. In particular, I have

---

[169] Ibid, 1167.
[170] I return to this point below in the text accompanying n 183.
[171] Eg, Hill (above n 95).
[172] See Wolkind et al (above n 117).

demonstrated how Emery's research, generated within a welfarist framework and insistent upon the distinction between legal reasoning and scientific research, was co-opted into a punitive, criminalising narrative that emerged in the late twentieth century. This latter narrative enabled a belief that recurrent death is *prima facie* murder: first within the medical literature regarding mothers whose infants suffer repeated unexplained illness; later in literature regarding mothers who suffer repeated infant death; and eventually in the expert evidence delivered during criminal trials themselves. From this review, it becomes apparent that Folbigg was tried at a moment in which there was a particularly strong emphasis on homicide as the most likely explanation of recurrent unexplained infant death within a family. Even in 2003 at the time of Folbigg's trial and conviction, however, there were pathologists who resisted the rush to criminalise mothers, pointing to the limits of contemporary scientific knowledge as a reason to proceed cautiously.

Despite the naysayers, at a certain moment in the mid- to late 1990s the belief that mothers can and do murder their children without leaving physical signs became something of a self-fulfilling prophecy. Convictions such as Hoyt's, Clark's and Cannings' vindicated the suspicions of those (pathologists, paediatricians, prosecutors, police and journalists) who were in truth integrally involved with securing these convictions. Meadow similarly drew upon law's ideological power when he asserted that if a court agreed with his findings, those findings were very likely to be correct.[173] By virtue of being objectified[174] through the criminal trial process, the belief that mothers can and do murder their children without detection was discursively detached from the expert communities who initially promoted the idea.

After some mothers were convicted, individual pathologists, lawyers, police officers and journalists continued to sound the alarm, relying now upon the 'general legitimacy accorded to law'[175] to entrench their argument that mothers kill their children and often get away with it. A very clear example of this phenomenon arose when Melbourne newspaper *The Age* went murder-shopping in the aftermath of Folbigg's conviction. On the day that counsel in Folbigg's case appeared before the NSW Supreme Court to make sentencing submissions, *The Age* published a front-page article about a Victorian case in which a mother (Carol Matthey) had been investigated but not (yet) charged, in the deaths of four children.[176] Folbigg's conviction was cited as support for the proposition that these children's deaths were highly suspicious, and an op-ed piece published the follow-

---

[173] Meadow, 'Unnatural Sudden Infant Death' (above n 133) esp 8 and 10.

[174] In Dorothy Smith's sense of the word, ie, given institutionally authorised status as fact through a process that conceals the socially constructed nature of institutional knowledge. Smith (above n 19) 210–14. See also Cunliffe and Cameron (above n 19) 14–16.

[175] A Hunt, 'Marxism, Law, Legal Theory and Jurisprudence' in P Fitzpatrick (ed), *Dangerous Supplements: Resistance and Renewal in Jurisprudence* (London, Pluto Press, 1991) 102, 115.

[176] 'Authorities were Told of Child Deaths' *The Age* (29 August 2003) 1. Carol Matthey was not named in this article, which clearly relates to her case. See the discussion of *Matthey* above ch 1, text accompanying nn 22–28.

ing day argued that the deceased children of this family had been failed by the child protection system.[177] These claims rested on the belief that this mother must have murdered her children, although her eventual trial was discontinued for lack of reliable evidence against her.[178]

Since 2003, the dominant posture towards recurrence of unexpected infant death has arguably shifted. The *Clark, Cannings* and *Anthony* cases have demonstrated the danger of an uncritical acceptance of expert evidence. Carpenter et al's study of recurrent infant death has reaffirmed the former belief that many, if not most, recurrent unexpected infant deaths are natural. In addition, the 2000 CESDI SUDI observation that some review teams judge parents more harshly than others when ascribing cause of death demonstrates the subjective and perspectival nature of the child death investigation process. Roger Byard and Henry Krous have warned that carving out a field of paediatric forensic pathology may have obscured more than it illuminates:

> [T]he mere naming of an area of medicine does not automatically ensure that there are accepted standards of practice, or that there are specialist training programs for subsequent practitioners. Naming may in fact confer superficial acceptance of an area that may not have an agreed upon content and defining characteristics.[179]

The need to proceed cautiously before claiming certainties within this field has become increasingly apparent.

Another important theme emerging from this literature review is the extent to which high-profile cases generate and constrain both the questions posed by research pathologists and the range of acceptable answers to those questions. In 1997, after Waneta Hoyt was convicted of murdering her children, Abraham Bergman wrote:

> The Hoyt case, along with others where homicide was thought to have been misdiagnosed as SIDS, has given new strength to those who have always suspected parents of being responsible for a high proportion of the deaths of infants who die suddenly and unexpectedly.[180]

Bergman, one of the pioneers of SIDS research, cautioned against drawing punitive conclusions about the relationship between SIDS and homicide: 'It would be sad if publicity about the infanticide cases results in a return to the aura of suspicion that surrounded the families of SIDS victims in the past.'[181] At least for a period of time, and at least in relation to families who experience multiple infant deaths, Bergman's warning seems to have gone unheeded. Hoyt's conviction lent credibility to those experts who adopted a sceptical approach to unexpected infant

---

[177] E Hannan and P Murphy, 'Police Knew, the Coroner Knew, but Not the Department of Child Services' *The Age* (30 August 2003) 4.

[178] *Matthey* (above n 1).

[179] RW Byard and HF Krous, 'Pediatric Forensic Pathology in Crisis' (2004) 7 *Pediatric and Developmental Psychology* 212, 212.

[180] AB Bergman, 'Wrong Turns in Sudden Infant Death Syndrome Research' (1997) 99 *Pediatrics* 119, 119 (emphasis added).

[181] Ibid.

death and probably embarrassed some who had formerly insisted upon a high standard of proof before criminal accusations should be made.

Clark, Cannings and *Anthony* have reminded those who work in paediatric pathology that excessive suspicion carries its own costs. The predominant focus on individual 'rogue' experts arguably overlooks the legal, institutional and cultural factors that have enabled Meadow and other researchers to wield such persuasive influence. These factors include the general cultural trend toward reconstructing questions that were formerly considered through a welfarist lens as fitting properly within the realm of criminal responsibility. This trend was explicitly tied to a suspicion of mothers and a belief that when infant death remains unexplained,

> [i]f it can be shown that a mother had not 'truly' loved her child – that is had not given her infant adequate care and devotion – then this might help to explain why she should have committed this heinous act. Alternatively, if it can be shown that she was a good and loving mother, then this would speak to her innocence.[182]

Focusing on the failings of individual expert witnesses without considering institutional and cultural factors risks perpetuating patterns that enabled justice to miscarry in English homicide prosecutions. In describing the historical background and scientific context of the punitive theory of recurrent infant death that is most often associated with Meadow, I have endeavoured to reintroduce some relevant systemic and cultural aspects of infant death investigation. Others are explored in greater detail in the ensuing chapters.

Clark, Cannings and Anthony were wrongly convicted in part because juries and judges readily accepted expert evidence that was controversial within its own field. The adversarial model of expert testimony failed to reveal the extent of the controversy in these trials, despite the fact that alternative expert opinions were introduced via the defence. Recent experience therefore underscores the importance of a more reflective approach to admitting expert evidence, particularly when that evidence is both controversial within its own field and adverse to an accused person.

It seems consistent both with the criminal requirement of proof beyond a reasonable doubt and with the principles of natural justice to require a pathologist who ascribes an unnatural cause of death to describe the investigations and reasoning process that led to his or her conclusion. The expert should be capable of situating that reasoning process within the medical literature. Arguably, an expert should also be capable of relating his or her reasoning to the principle of proof beyond a reasonable doubt, or at least of assisting the court to understand his or her own standards of certainty.[183] Minimally, this requires an expert to be familiar with relevant published literature, able to explain the limits of knowledge within the field and capable of delineating differences of opinion within the field.

---

[182] Raitt and Zeedyk (above n 102) 265.
[183] The delineation of responsibility for bridging the gaps between legal and scientific reasoning is a subject that warrants careful study. In this book, I only touch on the difficulties that arise because the gaps are often overlooked.

Arguably, all this could have been accomplished in *Clark* and its companion cases while still enabling convictions – because in those cases, the experts could have provided persuasive narratives about how the published literature supported their findings. The *Cannings* principle that a prosecution should not proceed when reputable experts disagree about whether a natural cause of death can reasonably be excluded seems a sound one when connected with the *Cannings* caveat that cogent evidence of deliberate harm may supplement an ambiguous pathological record or resolve expert disagreement.[184] While the Court of Appeal of England and Wales (Criminal Division) seems to have retreated from this proposition in subsequent cases,[185] a reasonable doubt must arise when reputable experts disagree about the inferences to be drawn from a pattern of deaths and there is no other cogent evidence of harm. The devil lies in the question of what else might constitute other cogent evidence of deliberate harm.[186]

As I next describe, the prosecution experts who testified at Folbigg's trial generally did not meet the criteria laid out in the preceding paragraphs. In particular, some experts commenced their analyses with the presumption that is commonly called 'Meadow's Law' (three unexplained deaths are murder unless proven otherwise). All experts, including defence expert Byard, arguably responded too casually to questions about the pre-existing scientific literature. While the particular form of statistical reasoning that was impugned in *Clark* did not directly enter the *Folbigg* trial courtroom, ensuing chapters will demonstrate that it seems to have framed at least some of the expert evidence; it also framed news reports about the case. In the next chapter, I reconsider the scientific evidence in *Folbigg* in light of the principles I have sketched out for expert testimony and in light of the current debates about the causes of recurrent infant death.

---

[184] *Cannings* (above n 1) para 178. See above ch 1.

[185] See *R v Kai-Whitewind* [2005] EWCA 1092, para 84. It seems clear on the facts of *Kai-Whitewind* that additional cogent evidence of harm existed; however, the Court of Appeal of England and Wales did retreat from what it described as an 'overblown' interpretation of *R v Cannings*. The reading that I propose of the *Cannings* principle is not the same as that offered by the defence counsel on appeal in *Kai-Whitewind*.

[186] Commissioner Stephen Goudge also suggested a comprehensive reliability analysis in his Report on Forensic Pediatric Pathology in Ontario, Canada: Goudge (above n 22) 487–96.

5

The Scientific Case against Folbigg

THE *FOLBIGG* TRIAL,[1] held over six weeks starting 1 April 2003, occurred just at the time that the punitive understanding of recurrent infant death was starting to shift in English courtrooms. The Court of Appeal for England and Wales published its decision in *R v Clark* on 11 April 2003.[2] All of the *Folbigg* parties were aware of this context – the defence applied unsuccessfully to have the trial stayed until the *Clark* judgment was released, and *Folbigg* prosecution expert pathologist Peter Jeremy Berry had given evidence in Sally Clark's favour.

Despite efforts made by the defence and trial judge to exclude prejudicial reasoning such as Meadow's law from the *Folbigg* courtroom, individual expert witnesses allowed that reasoning to influence their testimony.[3] Further, the complex scientific debate about the relationships between natural death from known causes, SIDS, and homicide was flattened and simplified in ways that ultimately benefited the prosecution. By the time the jury considered its verdict, the totality of evidence before them arguably made the scientific knowledge about infant death appear far more certain than many pathologists would accept. Two pathologists sought to contest the proposition that scientific knowledge was reasonably conclusive. In response, Mark Tedeschi SC, representing the prosecution, and some prosecution experts, demeaned the reasoning processes and qualifications of those pathologists.

The medical-scientific evidence occupied more than half of the court's time, generated all but one of Grahame Barr J's interim judgments and accounted for most of counsels' closing addresses and Barr J's summing-up. The prosecution called 19 doctors and specialists to testify about the lives and deaths of the four Folbigg children.[4] Two further specialists were called by the defence to answer the prosecution case and provide additional context. The medical-scientific witnesses ranged from two general practitioners who had attended Kathleen Folbigg and the children to numerous pathologists and paediatricians, two sleep specialists, an epidemiologist, a paediatric cardiologist and a paediatric neurologist, among others.

---

[1] The *Folbigg* trial was conducted in the New South Wales Supreme Court, Grahame Barr J presiding. The *Folbigg* case files are held by the NSW Court of Criminal Appeal registry under file numbers 60496 of 2002, 2002/70046, 60279 of 2004 and 2004/1814.

[2] *R v Clark* [2003] EWCA Crim 1020.

[3] For discussion of Meadow's law, see above ch 4, s III.

[4] For an outline of the lives and deaths of the Folbigg children, see above ch 2 and Appendix.

Each child's death raised slightly different medical questions, but common threads arose. These common issues included whether there was any positive evidence of suffocation; whether there was positive evidence to support the conclusion that any child died naturally; and when and how it is appropriate for a pathologist to diagnose SIDS rather than concluding that the child's death was of undetermined causes. One pathologist called by the prosecution, John Napier Hilton, had conducted the autopsy on Sarah Folbigg after her death. At trial, Hilton refused to accept that Sarah had probably been suffocated, preferring his original SIDS diagnosis. The prosecution was permitted to cross-examine Hilton in relation to those parts of his evidence that were unfavourable to its case.[5] In contrast, two other experts claimed the capacity to diagnose smothering based on a pattern of infant deaths in a single family 'beyond a reasonable medical doubt'[6] or 'until proven otherwise', [7] seemingly seeking to obviate the necessity for any supporting behavioural evidence or additional fact-finding. These latter opinions were, in the wake of *Clark*, unsurprisingly never placed before the jury. Nonetheless, the reasoning underlying those opinions structured some of the admissible medical-scientific evidence in troubling ways.

The primary disputes that arose between the parties included the extent to which experts could testify about the collective import of four deaths in a single family; the admissibility and proper use of an American Academy of Pediatrics (AAP) policy statement; and the shifting use of the term 'SIDS' over the course of the trial. The disputes over these issues exemplify the challenges presented by the medical-scientific evidence in the *Folbigg* case. In this chapter, I consider each of these disputes in turn.

I. Collective and Individual Approaches to Infant Death

Before Folbigg's trial started, her defence counsel applied for an order to sever the counts against her into separate trials. The defence argued that the prosecution could not persuade a jury beyond a reasonable doubt that any single Folbigg child had been murdered. Instead, the Crown was seeking to 'rely upon the concatenation of events to prove the cause of death in each case'.[8] The defence argued

---

[5] Prof John Napier Hilton, voir dire, *R v Folbigg* (14 Apr 2003) 643–45. The *Folbigg* trial transcript is contained in the *Folbigg* case files (above n 1). See Evidence Act 1995 (NSW) s 38 for the NSW rules regarding 'unfavourable' (hostile or adverse) witnesses. For a review of this provision, see Australian Law Reform Commission et al, 'Uniform Evidence Law' (ALRC Report No 102, 2005) ch 5.

[6] Memorandum to Peter Barnett (Crown Prosecutor) from Gregory Coles (Crown Solicitor) dated 15 Feb 2002 re Dr Janice Ophoven, contained in *Folbigg* case files (above n 1).

[7] SM Beal, *Expert Report* in *R v Tracey Louise Scotchmer* (trial conducted in Western Australian Supreme Court in January 2003, contained in *Folbigg* case files (above n 1)). This report was discussed and the witness adopted this position in Professor Beal's voir dire: *Folbigg* trial transcript (above n 5) 986–87.

[8] Peter Zahra SC, 'Appellant's submissions, *R v Folbigg*, Court of Criminal Appeal for Hearing 6 February 2003', para 51. See also Zahra SC, 'Defence submissions, *R v Folbigg* application for severance of indictment', 7 Nov 2002.

that this approach would contravene both the prima facie rule against coincidence evidence and the principle that the probative value of tendency evidence used against a criminal defendant must substantially outweigh its prejudicial effect.[9] Defence counsel Peter Zahra SC also argued that opinion evidence (of prosecution witnesses Janice Ophoven and Susan Mitchell Beal) that relied solely on the improbability of four unexpected infant deaths was not based on expert knowledge and should be excluded because it went to the ultimate issue for the jury.[10]

The prosecution resisted this application on two bases. First, it argued that the medical evidence would establish that a conclusive natural cause of death could not be ascribed to any of the Folbigg children and that SIDS and metabolic disorders could be excluded in each instance. Second, it argued that other evidence, particularly the diaries and the behavioural evidence, was sufficiently strong that when combined with the medical evidence and the fact that there were four deaths and an apparent life-threatening episode (ALTE),[11] the jury would be left with no rational explanation for the events but homicide.[12]

Wood J, who heard the interlocutory argument, dismissed the defence application.[13] The defence then appealed to the NSW Court of Criminal Appeal, which upheld Wood J's decision.[14] Hodgson JA concluded that the medical reports disclosed:

> little, if any, dispute in the medical evidence, insofar as it indicated that in each case medical considerations alone left a possibility that the cause was asphyxiation, this being a reasonable possibility and not a possibility which was merely remote or fanciful; and that there was no other cause which could be considered as something more than a reasonable possibility.[15]

The appellate court held that the jury could use the fact that there were five events when considering whether there was a reasonable possibility that all of the deaths and the ALTE occurred naturally. If the jury concluded that this was not a possibility, it should then proceed to consider each individual event separately in reaching a conclusion about whether the Crown had established each count beyond a reasonable doubt. In relation to each count, the jury could use evidence about the other deaths and the ALTE to decide whether that count had been proved.[16] The appellate judgment directed that the trial judge should give precise instructions to the jury about how to deal with the collective evidence. Those instructions were eventually distributed to the jury in written form, as well as

---

9 See ss 97, 98 and 101 of the Evidence Act 1995 (NSW).
10 *R v Folbigg* [2003] NSWCCA 17 (13 Feb 2003) para 20 [Folbigg pre-trial appeal].
11 For discussion of ALTEs, see above ch 1, n 19.
12 MG Sexton, 'Crown's submissions, *R v Folbigg*, Court of Criminal Appeal for Hearing 6 February 2003' contained in *Folbigg* case files (above n 1).
13 *R v Folbigg* (29 Nov 2002) NSW 70046/02 (NSWSC).
14 Folbigg pre-trial appeal (above n 10).
15 Ibid, para 29.
16 Ibid, paras 33 and 34.

being verbally delivered. An application to stay the trial pending an appeal to the High Court of Australia was denied in February 2003.[17]

When Folbigg's trial began, the defence raised a further objection to the prosecutor's attempts to introduce evidence about the collective import of the deaths. The prosecution intended to question each expert witness about whether his or her opinion about the cause of each child's individual death would be different when all four deaths were taken together.[18] The defence strongly opposed this question, arguing that it would permit the expert witnesses to introduce the reasoning that multiple unexplained infant deaths in the same family constituted murder unless proven otherwise.[19] Barr J ruled that the answer to the prosecution question was not founded on training, study or experience and therefore was inadmissible on the basis that it did not fit within the expert opinion evidence rule.[20]

This ruling effectively endorsed the defence position that the prosecution evidence was common sense rather than expertise. Neither the defence nor Barr J adverted to the reliability of this reasoning – if anything, the argument that the opinion depended on common sense tended to give more credence to prosecution experts' views that recurrent unexplained deaths were necessarily suspicious, while serving the immediate purpose of excluding that reasoning. The prosecution was required to formulate its questions in a manner that isolated the cause of each infant's death from the familial pattern of multiple infant deaths. Barr J did not comment on the defence argument regarding the implicit reversal of the onus of proof.

Over the course of the trial, the prosecution adopted an alternative strategy to cope with Barr J's ruling. Several of the expert witnesses were asked whether they had ever treated, heard or read in the medical literature about a family that experienced three or more sudden unexplained infant deaths from natural causes. For example, the prosecution question to Susan Mitchell Beal was phrased and answered in the following manner:

> Q. In your experience, and in the experience of your col-
> leagues that have been related to you and in the medical
> literature that you have read over the years, have you ever
> come across a family in any of that experience or any of
> that reading or research, a single family in which there
> have been three or more children who have died suddenly
> from a natural causes in the way that these children died?
>
> A. No.[21]

---

[17] *Folbigg v R* [2003] S59/2003 (19 Feb 2003). Transcript and judgment available electronically at www.austlii.edu.au.

[18] Eg, AD Cala, voir dire, *Folbigg* trial transcript (above n 5) 731.

[19] Ibid, 733–35.

[20] *R v Folbigg* (16 Apr 2003) NSW 70046/02 (NSWSC).

[21] SM Beal, Examination in Chief, *Folbigg* trial transcript (above n 5) 1143–44.

This question is ambiguously phrased – in particular, the last clause 'in the way that these children died' complicates things greatly because Beal had already testified to her belief that all four Folbigg children were murdered. The question was not identically phrased each time it was asked, but the general direction was the same. All of the prosecution's expert witnesses who were asked this question replied 'no'. These experts included Peter Jeremy Berry, who subsequently testified in *R v Cannings* that one of his colleagues had cared for three families who had each lost three infants suddenly and unexpectedly but to natural causes.[22] The defence expert, Roger Byard, initially pointed to some examples of three or more SIDS deaths documented within the literature but ultimately agreed that medical professionals no longer considered these cases to be true SIDS deaths.[23] The prosecution did not ask, and Byard did not say, whether these cases were now categorised by medical researchers as murder.

The dispute over the admissibility of medical evidence regarding multiple infant deaths exemplifies the mutual negotiation between lawyers and experts about what constitutes medical-scientific evidence and what medicine can offer the legal process.[24] The technical exclusionary rules of criminal evidence law and the rhetorical appeal to the principle 'innocent until proven guilty' seemed to provide the defence with a means of excluding the reasoning that multiple unexplained infant deaths within the same family are probable homicides. Barr J classified this form of reasoning as falling within the realm of common-sense rather than expert determination; and he therefore reserved it to the jury's consideration.[25] The reasoning was not, however, entirely excluded. The defence did not make full use of Byard's observation that it was inappropriate to make any assessments about the probability of four somewhat different infant deaths arising from a single natural cause.

The prosecution method of dealing with Barr J's ruling also illustrates that the boundaries between scientific expertise, legal procedure and lay knowledge do not remain fixed – in a trial such as *Folbigg*, the boundaries are constantly renegotiated and redrawn. The prosecution was able to reframe its desired question in a manner that was arguably more damaging to the defence case than the original version. The question whether the medical literature documented another case of

---

[22] *R v Cannings* [2004] EWCA Crim 1, para 146. Berry expressed some reservations about his colleague's conclusions. He presumably became aware of this information after testifying in *Folbigg*. For further discussion of *Cannings*, see below s IV.

[23] RW Byard, cross-examination, *Folbigg* trial transcript (above n 5) 1222.

[24] See S Jasanoff, *Science at the Bar: Law, Science and Technology in America* (Cambridge, Harvard University Press, 1995) ch 10.

[25] Redefining the issue in this way, Barr J did not consider the question of whether 'common-sense' reasoning might nonetheless be discriminatory or just plain wrong. This question deserves a paper of its own, but see generally C Boyle and M MacCrimmon, 'To Serve the Cause of Justice: Disciplining Fact Determination' (2001) *Windsor Yearbook of Access to Justice* 55; and J Nyman and C Boyle, 'Finding Facts Fairly in Roberts and Zuckerman's *Criminal Evidence*' (2004) 2 *International Commentary on Evidence*, www.bepress.com/ice/vol2/iss2/art3/. Compare: T Ward, 'Law's Truth, Lay Truth and Medical Science' in H Reece (ed), *Law and Science: Current Legal Issues 1998* (Oxford, Oxford University Press, 1998) 243–64.

three sudden unexpected but natural deaths in a single family was predicated on questionable assumptions about the experts' capacity for instant recall, about the nature of truth within published medical literature and about the completeness or coverage of that literature. The question elicited answers from the experts that were simply wrong.

The difficulty of remembering what information is contained within the SIDS literature is apparent from the size and complexity of the literature described above in chapters three and four. Perhaps more revealingly, defence expert Byard and Crown witness Beal co-authored a paper in which they questioned three medical reports of five or more SIDS deaths in single families, suggesting that these deaths may have been serial murders.[26] Beal answered 'no' to the Crown's question whether she had ever read or heard of more than three natural deaths in a single family; [27] Byard initially pointed to these other cases in the literature before agreeing that it 'is now considered by the medical profession that they were not SIDS'.[28] As I describe in this chapter, by the time Beal and Byard testified, the spectrum of causes of infant death had collapsed into a binary between SIDS and murder.

One of the cases Beal and Byard cited in their 1993 article involved Waneta Hoyt, who was subsequently convicted of murdering her children.[29] To the best of my knowledge and research, however, the other incidents have not given rise to criminal convictions.[30] Byard and Beal did not appear to have revisited the original death investigation records before raising the possibility that the three referenced examples might actually constitute serial murder. The Beal and Byard article redefined these previous case studies in light of then-current understandings, as did the prosecution's proposition that the medical community no longer considers these incidents true SIDS. While doubts may exist about these published cases, as they

[26] RW Byard and SM Beal, 'Munchausen Syndrome by Proxy: Repetitive Infantile Apnoea and Homicide' (1993) 29 *Journal of Paediatrics and Child Health* 77–79, 78.

[27] SM Beal, examination in chief, *Folbigg* trial transcript (above n 5) 1043–44.

[28] Mark Tedeschi SC, question posed to Roger William Byard, cross-examination, *Folbigg* trial transcript (above n 5) 1222.

[29] R Firstman and J Talan, *The Death of Innocents: A True Story of Murder, Medicine, and High-Stakes Science* (New York, Bantam Books, 1997); and G Pinholster, 'Multiple "SIDS" Case Ruled Murder' (1995) 268 *Science* 494. For discussion of this case, see above ch 3, s III.

[30] The three articles cited in RW Byard and SM Beal, 'Munchausen Syndrome by Proxy: Repetitive Infantile Apnoea and Homicide' (1993) 29 *Journal of Pediatrics and Child Health* 77 are: A Steinschneider, 'Prolonged Apnea and the Sudden Infant Death Syndrome: Clinical and Laboratory Observations' (1972) 50 *Pediatrics* 646–54; EF Diamond, 'In Five Consecutive Siblings Sudden Infant Death' (1986) 170 *Illinois Medical Journal* 33–34; and CE Hunt and RT Brouillette, 'Methylxanthine Treatment in Infants at Risk for Sudden Infant Death Syndrome' (1988) 533 *Annals of the New York Academy of Science* 119–26. Hunt and Brouillette identify two SIDS deaths occurring in families with multiple previous SIDS deaths – in one case the family had experienced three previous deaths, and in the other case the family had experienced five previous deaths. See also J Oren, DH Kelly and DC Shannon, 'Familial Occurrence of Sudden Infant Death Syndrome and Apnoea of Infancy' (1987) 80 *Pediatrics* 355–58. The authors identified five deaths in infants who had previously had two or more siblings die unexpectedly in infancy, from a study population of 73. Two of these families experienced four SIDS deaths, and two families experienced three SIDS deaths. The authors specifically consider – and exclude – the possibility that these children were murdered at p 357.

may about the Clark, Cannings, Patel, Anthony, Phillips and Matthey children,[31] the case law and medical literature that had been published in April 2003 supplied at least eight documented instances in which three or more infants died in the same family, and a murder conviction did not ensue.[32] In most if not all of these cases, the families were subjected to close forensic and criminal investigation.[33]

The prosecution reasoning, abetted by the expert witnesses' answers, was that medical literature which reported multiple SIDS deaths could be disregarded if the prevailing belief was that these deaths would now no longer be ruled SIDS. This strategy raises two concerns. First, there is an implicit duplicity in concealing (consciously or otherwise) the existence of literature that had been peer reviewed and conclusions that had been vigorously defended by those who investigated the relevant deaths. Second, the assertion that 'medical professionals' no longer consider these deaths SIDS simply denied the live debate among pathologists over how multiple unexplained infant deaths should be characterised.

It is also far from clear that multiple infant deaths will necessarily be reported within the medical literature. This seems to depend in part on the particular inclinations of the investigating pathologist and on the existence of any apparent pattern beyond the coincidence of death within a single family. For example, the Matthey family's case has not been written up by those pathologists who believed the deaths were natural,[34] perhaps because the mechanisms of death in that case were so different from one another that few generalities emerged. It is only relatively recently that Western concepts of infant death have shifted to encompass the expectation that virtually no live-born infant will die. There are good reasons for this shift, in terms of advances in public health and the medical profession's enhanced capacity to identify and treat childhood illnesses that were once often fatal. Still, it was only once SIDS was identified as a social problem that medical researchers began to focus and publish on the question of why infants die suddenly and unexpectedly.[35] Multiple unexpected deaths that seem to arise from disparate causes are insignificant to this research agenda and may therefore be unlikely to warrant publication.

Nonetheless, expecting that multiple infant deaths would necessarily be reported within the medical literature, the prosecution deployed the more general notion that science provides scientists with the tools by which to 'construct an accurate (ie, reliable, consistent and non-arbitrary) representation of the world'.[36] The Crown's question therefore ties the presumption that scientific knowledge is

---

[31] For discussion of these cases, see above ch 1, s I.

[32] Carpenter et al's 2005 study identified a further 11 instances: Carpenter et al, 'Repeat Sudden Unexpected and Unexplained Infant Deaths: Natural or Unnatural?' (2005) 365 *The Lancet* 29.

[33] Eg, D Kelly, 'SIDS or Murder? Reply to Vincent DiMaio' (1988) 81 *Pediatrics* 747–48.

[34] See discussion of the case above ch 1, s I.

[35] MP Johnson and K Hufbauer, 'Sudden Infant Death Syndrome as a Medical Research Problem since 1945' (1982) 30 *Social Problems* 65–81.

[36] AD Gold, *Expert Evidence in Criminal Law: The Scientific Approach* (Toronto, Irwin Law, 2003) 79. I provide a sustained criticism of this assumption in E Cunliffe, 'Without Fear or Favour? Trends and Possibilities in the Canadian Approach to Expert Human Behaviour Evidence' (2006) 10 *International Journal of Evidence and Proof* 280, 305–15.

accurate and complete with the expectation that expertise connotes universal knowledge of a particular field. Implicitly, according to the prosecution logic, if the experts are not aware of a case in which three or more infants died naturally in the same family, it probably hasn't happened. The reference to medical literature is diversionary, lending authority to individual expert's answers, in light of the fact that all experts either disclaimed knowledge of any reports or negotiated reports of recurrent natural infant death out of the equation. The experts' consensus that the medical literature did not include reports of multiple natural infant deaths correspondingly served to increase the apparent likelihood that the four Folbigg children were murdered and therefore may well have been given more weight than it deserved. Although the defence argued vigorously that the prosecution question was more prejudicial than probative, Barr J overruled that objection. He did not provide reasons for his decision, although he offered to provide those reasons if the defence required them.[37]

The development and resolution of this debate over the medical experts' capacity to testify about familial patterns of infant death illustrate that the content and limits of 'scientific knowledge' were co-constructed with the evidence itself as the trial unfolded. As I next explain, when the scientific evidence moved beyond the apparently consensual understanding about familial patterns, both parties needed to provide the jury with tools to resolve disputes between scientists.

II. The American Academy of Pediatrics (AAP) Policy Statement

In chapter four, I mentioned the 2001 AAP Policy Statement when describing the range of ways in which pathologists and other infant death experts have sought to come to terms with recurrent infant death.[38] In that Policy Statement, the AAP reviewed then-current understandings of SIDS and its relationship to cases in which an infant is smothered. The Policy Statement explained that 'it is impossible to distinguish at autopsy between SIDS and accidental or deliberate asphyxiation with a soft object', but certain circumstances 'should indicate the possibility of intentional suffocation'.[39] The AAP recommended that a SIDS diagnosis should not be used unless there has been a post-mortem examination, death scene investigation and clinical review of case records, and these investigations are 'negative'. When investigations 'reveal substantial and reasonable uncertainty regarding the cause or manner of death', including uncertainty about the possibility of deliberate asphyxiation, a pathologist should use the diagnosis 'undetermined'.[40]

---

[37] SM Beal, voir dire, *Folbigg* trial transcript (above n 5) 1128.
[38] American Academy of Pediatrics (AAP), 'Distinguishing Sudden Infant Death Syndrome from Child Abuse Fatalities' (2001) 107 *Pediatrics* 437–41 [2001 AAP Policy Statement].
[39] Ibid, 438.
[40] Ibid.

The 2001 AAP Policy Statement gave no guidance about what constitutes a 'substantial and reasonable uncertainty'. In particular, it did not suggest what circumstances warrant a pathologist elevating suspicions about *possible* smothering to the 'substantial and reasonable uncertainty' that requires a diagnosis of 'undetermined'. The Policy Statement therefore left a grey area between a SIDS death that must conform to very strict criteria and an 'undetermined' death.

The 2001 AAP Policy Statement entered the *Folbigg* trial when prosecution pathologist John Napier Hilton was giving evidence in chief about the postmortem examination he conducted on Sarah Folbigg.[41] It was never formally received into evidence because the defence objected to its tender. The prosecution withdrew the physical document from tender but was permitted to use the Policy Statement's contents to cross-examine Hilton and when examining other pathologists over the course of the trial.[42]

The prosecution used the 2001 AAP Policy Statement to establish a normative framework according to which the varying opinions offered by pathologists could be assessed, thereby defining and stabilising the range of reasonable opinions within pathology. This normative framework was a particular mobilisation of the more generalised ideological commitment to science as the most effective truth-seeking mechanism in contemporary society, drawing on the presumptive reliability of a peak professional body's pronouncements.[43] Because the document was never given to the jury, it operated indirectly to structure prosecution counsel's logic, to bolster the prosecution's case theory and to disparage those pathologists who disagreed with the Policy Statement. Notably, the fact that the 2001 AAP Policy Statement was not admitted into evidence did not prevent the prosecution from using the document in these ways. This is an example in which hierarchies of credibility between experts are negotiated through a text issued by an apparently authoritative professional organisation, but the text itself never properly enters the field.

The notion of hierarchies of credibility was first proposed by Howard Becker:

> In any system of ranked groups, participants take it as given that members of the highest group have the right to define the way things really are. . . Members of lower groups will have incomplete information, and their view of reality will be partial and distorted in consequence. Therefore, from the point of view of any well socialized participant in the system, any tale told by those at the top intrinsically deserves to be regarded as the most credible account obtainable of the organization's workings. And since . . . matters of rank and status are contained in the mores, this belief has a moral quality.[44]

[41] The 2001 AAP Policy Statement was briefly mentioned in pre-trial arguments: *R v Folbigg* 70046/02, transcript of pre-trial arguments (26 Mar 2003) [Pre-trial transcript] contained in *Folbigg* case files (above n 1) 2.

[42] J Hilton, examination in chief, *Folbigg* trial transcript (above n 5) 633.

[43] See Jasanoff (above n 24); and P Roberts, 'Science in the Criminal Process' (1994) 14 *Oxford Journal of Legal Studies* 469. Slightly different critical understandings of scientific rationality are offered by S Haack, *Defending Science within Reason: Between Scientism and Cynicism* (Amherst, Prometheus Books, 2003); and J Sanders, '*Kumho* and How We Know' (2001) 64 *Law and Contemporary Problems* 373.

[44] H Becker, 'Whose Side Are We On?' (1967) 14 *Social Problems* 239, 241 (citations omitted).

In this passage, Becker suggests that those who participate in a particular social system tend to accept that authoritative figures are best able to define 'the way things really are'. The narratives presented by those at the top of the hierarchy are therefore more likely to be accepted than conflicting narratives delivered by their subordinates. Importantly, accepting the account provided by authoritative actors is a morally appropriate action.

In the context of the *Folbigg* trial, those given the task of choosing between competing medical narratives about infant death (ie, the judge and jury) presumably knew relatively little about the professional hierarchies within paediatric pathology. Accordingly, each party was faced with two interrelated tasks. First, each needed to educate the judge and jury about the hierarchy of credibility within paediatric forensic pathology. Second, each party needed to harness that hierarchy to a narrative about the causes of infant death that fit with its overall case theory. Both the identity of the authoritative definer and the content of the authoritative narrative were open to discussion. The prosecution used the 2001 AAP Policy Statement to entrench its preferred experts and to prioritise its preferred account of how a competent pathologist determines the cause of a particular infant's death.

The 2001 AAP Policy Statement was first mentioned before the jury when Tedeschi SC asked Hilton whether he agreed with the document and whether it reflected his approach to concluding Sarah's cause of death.[45] Hilton explained that he agreed with much of the document but had reservations about certain parts. Tedeschi pressed Hilton to explain these reservations:

> Q. Does the document state 'Certain circumstances should indicate the possibility of intentional suffocation', including that which you have read?
>
> A. Yes.
>
> Q. Do you disagree with that?
>
> A. I agree that it is a possibility but no more than a possibility.
>
> Q. But do you disagree with the statement 'Certain circumstances should indicate the possibility of intentional suffocation'?
>
> A. I have already said I agree it is a possibility, but I would put it no higher than a possibility.
>
> Q. But isn't that exactly what is stated in the policy?
>
> A. That is the form of words used, but I am a bit concerned about the intent.[46]

---

[45] J Hilton, examination in chief, *Folbigg* trial transcript (above n 5) 633.
[46] Ibid, 632.

A theme emerged in this passage that developed over the course of Hilton's evidence and the evidence subsequently given by other pathologists. All of the pathologists adverted to the limits of their professional knowledge, and their opinions were informed by competing notions of professional responsibility; but they differed about where to locate those limits and about the content of professional responsibility. In particular, while all of the pathologists agreed that the pathology of a SIDS death is often indistinguishable from a smothering, they disagreed about the consequences of this indeterminacy.

When Hilton said that he was 'a bit concerned about the intent' of the 2001 AAP Policy Statement, he sought to draw a boundary between the pathologist's capacity to reach a particular conclusion about cause of death in the face of other *possible* explanations on the one hand and the (criminal investigative) function of identifying child homicide absent physical signs on the other hand. Hilton struggled to explain his disagreement with the precise words used in the Policy Statement – he agreed that smothering is a 'possibility'. Nonetheless, he questioned how best to fill the gap within the Policy Statement between the circumstances that should alert a pathologist to the possibility of smothering and the direction that an undetermined cause of death must be given when there is 'substantial and reasonable uncertainty'[47] about whether an apparent SIDS death might have been caused by smothering. Hilton's particular method of filling the gap eventually became apparent from the prosecution's cross-examination. The prosecution asserted that Hilton's diagnosis that Sarah died from SIDS was wrong, not just with the benefit of hindsight but also at the time Hilton delivered the diagnosis:

> Q. Professor Hilton, would you tell us whether or not you agree with this proposition, that there are certain circumstances which should indicate to a pathologist conducting a post-mortem the possibility of intentional suffocation and that they include the following: the previous unexpected or unexplained death of one or more sibling, that is, a brother or sister, of the deceased. What do you say to that?
>
> A. Yes.
>
> . . .
>
> Q. And would you agree with this proposition, that when conducting a post-mortem examination one should give consideration to the possibility of intentional asphyxiation, that is smothering, in cases of unexpected infant death with a history of ALTEs, or one ALTE, witnessed only by a single caregiver in a family, or of previous unexplained infant deaths. Do you agree with that?
>
> A. Broadly, yes.

[47] 2001 AAP Policy Statement (above n 38) 438.

Q. Now, I want to suggest to you that in the light of those propositions which I have just put to you, that you ought not to have diagnosed Sarah Folbigg's death as being due to SIDS and that you ought to have diagnosed it as being a death from unknown or undetermined causes. What do you say?

A. With respect, I would disagree with that.

. . .

Q. Do you agree with the proposition that it is extremely difficult, if not improper, at autopsy to distinguish between SIDS on the one hand and accidental or deliberate asphyxiation with a soft object on the other hand?

A. It may well be.

Q. Do you agree with that proposition?

A. I agree it may well be.

Q. And would you agree with this proposition, that Sarah Folbigg in essence died from an acute catastrophic asphyxiating event of unknown cause?

A. No, it was my opinion then that the most likely diagnosis on the balance of probabilities was sudden infant death syndrome.[48]

In this lengthy passage, the prosecution methodically put parts of the 2001 AAP Policy Statement to the witness. Hilton's responses illustrate the point at which the prosecution's preferred construction of medical professionalism departed from Hilton's construction. While Hilton accepted that it is 'difficult, if not improper' to distinguish between suffocation and SIDS, he did not accept that it is improper to diagnose SIDS when circumstances 'should indicate the possibility of intentional suffocation'. Hilton insisted on the gap between a 'possibility' and a 'substantial and reasonable uncertainty'. In his final answer, he also reasserted his understanding that a pathologist's duty is to record the 'most likely diagnosis'.

Gary Edmond identifies several techniques employed by lawyers and scientists in the courtroom to buttress favourable expert evidence and attack unfavourable evidence. Drawing professional boundaries establishes and manages areas of professional competence, by reference to matters such as expertise, methodology and credibility.[49] Faced with a professional disagreement between pathologists over what circumstances warrant abandoning a SIDS diagnosis for 'undetermined' (or vice versa), prosecution counsel sought to draw the boundaries of professionalism in a manner that rendered Hilton out of step with contemporary scientific practice. The prosecution used the putatively authoritative pronouncements of the

---

[48] J Hilton, examination in chief, *Folbigg* trial transcript (above n 5) 648–49.
[49] G Edmond, 'Azaria's Accessories: The Social (Legal-Scientific) Construction of the Chamberlains' Guilt and Innocence' (1998) 22 *Melbourne University Law Review* 396.

AAP as a normative framework by which to counter Hilton's credentials as the most senior forensic pathologist in New South Wales. Hilton was the head of the NSW forensic pathology service and had conducted more than 2,000 autopsies on children. The defence sought in turn to rehabilitate Hilton's reputation by pointing to his standing in the community of SIDS experts, seeking to establish that Hilton stood at the peak of his professional hierarchy:

> Q. Have you had particular experience in your professional career in dealing with SIDS cases?
>
> A. Yes. In fact at one stage I was chairman of the SIDS International Pathology Committee. I've published on SIDS, both in journal articles and in a textbook. I have been a member of a child death review team here in New South Wales, I've been a member of SIDS associations in Perth, here and in Western Australia. I have attended a number, a good number of local and international conferences on examining unexpected infant death and exchanging information about the latest techniques and theories of causation of SIDS in particular.[50]

Each of these markers of seniority and competence was marshalled to dispel the prosecution argument that Hilton's practices were incongruent with contemporary medical-scientific understandings of SIDS.

The 2001 AAP Policy Statement also served a positive purpose in the prosecution case – it helped to establish Crown witness Allan David Cala, who had autopsied Laura Folbigg, as the primary definer in relation to the question of when an unexplained infant death should be ruled undetermined. Stuart Hall et al built on Becker's hierarchy of credibility to suggest that in the context of news reporting, journalists systematically prioritise opinions and credibility of 'those in powerful and privileged institutional positions'.[51] These people become primary definers in relation to particular social disputes, and their interpretative framework 'covers the field', forcing others to respond within the framework that the primary definer prefers.[52]

The 2001 AAP Policy Statement provided Cala with an opportunity to assert the contemporeity and relevance of his credentials. Before opening statements were delivered, the prosecution applied to open its case with specific references to Cala's opinions about the cause of Laura's death. This application was denied on the basis that Cala's statement had not been served on the defence until two days before the trial began.[53] When Cala did testify, it emerged that his interpretation of the professional responsibilities of a pathologist faced with the unexpected

---

[50] J Hilton, cross examination, *Folbigg* trial transcript (above n 5) 649.
[51] S Hall et al, *Policing the Crisis: Mugging, The State, and Law and Order* (London, Macmillan, 1978) 58.
[52] Ibid.
[53] *R v Folbigg* (1 Apr 2003) NSW 70046/02 (NSWSC).

death of a second or subsequent sibling was very different from Hilton's. Dr Cala expressly adopted the 2001 AAP Policy Statement:

Q. What do you say about the contents of that article and any generally accepted views in the medical community worldwide about criteria that must be met before a medical diagnosis of SIDS can be made?

A. Well, I agree with this document, and this document does set out those criteria with which I do agree.

Q. And what do you say about the medical community in general worldwide and their attitude to what criteria must be met?

A. I would think that this document would be generally accepted by all people in paediatrics and in my area of forensic pathology. I would think there might, for example, be some people, a very small minority, who may argue with parts of it, but I think that in the main the entire medical community who looks at this area would be in agreement with this document.[54]

In this passage, Tedeschi SC sought to go beyond establishing that *this particular expert* agreed with the 2001 AAP Policy Statement. The evidence he elicited from Cala established that the Policy Statement represents a worldwide consensus and that pathologists and paediatricians who argue with part of the document place themselves within 'a very small minority' in their profession. This tactic reinforced the prosecution's suggestion that Hilton's compunctions were out of step with contemporary practice and that his evidence should therefore be discounted. It correspondingly entrenched the framework putatively established within the 2001 AAP Policy Statement as the appropriate framework for concluding cause of death, while concealing that even this framework was being interpreted in particular ways within the prosecution case.

Relying in part on the 2001 AAP Policy Statement, Cala testified that he would have ruled each of the Folbigg children's deaths undetermined because he could not exclude his suspicion that they had been smothered, even looking at each child's death in isolation.[55] Cala particularly testified that he would not have ruled Sarah's death a SIDS death, though Barr J ordered that he could not refer to the other children's deaths in justifying that opinion.[56] I return to this aspect of Cala's evidence below.

The power to define the terms of engagement is the end to which the struggle to identify an authoritative definer is directed. Cala became the prosecution's

---

[54] AD Cala, voir dire re admissibility of 2001 AAP Policy Statement, *Folbigg* trial transcript (above n 5) 724.

[55] AD Cala, examination in chief, *Folbigg* trial transcript (above n 5) 746–55.

[56] Ibid, 744.

preferred primary definer, and this position was partly secured using the 2001 AAP Policy Statement. This is most apparent in the Crown's closing address to the jury:

[M]y submission to you is that it was not appropriate for Professor Hilton to find that Sarah had died from SIDS because, in effect, what that did is it excluded a possible view that she may have died from unnatural causes, that is from accident or from homicide. . .

You will see from the summary of the evidence that Dr Cala did not believe that Professor Hilton excluded deliberate or accidental trauma. He said that in his view it was inappropriate for Professor Hilton to diagnose SIDS.[57]

Cala is positioned in this passage as a pathologist who is not merely expert in his own right but also better able than Hilton to judge what constitutes appropriate professional practice. The adversarial form also permitted the defence in this case to contest that preference using its own privileged actors – Hilton and Byard. Leading defence counsel Zahra SC sought to rehabilitate Hilton's evidence by pointing to his credentials and referring to Crown pathologist Berry's evidence that SIDS was an acceptable cause of death for Sarah; but he did not challenge Cala's professionalism as Cala and Tedeschi SC had challenged Hilton.[58]

In contrast, in his cross-examination of Hilton and closing address, prosecution counsel used the 2001 AAP Policy Statement to disparage Hilton's professionalism. Hilton and Folbigg's counsel resisted that construction using alternative constructions of medical professionalism and by deploying criminal procedure to exclude some prejudicial reasoning. In the process, the hierarchies and knowledges that govern pathology professionalism were introduced into the courtroom, via a mixture of evidence about professional organisations, lines of authority within forensic institutes and relative experience. Those hierarchies and associated knowledges were also altered.[59] For example, Tedeschi SC and Cala strained the language contained in the 2001 AAP Policy Statement, interpreting factors indicating the 'possibility' of smothering as circumstances that necessarily amounted to 'substantial and reasonable uncertainty'. As the defence tried to point out, the general recommendations contained within the 2001 AAP *Policy* Statement were thereby elevated to inviolable professional rules.

Hilton's compunctions and those of the defence were arguably vindicated when in 2006 the AAP revised the 2001 Policy Statement. The abstract to the revised statement explains that this revision 'addresses deficiencies and updates recommendations' in the 2001 Policy Statement.[60] The language contained in the 2006

---

[57] Tedeschi SC, closing address, *Folbigg* trial transcript (above n 5) 1340.

[58] Zahra SC, closing address, *Folbigg* trial transcript (above n 5) 1492–96.

[59] Jasanoff (above n 24) 52–53.

[60] American Academy of Pediatrics (AAP), 'Distinguishing Sudden Infant Death Syndrome from Child Abuse Fatalities' (2006) 118 *Pediatrics* 421 [2006 AAP Policy Statement] 421.

Policy Statement has been softened. For example, the list of factors that 'should indicate the possibility of intentional suffocation'[61] has become a list that 'could indicate the possibility of intentional suffocation'.[62] Similarly, the statement that '[i]t is impossible to distinguish at autopsy between SIDS and accidental or deliberate asphyxiation'[63] now reads:

> In some cases, it may be difficult or impossible to differentiate between a natural unexplained infant death, an unintentional or accidental infant death, and an unnatural (intentional) infant death. Recent literature has suggested that the index of suspicion for unnatural death should be higher, particularly in families in which an unexplained infant death has occurred previously. More recent publications, however, provide some reassurance that a percentage of recurrent, unexplained infant deaths may be, in fact, natural.[64]

The 2006 revisions could be read as a victory for medical truth over the formerly excessive emphasis on the risk that SIDS might mask intentional suffocation. I resist this reading, however, because it reinforces the grand progress theory of scientific evidence in a way that falsely positions exculpatory science as inherently more robust than inculpatory scientific evidence.[65] Nonetheless, the 2006 revision is an improvement over its predecessor in two ways. First, it provides a less selective accounting of the literature. Additionally, it sets out an investigative framework that is more consistent with the requirement of proof beyond a reasonable doubt and therefore more appropriate to criminal proceedings.

Sheila Jasanoff has argued that scientific debate within the courtroom 'exposes the cognitive and social commitments of individual expert witnesses more predictably than it identifies structurally or institutionally conditioned contingencies in scientific knowledge'.[66] A juror who heard and understood the evidence given by Hilton, Cala and other pathologists would have been able to conclude that some pathologists will not diagnose SIDS when another infant from the same family has already died in an unexpected and unexplained manner but that others will make the diagnosis. The juror would likely have believed (wrongly) from the prosecution's questions and Cala's evidence that the 2001 AAP Policy Statement *required* a pathologist to enter the diagnosis 'undetermined' when there has been a previous SIDS death in the family. And he or she would have understood that while Cala accepted and applied this practice in determining cause of death, Hilton did not. Although Hilton and the defence sought to point the jury to the slippage inherent in the prosecution reasoning, there is no way of knowing how the jury dealt with this essentially professional disagreement. Contemporary socio-legal theory suggests, however, that the jurors likely favoured the narrative

---

[61] 2001 AAP Policy Statement (above n 38) 438.
[62] 2006 AAP Policy Statement (above n 60) 423.
[63] 2001 AAP Policy Statement (above n 38) 438.
[64] 2006 AAP Policy Statement (above n 60) 422 (citations omitted).
[65] G Edmond, 'Constructing Miscarriages of Justice: Misunderstanding Scientific Evidence in High-Profile Criminal Appeals' (2002) 22 *Oxford Journal of Legal Studies* 53.
[66] Jasanoff (above n 24) 211.

that was most congruent with their pre-existing understandings about medicine and scientific truth.[67]

III. The Shifting Use of SIDS

A third striking aspect of the medical-scientific evidence in *Folbigg* is the extent to which the various actors disagreed about the proper use of the phrase 'sudden infant death syndrome'. The prosecution opened its case with a particular definition of SIDS and its relation to 'undetermined' deaths:

> SIDS, or cot death as it is sometimes called, is a mysterious illness or combination of illnesses which causes the sudden and unexpected death of an otherwise healthy infant during sleep. It occurs predominantly in babies between the ages of two and six months, with most of them being within the ages of two months to four months. It is very rare after six months and absolutely unknown after 12. . .
>
> SIDS is basically what is known as a diagnosis of exclusion. That is, where you have a baby that suddenly and unexpectedly dies that otherwise has been well and where the pathologist can find no cause of death, and where that baby is within the appropriate age range, in the absence of any other suspicions, such as child abuse or smothering or some other cause of death like a genetic defect, in the absence of any other cause of death, a pathologist will often certify SIDS as the cause of death. So SIDS equals undetermined cause of death. That is what it means.[68]

In this passage, SIDS is quite plainly equated with an undetermined death. The prosecution also emphasised that SIDS and deliberate smothering 'can often appear exactly the same' on autopsy.[69]

Over the course of the trial, the prosecution's working definition of SIDS shifted. For instance, although the SIDS definition extracted above is quite consistent with the notion that SIDS can be applied to a (possible) smothering, Tedeschi SC later sought to exclude that idea. Two weeks into the trial, the prosecution requested to cross-examine Hilton on the contents of the 2001 AAP Policy Statement:

---

[67] Eg, J Schklar and S Seidman Diamond, 'Juror Reactions to DNA Evidence: Errors and Expectancies' (1999) 23 *Law and Human Behavior* 159, 180–81; and V Hans et al, 'Science in the Jury Box: Jurors' Views and Understanding of Mitochondrial DNA Evidence', Cornell Law School Research Paper 07-021 (SSRN).

[68] Tedeschi SC, opening address, *Folbigg* trial transcript (above n 5) 30.

[69] Ibid, 32.

HIS HONOUR: That's what SIDS is, isn't it? You have been calling SIDS a disease. That's not what I understand SIDS to be. SIDS is a label which is put upon a death which is believed to be natural to which its cause cannot be attributed. Isn't that all SIDS is?

CROWN PROSECUTOR: But it is the belief that it is a natural death that is of significance. By ascribing it to SIDS Professor Hilton is, in effect, saying this was a death from natural causes to a disease that we know nothing about . . . What I wish to say is that he ought not to have ascribed it to SIDS, which is a death from natural causes, but he should have determined that it was from undetermined causes, which includes the possibility of deliberate suffocation.[70]

The disjuncture between Barr J's language – 'believed to be natural' – and prosecution counsel's language – 'saying this *was* a natural death'; SIDS '*is* a death from natural causes' – illustrates a shift in the prosecution's usage of the phrase 'SIDS'. In his judgment on the prosecution's application, Barr J wrote:

> As I understand it, SIDS is an acronym which is susceptible of fundamental misunderstanding. It has been called a syndrome, and indeed that is what the final letter stands for. It has been called a disease. I confess that I do not fully understand what it does mean. It seems clear that it is not a disease and I understand it to be no more than a label which is attributed to a death which is believed to have been natural but the cause of which cannot be assigned. I think the other necessary part of the definition is that the dead person must be a very young child.[71]

Over the course of the trial, the prosecution became more strongly committed to the notion that a SIDS diagnosis represents a positive conclusion that unnatural causes of death have been excluded. By the time Barr J gave the judgment quoted above, the prosecution had called nine medical witnesses and asked each for his working definition of SIDS.[72] The witnesses had given conflicting evidence about the age of peak incidence, the upper and lower age limit of SIDS diagnosis and the effect of various risk factors on the incidence of SIDS. The tenth expert witness, Cala, came closest to defining the boundary between SIDS and undetermined death in a way that supported the prosecutorial insistence that SIDS 'is a death from natural causes'. Even Cala, however, was not so absolute: 'SIDS is thought to be due to some natural process. It is not known what it is.'[73]

---

[70] Tedeschi SC, application for order under s 38 of the Evidence Act 1995 (NSW), *Folbigg* trial transcript (above n 5) 635–36. The defence immediately pointed to the Crown's intention to 'elevate an issue of caution or an issue of protocol to in fact a suggested finding of fact': Zahra SC, re: application for order under s 38 of the Evidence Act 1995 (NSW), *Folbigg* trial transcript (above n 5) 656. See also 739.

[71] *R v Folbigg* (14 Apr 2003) NSW 70046/02 (NSWSC).

[72] The masculine pronoun is correct at this point in the trial.

[73] AD Cala, voir dire, *Folbigg* trial transcript (above n 5) 721.

Ultimately, the prosecution's position that a SIDS death is necessarily a natural death stood at odds with the bulk of its own expert evidence. Testifying in voir dire, Susan Beal explained that the SIDS label has always included murder:

> Q. Can I just ask you, in relation to Sarah, this question appears on the second page of the questions and answers, as I have them? You were asked this question at about .7:
>
> 'Moving now to Sarah, if you had conducted the post-mortem examination of Sarah, again without any knowledge of what had happened to the other children, what in your view would have been the diagnosis of her cause of death?'
>
> And you answered:
>
> 'Most likely diagnosis was that this child had been intentionally suffocated, as not found prone, and her head wasn't covered and no hard[74] lesions found.'
>
> Do you recall saying that?
>
> A. Hmm, hmm.
>
> Q. Is that your opinion as to why you would disagree with Professor Hilton's finding that Sarah died of SIDS?
>
> A. I'm happy to accept SIDS. That's fine. I've always known that SIDS includes some murders. That has always been so, ever since I started working in SIDS.[75]

In her final answer above, Beal reasserted the difficulty of distinguishing between deliberate suffocation and SIDS. Nonetheless, the prosecution continued to insist that a SIDS diagnosis could never be given in a circumstance where the possibility of smothering exists. Logically, this position does not make sense – if, as the prosecution asserted, SIDS and smothering are truly indistinguishable, the possibility of smothering must always exist.

Barr J used Beal's testimony to challenge the prosecution's reasoning on voir dire:

> [CROWN PROSECUTOR] What I wish to elicit from Professor Herdson is his view that if he had conducted that post-mortem — firstly, that he agrees with that difference between SIDS and undetermined; and, secondly, that if he had conducted that post-mortem, and in the knowledge that Professor Hilton had found the physical findings that Professor Hilton had, he would have found a diagnosis of undetermined causes rather than SIDS.

---

[74] Later corrected to 'heart'.
[75] SM Beal, voir dire, *Folbigg* trial transcript (above n 5) 988.

There is not much difference between the two, but the difference is of great significance. They are both death from undetermined causes, but one acknowledges that it is death from undetermined natural or unnatural causes, whereas the other one does not.

. . .

HIS HONOUR: I wonder whether you can maintain that distinction any longer, in the light of Dr Beal's evidence? That evidence, of course, has only been given in the absence of the jury, but she made — most of Dr Beal's statements were strong statements, but one particularly that impressed itself upon me was that 'We recognise that a number of SIDS deaths are murder.' Now, that does not sound like SIDS being so restrictively defined.

CROWN PROSECUTOR: I understood Dr Beal's evidence to be this, your Honour: That inevitably —

HIS HONOUR: Well, it is an answer she gave.[76]

As Barr J observed, the Crown could not credibly sustain its adherence to a distinction between the putatively natural category of SIDS deaths and the more murky diagnosis of 'undetermined'. Nonetheless, in his closing address, prosecution counsel Tedeschi SC told the jury:

You might think a diagnosis for SIDS that said [sic] 'I do not know why this child died. I can't tell, because I have been unable to find any cause of death.' Numerous doctors came and gave evidence and explained to you that that is what SIDS means. SIDS means: We don't have any suspicious circumstances, we don't have any doubts about this case, but we cannot find a cause of death. So we write it down as 'SIDS'.

'Undetermined' is a little bit different, because 'undetermined' means we can't find a cause of death, but we cannot exclude some suspicions that we might have, and it might be a natural death or unnatural death. We don't know. 'Natural death' of course means death from disease or illness. Unnatural death really means homicide or accident.[77]

The prosecution's persistence with this demarcation in light of all the contrary evidence begs the question what purpose the demarcation served. An answer to that question is suggested by the evidence given by prosecution pathologist Berry about his reluctance to use the diagnosis 'undetermined':

---

[76] Folbigg trial transcript (above n 5) 1028–29.
[77] Tedeschi SC, closing address, *Folbigg* trial transcript (above n 5) 1310–11.

My background is very much in helping parents. I came to all this via cot death, SIDS, and researching that. I know that to use the term 'undetermined' or 'unascertained', certainly in the jurisdictions I work in, and I believe here, will trigger an inquest, so one does this with great reluctance because it does cause distress to families. I know that the organisations that represent families do not like us doing it.

My reply to that, and please stop me if I am going into more detail than you want, is that what we must do is go as far as we can to protect those parents who have lost their children suddenly, tragically and naturally, that is with SIDS, from being tarred, as it were, with the same brush as those very small numbers of carers who may actually have harmed the child . . .[78]

In seeking to retrieve certainty from a branch of medicine that is still by no means settled, the prosecution was attempting to draw a clear boundary between tragically bereaved families and murderous parents. Parents who lose their children suddenly and unexpectedly are here constructed as deserving protection from their differentiated other, murdering carers. In the absence of a medical-scientific explanation for SIDS, the next best thing is to police the boundaries of public sympathy.

SIDS and Kids Australia® is one of the most successful fundraising charities in Australia.[79] The successes of its programmes demonstrate the force of public sympathy for families whose children inexplicably die. It was essential to the prosecution case that Kathleen Folbigg be cast beyond the ambit of that sympathy. In fact, as I explain below in chapter eight, Folbigg was constructed in the news media as a direct threat to truly bereaved families. The grief that Folbigg displayed after her children's deaths was read as a calculated ploy to attract the sympathetic attention that should be reserved for deserving bereaved mothers. This perception was reinforced by the evidence of her husband, Craig Folbigg, described below in chapter six. Drawing a bright line between SIDS deaths and 'undetermined' deaths, prosecution counsel sought to distance Kathleen Folbigg as much as possible from the bereaved mothers who are the stalwart of the SIDS and Kids Australia® marketing campaign. Tedeschi SC also sought to engage the frustration that underpinned Crown pathologist Berry's concern to protect genuinely bereaved parents from being 'tarred with, as it were, the same brush' as those who kill their children.

At the same time as Tedeschi sought to limit SIDS to 'natural deaths', he narrowed the range of deaths that might be classified as 'undetermined.' The 2006 and 2001 AAP Policy Statements both direct that an undetermined diagnosis should be used when there is 'substantial and reasonable uncertainty' about the

---

[78] J Berry, examination in chief, *Folbigg* trial transcript (above n 5) 1064.
[79] See the SIDS and Kids® corporate profile at www.sidsandkids.org/wp-content/uploads/SIDSKIDS-20pp.pdf.

cause of death.[80] It is apparent from the policy statements and from the expert evidence given in Folbigg's trial that this uncertainty may come from a range of circumstances, including uncertainty about whether a natural condition such as myocarditis might have caused an infant's death. By the end of the second week of trial, however, prosecution counsel consistently used 'undetermined' to mean only a death in which homicide is suspected.[81] When examining Cala before the jury, Tedeschi SC took care to ensure that Cala excluded Laura's myocarditis from his decision to record Laura's death as 'undetermined':

> Q. Is it a reasonable possibility in your opinion that [Laura] died from myocarditis?
>
> A. I don't believe it is.[82]

By this point, both Cala and the prosecution had adopted a considerably more definite style when narrating the likely cause of Laura's death than they had previously employed. In Cala's original autopsy report, he was content to observe that the myocarditis 'may be an incidental finding'.[83] On 19 June 2001, Cala wrote:

> If I had examined the body of Laura Folbigg in isolation, without the knowledge I had at the time of previous infant deaths in the family, I might give the cause of death as myocarditis.[84]

By the time Cala testified that it was not 'reasonably possible' that Laura Folbigg had died of myocarditis, Barr J had directed that Cala must not consider the other deaths when testifying about the cause of any particular child's death. Cala's testimony therefore directly contradicted the statement made in his letter of 19 June 2001. During voir dire Barr J characterised Cala's ultimate testimony as '[a]n opinion, I might say, that surprises me'.[85] The defence cross-examined Cala at some length on this aspect of his evidence, although it did not directly put Cala's letter before the witness. To put this letter to Cala would have undermined the defence's strategy of keeping the expert opinion evidence confined to the cause of each individual child's death in isolation, because it necessarily introduced Cala's reasoning that previous infant deaths in the same family affect his decisions about cause of death.

When the broader context is reintroduced, the prosecution's efforts to maintain a logically impossible definition of SIDS begin to make more sense. During the trial, SIDS came to serve as an interpretive category. Genuinely bereaved parents who fit within this category deserve to access public sympathy and a great deal of support. The alternative diagnosis, 'undetermined', was narrowed by the prosecution and by Cala until its only meaning was suspected homicide. Excluding

---

[80] 2001 AAP Policy Statement (above n 38) 438; and 2006 AAP Policy Statement (above n 60) 422.

[81] See, eg, *Folbigg* trial transcript (above n 5) 634 and 721.

[82] DA Cala, examination in chief, *Folbigg* trial transcript (above n 5) 719.

[83] AD Cala, 'Coroners Act 1950 Autopsy Report re Laura Elizabeth Folbigg' (1 March 1999) contained in Folbigg case files (above n 1).

[84] Cala, quoted in *R v Folbigg* (1 Apr 2003) NSW 70046/02 (NSWCA).

[85] AD Cala, voir dire, *Folbigg* trial transcript (above n 5) 740.

the Folbigg children's deaths from the category of true SIDS, the Crown both reinforced its argument that the children did not die naturally and demonised Kathleen Folbigg for seeking to fit herself within the class of truly deserving bereaved parents.

This usage of the label 'SIDS' had the potential to carry far greater discursive power within the trial than the contested and confusing technical connotations of SIDS. Hamstrung by its strategy of preventing the expert witnesses from testifying about the collective import of the Folbigg children's deaths, the defence seemingly found it difficult to resist the prosecution's characterisation of the medical evidence. While the defence was able to offer an alternative conception of medical professionalism, it was unable to point effectively to the distorting effects of the adversarial process on the prosecution's medical case.

IV. Conclusion

In *Cannings*, the English Court of Appeal concluded that a prosecution should not be started or continued when there is:

> a serious disagreement between reputable experts about the cause of death, and a body of such expert opinion concludes that natural causes, whether explained or unexplained, cannot be excluded as a reasonable (and not a fanciful) possibility.[86]

The conclusion there was that unless pathological evidence is accompanied by 'additional cogent evidence' that supports the proposition that children were harmed, prosecution cannot proceed.

The NSW Court of Criminal Appeal rejected the proposition that the *Cannings* reasoning applied to *Folbigg*, on the basis that *Cannings* was a 'case-specific' decision that could be distinguished from *Folbigg*.[87] The features on which the Court distinguished *Cannings* were that an expert in *Cannings* (Roy Meadow) had given seriously flawed evidence in another trial, which could have formed a basis of cross-examination during Cannings' trial; the *Cannings* Court of Appeal received a fresh body of medical evidence; Cannings had evidence supporting a pattern of infant death in her extended family while Folbigg did not; and the evidence against Cannings did not disclose any history of ill-temper, 'let alone violence'.[88]

The *Folbigg* appeal judgment, written before the Victorian Supreme Court decision in *R v Matthey*,[89] refused the defence's invitation to contemplate the possibility that Crown experts Cala, Beal and Ophoven might be vulnerable to the

---

[86] *Cannings* (above n 22).

[87] *R v Folbigg* (2005) 152 A Crim R 35, [2005] NSWCCA 23 (17 February 2005) para 137 [*Folbigg* conviction and sentencing appeal].

[88] Ibid, paras 138–42.

[89] *R v Matthey* [2007] VSC 398.

same criticism as that made of Meadow in *Clark*[90] and *Cannings*.[91] Given that Folbigg is effectively an orphan who was raised without contact with her biological family, the negative comparison with Cannings' family history of infant death seems unfair. This judicial reasoning reinforces Mark Cooney's proposition that evidence is a currency that is more readily generated and used by those with positively valued social characteristics or institutional ties.[92] The evidence underpinning the Court's implication that Folbigg was violent towards her children is considered more closely below in chapters six and seven. For present purposes, it suffices to note how quickly the *Folbigg* appeal court veered away from engaging with the expert disagreement that was disclosed on the *Folbigg* trial record, despite having the benefit of the decision in *Cannings*. After *Matthey*, the NSW Court of Criminal Appeal's reasoning warrants reconsideration.

[90] Above n 2.
[91] For further discussion of *Matthey*, *Clark* and *Cannings*, see above ch 1.
[92] M Cooney, 'Evidence as Partisanship' (1994) 23 *Law & Society Review* 833.

6

A Mother Who Would Kill Her Children

The Crown case is that this accused had the following possible motives. The accused had a very low threshold for
stress, and she was also deeply resentful at the intrusions
that her children made on her own life and, in particular,
on her sleep, her ability to go to the gym, and her ability
to socialise, including going out dancing.

She was constantly tired, resentful against her husband,
Craig, for not providing her with what she considered to be
adequate help, and she was constantly, we say, constantly
preoccupied, to an exaggerated degree, with her weight-gain
due, in part, to the fact that she couldn't get to the gym
as much as she liked because of her children.

Crown opening statement, *R v Folbigg*[1]

I. Introduction

THE CASE FOR convicting Kathleen Folbigg depended on constructing her as a certain type of mother – a mother with few coping skills and relatively little support, but also one who was sufficiently organised and intelligent to murder her children and almost get away with it. This chapter traces the genesis and development of the prosecution argument that Kathleen Folbigg was the kind of mother who could murder her children and conceal her actions. The prosecution relied on several sources of evidence to make this case: information about the domestic structures within the Folbigg household; coincidence evidence about the five charged incidents; Craig Folbigg's testimonial evidence about Kathleen Folbigg's personality and mothering skills; and Kathleen Folbigg's diaries. In this chapter, the evidence about Kathleen Folbigg is considered, while chapter seven contains a closer analysis of the diaries, which were taken by the prosecution to

---

[1] M Tedeschi SC, Crown opening statement, *R v Kathleen Megan Folbigg*, trial conducted in the NSW Supreme Court between 1 Apr and 21 May 2003 before Grahame Barr J [*Folbigg* trial transcript] 26. The trial transcript is contained in the Folbigg court record, held by the NSW Court of Criminal Appeal registry under file numbers 60496 of 2002, 2002/70046, 60279 of 2004 and 2004/1814 [*Folbigg* case files].

encapsulate Kathleen Folbigg's lived experience of motherhood. Prosecutor Mark Tedeschi SC encouraged the jury to make sense of the evidence by drawing on their understandings of 'normal' mothering, thereby filtering the evidence through the dominant ideology of motherhood.

Evidence about the gendered family arrangement served multiple functions in Folbigg's trial. On the prosecution case, Kathleen's childcare responsibility provided her with the opportunity to murder her children. Kathleen's occasional resistance to full-time caregiving became evidence of indifference or even antipathy towards her children, as well as evidence of her inability to cope with the children. Ironically, even while Kathleen's resistance to full-time mothering was cast as suspect, the prosecution schedule of coincidence evidence rendered generic incidents of the gendered childcare arrangement into distinctive markers of similarity between the children's deaths. Finally, the prosecution positioned Craig as the authoritative definer of Kathleen's mothering skills, to the exclusion of her close friends, who arguably had more direct experience with the daily challenges of mothering.

The defence endeavoured to challenge each of these tactics, arguing in particular that Craig was fabricating evidence in an effort to make Kathleen falsely appear to be an uncaring and abusive mother. The defence also downplayed the distinctiveness of the coincidence schedule, identifying the extent to which the prosecution's posited similarities were necessarily consequent to Kathleen's role as primary caregiver. However, the defence was surprised by some of Craig's testimony. In the opening submission, it framed the case as one in which there would be no direct evidence that Kathleen was ever physically violent towards the children. The defence therefore found itself in an invidious position when Craig testified to some incidents in which Kathleen was rough with a child; Craig had not mentioned these incidents in previous interviews with police or prosecutors.

The common thread throughout both parties' arguments was the extent to which Kathleen Folbigg met or violated the expectations imposed by broadly held normative conceptions of motherhood. Both prosecution and defence deployed these normative conceptions in order to make sense of the coincidence evidence, Craig's testimony and the insights provided by Kathleen's friends. However, the ideology of motherhood inscribed within the trial was more constrained than may be the case outside the courtroom.

The logic adopted at trial was that an inadequate mother was more likely to commit murder. 'Inadequate' in this context should be understood broadly – there was no sustained suggestion that the children were physically abused or neglected, despite some evidence from Craig Folbigg that Kathleen was often angry and occasionally even physically rough in disciplining Laura in particular. Kathleen's posited inadequacies lay in what the prosecution depicted as a lack of patience with the children, her excessively rigid parenting style and her lack of tolerance for behaviour that she construed as naughty or disobedient. The defence resisted this construction by arguing that Craig's evidence lacked credibility and by pointing to the unanimous testimony of Kathleen's friends and treating medical staff that she was caring and appropriate in her dealings with the children. Neither friends nor doctors noticed unusual bruises, aversive behaviour or other hints of abuse or neglect during the children's lives. No child had bruises or other indicia of abuse or failure to thrive on post-mortem examination.

The quote that opens this chapter is drawn from Tedeschi SC's opening statement to the jury. It neatly demonstrates how the prosecution went about the task of constructing Kathleen Folbigg as the kind of mother who would murder her children. Tedeschi asserted that Kathleen Folbigg had a low threshold for stress, implying that she may have killed the children at times when she felt particularly stressed about mothering. This sounds plausible enough, except that the prosecution had relatively little evidence for the proposition that she was stressed at the relevant times.[2] Equally, Tedeschi suggested that Kathleen Folbigg felt unsupported in her mothering role. Finally, and most bizarrely, Tedeschi asserted that Kathleen Folbigg was worried about gaining weight, missing her regular trips to the gym and sorry that she could no longer go out dancing at nightclubs. This suggestion was drawn from Kathleen Folbigg's diaries and is explored in chapter seven.

Over the course of the trial the prosecution sought to develop a picture of a mother who could not put selfish things aside for the good of her children and who was in fact so incapable of love that she killed her children to return to her nightclub-dancing, gym-obsessive ways. The difficulty with this theory is that on the evidence Kathleen Folbigg had been 'out dancing' only a few times in ten years, and she did not take up the gym until several months after her third child died.[3] Nonetheless, the press in particular lapped up the image of Kathleen Folbigg as a partygoer who never wanted to stop. While Kathleen Folbigg seemed to insist upon the differences between angry thoughts and violent actions, and between self-blame and causation, these distinctions were largely lost within the evidence given at trial.

II. The Dominant Ideology of Motherhood

The trial is in part a hegemonic process: 'an apparatus, or ensemble of practices, discourses, experts and institutions, that actively contributes to the legitimation of a social order'.[4] In the case of Kathleen Folbigg's trial, the part of the social order that was engaged and generally reinforced was the privatised, gendered

---

[2] See, eg, C Folbigg, examination in chief and cross-examination, *Folbigg* trial transcript (ibid) 108–9, 114–15, 219–20 and 254–55. In *R v Sally Clark* [2003] EWCA Crim 1020, para 15, the Court of Appeal remonstrated with the prosecution for gratuitously introducing the suggestion that Clark was driven to murdering her children by the stress of her husband's absence. For more discussion of the relevance of *Clark*, see below n and above ch 1.

[3] *Folbigg* trial transcript (above n 1) 383–90, 1487–88 and 1501–2.

[4] DE Chunn and D Lacombe, 'Introduction' in DE Chunn and D Lacombe (eds), *Law as a Gendering Practice* (Toronto, Oxford University Press, 2000) 10.

ordering of childcare responsibilities within the heterosexual nuclear family.[5] Before police found Kathleen Folbigg's diaries, their suspicions focused on her as the primary caregiver to the four Folbigg children and as the person who found each of them dead. The police efforts to enlist Craig Folbigg into the investigation were predicated on the expectation that, as Kathleen Folbigg's husband, he possessed unique insight into her personality, motivations and actions. During the trial, Craig Folbigg asserted this status as an authoritative knower in response to defence suggestions that he was fabricating domestic incidents that cast Kathleen Folbigg as an aggressive, short-tempered mother. Other witnesses, including the family's doctors and nurses, friends and extended family, gave differing but largely positive accounts of Kathleen's care for her children.

The evidence elicited by both parties about Kathleen Folbigg's mothering went well beyond the relatively straightforward question of whether Folbigg had the opportunity to kill or cause harm to her children. Prosecution and defence counsel each spent considerable time with lay and clinical witnesses seeking to establish how Folbigg related to her children, whether she was prone to anger with them and how she cared for and about them during their lives and after their deaths. Given that some ambiguity arose within the scientific evidence at trial, prosecution counsel drew upon the ideology of motherhood to make sense of the conflicting evidence about Folbigg's mothering capacity.

Ideology is a complex concept that cannot be thoroughly defined in a brief discussion.[6] However, in this context, I take ideology to mean the institutional aggregation and coalescence of ideas about the social world.[7] One effect of coalescence and aggregation is that ideas which describe how the world often is (eg, 'many mothers behave in the following manner') attain a normative dimension ('mothers should behave in the following manner'). On this understanding, ideology is not necessarily wrong or distorted, as is often implied. However, ideology has a strong connection with social and economic power relations. It values some experiences or forms of life over others; and the process of selection tends to replicate other social hierarchies.[8] Marxist accounts of law emphasise that law participates in the creation and perpetuation of particular ideologies, in part by lending its own institutional prestige to the task of selective valuation.[9] Ideology therefore both helps to explain why some legal cases have social and institutional impact that far exceeds their immediate outcomes, and assists researchers in understanding the decision-making within individual cases.

---

[5] SB Boyd, 'Is There an Ideology of Motherhood in (Post)Modern Child Custody Law?' (1996) 5 *Social & Legal Studies* 495; and DE Roberts, 'Welfare Reform and Economic Freedom: Low-Income Mothers' Decisions about Work at Home and in the Market' (2004) 44 *Santa Clara Law Review* 1029.

[6] See T Eagleton, *Ideology: An Introduction* (London, Verso, 1991) ch 1.

[7] A Hunt, 'Marxism, Law, Legal Theory and Jurisprudence' in P Fitzpatrick (ed), *Dangerous Supplements: Resistance and Renewal in Jurisprudence* (Durham, NC, Duke University Press, 1991) 102, 107.

[8] SB Boyd, 'Some Postmodern Challenges to Feminist Analyses of Law, Family and State: Ideology and Discourse in Child Custody Law' (1991) 10 *Canadian Journal of Family Law* 79, 97.

[9] Hunt (above n 7) 115.

The *Folbigg* prosecution submission that Folbigg was an identifiably inadequate mother was presumably intended to help the jury to resolve any residual uncertainty about how the Folbigg children died. The defence meanwhile used other evidence to suggest that Folbigg complied with normative conceptions of good mothering and that she was therefore unlikely to have killed her children. Given that social constructions of good mothering are ubiquitous, it is not my intention to suggest that the parties used the ideology of motherhood in a fully conscious or deliberately strategic way. Rather, the lawyers engaged in the profoundly social process of combining experience and ideology to select among competing and conflicting accounts of Folbigg's motherhood. They invited the jury to do likewise.

The dominant ideology of motherhood imposes particular norms and behavioural expectations on all women, constructing a standard by which women's lives are judged.[10] Dorothy Roberts has written:

> Women's criminal conduct is of growing interest to both criminologists and legal scholars. Feminist legal theorists recently have embraced the concept of motherhood. There is important insight into the social construction of women's identities where these two topics meet.[11]

When enacted within criminal processes, legal discourses both draw upon and reconfigure the ideology of motherhood as a means to the end of categorising particular mothers. Commonly, as is particularly evident in the competing interpretations of Craig Folbigg's testimony at trial, the ideology of fatherhood is co-constructed with and helps to inform the ideology of motherhood.[12]

There are relatively few published feminist legal analyses of the relationship between motherhood and murder.[13] Fiona Raitt and Suzanne Zeedyk[14] provide a relevant discussion in their consideration of the mothering discourses that may be discerned from the English Court of Appeal decisions in *R v Clark*[15] and

---

[10] M Kline, 'Complicating the Ideology of Motherhood: Child Welfare Law and First Nation Women' in MA Fineman and I Karpin (eds), *Mothers in Law: Feminist Theory and the Legal Regulation of Motherhood* (New York, Columbia University Press, 1995) 119.

[11] DE Roberts, 'Motherhood and Crime' (1993) 79 *Iowa Law Review* 95 (citations omitted).

[12] While I seek to remain attentive to the relationship between ideologies of motherhood and fatherhood, this relationship is not the core focus of this discussion. For an extended consideration of the construction of fatherhood within law, see R Collier, '"Waiting Till Father Gets Home": The Reconstruction of Fatherhood in Family Law' (1995) 4 *Social & Legal Studies* 5.

[13] I distinguish between murder and the crime of infanticide. Infanticide has received a tremendous amount of scholarly attention. See, eg, C Backhouse, *Petticoats and Prejudice: Women and Law in Nineteenth-Century Canada* (Toronto, Women's Press for the Osgoode Society, 1991); C Smart, 'Disruptive Bodies and Unruly Sex: The Regulation of Reproduction and Sexuality in the Nineteenth Century' in C Smart and J Brophy (eds), *Regulating Womanhood: Historical Essays on Marriage, Motherhood and Sexuality* (London, Routledge, 1992) 7–32; and S Gavigan, 'The Criminal Sanction as it Relates to Reproduction' (1984) 5 *Journal of Legal History* 20–43. An empirical study that includes more contemporary infanticide cases is KJ Kramar, *Unwilling Mothers Unwanted Babies: Infanticide in Canada* (Vancouver, University of British Columbia Press, 2005).

[14] F Raitt and MS Zeedyk, 'Mothers on Trial: Discourses of Cot Death and Munchausen's Syndrome by Proxy' (2004) 12 *Feminist Legal Studies* 257.

[15] Above n 2.

R v Cannings.[16] Raitt and Zeedyk suggest that although commentators have tended to focus on the failure of expert evidence within these cases, it is also important to attend to the role of social expectations of mothering. Raitt and Zeedyk particularly link Clark's and Cannings' wrongful convictions to the deployment of gendered standards of childcare and expectations about a mother's emotional states. They suggest that in both cases the parties implicitly relied on assumptions that a murderous mother is identifiable through her lack of care for and attention to her child and through the nature and quality of her emotional reaction to a child's death or illness. Crucially, these assumptions did not only frame the contest at trial; they also provided the discourses with which appellate judges exonerated the two defendants.

The Australian murder trial of Lindy Chamberlain displays a similar logic.[17] Prosecution and defence lawyers, as well as appellate judges, proceeded on the assumption that a murderous mother would depart in identifiable ways from the behaviours stipulated by the ideology of motherhood. I have suggested elsewhere that the ideology of motherhood is sufficiently flexible to accept that a mother may become angry or frustrated, although generally only towards those who threaten or harm her children.[18] Within a contested criminal trial, social expectations about mothering therefore operate as an implicit comparator by which a particular mother's behaviour can be judged. This comparator persistently extends beyond the charged acts – a mother who kills her children is plainly a bad mother – to other aspects of her behaviour, particularly her caregiving. A mother whose behaviour fails to comply with the ideology of motherhood in identifiable ways may therefore become more vulnerable to being found to have committed the particular acts with which she is charged.

Whereas Raitt and Zeedyck, and my previous work, focus on the ways in which the ideology of motherhood can help to prove murder or to vindicate a wrongly convicted mother, most research in this field is more concerned with understanding and explaining maternal violence. This literature provides a useful counterpoint. The feminist quest to understand criminal mothers takes two forms: mapping the interaction of criminal law and motherhood; and understanding why some mothers harm their children. Roberts conceptualises the relationship between motherhood and crime as possessing two characteristics. First, laws criminalising maternal behaviour help to 'construct the meaning of motherhood' by defining the outer limits of acceptable behaviour.[19] Murdering a child is an extreme example of this proposition, and Roberts is more concerned with 'failure to protect' a child from abuse by another adult (most often a father or boyfriend) and other crimes of omission. Second, and more saliently, criminal law enforces

---

[16] *R v Angela Cannings* [2004] EWCA Crim 1.
[17] See *Re: Alice Lynne Chamberlain and Michael Leigh Chamberlain and: the Queen* (1983) 72 FCR (Australia) 1; E Cunliffe, 'Weeping on Cue: The Socio-legal Construction of Motherhood in the *Chamberlain* Case' (LLM thesis, University of British Columbia, 2003).
[18] Cunliffe, 'Weeping on Cue' (ibid) 60–61.
[19] Roberts, 'Motherhood and Crime' (above n 11) 100.

the subordinating aspects of motherhood, punishing women who resist their maternal role.[20]

Roberts proposes that feminist research should strive to understand why some mothers harm their children, but cautions that '[a] feminist praxis based on identification with criminal mothers must recognise the damage criminal mothers inflict on children, while criticising society's construction of mothers and celebrating positive resistance.'[21] Marie Ashe tentatively proposes that narrative depictions of murderous mothers may help lawyers and law students come to terms with the difficult task of representing abusive mothers, allowing lawyers to tell women's stories to courts.[22] Susan Ayres argues that when faced with murderous mothers, lawyers and judges 'should make every effort to give recognition to the "other" and should try both to represent and to judge mothers accused of infanticide with other love'.[23]

Roberts, Ashe and Ayers identify a pervasive incomprehension of maternal violence against children, and they propose various means of countering that incomprehension. This lack of understanding arguably originates in the ideology of motherhood. A central tenet of this ideology is that mothers are expected to sacrifice their own interests in favour of their children.[24] An act of direct violence perpetrated by a mother against a child is the clearest contravention of this principle, and within criminal law it warrants significant sanction. As Roberts, Ashe and Ayres identify, incomprehension frequently justifies a refusal to engage fully with the reasons why women might be driven to harm or kill their children – with the consequence that these mothers are punitively punished, and their violence is severed from its material context.[25] This material context is the normative isolation of the nuclear family unit as a site for 'proper' child-raising, as well as the displacement of financial and emotional responsibility for children onto the family unit, especially onto mothers.

The refusal to understand frames many of the longer published treatments of child homicide. For example, Lita Schwarz and Natalie Isser ask rhetorically:

---

[20] Ibid.

[21] Ibid, 138.

[22] M Ashe, 'The "Bad Mother" in Law and Literature: A Problem of Representation' (1992) 43 *Hastings Law Journal* 1017. See also M Ashe, 'Postmodernism, Legal Ethics, and Representation of "Bad Mothers"' in Fineman and Karpin (eds) (above n 10) 142–67.

[23] S Ayres, '[N]ot a Story to Pass On: Constructing Mothers Who Kill' (2004) 15 *Hastings Law Journal* 39, 110. By 'other love', Ayres seems to mean an attempt to judge mothers who kill with compassion and an effort to understand their worldview, as opposed to a decision to exclude these mothers from the realms of compassion or understanding.

[24] MM Slaughter, 'The Legal Construction of Mother' in Fineman and Karpin (eds) (above n 10) 79; Boyd, 'Is There an Ideology of Motherhood?' (above n 5) 508; and JC Murphy, 'Legal Images of Motherhood: Conflicting Definitions from Welfare "Reform", Family and the Criminal Law' (1998) 83 *Cornell Law Review* 688.

[25] The contemporary trend towards punitive charging and sentencing practices in relation to maternal violence has been documented elsewhere, including in the context of wrongful convictions that arose in the United Kingdom and Canada. I have specifically documented this trend in Canada in E Cunliffe, 'Infanticide: A Legislative History and Current Questions' (2009) 55 *Criminal Law Quarterly* 21–46.

Why do these parents (or those serving in that role) batter and kill children who cannot control their behaviour because they are too young to do so? When social welfare agencies exist in virtually every community in the United States, why are some parents so overwhelmed by child care that they can murder a child rather than seek outside help?[26]

Shwarz and Isser go on to explain that mothers' motives for murdering children are 'beyond the ken of most people'.[27] Melissa Prentice has taken this observation one step further, suggesting that American prosecutors find it difficult to persuade 'skeptical jurors' that seemingly devoted mothers would harm or kill their children.[28] Prentice's own empirical data belies this assertion – in the cases she reviewed, prosecutors secured 15 convictions from 15 charges, and 19 child protection orders from 19 applications.[29] Some commentators blame the cultural incomprehension of maternal violence for the professed under-reporting of child homicide and for the asserted frequency with which infant smothering is mistaken for sudden infant death syndrome.[30]

The dissonance between Prentice's empirical data and her assertion that it is difficult to secure convictions against abusive mothers hints at one of the more elusive features of this area of research. Although cases such as *Folbigg* are tremendously complex and consume significant amounts of trial time, jurors are plainly capable of reaching the conclusion that certain mothers have murdered their children.[31] Similarly, while pathologist John Napier Hilton was sure that he had correctly diagnosed Sarah Folbigg's death as SIDS, his former colleague Allan Cala was equally convinced that the four Folbigg children were murdered.[32] These differing opinions, coupled with the broad assertion that it is difficult to convict mothers who have killed children, re-enliven the insistent question about the extent to which lay and expert ascriptions of responsibility for infant death rely on cultural preconceptions about motherhood. If cultural notions of good mothering play a role, it is important to investigate whether this reasoning is founded in an empirical link between perceived emotional or behavioural inadequacies and homicidal actions.

In this chapter, I interrogate the process and effects of categorising the Folbigg children's deaths as murder. Rather than focusing on the task of rendering homicidal actions explicable within legal discourse, I investigate the ways in which

[26] LL Schwarz and NK Isser, *Child Homicide: Parents Who Kill* (Boca Raton, Taylor & Francis, 2007) 57. Despite the gender-neutral phraseology, Schwarz and Isser's examples in the ensuing passage are all mothers who kill their children.

[27] Ibid, 58.

[28] MA Prentice, 'Prosecuting Mothers who Maim and Kill: The Profile of Munchausen Syndrome by Proxy Litigation in the Late 1990's' (2001) 28(3) *American Journal of Criminal Law* 373, 412.

[29] Ibid.

[30] Eg, A Wilczynski, *Child Homicide* (London, Greenwich Medical Media, 1997) 33–34; and the review provided in K Polk and C Alder, *Child Victims of Homicide* (New York, Cambridge University Press, 2001) 5–9. See also AW Craft and DMB Hall, 'Munchausen Syndrome by Proxy and Sudden Infant Death' (2004) 328 *British Medical Journal* 1309, 1311; and J Stanton and A Simpson, 'Murder Misdiagnosed as SIDS: A Perpetrator's Perspective' (2001) 85 *Archives of Disease in Childhood* 454.

[31] Confining myself to examples in which jurors wrongly convicted mothers, see *Re: Alice Lynne Chamberlain* (above n 17); *Clark* (above n 2); and *Cannings* (above n 16).

[32] See above ch 5, esp s II.

the dominant ideology of motherhood informs fact determination and is also re-inscribed by the terms on which a murder case is argued. I set the scene by explaining how the Folbigg family unit functioned and then trace the ways in which the prosecution drew upon aspects of Kathleen Folbigg's mothering practices to suggest that she was a suspect mother. Focusing on Craig Folbigg's testimony, I next explain how these suspicions were given form and substance.

III. The Folbigg Family Unit

The Folbiggs appear to have had what I will loosely term a traditional marriage; Kathleen worked at times, but generally after a child was born, Kathleen resigned her job to take care of the baby while Craig continued to work outside the home. While the terms of the arrangement varied somewhat over time, Craig explained their usual family organisation on cross-examination:

Q. That was your attitude at the time that Laura was born — that you were the provider?

A. Kathy and I made a deal; she wanted to be a mum; she wanted to leave her job, so we made a deal. I put 150 per cent into what I could do in my life to provide for her and this baby, and me to provide a tidy life and she would put 150 per cent into her life as a mother. I did help out at home, but not very much.[33]

An exception to this description of Craig's role is that when their second child, Patrick, was born, Craig resigned from his paid employment to spend time with his son.[34] He returned to work when Patrick was four months old.[35] At trial, the prosecution pointed to the fact that Patrick's acute life-threatening episode (ALTE) occurred two days after this return to work as evidence that Kathleen had caused the ALTE by smothering Patrick.[36] There was, however, no evidence that Craig's decision to return to paid employment distressed Kathleen nor that she was having any difficulty caring for Patrick before his ALTE.[37] In fact, Craig testified that Kathleen was Patrick's primary caregiver even during the months when Craig remained at home.[38]

---

[33] *Folbigg* trial transcript (above n 1) 234.

[34] Craig Folbigg, examination in chief, *Folbigg* trial transcript (above n 1) 108.

[35] Letter from Craig Folbigg, 1 July 1991, contained in *Folbigg* case files (above n 1).

[36] Craig Folbigg, examination in chief, *Folbigg* trial transcript (above n 1) 108–9. For discussion of the term 'ALTE', see above ch 1, n 19.

[37] As described below, the English Court of Appeal warned prosecution counsel that it should not make unfounded assertions about a mother's emotional response to her husband's absence in circumstances such as these: *Clark* (above n 2).

[38] *Folbigg* trial transcript (above n 1) 107.

Kathleen was primarily responsible for attending to the children, although Craig spent time bathing and playing with Sarah and Laura most evenings. Kathleen was always the one who responded to the children at night, a responsibility partly explained at trial by the fact that Craig was a heavy sleeper and partly by the fact that Kathleen was the primary caregiver. After Sarah was born, Kathleen returned to part-time paid employment on weekend mornings. When she worked, Craig cared for Sarah or, after he also began working on Saturday mornings, a family member babysat. Craig testified that Kathleen quit this job after members of his extended family chastised her for missing too much of Sarah's life by working in paid employment.[39]

Contemporary empirical research suggests that the gendered allocation of childcare and financial responsibilities within the Folbigg family fits a fairly typical pattern for a two-parent, heterosexual Australian family. Janeen Baxter, Belinda Hewitt and Michele Haynes report:

> From a gender perspective, parenthood is likely to be associated with an increased production or display of gender, as doing housework is a major component of being a good mother, and the birth of children is likely to generate a greater amount of housework. For men this is likely to be expressed in terms of greater involvement in paid work, whereas for women it is likely to be expressed in terms of greater involvement in domestic work. [40]

Kathleen's engagement in part time paid employment while Sarah was still quite young is not unusual within contemporary Australian families.[41] Nonetheless, the prosecution suggested that Kathleen's decision to seek paid employment was explained by a desire to escape her maternal role. At the same time, the prosecution submitted that quotidian aspects of the Folbigg family arrangements constituted distinctive and highly suspicious similarities between the four deaths and Patrick's ALTE.

A Working Mother

Within Western societies it is increasingly common, even expected, for a mother to combine caregiving responsibilities with paid employment at a time when her children are still young.[42] This aspect of the ideology of motherhood does not operate evenly across fields of law, however. Mothers who seek to rely on welfare or social security payments are pushed into the paid workforce,[43] yet mothers

---

[39] Ibid, 122–23.

[40] J Baxter, B Hewitt and M Haynes, 'Life Course Transitions and Housework: Marriage, Parenthood, and Time on Housework' (2008) *Journal of Marriage and Family* 259–72, 262 (citations omitted). See also J Baxter, B Hewitt and M Western, 'Post-Familial Families and the Domestic Division of Labor: A View From Australia' (2005) 36 *The Comparative Journal of Family Studies* 583–600.

[41] Baxter, Hewitt and Western (ibid) 587.

[42] See, eg, Roberts, 'Welfare Reform and Economic Freedom' (above n 5); Boyd, 'Is There an Ideology of Motherhood?' (above n 5).

[43] Roberts, 'Welfare Reform and Economic Freedom' (above n 5).

whose children suffer harm while they are working outside the home are distinctly at risk of being blamed for that harm.[44]

During the *Folbigg* trial, the prosecution took advantage of this ambivalence within the ideology of motherhood to cast Kathleen's desire to engage in paid employment while mothering as suspect. Craig testified that Kathleen chose to return to work after Sarah was born because 'she was sick of being broke, sick of being stuck at home.'[45] It is unclear from this assertion whether the family was struggling to meet its financial commitments, or whether Kathleen wanted to earn some money of her own. Craig had previously told police that Kathleen worked after Sarah's birth because it was financially necessary.[46] On cross-examination, Craig testified that this passage in his police statement was untrue and that Kathleen did not need to return to work at that time.[47]

The exchange between Craig Folbigg and Tedeschi SC over Kathleen's decision to work part-time implies that in her desire to work outside the home, Kathleen was breaching the marital consensus regarding the division of responsibilities within the family. Furthermore, Craig suggested that Kathleen was not adequately concerned about providing Sarah with stable or high-quality care while she was working. Craig testified that he eventually enlisted his sister and brother-in-law to help persuade Kathleen to accept responsibility to care for Sarah fulltime.[48] In his closing address, defence counsel Peter Zahra SC suggested that the jury should not believe Craig Folbigg's evidence on this point, because he had earlier provided an inconsistent account to police.[49] The defence strategy, predicated on questioning Craig's evidence rather than explaining any desire Kathleen had to engage in paid work, affirmed the underlying class-based logic that a mother who works outside the home when her baby is young compromises the child's wellbeing, and such work should only occur when it is financially necessary. If Kathleen wanted to work for other reasons, she would hardly be unique in this regard, yet there was no broader challenge to the prosecution characterisation of a desire to work outside the home as inherently suspect.

Craig's evidence about Kathleen's desire to work outside the home cast her actions as a selfish repudiation of her husband's capacity to provide financially for the family. Worse, it suggested that Kathleen was looking for ways to escape the shackles of motherhood. Implicitly, having been denied an exit via paid employment, Kathleen may have elected to murder Sarah as a means of freeing herself. This version does not make a whole lot of sense in isolation, but it contributed to a developing picture of Kathleen as a woman who had trouble meeting the broader demands of motherhood.

[44] Roberts, 'Motherhood and Crime' (above n 11).
[45] Craig Folbigg, examination in chief, *Folbigg* trial transcript (above n 1) 122.
[46] Craig Folbigg statement (23 May 1999), *Folbigg* case files (above n 1).
[47] Craig Folbigg, cross-examination, *Folbigg* trial transcript (above n 1) 251–52 and 290–91.
[48] Ibid, 122–23.
[49] P Zahra SC, defence closing address, *Folbigg* trial transcript (above n 1) 1469.

The Coincidence Evidence

The prosecution case for convicting Kathleen Folbigg relied in part on a number of similarities between the circumstances in which each child died or was found dead. The admissibility of this coincidence evidence was hotly contested by the defence pre-trial. The NSW Court of Criminal Appeal affirmed the admissibility of the coincidence evidence after the defence appealed from a pre-trial order that permitted the evidence.[50] The defence was denied a stay of proceedings pending leave to appeal the NSW Court of Criminal Appeal decision to the High Court of Australia.[51]

Coincidence evidence is relevantly defined in section 98(1) of the Evidence Act (NSW) 1995 as evidence of two or more related events introduced to 'prove that, because of the improbability of the events occurring coincidentally, a person did a particular act'. A party who seeks to introduce coincidence evidence must serve notice before trial and must also persuade the trial judge that the coincidence evidence, alone or in combination with other evidence, possesses 'significant probative value'.[52] Events are related when they are substantially and relevantly similar and they occur in similar circumstances.[53] In *Folbigg*, the prosecution relied on several asserted similarities between the four deaths and the ALTE in order to raise the inference that the incidents were related.

The heart of the prosecution coincidence reasoning was that when taken with the medical, behavioural and diary evidence, the occurrence of four unexplained infant deaths in a single family proved that the children were murdered, rather than dying of natural causes. Since Kathleen was the only person who could have precipitated all five events, and since she was demonstrably an inadequate mother, she must have killed her children.

In support of the contention that the deaths were substantially and relevantly similar and that they occurred in similar circumstances, prosecutor Tedeschi ultimately relied on ten enumerated similarities between the charged events. These similarities were summarised in a chart that was served on the defence and supplied to the jury.[54] This reasoning was reconstituted several times over the course of the trial – originally, 19 similarities were flagged.[55] The coincidence reasoning engaged a mélange of factors, some originating from medical science (eg, the assertion that each child's death occurred unexpectedly, in the sense that no child had been diagnosed with a life-threatening illness) and others drawn more from common sense. As I have already discussed the medical evidence in other chapters, I will focus here on those factors that relied on common-sense reasoning. It is, however, somewhat artificial to disaggregate the medical similarities from the

---

[50] *R v Kathleen Megan Folbigg* [2003] NSWCCA 17.
[51] *Kathleen Folbigg v The Queen High Court of Australia,* transcript S59/2003 (19 February 2003).
[52] Evidence Act (NSW) 1995 s 98(1)(b).
[53] Ibid, s 98(2).
[54] Crown schedule of coincidence evidence, *Folbigg* case files (above n 1).
[55] The original list is reproduced in *R v Folbigg* [2003] NSWCCA 17, para 11.

'common-sense' similarities, since both types rely to some extent on generalities about usual or proper maternal behaviour.[56]

Table 6.1 summarises the 'common-sense' similarities pressed at trial. The defence contested the evidentiary basis of one proposition, and in several instances the defence directly challenged the prosecution's underlying logic.

Table 6.1 Summary of 'Common-Sense' Coincidence Reasoning Used by the Prosecution in *Folbigg* [*]

Proposed Similarity	Evidentiary Basis Contested by Defence?	Logic Contested by Defence?
1 Each death and the ALTE occurred at the Folbigg home.	No	No†
2 Each incident occurred during a sleep period.	No	No†
3 Each incident occurred while the child was in bed.	No	No†
4 Each child was found dead or moribund by the accused.	No	Yes
5 Each time an incident occurred, the child was found in the course of a 'normal check' by the accused.	No	Yes
6 Three incidents occurred at night when the accused was coming back from the toilet.	No	Yes
7 Each child was warm to the touch when found, and in two incidents the child still had a heartbeat.	Yes	Yes
8 The accused failed to pick up or attempt to resuscitate any of the children except Laura after discovering that the child was not breathing.	No	Yes

* M Tedeschi SC, Crown closing address, *Folbigg* trial transcript (above n 1) 1362–64.
† Defence counsel Zahra SC observed in passing that propositions 1–3 were logically explicable given Kathleen Folbigg's role as primary caregiver: *Folbigg* trial transcript (above n 1) 1399.

In evaluating the coincidence evidence, it is important to have regard to the purpose for which it was introduced. Kathleen Folbigg's opportunity to cause death and injury in relation to each count was established without relying on coincidence evidence, and therefore coincidence evidence was not needed for this purpose. There was no suggestion at trial that anyone else could have killed the children – if they died unnaturally, it could only have been at Folbigg's hand. If the prosecution proved that Folbigg had killed each child and caused Patrick's ALTE, Folbigg's intention was potentially a proper subject for coincidence evidence. However, the defence broadly conceded that if Folbigg had smothered her

[56] See also Raitt and Zeedyck (above n 14).

children, she had done so with the requisite criminal intention.[57] Accordingly, the coincidence evidence was not probative of mens rea.[58] Therefore, the only purpose to which the coincidence evidence was material at trial was to help the prosecution prove that because of the sheer number and similarity of deaths in the Folbigg family, those deaths and Patrick's ALTE must have been inflicted rather than natural. To re-couch this point in the statutory language, the coincidence evidence was used to establish that Folbigg performed acts (smothering) that caused the deaths and Patrick's ALTE. In the ensuing paragraphs, I assess the prosecution's coincidence evidence according to the extent to which it both serves and over-reaches this purpose.

Of the similarities listed in Table 6.1, similarities 1–5 are strikingly general and somewhat repetitive. For example, the observation that each incident occurred while the child was in bed adds virtually nothing to the observation that each incident occurred during a sleep period, when the child was at home. Like many Australian infants, the Folbigg children spent much of their lives at home, in the sole care of their mother. The caregiving arrangement is here transformed into a reason to suspect that Kathleen Folbigg killed her children. The prosecution argument denies the accused the trust implicit within the standard arrangement. Kathleen Folbigg is rendered dangerous, while the normalcy of private gendered caregiving is reinforced – these events would not be 'substantially and relevantly similar' if home were a common place for a child to suffer natural death or serious illness. The prosecution did not introduce any evidence to support the contention that it is unusual for infant death to occur at home while the child was asleep. Nor did the defence contest this reasoning, however.[59] The net result was that some factual circumstances which were nearly inevitable incidents of Kathleen Folbigg's primary caregiving role were decontextualised and rendered singular by the prosecution, thereby becoming evidence of a pattern of malevolent mothering.

Similarities 4–6 also draw upon the gendered childcare pattern. Given that Kathleen Folbigg was the primary caregiver and the only parent who attended the children for around 18 hours a day, it is relatively unsurprising that she was the one to find each child dead. The English Criminal Court of Appeal criticised a similar line of reasoning in its decision exonerating Sally Clark:

> Children frequently spend the majority of the early part of their life in the sole care of their mother, and hence it cannot in any way be said to an unusual feature for just two events to occur when the babies are in the mother's sole care.[60]

[57] Barr J, summing-up, *Folbigg* case files (above n 1) 46.

[58] Barr J directed the jury that it could use tendency reasoning to find intention in respect to the second and subsequent counts but not in relation to Caleb. This was plainly proper, and this discussion is not concerned with this aspect of the jury's reasoning. See ibid and also Evidence Act (NSW) 1995 s 97. Note that the NSW legislation distinguishes between tendency and coincidence evidence, unlike some common law jurisdictions.

[59] I am grateful to Professor Paul Roberts for pointing out that such 'manufactured similarities' are commonly deployed by the prosecution in order to make the circumstances of putatively related events seem more distinctive than they might otherwise appear.

[60] *Clark* (above n 2) para 15.

Folbigg was different from *Clark* in that there were five incidents under scrutiny, but Craig's testimony regarding the childcare arrangements was unambiguous: Kathleen attended to the children, even when Craig was home, and especially at night. Craig worked long hours during the day and often returned home after the children's bedtime. This testimony was supported by passages in Kathleen's journals, which are discussed below in chapter seven. The asserted 'pattern' of Kathleen discovering the children dead or moribund becomes, in this light, little more than an incidence of the allocation of responsibility within the Folbigg household.

In his closing address, Tedeschi SC made a great deal of Kathleen Folbigg's propensity to find her children dead as she was going to the toilet at night (similarity 6 in Table 6.1):

> God, her going to the toilet was very dangerous for these
> children. Three out of her five children had incidents when
> she happened to go to the toilet. God, you would be locking
> up the toilet, wouldn't you? Every one of them was during a
> normal check of their well-being. Gosh, you would be tell-
> ing her not to check on them, wouldn't you? What an amazing
> coincidence, or is it?[61]

This similarity is unlike similarities 1–5 in that it is less generic. The prosecution repeatedly asked why Kathleen, sleep-deprived from caring for an infant, would wake in the middle of the night to visit the toilet. The defence did not directly respond to this question. Kathleen's diaries record that she frequently had trouble sleeping – many entries are written between midnight and 6 am. Folbigg's experience is arguably consistent with medical research which suggests that while almost all mothers experience interrupted sleep after giving birth, mothers (such as Folbigg) who do not breastfeed sleep more lightly and have lower sleep quality.[62]

Tedeschi's sarcasm was partly designed to help the jurors see that a seemingly humdrum domestic moment – checking on a child after visiting the washroom – can provide the opportunity to commit murder.

In his closing address, Zahra SC made the following suggestion about how the jury should assess similarities 1–6:

> Looking at these elements of coincidence we would obviously
> need to look at her role, her role as the primary caregiver
> and see in fact when we look at these in total that we need
> to factor that into account. When we factor those types of
> situations we can in fact obviously see that they don't
> appear, the coincidences or the lack of coincidences that
> the Crown has suggested.[63]

---

[61] Tedeschi SC, closing address, *Folbigg* trial transcript (above n 1) 1363.

[62] KA Lee and AB Coughley, 'Evaluating Insomnia during Pregnancy and Postpartum' in HP Attarian (ed), *Sleep Disorders in Women* (Totowa, NJ, Humana Press, 2006) 185, 192.

[63] Zahra SC, defence closing address, *Folbigg* trial transcript (above n 1) 1399.

In this passage and briefly elsewhere, Zahra SC appealed to the jurors' capacity to understand that the prosecution's asserted distinctive similarities were incidents of Kathleen's familial role as primary caregiver.

Similarity 7 is that each child was warm to the touch when found. This issue was contested at trial, on two grounds. First, there was disputed documentary and testimonial evidence to suggest that Caleb's body[64] and Sarah's body[65] were cool or cold when ambulance officers attended these deaths.[66] Other evidence suggested that the bodies were warm. This was particularly important because these were the two deaths that occurred at night. Patrick's ALTE also occurred at night, and the fact that Folbigg found him moribund was used by the prosecution as evidence that she had harmed him.

Grahame Barr J's summing-up obscured the dispute over Sarah and Caleb's body temperatures, particularly in relation to Caleb: 'The prosecution also said that it is remarkable that the accused was in the presence of the dead child not long after the time when he must have died. His body was still warm.'[67] However, Zahra SC did not point specifically to the evidence that Caleb and Sarah may have been cool to the touch in his closing address. Recently, in *HML v The Queen*, the High Court of Australia suggested that the prosecution must prove facts underlying coincidence evidence beyond a reasonable doubt before the jury may draw the proposed inference.[68] At a minimum, it seems appropriate to direct the jury to any conflict within the evidence about a fact on which coincidence evidence relies. The defence contested similarity 7 at trial on the basis that the prosecution had not introduced any evidence about how quickly an infant's body will cool after death. Zahra SC pointed out that it was therefore difficult to sustain the contention that a warm body was evidence that the child had only recently died.[69]

Some time after Folbigg was convicted, it emerged that a juror had asked a friend who was a nurse how long it would take a child's body to cool after death. The information that it would take 'an appreciable period of time' was subsequently discussed among some jurors.[70] The NSW Court of Criminal Appeal dismissed an

---

[64] AA Reed (ambulance officer who attended Caleb's death), examination in chief, *Folbigg* trial transcript (above n 1) 1151–52. The contemporaneous ambulance report recorded that Caleb's body was cold.

[65] DA McDermid (ambulance officer who attended Sarah's death), examination in chief, *Folbigg* trial transcript (above n 1) 570.

[66] The prosecution disputed that Caleb's body was cool, and neither party dealt expressly with McDermid's evidence in closing addresses. See Tedeschi SC, Crown closing address, *Folbigg* trial transcript (above n 1) 1311.

[67] Barr J, summing-up, *Folbigg* case files (above n 1) 36.

[68] *HML v The Queen* [2008] HCA 18 (24 April 2008). The status of this rule in New South Wales is presently uncertain. See *DJV v R* [2008] NSWCCA 272; *FDP v R* [2008] NSWCCA 317; and *DTS v R* [2008] NSWCCA 329. The principles underlying *HML* have been criticised on the basis that they operate too stringently when tendency evidence is offered to help prove lack of consent in sexual assault cases, eg: D Hamer, 'Similar Fact Reasoning in *Phillips*: Artificial, Disjointed and Pernicious' (2007) 30 *UNSW Law Journal* 609. Arguably, this criticism reflects the need to attend to the evidentiary context in which the coincidence inference is being advanced.

[69] Barr J, summing-up, *Folbigg* case files (above n 1) 37.

[70] *Kathleen Folbigg v R* [2007] NSWCCA 371 (21 December 2007) [*Folbigg* jury appeal] para 8.

appeal based on this and a second jury irregularity on the basis that the irregularities were not material. Without mentioning the two ambulance officers' evidence or Caleb's ambulance report, McClellan CJ stated that the evidence at trial had established that each infant was warm to the touch when found. He held, 'I do not believe [the information about cooling time] could have affected the jury's verdicts.'[71]

The disappearance of the ambulance drivers' testimony about the state of Caleb and Sarah's body temperatures from the judicial account is significant. It was inappropriate for the jury to conclude that Caleb's body was warm unless they decided that Allan Albert Reed, the responding ambulance officer, was mistaken or lying in his testimony and that the ambulance report was also wrong. Similarly, before concluding that Sarah's body was warm it was necessary for the jurors to consider the evidence of Deborah Ann McDermid, the ambulance driver in that case, to the contrary. The prosecution made a great deal of the evidence that Folbigg discovered each of her children relatively soon after death, inviting the jury to reason that this was more consistent with the behaviour of a mother who had killed her children than with that of an insomniac, perhaps over-concerned, parent. The defence did relatively little to contest the assertion and did not direct the jury's attention to the inconsistent evidence.

The prosecution suggestion that it was unlikely for Kathleen Folbigg to have spontaneously checked on her children at about the time of their deaths was also enabled by the 'bad mother' discourse. Had Folbigg been accepted as a good mother, it would be more plausible that she would check on her children in the middle of the night. Furthermore, Folbigg's vulnerability to an adverse inference was greater *because* of her caregiving role – as the person who held primary responsibility for the children, she was most likely to find them moribund or dead.[72] While the defence asserted this proposition, it did not mount a sustained attack on the ways in which the prosecution logic decontextualised the Folbigg children's deaths from the pattern of their lives.

While the prosecution reasoning about the importance of body temperature is far from unassailable, it was one of the more distinctive similarities remaining at the end of the trial. The proposition that Folbigg killed her children and then immediately raised the alarm was central to the prosecution theory of the case, because it explained why Patrick was moribund after his ALTE and why Laura had residual electrical signals in her heart when ambulance officers first attended her. The defence suggested that Patrick's condition was due to the virus that was subsequently diagnosed in hospital and that Folbigg had checked on Laura because she had heard her cough a few minutes earlier. On these case stories, if Caleb and Sarah were cool to the touch, the prospect that Folbigg had smothered them becomes more remote. These deaths, which were the two that most resembled SIDS in their absence of positive pathological findings, then fall more

---

[71] Ibid, para 56.
[72] See *Clark* (above n 2).

squarely within the expected pattern of SIDS discovery described in much of the scientific literature, whereby a parent checks on an infant to find that s/he has died some time earlier.

Similarity 8 from Table 6.1 above invited the jury to identify a pattern within Kathleen Folbigg's failure to touch her children or administer cardiopulmonary resuscitation (CPR) after finding them dead or moribund. In its initial coincidence schedule, the prosecution cast doubt on Folbigg's statement that she had rendered CPR to Laura. This doubt was plainly removed by the tape of the accused's emergency call, and the prosecution dropped that contention at trial. The asserted similarity within Folbigg's reactions is interesting because it relates less to the distinctive similarities between the children's deaths and Patrick's ALTE than to the similar way in which the accused responded to each incident. The accused's reaction may be a relevant circumstance when enquiring whether the accused caused the incidents but not to the question of whether the deaths and ALTE were so similar that they must be related.

As Bell J observed in *R v Phillips*, it is improper to strengthen the similarity inference by assuming that the accused has performed the charged act.[73] Even more strongly, Judge LJ held in *R v Cannings*:

> It will immediately be apparent that much depends on the starting point which is adopted. The first approach is, putting it colloquially, that lightning does not strike three times in the same place. If so, the route to a finding of guilt is wide open. Almost any other piece of evidence can reasonably be interpreted to fit this conclusion. For example, if a mother who has lost three babies behaved or responded oddly, or strangely, or not in accordance with some theoretically 'normal' way of behaving when faced with such a disaster, her behaviour might be thought to confirm the conclusion that lightning could not indeed have struck three times. If however the deaths were natural, virtually anything done by the mother on discovering such shattering and repeated disasters would be readily understandable as personal manifestations of profound natural shock and grief. The importance of establishing the correct starting point is sufficiently demonstrated by this example.[74]

This passage is particularly apposite because Tedeschi SC used the lightning metaphor in his closing address to the jury.[75]

Similarity 8 depended upon the reasoning that since a mother who had murdered an infant would presumably be reluctant to resuscitate the child, a mother who does not try to resuscitate her child is more likely to have caused the child's death or illness. Zahra SC attacked this logic, reminding the jury that Kathleen Folbigg invariably sought emergency help, and in three instances, Craig Folbigg conducted CPR. Kathleen's actions in raising the alarm first were appropriate in

---

[73] *R v Phillips* [1999] NSWSC 1175 (17 December 1999) para 76. In New South Wales as in the United Kingdom, the Court must assume that the coincidence evidence is true when assessing its relevance and the inferences that may reasonably be drawn. See Evidence Act (NSW) 1995 ss 55 and 57; and Criminal Justice Act (UK) 2003 s 109.

[74] *Cannings* (above n 16) (19 January 2004) para 11.

[75] Tedeschi SC, closing address, *Folbigg* trial transcript (above n 1) 1364.

part because it was rational to seek assistance but also because she was too distressed to perform CPR herself.[76]

Similarity 8 is predicated on the expectation that a normal mother will respond to a baby's illness or death in identifiable ways. Correspondingly, a mother's love for her child can be measured in the nature and quality of her response to crisis. The defence pointed to other evidence that Kathleen Folbigg had been grief-stricken and distressed at the time of the five incidents.[77] The prosecution agreed that Kathleen Folbigg was truly upset but suggested that this affect was 'not an unambiguous grief reaction'; rather it was evidence of grief mixed with guilt.[78]

The prosecution acknowledgment that Kathleen Folbigg grieved her children's deaths reinforced its refusal to suggest a motive for the alleged crimes, as well as its characterisation of the accused as so damaged that she was literally unable to prevent herself from murdering her children:

> This accused had an overriding need to control — particularly the sleeping and eating patterns of the children — and when she could not do that she imposed her will upon them, to the extent of murdering them. She was going to win that battle of wills, and when they wouldn't comply with her she murdered them. With each child, she was able to cope just a little better. That is why each child lasted a little longer than the previous one.[79]

The remarkable aspect of this submission is that acknowledging Kathleen Folbigg's grief did not function as a reason for compassion or mitigation but as a warrant for punitive response. Kathleen Folbigg's posited emotional inadequacy was thereby decontextualised from the circumstances in which she mothered, stripped of its potential to explain or justify her experience and subjected to the neoliberal construction of individual responsibility with a vengeance.[80]

I explained above in chapter five that the NSW Court of Criminal Appeal decision to admit coincidence reasoning depended in part upon the expectation that certain evidence would be adduced at trial. In the event, some of that evidence was never led, and other parts were introduced in more guarded terms than the prosecution expected. The same phenomenon arose with the common-sense similarities outlined above in Table 6.1. When the prosecution initially served its coincidence notice, the similarities were more precise and more distinctive than those on which it ultimately relied. For example, the initial list included the following similarities:

---

[76] Zahra SC, closing address, *Folbigg* trial transcript (above n 1) 1485.

[77] Ibid, 1485.

[78] Tedeschi SC, closing address, *Folbigg* trial transcript (above n 1) 1373.

[79] Ibid, 1373–74.

[80] J Simon, '"Entitlement to Cruelty": The End of Welfare and the Punitive Mentality in the United States' in K Stenson and RR Sullivan (eds), *Crime, Risk and Justice: The Politics of Crime Control in Liberal Democracies* (Cullompton, Willan Publishing, 2001) 125–43.

- 'There was, in each case, a short interval between the time when the child was last claimed to have been seen alive by the accused and the time when he or she was found lifeless or not breathing properly';
- 'sleep monitors, which had been provided following the earlier deaths and ALTE, were not in use at the time of death in the case of Sarah and Laura'; and
- 'the accused had shown acute irritation in relation to each child or appeared to have been in a condition of stress before the deaths or ALTE.'[81]

While each of these notions arose at some point during the trial, none of them was fully established. The prosecution properly removed these propositions from its ultimate coincidence schedule.

The NSW Court of Criminal Appeal held when deciding to allow the coincidence evidence:

[I]f, as the trial progresses, there are grounds for contending that the evidence as presented turns out to be substantially different from how it appeared at the time of the determination of admissibility or the joinder of counts, there may be a ground to apply for those questions to be reconsidered.[82]

The defence did not make an application along these lines during trial. As things turned out, however, the prosecution's coincidence schedule looked very different by the time closing addresses were delivered than it did when the Court of Criminal Appeal decided to admit the coincidence evidence. In particular, it seems appropriate to revisit the question whether the eight enumerated common-sense similarities, coupled with the two medical-science similarities, were enough to make the five charged incidents 'substantially and relevantly similar' and to establish that they occurred in 'substantially similar' circumstances.[83] The two medical-science similarities were that the deaths were all sudden, in the sense that they were not precipitated by major illness; and unexpected, in that no child had been diagnosed with a life-threatening condition. The distinctiveness of these similarities was never as great as the expert evidence at trial seemed to suggest and has diminished in light of the paper published by Robert Carpenter and colleagues in 2005.[84]

Boiled down, the prosecution's asserted similarities are that: each death was sudden and unexpected; the deaths occurred at home during sleep periods, while the children were in their mother's care and Craig Folbigg was absent or asleep; Kathleen Folbigg found each child moribund or dead, three of them while returning from a trip to the toilet at night; despite evidence to the contrary, the children were all warm to the touch when found; and Kathleen Folbigg's reactions made the circumstances of the deaths more similar than they would otherwise be.

---

[81] Crown coincidence evidence notice, quoted in *R v Folbigg* [2003] NSWCCA 17 (13 February 2003).

[82] *R v Folbigg* (ibid) para 28.

[83] Evidence Act (NSW) 1995 s 98(2).

[84] RG Carpenter et al, 'Repeat Sudden Unexpected and Unexplained Infant Deaths: Natural or Unnatural?' (2005) 365 *The Lancet* 29.

In *Phillips*, Bell J criticised the prosecution for relying on 'criteria of consider-able generality'.[85] These criteria included the facts that the Phillips children were all the natural children of the accused, that Tracy Phillips had found each of the children dead or in distress and that she had taken each child to hospital. In *Clark*, Kay LJ observed that '[i]n the ordinary incidence of family life, it could be antici-pated that some imprecise similarity . . . could always be found.'[86] The prosecu-tion had relied on similarities that included the facts that the dead Clark children were in their mother's care at the time of their deaths and that in each case Sally Clark had been alone with the children before finding them dead. While the admissibility of similar fact evidence is always a question decided within the con-text of a particular case, *Phillips* and *Clark* provide germane warnings against rely-ing on generic similarities that may well reflect the innocuous organisation of family affairs rather than constituting evidence of a criminal pattern.

In *Folbigg*, the prosecution's coincidence reasoning transformed the gendered allocation of childcare responsibility within the Folbigg family unit into a circum-stance that provided Kathleen Folbigg with the distinctive opportunity to commit murder. This line of reasoning ultimately relied on a misunderstanding of the purpose of coincidence evidence. Simply put, the prosecution may rely on coinci-dence evidence to prove that because of the improbability of events occurring coincidentally, the accused performed acts that killed her children. This evidence may be adduced only when it has significant probative value[87] – that is, when it could 'rationally [significantly] affect the assessment of the probability of the existence of a fact in issue'.[88]

Relying on factors linked inextricably to the gendered allocation of caregiving responsibility within the Folbigg family was improper because the prosecution did not demonstrate that these factors rationally affect the probability that the Folbigg children were smothered rather than dying naturally. Similarly, I find it difficult to accept that the jury turned its mind to whether Caleb and Sarah were in fact warm to the touch when they were found. The jury was not directed on this issue, and the NSW Court of Criminal Appeal seems to have overlooked the con-tradictory evidence on this point. Finally, the distinctiveness of four sudden unex-pected infant deaths has arguably taken on a more complicated complexion than was apparent from the evidence at trial – both because of the over-simplification of the medical knowledge and because of subsequent research in the field. Nonetheless, the coincidence evidence was allowed to stand at trial and in subse-quent appeals. It may be time to reconsider this aspect of the case against Folbigg far more closely.

---

[85] *Phillips* (above n 73) para 71.
[86] *Clark* (above n 2) para 15.
[87] Evidence Act (NSW) 1995 s 98(1)(b).
[88] Ibid, dictionary section.

IV. 'Something I Carried in My Heart': Craig Folbigg's Evidence

A relatively unusual feature of the *Folbigg* case was that Kathleen Folbigg's ex-husband Craig was convinced that the accused had murdered her children.[89] Craig became a central witness at Kathleen's trial, testifying for almost 12 hours over six days. His testimony represented more than a quarter of the transcribed evidence. In the prosecution case, Craig became the primary definer of Kathleen's personality, motivations and mothering practices.[90] The defence contested this construction, cross-examining Craig at great length. The defence also attacked Craig's credibility, repeatedly asserting that he had exaggerated Kathleen's negative traits and behaviours. In this section, I explore the prosecution position that Craig had a unique insight into Kathleen Folbigg's personality and mothering capacity. I also describe how the defence resisted that ascription, before explaining the ways in which the defence attacked Craig's honesty and motivations as a means of impugning his credibility. Throughout, I reflect on when and why both parties' tactics mobilised familial ideology and the dominant ideology of motherhood.

Crown prosecutor Tedeschi relied upon Craig's evidence for several purposes. Most obviously, Craig provided the jury with information about the four Folbigg children's births, lives and deaths: in examination in chief, Tedeschi SC took Craig through the events of each child's life in great detail. Secondly, the prosecution sought to construct Craig as an authoritative knower in relation to Kathleen's practical mothering skills: disagreements between the Folbiggs about how to parent Sarah were particularly relevant to this construction. Thirdly, the prosecution relied on Craig's insights into Kathleen's emotional capacities: during examination in chief, Tedeschi asked Craig about Kathleen's responses to each birth and elicited testimony regarding Kathleen's difficulty remaining calm when the children were disobedient. Finally, the prosecution elicited testimony about a number of specific incidents in which Kathleen lost her temper with a child. This testimony was particularly strongly contested by the defence, who pointed to inconsistencies within Craig's accounts.

The Folbigg Children

Most of the details Craig Folbigg related about the children's births and lives were mundane – rooms painted to prepare a nursery, furniture borrowed from friends

---

[89] In every similar case I have investigated, a husband has supported the mother-defendant's claim to innocence, eg, *Re: Alice Lynne Chamberlain* (above n 17) 1; *Clark* (above n 2); *Cannings* (above n 16); *R v Matthey* [2007] VSC 398. Trupti Patel's trial presents another example. See A Holt, 'Patel Case Raises Questions', BBC News, 11 June 2003, news.bbc.co.uk/2/hi/uk_news/england/2982302.stm.

[90] See H Becker, 'Whose Side Are We On?' (1967) 14 *Social Problems* 239, 241; and above ch 5, text accompanying n 44.

and family, visits to family doctors. This evidence was filtered through the gendered allocation of caregiving within the Folbigg household – for example, Craig testified 'I hadn't really spent much time with Caleb at all'.[91] Similarly, Craig recounted that he had asked Kathleen to discuss Caleb's feeding difficulties during a routine visit to a paediatrician, because he had not attended that appointment.[92] The prosecution relied on the domestic incidents Craig recounted as established fact, even when Craig had not personally observed or experienced those events. The prosecution's approach fits with the general principle that an accused's relevant and material statements are directly admissible despite the general prohibition against hearsay. It also overcame the difficulties presented by the need to give the jury a picture of the Folbiggs' domestic affairs without testimony from Kathleen.

Beyond the usual evidentiary rules, the reasoning underlying the prosecutorial reliance on Craig's evidence about domestic tasks he did not perform is that, as Kathleen's husband and the Folbigg children's father, Craig had an inherent understanding of the family's domestic affairs – despite his not being the primary caregiver.[93] This strategy recalls the distinction Carol Smart has drawn between 'caring for' and 'caring about' children in the context of family law.[94] Smart has identified that when a custody dispute arises between parents, fathers tend to adopt a discourse of 'caring about' the children, while mothers describe 'caring for' the children, in the sense that women tend to point to their caregiving work. Smart has suggested that these two modes of caring are perceived as being of at least equal value to children, reinforcing a presumption that children's best interests are secured by retaining a continuing relationship with both parents. The work and expertise involved in daily caregiving are thereby discounted.[95] Similar ideological commitments to shared (yet asymmetrical) parenting expertise are identifiable within the prosecution case in *Folbigg*. These commitments become clearer when one looks at two further aspects of the evidence – Craig's testimony regarding Kathleen's domineering and rigid mothering style; and the prosecution's submissions regarding the relative merits of evidence given by Kathleen's female friends about her mothering.

---

[91] Craig Folbigg, examination in chief, *Folbigg* trial transcript (above n 1) 108.

[92] Craig Folbigg, cross-examination, *Folbigg* trial transcript (above n 1) 209.

[93] For a description of the history of the notion that a father possesses authority over his wife and children and the contemporary manifestations of that proposition, see Collier (above n 12). I am more interested here in the assumption that Craig Folbigg was an authority about his family, despite being a largely absent father.

[94] C Smart, 'Losing the Struggle for Another Voice: The Case of Family Law' (1995) 18(2) *Dalhousie Law Journal* 173.

[95] Susan B Boyd similarly argues that an ideology of equality operating within family law equates a mother's track record of providing childcare with a father's expressed intention to parent in the future, particularly when the mother is non-traditional in certain ways (eg, because she engages in paid employment outside the home): SB Boyd, *Child Custody, Law, and Women's Work* (Toronto, Oxford University Press, 2003).

Parenting the Folbigg Children

Craig testified about mounting disagreements between him and Kathleen about the best way to raise children. He described Kathleen's parenting style as regimented and authoritarian, particularly with Sarah and Laura. For example:

> She was a very rigid, regimented type of person, and so times were always a factor, so if you went beyond the boundaries of those times, it was very hard for me because working in Singleton was an hour away and it was very hard for me because I was that much further and much longer, and so you would come home and if you got home late that was tough for you, the baby [Sarah] was going to bed at 8, 8.30, and that was it. So she just got sort of like harder about things.[96]

On cross-examination, Zahra SC suggested that the traits Craig perceived as rigidity were actually good parenting, and the conflict between the Folbiggs resulted from Craig's lack of understanding about children's need for routine:

> Q. Did she indicate to you that, obviously being with the child all day, it was important for the child to have a regular sleep pattern?
>
> A. Not that I recall.
>
> Q. Did you understand that it was important that after 8.30 she may be tired at that point?
>
> A. She could have gone to bed at any time, and she always knew that.
>
> Q. That this may have been a concern of hers to have the child with a regular sleeping pattern so she herself could properly attend to the child?
>
> A. But I was home and it was one thing that was always a contentious issue with us. I was home. I was quite happy to take on that responsibility, bathing her, giving her her dinner, playing with her, putting her to sleep. It was never an issue to me. And that's why we constantly argued over this 8.30 affair. But Kathy could have gone on her merry way and done whatever she wanted to, because I had Sarah.[97]

This passage is interesting because it reveals the selective way in which Craig engaged with the gendered allocation of caregiving responsibility. Although Kathleen was the primary caregiver and was at times persuaded into that role by her extended family, Craig here constructed this demarcation as a matter of

---

[96] Craig Folbigg, examination in chief, *Folbigg* trial transcript (above n 1) 123.
[97] Ibid, 292. See also Zahra SC, defence closing address, *Folbigg* trial transcript (above n 1) 1467.

choice on Kathleen's part. In asserting that he was 'quite happy to take on that responsibility',[98] Craig countered the defence suggestion that his actions interfered with Kathleen's attempts to care for Sarah's material needs, such as her need for adequate sleep. Craig possibly misunderstood Zahra SC's suggestion 'she might be tired at that point', taking the feminine pronoun here as a reference to Kathleen when, in context, 'she' may equally refer to Sarah. Craig's interpretation is revealing because it demonstrates his belief that the children's routines were designed to relieve Kathleen of her mothering duties rather than being for the children's benefit. The defence subsequently softened its interpretation of Craig's responses to Kathleen's desire for routine to a disagreement about appropriate parenting.[99] This subtle shift is quite important because it implicitly concedes that Craig's practical parenting expertise was equivalent to his wife's, at least in relation to the children's routines.

Craig resisted the defence suggestion that Kathleen was an organised and attentive mother who attended diligently to the children's needs. Zahra SC took Craig to passages within Kathleen's diaries as evidence of her skill, suggesting for example that the act of documenting Caleb's daily routines reflected careful and caring mothering practice:

Q. In the days that Caleb was alive your wife essentially made entries almost on the half hour about the child?

A. Almost.

Q. She noted everything, at times whether he had done a number two, absolutely everything; would you agree with that, Mr Folbigg?

A. Yes.

Q. Have you ever seen anything like that before, any other person that you know filling out a diary about every half hour what the child was doing?

A. Yeah, I have seen other people do it.

Q. But your wife appeared to be watching that child intently; yes or no?

A. Pretty much about every time any other mum would have looked at her kid.

. . .

Q. You are suggesting it means nothing?

A. It is just a mum writing stuff down about her baby.[100]

---

[98] As I explain below in ch 8, Kathleen Folbigg's diary suggests that she was less certain about Craig Folbigg's willingness to help with caregiving and housekeeping responsibilities.

[99] Zahra SC, defence closing address, *Folbigg* trial transcript (above n 1) 1467.

[100] Craig Folbigg, cross-examination, *Folbigg* trial transcript (above n 1) 230–31.

The defence suggested that this and other passages proved Craig's reluctance to admit to any positive aspect in Kathleen Folbigg's mothering. I return to that submission later. For the time being, what is notable about Craig's responses is that he demeaned Kathleen's mothering work by reference to its ordinariness and, implicitly, its low value to the child.[101] Denying that Kathleen was a diligent mother formed an important part of the prosecution's strategy to render her murderous tendencies apparent through her inherent incapacity to mother her children to anything more than a most basic standard.

The prosecution's effort to position Craig as a person who possessed considerable knowledge about parenting, particularly about Kathleen's parenting skills, is most apparent when contrasted with the prosecution's submissions regarding other evidence that suggested Kathleen was a good mother. In total, seven women testified that they had spent time with Kathleen and her children and observed that she was a good mother.[102] The defence called three of Kathleen's female friends to testify about her care and regard for Laura, as well as the appropriateness of Kathleen's interactions with her daughter. Kathleen and Laura saw these women every day at the gym. Two of these witnesses were mothers who occasionally babysat Laura, and they all met Kathleen for coffee at times. Their evidence about Kathleen's mothering capacity was uniformly positive – Laura was always clean, well turned out and happy in her mother's care, and Kathleen was attentive and caring towards her child.[103] The prosecution asked the jury to disregard these witnesses' evidence:

> No doubt [Zahra SC] will point to some evidence that was called in the defence case from the girls at the gym, that the accused was a good mother. Well, ladies and gentlemen, the girls from the gym, you might think, would have no real idea what sort of a mother Kathleen Folbigg was. You would give their evidence, in our submission, very little weight. None of them had any idea that she harboured the thoughts that are expressed in her diaries, and those aren't the kind of thoughts that you would confide in casual acquaintances that you meet at the gym, or even better friends than that.[104]

This passage served two purposes. Tedeschi suggested to the jury that Kathleen's friends were 'casual acquaintances' or, at best, friends in whom the accused did not confide her deepest thoughts. This prefigures a distinction Tedeschi drew between the true Kathleen of the diary evidence and the false, social face that

---

[101] See generally L Turnbull, *Double Jeopardy: Motherwork and the Law* (Toronto, Sumach Press, 2001).

[102] See 'Evidence regarding Kathleen Folbigg as a Good Mother', document submitted by defence to Barr J in sentencing phase, *Folbigg* case files (above n 1).

[103] Jan Bull, evidence in chief, *Folbigg* trial transcript (above n 1) 1185; Debbie Goodchild, evidence in chief, *Folbigg* trial transcript (above n 1) 1282; and Judith Patterson, evidence in chief, *Folbigg* trial transcript (above n 1) 1288.

[104] Tedeschi SC, Crown closing statement, *Folbigg* trial transcript (above n 1) 1376.

Kathleen presented to most of the world, most of the time. On the prosecution case, Craig is the only living person who repeatedly saw this mask slip.[105] Equally importantly, Tedeschi here belittled the women's knowledge about Kathleen's mothering practices and the depth of many friendships between women. Debbie Goodchild and Judith Patterson drew explicitly on their own experiences of mothering when offering their opinion that Kathleen Folbigg was a good and caring mother, and all three women characterised themselves as reasonably close to Kathleen. In Tedeschi's submission, however, they were transformed into 'the girls from the gym', and their experience and knowledge of good mothering were correspondingly devalued.

The Emotional Mother

In contrast to the testimony offered by Kathleen Folbigg's female friends, Craig painted a picture of a mother who loved her children but had trouble yielding centre stage to them. With the benefit of hindsight, Craig suggested that this conflict was apparent from the time of Caleb's birth:

> Q. Are you suggesting now that there are things that you want to say about the way she treated Caleb that were of concern to you?
>
> A. It wasn't so much necessarily how she treated Caleb.
>
> Q. What was it?
>
> A. It might have been her disposition at being a mother. It might have been what I viewed as — okay, it sort of kind of boils down like this: When Kathy was pregnant with the boy, she was special and everybody looked on her as special because she was having this baby. When the baby was born he became special and Kathy wasn't special any more. It is something that I saw back then. It is something I carried in my heart. I don't know what to do with it, I didn't know where to it [sic] take it. I just lived with it. Then more things go on in life that make Kathy special and then things happen that keep her being special. Whether it is engineered by her or it is just the nature of it happening, along its course. That is what I'm trying to explain to you.
>
> Q. What are you suggesting by that? What are you suggesting, that that was apparent by her demeanour at that time?
>
> A. After Caleb was born.

---

[105] Kathleen's foster sister, Lea Bown, also related an incident in which Kathleen lost her temper with Laura for the first time at trial. Bown alleged that Kathleen had pulled Laura out of her highchair by an arm: *Folbigg* trial transcript (above n 1) 769.

Q. Yes.

A. Everybody was ripping around and yahooing that I had a son; Craig had a son. It put the spout on it. All that sort of stuff. Where was Kathy in all that?[106]

While Kathleen initially seemed happy to be a mother to Caleb and later Patrick, Craig testified that her behaviour changed profoundly once Patrick was diagnosed with epilepsy. The stresses of coping with a sick child made Kathleen lose her temper and become frustrated with both Craig and Patrick.[107] Craig testified that Kathleen began to leave Patrick in her sister-in-law's care and that Kathleen considered leaving Patrick and her husband.[108] As they would later do during Sarah's life, Craig and his sister talked to Kathleen about her duty to remain with her family despite the difficulties of motherhood. Craig testified that by the time that she was caring for Sarah, Kathleen was short-tempered and angry, 'growling' almost daily at the baby and at Craig.[109] This pattern recurred during Laura's life.[110]

Relying on Craig's evidence, the prosecution case at trial highlighted Kathleen's reluctance to allow her children or husband to detract from the attention she purportedly felt she deserved from others. This argument drew on the normative expectation that a mother will compromise her independent interests in favour of her children and husband and also resonates with the theory behind Munchausen's Syndrome by Proxy (MSbP). According to Roy Meadow, MSbP mothers classically thrive on the attention they receive from friends and medical staff when a child becomes ill or dies.[111] Craig identified a similar phenomenon when explaining Kathleen's response to her children's births and deaths – 'more things go on in life that make Kathy special and then things happen that keep her being special.'[112] The prosecution was careful to explain to the jury that there was no evidence to suggest that Kathleen Folbigg suffered from MSbP.[113] Nonetheless, the gendered discourses that organise the medical profession's understanding of MSbP are also apparent in Craig's evidence and in the prosecution case theory that Kathleen was incapable of making the sacrifices necessary to become a mother. The common link is that all these discourses are informed by normative conceptions of proper, self-sacrificial mothering.[114]

---

[106] Craig Folbigg, cross-examination, *Folbigg* trial transcript (above n 1) 221–22.

[107] Craig Folbigg, examination in chief, *Folbigg* trial transcript (above n 1) 112.

[108] Ibid, 112–14.

[109] Ibid, 126.

[110] Ibid, 162.

[111] R Meadow, 'Munchausen Syndrome by Proxy: The Hinterland of Child Abuse' (1977) 13 *The Lancet* 343–45; and R Meadow, 'Different Interpretations of Munchausen Syndrome by Proxy' (2002) 26 *Child Abuse & Neglect* 501–8.

[112] Craig Folbigg, evidence in chief, *Folbigg* trial transcript (above n 1) 112.

[113] Tedeschi SC, Crown opening statement, *Folbigg* trial transcript (above n 1) 67. Tedeschi presumably intended this strategy to secure the finding that Kathleen Folbigg was capable of forming the intent to commit murder.

[114] See Raitt and Zeedyk (above n 14) for a similar analysis of *Clark* and *Cannings*.

The assertion that Kathleen Folbigg had difficulty setting her own interests aside in favour of her children was underpinned by a suggestion that she was vain and selfish. Tedeschi SC said in his opening statement:[115]

> When she could get away from her kids, such as to the gym, she was on top of the world and she was very eager at all stages of all the babies lives to resume her social life, her sporting life, her working life, her sexual life that she had had when she didn't have children.[115]

This assertion was drawn in part from the diaries, but Craig also recounted the difficulties that Kathleen Folbigg had with her body image when she was pregnant and mothering. For example, he testified in cross-examination that after Sarah's death, Kathleen Folbigg was more upset about her weight than about the loss of her daughter:

> A. She didn't appear to be grieving. She was at loggerheads with herself about her appearance and —
>
> Q. You contributed to that, didn't you?
>
> CROWN PROSECUTOR: I don't think he had finished his answer.
>
> WITNESS: A. At her appearance and the fact she didn't seem to be able to make friends or fit in anywhere.
>
> ZAHRA SC: Q. But she was devastated during that time, wasn't she?
>
> A. By the fact that she was fat and couldn't fit in anywhere.[116]

Craig's perception that Kathleen was more upset about her weight than she was about Sarah's death was consistent with his evidence that Kathleen struggled to come to terms with her body during pregnancy: 'She did what I had seen every other mother I ever knew do, which was whinge about her belly.'[117] In this rendering, Kathleen becomes a shallow woman who is unable to feel deep emotion about anyone except herself. Revealingly, on Craig's account, this behaviour is at least partly in keeping with that of every pregnant woman. The misogynistic undertones here suggest that Craig was deeply unsympathetic to Kathleen's physical experience of motherhood and that he probably did not understand the nature of Kathleen's grieving process.

Notwithstanding this and other evidence that Kathleen mothered in an emotionally unsupportive environment, the prosecution posited Craig as possessing unique insight into Kathleen's emotions and motivations. The task before the court was to determine whether Kathleen had caused her children's deaths. This individualised inquiry into criminal responsibility excluded the question of how

---

[115] Tedeschi SC, opening statement, *Folbigg* trial transcript (above n 1) 67–68.
[116] Craig Folbigg, cross-examination, *Folbigg* trial transcript (above n 1) 383.
[117] Ibid, 219.

the dominant Australian culture's lack of understanding of and empathy for the negative or challenging aspects of mothers' experiences might influence Craig's interpretation of Kathleen's emotions and actions. The prosecution explicitly adverted to Kathleen's perception that Craig was unsupportive, transforming this perception into another reason to suspect Kathleen of having murdered her children.[118] This submission detached Kathleen's perception and allegedly murderous reaction from the material context in which she, like many women, mothered. The prosecution interpretation also denies the validity of Kathleen's perception that she was unsupported. The vulnerability created by a combination of normative social expectations and Craig's specific allegiance to a gendered allocation of family responsibility is thereby decontextualised, becoming Kathleen's individual failure and a potential motive to commit murder.

The defence resisted the prosecution assertion that Craig was in the best position to understand Kathleen's emotions and motivations. Zahra SC's cross-examination of Craig regarding Kathleen's response to Sarah's death provides an example of this resistance. Zahra SC suggested in the passage already quoted that Craig contributed to Kathleen's insecurity about her appearance.[119] Elsewhere, the defence pointed to Craig's daily absences from the family home and lack of involvement in providing childcare as reasons to discount Craig's account of Kathleen's material and emotional mothering skills.[120]

The Abusive Mother

At trial, for the first time, Craig Folbigg related several incidents involving Sarah and Laura that suggested that Kathleen Folbigg was occasionally physically aggressive towards her children. This evidence was crucial to the prosecution case because it provided the missing link between the emotions recorded in Kathleen's diary and the lack of evidence that any Folbigg child was poorly cared for or unhappy in their mother's presence. As I have explained, no child had any signs of abuse at autopsy, and they all appeared well nourished to every witness, including the pathologists. GPs and paediatricians who examined the babies while they were alive saw no signs that raised their suspicion that the children were being emotionally or physically abused or that they were not thriving.[121] Kathleen Folbigg's female friends testified that the children were always impeccably dressed and cared for and that they seemed to relate well to their mother. No lay or expert witness observed any unusual or unexplained bruises on any of the children.

Craig's evidence that Kathleen was occasionally physically aggressive towards Sarah and Laura surprised the defence. Zahra SC said in his opening statement:

---

[118] Tedeschi SC, Crown opening statement, *Folbigg* trial transcript (above n 1) 26.
[119] Craig Folbigg, cross-examination, *Folbigg* trial transcript (above n 1) 383.
[120] Zahra SC, defence closing address, *Folbigg* trial transcript (above n 1) 1400.
[121] Eg, Dr Christopher George Marley, evidence in chief and cross-examination, *Folbigg* trial transcript (above n 1) 538–42.

LIVERPOOL JOHN MOORES UNIVERSITY
LEARNING SERVICES

> There will be nothing, no evidence during the course of
> this trial, that there was in fact a history of physical
> abuse to any of these children at the hands of the accused.
>
> . . .
>
> This is not a situation where people will come to court and
> say 'I saw her even slap the child'. No evidence is expected
> to be called about that.[122]

This expectation was presumably based on the evidence disclosed before trial, including the statement Craig gave to police on 19 and 23 May 1999 and a pre-trial conference between Craig and the prosecution in October 2002.

At trial, Craig admitted he had lied in one paragraph of his 1999 statement and sought a certificate to protect him from being prosecuted for lying to police.[123] The lie related to whether Craig had woken to find Kathleen and Sarah outside their bedroom on the night of Sarah's death, a matter about which he had given conflicting statements. At the time of her death, Sarah slept in her parents' bedroom. In court, Craig said that the pair had been outside the bedroom on the night that Sarah died. The prosecution case was that Kathleen must have smothered Sarah during the time that they were in another room. During cross-examination, Craig testified that he had told several more lies in the statement, including downplaying several domestic incidents that he described in far more graphic detail in court. The defence suggested that Craig was exaggerating these events in order to make Kathleen seem more disposed to use physical force against her children than she really was.

A dispute over the nature of an argument between Kathleen and Craig on the morning of Laura's death gives the flavour of this evidence regarding Kathleen's alleged tendency to lose her temper with her children. Craig gave the following account of that morning in his evidence in chief:

> A. . . . I had heard Kathy growl. I didn't know what they
> were doing at the time. I wasn't in the room. I heard Kathy
> growl.
>
> Q. In the same way you described yesterday?
>
> A. Yes. I walked down the hallway to see what was happening
> because that alarmed me. I went down and Kathy had Laura in
> the highchair and she had both of Laura's hands pinned
> under her hand on the deck of the highchair and she was
> trying to feed her cereal.
>
> Q. Was she force-feeding her?
>
> A. Force-feeding her. Laura was twisting her head every-
> where and whinging. I said to Kathy, "For Christ's sake,

---

[122] Zahra SC, defence opening statement, *Folbigg* trial transcript (above n 1) 82.
[123] Evidence Act (NSW) 1995 s 128.

she's a bloody baby. If she doesn't want to have breakfast, don't bother trying to make her."

Q. Was Laura still in the highchair?

A. She was still in the highchair. I just started sort of into the dining room. Kathy told me to 'Fuck off'. Laura would have breakfast if she said she would. I said, 'You're just unreal.' I actually swore. I said, 'You're fucking unreal Kathy. I just can't figure this out.'

Q. Was there anything that Kathy said about the effect that you have on Laura?

A. 'She's only like this when you're around. You do this to her. You mollycoddle her and sook her up too much.' I said to Kathy — I recall saying to Kathy, 'It's better than having her cry.' Kathy grabbed Laura and just pulled her out of the highchair and plonked her on the ground and said, 'Go to your fucking father.' Laura started to come towards me and — at that time Laura was crossing the floor towards me and I heard this guttural growl and Kathy scream.

Q. Can you tell us what it sounded like?

A. Oh, 'grrh', and Kathy screamed, 'I can't handle her when she's like this' and she had both her arms in the air and Laura fell to the ground and Laura was crying and I just scooped Laura up and tore off down to the bedroom.

Q. How was Laura crying?

A. She was hysterical, shaking and sobbing. I took her down to the bedroom and sat on the bed with her in my lap. I was rocking her and trying to settle her down. 'Mummies and daddies argue. It doesn't mean they don't love you' and all that stuff. Kathy came to the door and said, 'Give me that baby.' And I said, 'Just fuck off.' She said, 'You give me that baby and get ready for work. Get out. You do this. This is your fault' and she grabbed Laura by the arm. I had Laura in my lap. I said, 'Kath, just let her go. Just leave her. Piss off. You look like you're going to punch somebody.' She said, 'If I'm going to punch anybody I'd punch you. Just give me that bloody baby.' So I let Laura go, followed her down the hallway.

She told me to bugger off and get ready for work. So I went in — I had a shower. I got dressed for work. I was listening intensely down the house. I walked down the house to see how everybody was. Kathy met me at the breakfast bar, which was just short of the family room. You could see from the

```
breakfast bar through the door into the family room. She
said, 'Look, she's fine now. She is just watching TV.'
```

```
She had Laura sitting on Laura's little banana lounge. She
was eating dry cereal, just watching 'Tele Tubby'. Kath
said, 'She's fine. She's only like this when you're around.
Blah, blah, blah. Just go to work.' So I did.
```

This long passage was central to the prosecution assertion that Kathleen had been intensely irritated with Laura shortly before her death. It also helped to counter the defence assertion that no one had ever seen Kathleen behave inappropriately towards her children. This episode became one of the most hotly contested issues in a trial that Barr J characterised as having 'few issues of fact'.[124]

Kathleen described the same morning in a handwritten statement to police:

> Morning was regular. Breakfast routine commenced at around 7 am while Craig was showing. This morning however. He didn't get into shower was playing & talking with Laura while she was in highchair attempting breakfast. I remember having words with Craig. Stating that she doesn't behave like this when he's not around. Telling him to go & get ready for work. I had relented & let Laura out of her chair & Craig was carring her I rember raising my voice & seeing Laura's face she was a little frightened. Craig & I rarely argued with loud voices & never in front of her. I rember Craig looking at me & saying I looked like I would like to punch someone. I interpreted that he was suggesting I'de hurt Laura. I said if I punched anyone it would be him never her. We calmed down. I think I said Ide see him later at work. Rest of the morning went smoothly.[125]

In Craig Folbigg's statement of 23 May 1999, he made no mention of an argument beyond providing the following account of Laura's last morning:

> Kathy got up about 7 am and Laura was in a very clinging whingey mood. I was walking around nursing her to keep her settled as every time I put her down she would cling. We were feeding the goldfish and the lid on the tank fell down and bumped Laura on the right shoulder, on the right side of the head. This made her cry and Kathy became angry with me and told me to put her down.[126]

On cross-examination, Zahra SC suggested that Craig had exaggerated his account of this and other incidents at trial:

```
Q. Could I take you to the morning that Laura died? Again,
I put to you that you have added and fabricated evidence
relating to the incident of this morning?
```

```
A. That's not correct.
```

```
Q. This was a very significant incident in the way you
related it?
```

---

[124] Barr J, summing-up, *Folbigg* case files (above n 1) 79.
[125] Kathleen Folbigg, handwritten statement, *Folbigg* case files (above n 1). I have left Folbigg's spelling, etc as it appears in this statement.
[126] Craig Folbigg, statement of 23 May 1999, *Folbigg* case files (above n 1) 18.

A. It was.

Q. You didn't refer to this in your original statement in May 1999?

A. No, I didn't.

Q. Did you have a conference with the Crown Prosecutor in October [2002]?

A. I did.

Q. 25 October?

A. I did.

Q. You didn't mention this incident to him at that time?

A. Not that I recall.[127]

Elsewhere, Zahra SC suggested that Craig had consistently 'taken what are otherwise normal domestic situations and . . . made them look sinister'.[128] Craig denied this assertion.

Before the trial, Craig repeatedly told friends, family and police that Kathleen was a good mother who loved and cared for her children.[129] After police approached Craig with their suspicions about Kathleen's role in her children's death, Craig told his sister that they were 'trying to assassinate Kath's character . . . [W]hat he's trying to do is trying to establish that she couldn't cope as a mother.'[130] Craig went on to say that the police had 'planted horrible things in my head' about Kathleen's role in her children's deaths and that he had fallen for this strategy because he was upset that Kathleen had initiated a separation:

> Suppose you feel pretty bad, you know. I mean, she's cleaned out, and she's going out with her girlfriends and going to the gym and you're all alone and got, haven't got, haven't your kid and your wife's, er, walked out on you and, you know, isn't it all pretty convenient for her and all that sort of shit?[131]

Later that day, he said to a female friend:

> I think what also narks [the investigating police officer] too is anybody sitting there waxing lyrical about how good a mother she was when they saw her as a mother. You know what I mean? Cause that's like he don't want to hear that.[132]

---

[127] Craig Folbigg, cross-examination, *Folbigg* trial transcript (above n 1) 407.

[128] Ibid, 405. See also 413 and 419.

[129] Craig Folbigg's telephone conversations were wiretapped in May 1999. Zahra SC cross-examined Craig Folbigg at length about these conversations: Craig Folbigg, cross-examination, *Folbigg* trial transcript (above n 1) 304–24.

[130] Ibid, 307.

[131] Craig Folbigg, transcript of telephone conversation on 26 July 1999 with Carol Newitt, reproduced in *Folbigg* trial transcript (above n 1) 309.

[132] Craig Folbigg, transcript of telephone conversation on 26 July 1999 with unidentified female, reproduced in *Folbigg* trial transcript (above n 1) 312.

On cross-examination, Craig explained that he had not believed these things when he said them, and the police had not manipulated his thoughts or suspicions about his wife. In fact, he observed:

> Detective Ryan was explaining to me that mothers do kill their children. I couldn't understand that and I couldn't accept that, but Detective Ryan told me that I really needed to open my eyes, that it wasn't just always drug addict mothers, housing commission women, and those type of people that killed their children. That loving, caring mothers did it as well.
>
> Q. Was he also saying things to you about Kathy leaving you, and you should reflect on that?
>
> A. He said it was awfully sad to see not only that I had lost Laura but she had cleared out and cleaned me out and I was sitting in an empty house all on my own. [133]

Even on voir dire when explaining why he had lied in his statement, Craig testified that Kathleen was loving towards the children at times – 'She was my wife, she was their mother and she – there were times – I mean, she loved them. That was evident. There were times that she loved them.'[134]

For Craig, as for the expert witnesses,[135] the experience of testifying at Kathleen's trial was one of being pushed towards a more extreme position. By the time he gave evidence in front of the jury, the closest Craig came to accepting that Kathleen loved her children was a double-edged statement he made when testifying about why he had lied in his statement:

> Kathy had said to me, you know, 'How could you say those things about me. You know I loved them' and, you know, 'you saw how much I loved those babies', and stuff, and we just talked about life together and parenting together, and Kathy had said, you know, 'You've got to tell them the truth. You've got to tell them. You know I loved those kids' and, yeah, I had seen how she had loved them. So, when I went back to Bernie, I asked him to rewind back through his machine, and told him what I wanted him to change.
>
> Q. Did you know at the time that you were telling him lies?
>
> A. Yes[136]

The defence pressed the argument that Craig was a jilted husband who coloured his evidence as a means of exacting revenge from Kathleen.[137] Craig claimed a

---

[133] Craig Folbigg, cross-examination, *Folbigg* trial transcript (above n 1) 305–6.
[134] Craig Folbigg, voir dire, *Folbigg* trial transcript (above n 1) 96.
[135] See above ch 5.
[136] Craig Folbigg, re-examination, *Folbigg* trial transcript (above n 1) 522.
[137] Zahra SC, defence closing address, *Folbigg* trial transcript (above n 1) 1408–9.

more basic truth, asserting that he was simply 'trying to tell the people how things were in that house'.[138] The prosecution case was that Craig lied because he needed time to come to terms with the awful realisation that his wife had killed their babies. On this account, Craig was also a victim of Kathleen Folbigg's manipulation: 'He was very much in love with Kathy. One would almost conclude that he was besotted by her.'[139] This interpretation allowed the jury to see that Kathleen's antisocial tendencies extended beyond having the capacity to murder her children – she was also able to manipulate and control her husband.

The defence and prosecution case stories drew upon tropes that are readily recognisable – was Craig Folbigg the bitter, lying, jilted husband or just an honest bloke who fell in love with the wrong woman, with tragic consequences for himself and his children? It is, of course, hard to know which of these readings the jury accepted, if either. It is certainly conceivable that the jury accepted the defence submission about Craig's tendency to exaggerate but nonetheless felt that they had enough other evidence to convict Kathleen Folbigg. Perhaps more revealingly, as I explain below in chapter eight, Craig Folbigg became something of a media darling – hailed by the *Daily Telegraph* as one of the 'trio who solved the deadly puzzle' of the Folbigg children's deaths, together with a police officer and Folbigg's adoptive sister.[140]

V. Conclusion

The prosecution submission that Kathleen Folbigg was an ill-tempered, domineering and selfish mother raises many questions, none of which was squarely faced within the trial. Is it true that an impatient or angry mother who is not physically abusive is more likely to kill a child by smothering that child without a trace of physical harm? There is nothing in the medical literature to suggest that this is so – not even in Meadow's work, let alone in the work conducted by the eminent researcher in this field, John Emery.[141] Rather, using even the broadest and most contested set of published works, the behavioural risk factors for filicide include past assaultive behaviour; fabricated illness in a child; a diagnosed maternal history of fabricating her own illness; a diagnosed personality disorder or mental illness in the allegedly filicidal parent; parental incompetence; financial difficulties or a crisis at the time of the child's death; and a poor bond between mother and child.[142] An additional factor, cited but unexplained by Elizabeth

---

[138] Craig Folbigg, cross-examination, *Folbigg* trial transcript (above n 1) 301.

[139] Tedeschi SC, Crown opening statement, *Folbigg* trial transcript (above n 1) 37.

[140] F O'Shea and L Knowles, 'Trio who Solved a Deadly Puzzle' *Daily Telegraph* (Sydney, 22 May 2003).

[141] See above ch 4.

[142] EM Taylor and JL Emery, 'Categories of Preventable Infant Deaths' (1990) 65 *Archives of Disease in Childhood* 535; Meadow, 'Munchausen Syndrome by Proxy' (above n 111) 343; R Meadow, 'Fictitious Epilepsy' (1984) ii *The Lancet* 25; and R Meadow, 'Suffocation, Recurrent Apnea and Sudden Infant Death' (1990) 117 *Journal of Pediatrics* 351.

Taylor and Emery, is 'mother's upbringing and home background'.[143] Thus perhaps Kathleen's early life could be relevant, though by most accounts she seemed a relatively settled child and teenager within her foster home. Certainly one would wish to be careful before generalising from an infant history of neglect and abuse to an adult finding of criminal guilt in homicide when there is an intervening history of largely unexceptional behaviour at school and work and a capacity to form and retain adult personal relationships. Otherwise, none of the behavioural risk factors was present in *Folbigg*.[144]

A second question involves the reliability of evidence. If one accepts that angry and rough behaviour, such as that described by Craig at trial, is correlated with an increased likelihood of murder, there should be reliable evidence of that behaviour before a jury can act upon it. The question therefore is how reliable the evidence must be. Notably, while Craig said that Kathleen had been rough with Laura on the morning of Laura's death (holding her hands down to force-feed her, then pulling Laura roughly out of the highchair), no bruises were found on autopsy by a pathologist who actively suspected murder. At trial, Craig's sworn account of that morning differed from those he had previously provided and rendered Kathleen far more dangerous and physically aggressive than previous statements suggested. Arguably, given the claims made by the prosecution that Craig alone knew Kathleen's true nature, this new account should have been carefully scrutinised before being admitted. The jury should perhaps have been warned to consider why Craig had given differing accounts before accepting his sworn evidence.[145]

In cross-examination and in its closing address, the defence suggested that Craig was motivated to lie because he was angry at Kathleen for leaving him. This motive was founded in evidence, including Craig's intercepted telephone conversations, but the judge did not remind the jury of this submission even when asked by the defence to do so.[146] The prosecution suggestion that Craig had been besotted with Kathleen to the point of being blind to her faults but was now clearsighted, should fairly have been treated with care. The failure to warn the jury about Craig's inconsistencies was particularly significant because in accordance with applicable law, the jury was directed how to treat Kathleen Folbigg's state-

---

[143] Taylor and Emery (ibid) 537.

[144] Kathleen Folbigg was subsequently diagnosed with a personality disorder, but this diagnosis came after conviction and was presumably predicated at least in part on her convictions. The medical literature that discusses the mental health of potentially filicidal mothers seems to contemplate mental illness that is either previously diagnosed or clearly identified at the time of a child's death, as a relevant risk factor.

[145] Barr J warned the jury to consider each piece of evidence carefully for credibility and reliability and to take due account of the submissions of both parties: Barr J, summing-up, *Folbigg* case files (above n 1) 14. He also reminded the jury of the defence argument that Craig was altering his accounts of family events with the benefit of hindsight: eg, 74–75, 83–84 and 106. However, he did not specifically warn the jury to consider why Craig had changed his accounts of some family events or to review the defence submission that Craig was motivated by revenge.

[146] Ibid, 89–90. S 165 of the Evidence Act (NSW) 1995 requires a trial judge to warn a jury about unreliable evidence upon a party's request, unless there are good reasons for not doing so. Zahra SC and Barr J discussed whether the trial judge should exercise this function, but the trial judge did not give the warning contemplated by s 165(2).

ment to police and about what inferences they might draw from a conclusion that she had lied in that statement.[147]

In sum, the behavioural evidence marshalled for and against Kathleen Folbigg was grounded in common sense, an area that Marilyn MacCrimmon and Christine Boyle have described as 'largely unexamined and uncontrolled' within common law.[148] As Boyle and Jesse Nyman have noted, 'Inaccurate fact finding may not be an equal opportunity social phenomenon.'[149] Untangling the mixture of truth and hyperbole that underpins the proposition that a mother who kills her child will be identifiably inadequate in certain ways is crucial to guarding against wrongful convictions. Subjecting behavioural evidence to a careful analysis of credibility and reliability is similarly fundamental. Whatever happened in the Folbigg household before Craig left for work on the morning of Laura's death, the prosecutors and judges in *Folbigg* were not as careful as one would wish about the inferences that could safely be drawn from Craig's evidence. No participant directly explored the proposition that a mother who behaves as Craig described is more likely to kill her child. Similarly, the assumptions underpinning both the prosecution evidence about Kathleen's desire to work outside the home when her children were young and the proposition that Kathleen struggled with her body image and a lack of attention after each child was born, remained largely unchallenged. As I explain in the next chapter, the quest to define what sort of mother Kathleen Folbigg was to her children was also profoundly influenced by her own personal narratives of motherhood – the diaries she kept during her children's lives.

---

[147] Barr J, summing-up, *Folbigg* case files (above n 1) 126–28.

[148] M MacCrimmon and C Boyle, 'To Serve the Cause of Justice: Disciplining Fact Determination' (2001) 20 *Windsor Yearbook of Access to Justice* 55, 82.

[149] C Boyle and J Nyman, 'Finding Facts Fairly in Roberts and Zuckermann's *Criminal Evidence*' (2005) 2(2) *International Commentaries on Evidence* article no 3, 6.

7

Reading Guilt: Kathleen Folbigg's Diaries

I. Diaries and Subjectivity

DURING HER CHILDREN'S lives, Kathleen Folbigg was a prolific diarist. When Caleb was born, she recorded every doctor's appointment, every feed, every sleep and every nappy change.[1] At trial, the defence pointed to this practice to suggest that Folbigg was a caring and diligent mother who was coping well with motherhood.[2] By the time Folbigg was trying to conceive her fourth child, she was recording her hopes and fears about motherhood as well as her feelings about the events of her life. After Laura died, Folbigg threw out most of her diaries, but two journals, a dayplanner and a calendar remained in her former house.[3] At trial the journals, comprising approximately 270 photocopied pages, formed a cornerstone of the prosecution case. The prosecution relied on several diary entries to make their case that Folbigg had killed her children, selectively extracting these entries into a written document that was supplied to the jury.[4] After Folbigg was convicted, the defence also prepared a document extracting selected entries in support of its submission that she should be leniently sentenced. In his sentencing judgment, Grahame Barr J reproduced extracts from both the prosecution and defence compilations.

Folbigg's diaries accordingly served two purposes in her trial. First, the prosecution used the diaries to advance its argument that the accused was guilty of murdering her four children and of causing Patrick's acute life-threatening episode (ALTE).[5] In this regard, the diaries helped the jury to determine the material facts in the case. Second, the prosecution, the defence and Barr J used the diaries as an aid when proposing and deciding the appropriate sentence. In this phase, the diaries helped the legal actors to gauge Folbigg's remorse for her children's

---

[1] Kathleen Folbigg, calendar for February 1989. Contained in *Folbigg* case files, which are held by the New South Wales Court of Criminal Appeal registry under file numbers 60496 of 2002, 2002/70046, 60279 of 2004 and 2004/1814 [*Folbigg* case files]. For an outline of the birth, lives and deaths of the Folbigg children, see above ch 2 and below the Appendix.

[2] Craig Folbigg, cross-examination, *R v Kathleen Megan Folbigg* trial transcript, 180 and 230–31. The *Folbigg* trial was conducted in the NSW Supreme Court between 1 Apr and 21 May 2003 before Grahame Barr J. The trial transcript is contained in the *Folbigg* case files (ibid).

[3] Folbigg told police that she threw the diaries out on Mother's Day 1999, after Laura died. See *Folbigg* trial transcript (ibid) 47.

[4] 'Kathleen Folbigg's Diaries (Extracts)', undated, *Folbigg* case files (above n 1).

[5] For a discussion of this term, see above ch 1, n 19.

deaths and also introduced some context to explain why she killed her children. There is of course no bright line between these two uses – both are inextricably connected with ascribing moral and legal culpability or, for the defence's part, with resisting that ascription.[6]

In what follows, I draw upon Folbigg's explanations of some diary entries as well as feminist work on the ideologies within which women make sense of their lives to examine how the diaries were used at trial. The prosecution submitted that the diaries' meaning was obvious, while the defence argued that the words 'guilt', 'responsibility' and 'mistakes' have multiple meanings and should not be understood as confessions to murder. Given the social and medical contexts I have already described in earlier chapters, the defence case was considerably more difficult to sustain, as it depended on interpreting the diaries in ways that were less accessible and seemed less literal than the prosecution's simplified narrative. Folbigg herself did not at any stage provide direct explanations for the troubling entries contained in the later diary. In particular, Folbigg did not testify at her trial.

Arguing on behalf of the defence, Peter Zahra SC faced an extremely challenging task when trying to construct a coherent interpretive principle for Folbigg's diaries. Women are more likely than men to keep personal journals, and much feminist literary criticism of diaries proceeds on the basis that diaries are a particularly gendered narrative site.[7] Feminist engagement with the role of diaries has, however, largely resisted seeking to understand the 'true meaning' of diary narratives or what role diaries might play in women's lives. This reluctance stems from a concern to preserve the autonomy and dignity of women's life narratives: commentators have focused either on protecting women's privacy by seeking to exclude diary evidence from criminal proceedings or alternatively on asserting the inherent truthfulness of the personal narratives contained in women's diaries. The first trend is particularly apparent in the heated Canadian debate over the admissibility of sexual assault complainants' diaries and therapeutic records.[8] The second, relatively unsophisticated, appeal to the literal truthfulness of women's diaries emerges from the difficulty of proving battering histories when women are killed by an assaulting partner.[9] Notably, both of these strands focus on women as victims of crime rather than women as alleged perpetrators of harm.

---

[6] M Valverde, *Law's Dream of a Common Knowledge* (Princeton, Princeton University Press 2003) 1; and J Katz, 'What Makes Crime "News"?' (1987) 9 *Media, Culture and Society* 47, 67.

[7] S Bunkers, 'What Do Women Really Mean? Thoughts on Women's Diaries and Lives' in DP Freedman, O Frey and FM Zauhar (eds), *The Intimate Critique: Autobiographical Literary Criticism* (Durham and London, Duke University Press, 1993) 207; and WJ Weiner and GC Rosenwald, 'A Moment's Monument: The Psychology of Keeping a Diary' in R Josselson and A Lieblich (eds), *The Narrative Study of Lives* (London, Sage Publications, 1993) 30.

[8] K Busby, 'Discriminatory Use of Personal Records in Sexual Violence Cases' (1997) 9 *Canadian Journal of Women & the Law* 148; and KD Kelly, '"You Must be Crazy if You Think You were Raped": Reflections on the Use of Complainants' Personal and Therapy Records in Sexual Assault Trials' (1997) 9 *Canadian Journal of Women & the Law* 178.

[9] Eg, L Ledwon, 'Diaries and Hearsay: Gender, Selfhood and the Trustworthiness of Narrative Structures' (2000) 73 *Temple Law Review* 1185.

Writing in a slightly different context, Patricia Ewick and Susan Silbey have questioned the essentialist concept of truth that is implicit within an instrumental understanding of autobiographical narratives. They argue that personal narratives cannot shed an unmediated light on lived experience:

> Even the most personal of narratives rely on and invoke collective narratives – symbols, linguistic formulations, structures, and vocabularies of motive – without which the personal would remain unintelligible and uninterpretable. Because of the conventionalized character of narrative, then, our stories are likely to express ideological effects and hegemonic assumptions. We are as likely to be shackled by the stories we tell (or that are culturally available for our telling) as we are by the form of oppression they might seek to reveal.[10]

Folbigg's diaries present many glimpses of a woman who is trying to live up to the self that the culture has already prepared.[11] Kathleen's concerns with her weight and her dissatisfaction with Craig, which sounded so sinister in the prosecution argument at trial, read to me like the meditations of a woman who has absorbed Western society's standard messages about femininity and motherhood:[12]

14 October 1996

Sitting in bed deciding wether to go back to sleep till whenever. Could save me walking, except I need to. I have gone back up to 67kg I'm sure. Must lose at least 2kg before Sat night. Don't want to look fat.[13]

19 January (?) 1997[14]

Not happy with myself lately finally starting to physically show that I'm pregnant. Doesn't do much for the self esteem. Don't get me wrong I couldn't be happier its just Craigs roving eye will always be of concern to me. I suppose this is a concept known to all women we are vulnerable emotionally at this stage. So everything is exagerated 10fold. I know he loves me, but I ask every now & then just for assurance anyway.

17 February 1997

. . . I also know that my lethargy & tiredness & continued rejection of [Craig] had a bad effect.

I have to accept that if he doesn't get sex regularly from me, he feels abandoned & unwanted.

---

[10] P Ewick and S Silbey, 'Subversive Stories and Hegemonic Tales: Towards a Sociology of Narrative' (1995) 29 *Law & Society Review* 197, 211–12. See also AM Coghlin, 'Regulating the Self: Autobiographical Performances in Outsider Scholarship' (1995) 81 *Virginia Law Review* 1231–32, 1251.

[11] Ewick and Silby (ibid).

[12] See, eg, A Rich, *Of Woman Born: Motherhood as Experience and Institution* (New York, Norton, 1986) ch 2; and B Wearing, *Ideology of Motherhood: A Study of Sydney Suburban Mothers* (Sydney, Allen & Unwin, 1984).

[13] Kathleen Folbigg, diary entry, *Folbigg* case files (above n 1). Folbigg's text is reproduced here exactly as it appears in the original document. In particular, no attempt has been made to draw attention to spelling, grammar and usage mistakes by using 'sic'. All diary entries quoted herein are taken from the diaries contained within the *Folbigg* case files unless otherwise specified.

[14] Kathleen Folbigg, diary entry (date obscure), *Folbigg* case files (above n 1).

20 September 1997

I can't even trust or depend on [Craig] to look after her properly. He refuses to bother to learn anything about her. He doesn't pay attention when feeding her, hasn't changed her nappy, doesn't do the washing or the ironing. Only washes up, once in a while. His life continues as normal. Work, come home and I look after him. He doesn't even cook, every now and then unless I ask him to. And then it is begrudgingly. What do I do. The only break I get is when I go to aerobics – 3½ hours a week. But there are times, it's not enough.

The hegemonic expectations society places on women within marriage and family are here refracted into Folbigg's personal narratives and the expectations she places on herself as a woman, wife and mother. As Mary Eaton observed in her classic study on women within the criminal justice system, familial ideology operates to isolate and control women within heterosexual relationships.[15] Far from presenting a threat to the ideology of motherhood, in these entries Folbigg seems to be trying hard to live up to its expectations.

In her police interview, Folbigg tried several times to explain the function served by the diary, but her explanation was cut off by the police officer who was questioning her:

```
Q581 Do you recognise that diary?

A. I do.

Q582 What can you tell me about it?

A. Just as I said before, it's just a book I used to spend
a couple of minutes or even only a minute jottin' down this
and jottin' down that in. It wasn't a –

Q583 So is this your diary?

A. It is, yes.[16]
```

In this passage and throughout the subsequent proceeding, the prosecuting authorities tended to assume that the diary's purpose and function in Folbigg's life was self-evident – it was a repository for the truth that she had killed her children, a truth she was otherwise unwilling or unable to admit.

Folbigg's description of the role her diary played in her life is augmented by observations that appear from time to time in the diaries themselves:

6 August 1996

Just a reminder note. . .

13 November 1996

Always write in here when I'm restless & not sleepy. Never regularly, like most other journal holders. . .

---

[15] M Eaton, *Justice for Women? Family, Court and Social Control* (Milton Keynes, Open University Press, 1986) ch 7.
[16] Record of interview with Kathleen Megan Folbigg, *Folbigg* case files (above n 1).

29 May 1997

Need new diary soon I've actually nearly filled up this one. Think it has helped, writing my thoughts and feelings down. regularly. Fell as though its become a friend that I can off load on. And it doesn't back answer me – thats the best thing. Laugh & stupid things I've written in Past, but they were important, to me back then as this is now.

The journal entries are often written late at night or very early in the morning and are accompanied by comments that Folbigg was having trouble sleeping. The range of entries suggests that the diaries may have served a multivalent purpose in Folbigg's life. As the entry above suggests, the journals provided an emotional repository for thoughts that she could not or would not share with her friends or husband. The prosecution cast this practice as inherently suspect, but it is proba- bly a fairly common reason for keeping a diary.[17] Feminist researchers often sug- gest that women's journals begin from the desire to define a sense of self beyond the familial roles of wife and mother.[18] Folbigg's observation that she only wrote in the journal when she was 'restless' and having trouble sleeping suggests that she tended to record the more negative or darker aspects of her emotional life rather than representing anything close to a complete picture of her lived experience. Nonetheless, certain entries in Folbigg's diaries do seem concerned with working through emotions and experiences that threaten her aspirations for her life. Other entries, particularly in the early dayplanners, are essentially factual, 'reminder notes', suggesting that the records were also a means of keeping track of the daily tasks of housework and childcare.

Folbigg was by no means unique in keeping a diary that was subsequently used to help prove that she murdered her children.[19] Given the evidentiary principle that defendants' out-of-court statements are routinely admissible and given the increasing criminalisation of women,[20] we may see more of this type of evidence in the future. Accordingly, feminist legal theory needs to engage with the nature of the truths contained within women's diaries. Providing an alternative set of interpretive principles, informed by work such as Ewick and Silbey's, may assist advocates who seek to make sense of marginalised women's narratives in future proceedings.

[17] Bunkers, 'What Do Women Really Mean?' (above n 7); Weiner and Rosenwald (above n 7); and JN Lensink, 'Expanding the Boundaries of Criticism: The Diary as Female Autobiography' in MW Brownley and AB Kimmich (eds), *Women and Autobiography* (Wilmington, Rowman and Littlefield, 1999) 151–62, 155–56. See also D Spender, 'Journal on a Journal' (1987) 10(1) *Women's Studies International Forum* 1–5, 3; and the other articles collected in issue 10(1) of *Women's Studies International Forum*.

[18] Eg, SL Bunkers, '"Faithful Friend": Nineteenth-Century Midwestern American Women's Unpublished Diaries' (1987) 10 *Women's Studies International Forum* 7–17, 9.

[19] Eg, in the aftermath of Madeleine McCann's disappearance in May 2007, her mother's diary became a central focus of the Portuguese police investigation. See D Batty and J Sturke, 'Madeleine Prosecutors Seek Diaries and Toys, Reports Say' *The Guardian* (12 September 2007) www.theguardian. co.uk. Kate McCann is no longer a suspect in her daughter's disappearance.

[20] G Balfour and E Comack, *Criminalizing Women* (Halifax, Fernwood Publishing, 2006).

Having said that, my reading of Folbigg's trial is necessarily my own, and it is not possible for me to represent her experience of the investigation and trial. Both Barr J and the prosecution tended to conflate the diary entries and their interpretation of those entries with Folbigg's consciousness, but as I have explained elsewhere, Folbigg's subjectivity cannot ultimately be reduced to her written words.[21] It is not wholly possible to avoid interpreting Kathleen Folbigg's words nor to circumvent constituting her as a subject within my depiction of her trial. I hope, however, to avoid displacing either the diary entries themselves or the various actors' interpretations of those entries with another putatively authoritative narrative about Folbigg's consciousness.

II. 'A Machine to Look into Her Mind': The Diary Entries

At trial, the prosecution posited the diaries as the truest possible expression of Folbigg's guilty consciousness:

These diaries are the strongest evidence that you could possibly have for this accused having murdered her four children.

. . . [I]t would not be as strong evidence if you had a machine to look into her mind, to read her mind as these diaries are. There is only one explanation for them. It is the only explanation that makes any sense at all.[22]

The striking image of the diaries as coming as close as possible to a mind-reading machine distilled the prosecution submissions regarding the diaries to a simple essence: in these diaries, written only for herself, Folbigg admitted having murdered her children. To the world at large, Folbigg maintained the pretence that she was a tragically bereaved mother, but the diaries revealed the truth. The prosecution argument thus raises a threshold question. Do the diaries contain a confession to murder? If not, what was the nature and extent of the admissions contained in the diaries?

The diaries contain more than 200 entries, dealing with a range of subjects, including the children, Kathleen's feelings about her marriage with Craig, issues with her paid employment and concerns about her weight. At least four of the entries are particularly unsettling because they seem to imply that the children's deaths were not entirely unexplained. These entries read:

---

[21] E Cunliffe, '(This is Not a) Story: Using Court Records to Explore Judicial Narratives in *R v Kathleen Folbigg*' (2007) 27 *Australian Feminist Law Journal* 71.

[22] Mark Tedeschi SC, Crown closing address, *Folbigg* trial transcript (above n 2) 1372–73. See also 1366.

25 August 1997

Off to bed, feeling sick, because I am really tired, must try a nap in the afternoon, if Laura will let me, or a sleep in or something.

Scary feelings, Ive realised I actually love her and have bonded with her, wish to protect her etc. Maternal instinct is what they call it. I now know I never had it with the others.

Monitor is a good idea. Nothing can happen without the monitor knowing & since I'm not game enough to not plug it in, because theyde want to know why I hadn't. Everything will be fine this time.

9 November 1997

Craig was pretty drunk Friday nite; In his drunken stupor he admitted that he's not really happy. There's a problem with his security level with me & he has a morbid fear about Laura – he well I know theres nothing wrong with her. Nothing out of the ordinary anyway. Because it was me not them.

Think I handle her fits of crying better than I did with Sarah – I've learnt to ace getting to me, to walk away & breath for a while myself. It helps me cope & figure out how to help her. With Sarah all I wanted was her to shut up. And one day she did.

31 December 1997

Getting Laura to be next year ought to be fun. She'll realise a party is going on. And that will be it. Wonder if the battle of wills will start with her & I then. We'll actually get to see. She's a fairly good natured baby – Thank goodness, it has saved her from the fate of her siblings. I think she was warned.

28 January 1998

Very depressed with myself, angry and upset.

I've done it. I lost it with her. I yelled at her so angrily that it scared her, she hasn't stopped crying. Got so bad I nearly purposely dropped her on the floor & left her. I restrained enough to put her on the floor & walk away. Went to my room & left her to cry. Was gone probably only 5 mins but it seemed like a lifetime.

I feel like the worst mother on earth. Scared that she'll leave me now. Like Sarah did. I know I was short tempered and cruel sometimes to her & she left. With a bit of help.

I don't want that ever to happen again. I actually seem to have a bond with Laura. It can't happen again. I'm ashamed of myself. I can't tell Craig about it because he'll worry about leaving her with me. Only seems to happen if I'm too tired her moaning, bored, wingy sound drives me up the wall. I truly can't wait until she's old enough to tell me what she wants.

None of these entries contains an unambiguous confession – Folbigg does not at any point write that she killed her children, nor that she took any action that might be construed as having smothered them. In all of these entries, however, Folbigg seems to indicate a direct sense of guilt or responsibility for her children's deaths, and she also seems to suggest that her behaviour was implicated in her children's deaths.[23] The statement that Sarah left 'with a bit of help' is particularly conspicuous, as is the statement that 'it was me not them'. Curiously, the prosecution made relatively little use of these phrases during the trial.[24] By contrast, Mark Tedeschi SC spent a lot of time analysing the notion that Laura 'was warned' by the other Folbigg children. In general, prosecution counsel adopted a practice of reading the more damaging entries aloud multiple times, over the defence's objections that this tactic served unfairly to emphasise the damaging evidence with no direct utility.[25]

When police interviewed Folbigg, they had not yet found the diary from which the above entries were extracted. They had, however, found an earlier diary that also contained troubling entries. The transcript of this interview was tendered at Folbigg's trial, and the video recording was played to the jury. The interview, which lasted more than nine hours,[26] spanned roughly three phases. In the first, Folbigg was asked to describe each child's life and death and was taken in detail through the circumstances in which she found each of her children dead. In the second phase, Kathleen was asked about the diary Craig had found and was invited to explain particular entries. In the final, brief phase Folbigg was asked directly whether she had killed each of her children and whether she knew how her children died. She denied having killed her children or knowing anything more about their deaths than she had already described.

During her police interview, the police officer took Folbigg through many of the diary entries. In her explanations of them, Folbigg described her frustration and anger and elaborated on her sense of responsibility for the first three children's deaths. The following lengthy quote from the transcript of the interview provides the flavour of these explanations, and I provide other examples over the course of this discussion. Each quote from the interview is preceded by the relevant diary entry to provide context to the questions and answers:

26 August 1996

Went to clarvoant last week – so did Craig. I always believed there is more going on than just human nature. I seem content now because I now know that even though I'm responsible Its alright. She accepts & is happy their. I've always felt her strongly. And now I know why. She is with me. I think my mother is too.

Nice to know Craig's mother & guardian angle are with him. He seems more relaxed now he knows they are still with him.

Q610 What do you mean by, Even though I am responsible it's all right?

A. I was still carrying around the thought that I could have done more or should have done more. So the word responsible in there sort of refers to that, my thoughts of I didn't try

---

[23] I suggest below, text accompanying n 32, that this is probably a common parental response to the death of an infant.

[24] See Tedeschi SC, Crown closing address, *Folbigg* trial transcript (above n 2) 1349 and 1372.

[25] Eg, *Folbigg* trial transcript (above n 2) 1190–91.

[26] Graham Barr J, summing-up, *Folbigg* case files (above n 1) 128.

enough or didn't do something, I should have done something. So to me that's what my word responsible means . . .[27]

14 October 1996

Children thing still isn't happening. Thinking of forgetting the idea. Nature, fate & the man upstairs have decided I don't get a 4th chance. And rightly so I suppose. I would like to make all my mistakes & terrible thinking be corrected & mean something though. Pluse Im ready to continue my family time now. . .[28] But I think losing my temper stage & being frustrated with everything has passed. I now just let things happen & go with the flow. An attitude I should of had with all my children if given the chance I'll have it with the next one.

Q641 What's your version of being responsible?

A. Just the thoughts of was I diligent enough? Was I watching? Was I listening? Was I, should I have walked in two minutes earlier, or should I've been somewhere else or done something else or spoken to someone else or got help from someone else? The list just goes on, it's just a never ending sort of thing.

Q642 What were your mistakes and terrible thinking?

A. Just the frustrations that I might have felt with Pat, and the occasional battles of will that I would have had with Sarah. To me that, looking back at that time I thought that was a terrible way of thinking. I kept telling myself that that shouldn't have happened.

Q643 Did you ever feel as though you hated the children?

A. Never, nuh. I don't, I know I've come across my versions of what I think atrocious parents are, watchin' them in plazas beltin' their kids till they're red, and hearin' about other parents that have done this to their kids or humiliating and embarrassing them in public and all the rest of it. To me, that's just not socially acceptable sort of behaviour, and I always wander whether they actually really want their kids or do they hate their kids to turn around and do that sort of thing? But no, I've never, never hated my children.

I have set Folbigg's words out at some length because they provide an important gloss on the diary entries. Throughout her answers, Folbigg insisted on a difference between her acknowledged sense of guilt or responsibility for failing to live up to her ideals about mothering on the one hand and, on the other hand, the police interpretation of the diaries as constituting an admission of responsibility

[27] All extracts of the police interview with Kathleen Folbigg (transcript 4313-99/0137) are drawn from the *Folbigg* case files (above n 1). Numbering is as it appeared in the original transcript.

[28] Part of this entry was excluded from jury consideration. I have reproduced those parts that were provided to the jury.

for physically causing her children's deaths. To the police, phrases such as 'mistakes and terrible thinking' become equated with homicidal actions, while Folbigg insisted that her thoughts and engagement with her children were negative at times but not violent. As I explain, the perspective reflected in these explanations was not wholly conveyed at Folbigg's trial.

III. Constructing a Murderous Mother

The diaries leave no question that Folbigg became angry at times, a theme that recurs in other less damaging passages than those extracted above. The prosecution used this evidence to suggest that Folbigg had a tendency to become uncontrollably enraged with her children, and it invited the jury to conclude that she smothered each of the children in a moment of such anger. The prosecution also asserted that Folbigg admitted to killing her children:

> [P]assages from the diary amounted to admissions by the Appellant that she had *caused* the deaths of Caleb, Patrick and Sarah and an appreciation by her that her tendency to lose her temper and control presented a similar danger to her last-born child, Laura.[29]

In this passage from the prosecution submissions on appeal and many times during the trial, Tedeschi SC conflated Folbigg's words with his interpretation of those words. Tedeschi cast the 'admissions' as expressions of Folbigg's authentic self, in contrast to the denials of guilt Folbigg made on other occasions.

Folbigg provided a different interpretation of her anger in her interview with police. For example:

> 1 January 1997
>
> Another year gone by & what a year to come. I have a baby on the way, which means major personal sacrifice for both of us. But I feel confident about it all going well this time. I am going to call for help this time & not attempt to do everything myself any more – I know that was the main Reason for all my stress before & stress made me do terrible things. . .

Q701 What terrible things?

A. Again, talking about the stress and frustrations and the odd growling and anything of that sort of nature.

Q702 You say that stress made you do terrible things.

A. Yeah, as in have an angry thought here or there. I don't think I've met a parent who doesn't have an angry thought every now and again if their child's arguin' with them or somethin's not goin' quite right . . .

---

[29] Crown submissions, *Folbigg* case files (above n 1) para 3.13 (emphasis added).

Q704 Do you really think that those odd angry thoughts were terrible things?

A. I used to.

Q705 It's a very strong expression isn't it, terrible things?

A. Yeah, yeah it is but, you know? I used to sort of think that the odd angry thought or the odd stress or the odd frustration didn't help the situation.

Q706 Mmmm.

A. Not that particular angry thought or the frustration or stress in general, it was actually what caused their death. But it didn't help the situation any was what I was probably trying to get at. So stress had made me do terrible things would probably mean I really didn't want to get to the stress level where I would have an angry thought and therefore exasperate the situation and make it worse sort of thing is what I probably meant . . .

Q710 But I guess I'm just trying to get you to clarify your own thoughts and maybe you can't do that. But I suppose the things that you were saying that you viewed as terrible things, the frustrations and that, the stresses that go along with being a parent of a young child particularly, you've said that every parent feels it at some time to some degree. And yet children don't die of it.

A. Yes, I know that, but after four what are you s'posed to think? You start thinkin' is it possible? Is, you just start (Tape beeping)

Q711 Always happens at the best possible time.

From this lengthy extract, a number of themes emerge. Here, as elsewhere in the record of interview, Folbigg emphasised that her anger manifested in thoughts rather than actions. Arguably, this is consistent with the diary entries from 14 October 1996 (regarding 'mistakes and terrible thinking') and 28 January 1998 (in which she records that she had 'lost it' with Laura), although that consistency was not expressly relied upon by the defence at Folbigg's trial. In fact, despite the fact that the journal entry on 28 January 1998 suggests that Folbigg's definition of 'lost it' consists of getting angry and walking away, the prosecution asserted in its closing address that this phrase self-evidently meant murdering a child or at the least committing physical violence.[30] Barr J specifically reminded the jury of this prosecution submission in his summing-up.[31]

---

[30] Tedeschi SC, Crown closing address, *Folbigg* trial transcript (above n 2) 1346.
[31] Barr J, summing-up, *Folbigg* case files (above n 1) 105.

During her police interview, Folbigg sought to normalise her emotions by referring to other parents, a tactic that was turned back on her at question 710. Both the accused and the police were drawing upon a particular aspect of the ideology of motherhood – the notion that a mother may have 'angry thoughts' about a child but must never act on those thoughts, however stressed, isolated or upset she might be. By the time Folbigg came to trial, Tedeschi SC extended the logic that underlies question 710 to assert that Folbigg's anger with her children manifested in physical actions, namely smothering. The defence response was to deny that Folbigg had ever been seen to physically harm her children and to suggest that the jury look to Folbigg's actions as a means of interpreting the diary references to anger.

Folbigg was careful to say throughout her police interview that her anger, frustration and stress did not actually cause her children's deaths; rather, it did not help their lived environment. This is in direct contrast to the prosecution assertion that Folbigg admitted to *causing* her children's deaths. Instead, Folbigg sought to articulate why she blamed herself for her children's deaths: 'after four, what are you s'posed to think?' This form of self-blame seems to be a common parental response to infant death,[32] and it certainly fits well with the proposition that a mother who cares adequately for her child will be able to protect that child from harm.[33] Tantalisingly, at the moment Folbigg seemed to come to the crux of how she has made emotional sense of her children's deaths, the tape ends. When the interview resumed, the police had moved on to a new entry and a new topic.

IV. The Quest for a Confession

Throughout Folbigg's trial, Tedeschi SC's submissions conflated Folbigg's words with his own interpretation of those words. For example, when discussing the defendant's apparent disregard for Laura's sleep monitor, the prosecutor made the following comments:

> Now, you should also compare that [evidence] with the diary entry for 9 November 1997 where she wrote this – she is talking about Craig:

---

[32] Eg, J DeFrain, 'Learning about Grief from Normal Families: SIDS, Stillbirth, and Miscarriage' (1991) 17 *Journal of Marital and Family Therapy* 215–32. Based on data from nearly 850 parents, the author observes, 'Almost everyone the researchers have interviewed or read testimony from over the years has felt some guilt. They blame themselves in some way for the death, even though they cannot rationally be held accountable' (216).

[33] M Kline, 'Complicating the Ideology of Motherhood: Child Welfare Law and First Nation Women' in MA Fineman and I Karpin (eds), *Mothers in Law: Feminist Theory and the Legal Regulation of Motherhood* (New York, Columbia University Press, 1995) 119, 119–22; and LA Lothian, 'Mapping Contesting Terrain: The Doctrine of Failure to Protect in Canadian Criminal Law' (LLM thesis, University of British Columbia, 2002).

'There is a problem with his security level with me, and he has a morbid fear about Laura. He, well, I know there is nothing wrong with her, nothing out of the ordinary anyway, because it was me. Not them.'[34]

What does that mean? What could that possibly mean other than this: Craig has terrible fear about losing Laura like he's lost the others. I know there is nothing wrong with her, nothing out of the ordinary anyway, because I killed them. They didn't just die". That is what it means.[35]

The striking aspect of this passage is that Tedeschi stitched Folbigg's words together with his interpretation of these words, inserting a direct confession into this passage in a way that makes it sound like it came from Folbigg: 'I killed them. They didn't just die.' The confusion between who said what is apparent from the court reporter's transcription: on the trial transcript, as in the quote above, this phrase is closed with inverted commas, but those inverted commas are never opened. Folbigg never said nor wrote those words.

The text itself may have been adequately damning, but the prosecution still sought to attribute a higher level of guilty consciousness to Folbigg – it was not enough that she be *found* guilty, she needed to *admit* her guilt.[36] Here, as elsewhere in the prosecution case, it is difficult to distinguish between submissions designed to prove that the defendant was guilty and submissions – predicated upon the assertion that the defendant had admitted to killing her children – designed to establish that Folbigg was an identifiably inadequate mother. The prosecution never fully engaged with the reasons why Folbigg might have left a virtual confession in her former marital home, unlocked and accessible to Craig. In fact, the available evidence suggests that Kathleen was not hugely protective of the privacy of her journals. Craig related the concern he felt after he read Kathleen's diary entry regarding her desire to leave her family during Patrick's life, but he did not suggest that Kathleen had banned him from reading her diary in the future or even that she had been particularly affronted by the fact that he had read the diary.[37]

Securing a confession serves a pragmatic purpose – it relieves the state of the need to prove a crime via other means such as by contested scientific evidence – but the pressure to confess or to find a confession goes beyond the merely strategic. The

---

[34] Note that the grammatical structure of this entry has shifted in transcription. Presumably this is attributable to a combination of the emphasis Tedeshi used and the court reporter's effort to make sense of a difficult sentence structure. However, 'It was me. Not them.' arguably reads differently from 'it was me not them.'

[35] Tedeschi SC, Crown closing address, *Folbigg* trial transcript (above n 2) 1349.

[36] See, eg, B Wood, 'The Trials of Motherhood' in H Birch (ed), *Moving Targets: Women, Murder and Representation* (London, Virago Press, 1993) 85–86; evidenced in this case in L Knowles, 'I'm the Most HATED Woman Alive' *Daily Telegraph* (Sydney, 9 July 2003) 5.

[37] See above ch 6, text accompanying n 108. Craig never suggested that Kathleen was upset by the intrusion of privacy implicit within his actions. In fact, he testified that she did not hide her diaries: *Folbigg* trial transcript (above n 2) 433–34.

prosecution's conflation of arguments that are designed to prove legal guilt and arguments that invited the jury to judge Folbigg's moral failures as a mother arguably resolved a tension between the indeterminate medical evidence and the social imperative to identify and punish mothers who kill their children. As the preferred primary caregivers in a society that prizes children, mothers enter a social contract of trust to put aside their own interests in favour of their children.[38] A mother who breaches that trust by killing her children not only harms those children but also threatens the social ordering of caregiving responsibility. This threat is doubled when the mother refuses to acknowledge the wrongness of her actions, and its horror is magnified by the difficulties medical science seems to have in identifying murder. 'Finding' (or, perhaps more accurately, constructing) a confession presents a way of managing the fear presented by the revelation that science cannot distinguish between natural infant deaths and homicide. In this context, the ubiquitous pressure imposed on *all* accused to confess coalesces with cultural fears about our capacity to detect and prevent malevolent mothering.

The expectation that a mother who is charged with her children's murders will admit her guilt is therefore informed by the ideology of motherhood. Writing about *Re: Chamberlain*,[39] Briar Wood has observed that the investigative narrative was founded on an assumption that 'as a mother [Chamberlain] *must* know and *must* be made to speak the truth' about her daughter's disappearance.[40] Chamberlain herself observed the same phenomenon: 'I was told so often "if you will only give up your fight for innocence and say you're guilty, you can go home."'[41] Folbigg similarly wrote to her foster sister, Lea Bown, about the pressure imposed on her by Craig and the police to confess.[42]

Richard Weisman has argued that expressions of responsibility and remorse help to establish society's moral boundaries:

> [E]xpressions of remorse and apology incorporate multiple meanings all of which come to signify in moments of public performance the fit or lack of fit in values among victim, offender, and the community in which they are engaged. The perpetrator who acknowledges responsibility for his or her transgressive act, who admits the wrongfulness of the act, and who shows through her/his feelings of pain and self-condemnation not just her/his empathy but her/his internalisation of the values of community, does more than merely create the possibility for reconciliation with the victim. Because of the epistemological privileging of feelings over words – that feelings more than words reveal the true identity of the person – such performances help constitute the moral boundaries of community by confirming their validity at what are perceived as the deepest levels of personal commitment. Correspondingly, the willingness to defy these expectations

---

[38] SB Boyd, *Child Custody, Law and Women's Work* (Toronto, Oxford University Press, 2003) 12–18 and 218.

[39] *Re: Alice Lynne Chamberlain and Michael Leigh Chamberlain And: the Queen* (1983) 72 FCR (Australia). For additional discussion of this case, see above ch 6, s II.

[40] Wood (above n 36) 85–86.

[41] L Chamberlain, *Through My Eyes: An Autobiography* (Port Melbourne, William Heinemann Australia, 1990) xi–xii.

[42] Kathleen Folbigg, letter to Lea Bown, reproduced in Knowles (above n 36) 5.

when expressions of remorse or apology are invited can convey not merely a rejection of the standpoint of the victim but also a challenge to the moral authority of the community as a whole.[43]

In the context of alleged filicide, a full confession and an associated expression of remorse by a mother who has apparently harmed her children reinforces the appropriateness of the privatised gendered order of caregiving responsibility for children.

Folbigg did not accede to the pressure to confess, and so the prosecution constructed a narrative that split the defendant's subjectivity into two. On the one hand, the 'true' Folbigg admitted within her journals that she had caused her children's deaths and could barely live with this knowledge. Picking up on the distinction Weisman identifies between the value culturally placed on feelings versus words, the prosecution constructed the (ironically textual) journal entries as a reflection of Folbigg's authentic emotional landscape, in direct contrast with the mere words she used to deny having murdered her children when interviewed by police.[44] Tedeschi SC's submissions to the jury regarding the diaries' inescapable meaning obscured the fact that the entries themselves, though troubling, were not straightforward confessions. Implicitly within the prosecution case, the guilty subject of Folbigg's diaries ascribed to and judged herself through the moral conviction that a mother who kills her children commits a monstrous, inexplicable act. Meanwhile, the 'false' Folbigg intransigently persisted in denying her responsibility, distracting herself with dancing and the gym. Tedeschi invited jurors to use their moral compass to navigate through Folbigg's equivocation, as in the following quote, wherein Tedeschi again conflates his own words with Folbigg's:

> 25 October 1997: 'Just watched a video of Sarah'. A little later on, 'I cherish Laura more, I miss her, yes, but I'm not sad that Laura is here and she isn't'. What a strange thing to say about your deceased child 'Is that a bad way to think? Don't know'. I do. Do you?[45]

The murderous mother here becomes identifiable again, and Tedeschi retrospectively reconstructed Folbigg's feelings about motherhood and about her children as indicative not just of criminal guilt but of innate unfitness to mother. This discursive move correspondingly secures the belief that good mothering, self-sacrificial mothering, is a natural female act.[46]

In partial answer to this submission, the defence pointed to the fact that no witness had suggested that Folbigg had failed to care for her children. Zahra SC

---

[43] R Weisman, 'Showing Remorse at the TRC: Towards a Constitutive Approach to Reparative Discourse' (2006) 24 *Windsor Yearbook of Access to Justice* 221, 231.

[44] Weisman, 'Showing Remorse at the TRC' (ibid). See also R Weisman, 'Showing Remorse: Reflections on the Gap between Expression and Attribution in Cases of Wrongful Conviction' (2004) 46 *Canadian Journal of Criminology and Criminal Justice* 121–38, 125–26.

[45] Tedeschi SC, Crown closing address, *Folbigg* trial transcript (above n 2) 1370.

[46] A Rich, *Of Woman Born: Motherhood as Experience and Institution* (New York, WW Norton & Co, 1986) esp the diary entries reproduced in ch 1.

emphasised that despite Craig's testimony, the greatest weight of the evidence pointed to Folbigg's skills as a diligent and caring mother:

> [T]his is in fact was [sic] really quite incongruous with the type of picture the Crown wants to paint about a woman with a low threshold of frustration, totally loses her cool, losing her control, venting high levels of anger, frustration and stress. Again incongruous with the picture that might be presented by Craig Folbigg in the sense the children were really quite an impediment to the accused, but really the accused was more inclined to in fact social-ise and want to go to the gym and in fact not in a sense carry out her functions and her role as a mother.
>
> So these observations by Craig Folbigg again, don't really fit into that pattern of a person as the Crown has sought to use the diaries. In fact there is nothing about the dia-ries, nothing in the diaries that can show itself to mani-fest itself in these excerpts of the evidence.[47]

And:

> It is important before you consider the conclusion that the Crown invites of you, that these diaries represent her true state of mind, whether in fact you can see any support for that. Again reflecting on what Craig Folbigg said in re-examination, a man who lived with his wife for some 16 years. With those attitudes you read in the diary — no. He saw no manifestations of them.[48]

The defence strongly submitted that no one, not even Craig, had ever seen Kathleen display the murderous anger and uncontrollable emotions posited by the prosecution.[49] Given the absence of any other reliable evidence that Kathleen Folbigg had ever failed to care properly for her children, let alone harmed them, the defence suggested that the jury should give little weight to the prosecution's interpretation of the diary entries. Instead, the entries were consistent with the guilt and self-blame that might be experienced by any grieving parent.[50]

Zahra SC's submissions were couched in guarded language, at times so guarded that it is difficult to follow them on the page. Zahra's complex language partly derives from his insistence on the legal principle that Folbigg must be presumed innocent until prosecution evidence proves her guilt:

> Now, in a sense what we flagged at that point in time was to, really, look critically at the motive when the evidence is

---

[47] Peter Zahra SC, defence closing address, *Folbigg* trial transcript (above n 2) 1464.
[48] Ibid, 1516.
[49] Ibid, 1391–94. This submission gave rise to a dispute over the nature and gravity of five incidents in which Kathleen Folbigg allegedly lost her temper with a child.
[50] Ibid, 1514.

```
called, test it. Now, I will take you to the evidence with
an amount of detail and precision and I would ask that you
bear with me during that process, because when we look at
the detail we can now conclude that that motive, as I said
to you at the outset, is very, very shaky.⁵¹
```

Holding the prosecution to its burden of proof has an honourable tradition within the criminal law, and rightly so. The potential difficulty with this tactic, however, is that empirical research into jury decision-making tends to show that jurors conceptualise evidence holistically, as part of a story about 'what happened'.[52] A defence that is predicated solely on holding the prosecution to its burden of proof may fare badly on this model because it does not provide jurors with an alternative story about the facts of the case. In fact, adopting this strategy may increase the risk that jurors will fall back on 'prevalent, often erroneous, stereotypical narratives' in reaching their decisions.[53] This presents a real conundrum to a defence that faces the enormously complex task of pointing out and countering stereotypes while arguing for a client's innocence.

V. Re-reading the Diaries: Looking for Interpretive Principles

The distinction Tedeschi SC drew between Folbigg's true guilty consciousness and her false denials is predicated on a particular conception of the 'truth' found within personal narratives.[54] In particular, the prosecution posited the diary entries as representing the most authentic and complete record of Folbigg's emotional response to motherhood and asserted that Folbigg must have acted upon the unbecoming emotions recorded in the journals. I have demonstrated that Tedeschi interpreted and thereby transformed the diary entries, yet he persistently characterised his reading as the most literal possible understanding of the words Folbigg had written. Accordingly, Tedeschi implied, his preferred interpretation corresponded with an unmediated truth. For example, Tedeschi parodied Folbigg's suggestions that Laura was warned by her (predeceased) siblings to be a good child, interpreting these statements as firmly held convictions and encour-

---

[51] Ibid, 1387.

[52] N Pennington and R Hastie, 'A Cognitive Theory of Juror Decision-Making: The Story Model' (1991) 13 *Cardozo Law Review* 519; and R Lempert, 'Telling Tales in Court: Trial Procedure and the Story Model' (1991) 13 *Cardozo Law Review* 559.

[53] D Menashe and ME Shamash, 'The Narrative Fallacy' (2008) 3 *International Commentary on Evidence* 1–47, 2–3, www.bepress.com/cgi/viewcontent.cgi?article=1034&context=ice; and MT MacCrimmon, 'Fact Determination: Common Sense Knowledge, Judicial Notice, and Social Science Evidence' (1998) *International Commentary on Evidence*, www.bepress.com/ice/vol1/iss1/art2/.

[54] AM Coghlin, 'Regulating the Self: Autobiographical Performances in Outsider Scholarship' (1995) 81 *Virginia Law Review* 1231–32.

aging the jurors to see this absurd 'belief' as yet another sign of the defendant's guilt.[55]

Tedeschi encouraged the jurors to read the diaries as akin to reportage, denying the possibility that the diaries represented emotional or metaphoric truth rather than admissions of criminal guilt:

> You would interpret the second diary, giving the words their ordinary English meanings. Would you [sic] interpret the diary as you interpret any document that you read, a letter that you received, a newspaper article that you read.[56]

These comparators – a document, a newspaper article, a letter (to whom?) – reinforce Tedeschi's construction of the diary entries as being readily understood and directly communicative of their author's intent. Tedeschi characterised the alternative interpretations that Folbigg offered in her police interview as 'glib, trite, evasive', 'just unbelievable', 'lame excuses'; and he implicitly invited the jurors to see the defence strategy of offering metaphoric or psychological explanations as similarly lame.[57]

The prosecution argument employed a common-sense understanding of diaries as inherently truthful, particularly as regards the more unpleasant self-revelations recorded by the author: 'this was a very serious diary with her innermost thoughts about the most intimate subjects.'[58] Lenora Ledwon has argued that the narrative structure of a diary lends itself to truthfulness, suggesting that a 'diary becomes a useful vehicle for self-help, a way to understand one's life journey . . . But all such progress reports only "work", that is, have a utility, *if they are recorded truthfully*.'[59] The question of why Kathleen Folbigg would lie or even exaggerate to *herself* about her role in her children's deaths similarly permeated much of the prosecution discussion of the diaries, although it was never stated in precisely those terms.

The defence sought to limit the damaging impact of the diary evidence, pointing to Folbigg's exculpatory explanations and emphasising the possibility of innocuous interpretations for the diary entries.[60] In particular, Zahra SC suggested that the diary entries reflected Folbigg's grief and self-blame about her children's deaths in an emotional sense, and they could not be interpreted as direct confessions. The following passage suggests, however, that the distinction was difficult to articulate:

---

[55] Tedeschi SC, Crown opening statement, *Folbigg* trial transcript (above n 2) 63–64; and Tedeschi SC, Crown closing address, *Folbigg* trial transcript (above n 2) 1367–68. Tedeschi SC's stance was at odds with Folbigg's explanation of her beliefs: in the record of her police interview, when asked whether she believes in clairvoyants, Folbigg answered 'Not really'. She agreed that she would like to think that her children were somewhere and that they were happy: police interview with Kathleen Folbigg (above n 27) interview questions 608–9.

[56] Tedeschi SC, Crown closing address, *Folbigg* trial transcript (above n 2) 1369.

[57] Ibid.

[58] Ibid, 48.

[59] L Ledwon, 'Diaries and Hearsay: Gender, Selfhood and the Trustworthiness of Narrative Structures' (2000) 73 *Temple Law Review* 1185, 1202 (emphasis added).

[60] Zahra SC, defence closing address, *Folbigg* trial transcript (above n 2) 1513–17.

The Crown says that you can look at these diaries and you can consider that they represent evidence of guilt or blame. It is submitted to you that that is a clear inference. It is able to be gleaned from these diaries that they may amount to an expression of guilt or blame. The question is, however, whether they are admissions of guilt or blame of having murdered or are they feelings that she had of blame, because of what might be recognised as a range of human emotion.

You may recall in my opening address to you when one looks at these diaries, one may need to consider the ranges of human emotions and at times people might ask 'what if' questions. They may feel blame, they may think they should have done something else and they might reflect on blame. If obviously these diaries could be looked at as evidence of feelings of blame or feelings of guilt, there is in fact the next step; are they feelings of blame and guilt of murder or are they feelings of blame and guilt because she continued over this time of many years to think about the 'what if' questions and thought in fact if she was to blame because certain parts of her behaviour. So there is really quite a difference there.

One needs to really not only consider they might be indications of blame or guilt, but the question ultimately has to be answered whether they are evidence of blame or guilt of murder or whether they are in fact another state of mind.[61]

I sympathise with Zahra's difficulty: given the dual work that words such as 'guilt', 'blame' and 'responsibility' perform in our language, it can be hard to untangle criminal guilt from emotional guilt. When spoken by the victims of sexual assault, these words persistently operate to undermine the complainant's credibility and cast doubt on the question of consent.[62] Zahra faced the task of articulating a nuanced narrative about gender, social expectations and self-blame that lacked the straightforward, seemingly intuitive, emotional impact of the prosecution's interpretation.

The defence was on more solid ground when submitting that the prosecution's interpretation of the journal entries was inconsistent with the behavioural evidence.[63] Arguing that the emotions seemingly documented in the diaries bore no relationship to Folbigg's mothering practices, Zahra cited the absence of a corre-

---

[61] ibid 1513–14.

[62] There is a vast literature on this topic. One recent one, eg, is L Gotell, 'When Privacy is Not Enough: Sexual Assault Complainants, Sexual History Evidence, and the Disclosure of Personal Records' (2006) 43 *Alberta Law Review* 743, 770–72. See also CA Ward, *Attitudes Toward Rape: Feminist and Social Psychological Perspectives* (London, Sage, 1995) esp 124–28.

[63] Zahra SC, defence closing address, *Folbigg* trial transcript (above n 2) 1392–93, 1398–99 and 1513–16.

sponding pattern of behaviour.[64] He also pointed towards the wealth of positive evidence regarding Folbigg's diligent care for her children.[65] In this regard, the defence employed much the same logic as the prosecution had when inviting the jury to judge Folbigg's preference for Laura over Sarah. Drawing on the ideology of motherhood, the defence invited the jurors to understand that a mother who murdered her children would be identifiably inadequate in other ways.[66] On the defence case, a mother such as Folbigg, who dressed her children neatly, kept her house tidy and appeared to be happy when she fell pregnant, would not murder her children. Each of these propositions is arguably founded in a common-sense truth, as was the prosecution's submission that a mother who is ambivalent about her children might be more likely to murder those children. The interesting aspect of both arguments is, however, the way in which they mobilise normative expectations about mothering to fill the gap left by the absence of conclusive medical evidence or a direct confession. Each drew upon and arguably reinforced a narrow conception of the ideology of motherhood. (Of course, the prosecution's response to the defence submission was to introduce evidence of several occasions on which Folbigg allegedly behaved aggressively towards a child.)

While the defence arguments regarding Folbigg's behaviour were relatively straightforward, the need to make subtle arguments about the journals themselves may have left the defence position ambiguous. Was the defence arguing that the diaries were a relatively unimportant outlet in which Folbigg vented her minor daily concerns; or that the diary contained deep emotional truths quite different from those the prosecution suggested? An apparent ambiguity within the defence position regarding how best to interpret the diary entries may have reinforced the perception that the prosecution had a more coherent and persuasive narrative.

Zahra SC was correct at Folbigg's trial to point to the complicated relationship between literal truth and the emotional exploration that may actually form the stuff of many women's diary narratives. This insight suggests a springboard for a careful analysis of women's personal narratives and their role in law. Recognising that law *will* judge these narratives, the key task for feminist engagement in this area is to identify interpretive principles for women's narratives that avoid the risks of pathologising women's emotional lives, denying women's capacity to define their own meaning or assessing women's narratives according to the degree to which they comply with normative expectations of gender performance.

---

[64] Ibid, 1516. See also 1392–93.

[65] Ibid, 1398–99.

[66] E Cunliffe, 'Weeping on Cue: The Socio-legal Construction of Motherhood in the Chamberlain Case' (LLM thesis, University of British Columbia, 2003); and F Raitt and MS Zeedyck, 'Mothers on Trial: Discourses of Cot Death and Munchausen's Syndrome by Proxy' (2004) 12 *Feminist Legal Studies* 257.

VI. Conclusion: Interpretive Principles for Diary Narratives

Identifying appropriate interpretive principles for diaries presents enormous challenges and warrants a project unto itself rather than a brief discussion. For want of a more comprehensive analysis elsewhere, some potential principles emerge from the ways in which Kathleen Folbigg's diaries were used during her trial. In offering these principles, I am elaborating on the defence use of diaries at trial while seeking to grapple with the subtle challenges of displacing stereotypes about the kind of mother who might kill a child.

First, the prosecution contention that the journals represented a more authentic or complete account of Kathleen Folbigg's relationships with her children than other narratives might be countered, not by suggesting the diaries' contents are untrue but by pointing to the fact that they represented one of many emotional truths within her life. In other words, while Kathleen Folbigg's diaries recorded some of her emotions, the entries are not complete – they are probably not even representative – records of her experience of motherhood. The diaries themselves provide significant suggestion that the diaries were a repository for Folbigg's fears and anxieties about life, motherhood and relationships – which is far from being synonymous with a confessional to the dark crime of murder.

Second, hegemonic discourses, such as normative conceptions of motherhood, form and frame diary narratives much as they do any other narrative.[67] This presents a fundamental challenge to the occasional tendency to represent journals as a more authentic or unmediated form of narrative than other, more 'public' communications. The prosecution made this assumption during Folbigg's trial, and some scholars who study women's diaries demonstrate a similar logic. Ideology's role becomes abundantly clear when Folbigg's diary is read in its entirety rather than through the selective extracts preferred by the prosecutor. I have sought to counter the prevailing reading by providing some examples of entries that reflect the influence of dominant ideologies of motherhood on Folbigg's writings.

Third, the prosecution case against Folbigg compounded emotion and action in a manner that warrants challenge. Normative conceptions of motherhood arguably account for the possibility that a mother will become frustrated or angry with her children, provided that she never acts on those emotions. In her police interview, Folbigg insisted upon a distinction between her occasional 'terrible thinking' and the acts of which she was accused. This distinction was denied by the prosecution.

Finally, while the defence identified the self-blame and guilt consequent to losing a child and distinguished between these feelings and criminal responsibility, the argument was a difficult one to make given the ethical and evidentiary constraints of legal representation. Folbigg possibly did a better job of describing the

---

[67] Ewick and Silbey (above n 10).

limits of these feelings in her police interview. This suggests that it may be ideal to permit women to explain the meanings of their personal narratives in their own terms; however, the choice whether to testify as an accused person is always risky, and the risks of testifying may well counteract this principle in a given case. Barr J directed the jury that it must not draw any inference from Folbigg's decision not to testify:

> You must understand that her silence is not evidence against her. You are not to treat it as though it were some kind of admission of guilt. You are not to use it to fill in any gaps you perceive in the Crown case or to top up the Crown case. You must not speculate about what the accused might have said in evidence. You must not speculate why she has not given evidence. There may be reasons of which the jury is unaware why an accused person exercises the right of silence.[68]

Nonetheless, it is possible that the decision not to call Folbigg created an explanatory vacuum that enabled the inculpatory interpretation of her personal narratives. It is, however, difficult to assess at a distance whether this was the less dangerous alternative for the defence case. If Folbigg had testified at her trial, it seems most likely that she would have given evidence much like the answers she provided to police in her interview. Whatever her testimony, it would almost certainly have been subjected to the same interpretive tactics as those that the prosecution used for the diaries and interview.

In her police interview, Folbigg did not have an opportunity to explain the meanings of the more damning entries contained in the later journal. This must have represented a conundrum for the defence. Given that she was never interviewed about the second journal, the defence faced a choice between eliciting Folbigg's testimony at trial or seeking to patch together an explanation from the police interview that the jury had already seen. The defence adopted the latter course, presumably as the least risky of two unappealing options given the social and medical context in which the case against Folbigg had been constructed. One shortcoming of this strategy is that the admissions contained in the second journal appear to refer to action rather than emotion: 'I'm not game enough to not plug it in, because theyde want to know why'; 'it was me, not them'; 'it has saved her from the fate of her siblings'; Sarah left 'with a bit of help'.

Reading these entries, it is easy to wonder whether Folbigg killed her children. However, to wonder is not to prove. The journals, read globally or selectively, do not provide sufficiently conclusive evidence of murder to compensate for other uncertainties within the case. There *was* ample evidence that Folbigg was troubled and upset in the period covered by the journals. Our cultural scripts do not provide us with the tools to understand how a mother might respond to experiencing multiple infant deaths,[69] why she might choose to try for more children after these deaths or what form a mother's self-blame might take when yet another child dies. Doron Menashe and Mutal Shamashe have observed that '[p]opular culture

---

[68] Barr J, summing-up, *Folbigg* case files (above n 1) 15.
[69] The medical research cited above at n 32 is confined to parents who have suffered one infant death.

offers more stories of guilt than of innocence, and the predominance of stories of guilt diminishes fact-finders' efforts to empathise with defendants.'[70]

Folbigg's expressions of responsibility and self-blame fit with both the neo-liberal and neoconservative tendencies to individualise responsibility and opened the door to a punitive criminal justice response.[71] Arguably, the prosecution conflation of Folbigg's text with its own preferred interpretation rendered the diary entries even more damning than they were. This tendency was not per se improper, although the lines between text and interpretation should perhaps have been signalled more carefully to avert the risk that the jury might mistake argument for evidence. Equally, the diaries were relevant and admissible evidence, and leaving the interpretation to the jury was not wrong in legal principle.

The diaries provided a pretext for punitive stereotypes about malevolent mothering to enter the trial and be connected directly with the accused. In answering the prosecution arguments, the defence necessarily sought to construct a complicated narrative that both answered the immediate arguments about the diaries' meaning and countered the operation of pervasive stereotypes about bad mothering. The jury was not warned by the trial judge that the absence of any broad cultural understanding of how a mother might respond to losing four children does not justify a default to inculpatory interpretations under the guise of common-sense reasoning.[72] The prosecution's use of the diaries to construct Folbigg as a self-confessed malevolent mother risked permitting the jury to adopt such a reading with relatively little consideration of alternative possible interpretations.

---

[70] Menashe and Shamash (above n 64) 11. See also C Boyle and M MacCrimmon, 'To Serve the Cause of Justice: Disciplining Fact Determination' (2001) *Windsor Yearbook of Access to Justice* 55.

[71] J Simon, '"Entitlement to Cruelty": The End of Welfare and the Punitive Mentality in the United States' in K Stenson and RR Sullivan (eds), *Crime, Risk and Justice: The Politics of Crime Control in Liberal Democracies* (Cullompton, Willan Publishing, 1999) 125–43; and D Garland, *The Culture of Control: Crime and Social Order in Contemporary Society* (Oxford, Oxford University Press, 2001) 8–12.

[72] *R v Cannings* [2005] EWCA Crim 1. See Boyle and MacCrimmon (above n 82); but compare T Ward, 'Law's Truth, Lay Truth and Medical Science' in H Reece (ed), *Law and Science: Current Legal Issues 1998* (Oxford, Oxford University Press, 1998) 243–64. See also earlier discussion of *Cannings* above ch 1, s I.

8

Media Monster

COURT RECORDS AND medical research are neither readily accessible to nor commonly accessed by the public. While judgments are now widely available through free online services, it is relatively rare for a person to find and read a judgment unless he or she has a personal or professional interest in the case.[1] Accordingly, press accounts, particularly those that are also published online, form a primary source of knowledge about particular criminal cases and about the criminal justice system in general.[2] Similarly, press accounts form a primary source of the knowledge that many people, even medically trained citizens, possess about particular scientific issues.[3] Research into the effects of media coverage reinforces the importance of the media as a source of public information about particular medical issues, individual trials and the criminal justice system. News articles are an important means by which law's ideological messages find their way to a broader public.

Despite its ostensible commitment to neutrality, the media is not a neutral transmitter of information. Journalists and editors selectively value certain information emerging from trials and omit other information from their accounts of particular cases. Richard Ericson, Patricia Baranek and Janet Chan have suggested that newspapers communicate 'public conversations about crime, law and justice', convincing readers to assimilate represented events within broader discourses about morality, institutional procedure and social hierarchy.[4]

The newspaper accounts of the *Folbigg* trial and sentencing process provide some insight into the ways in which infant death and maternal responsibility were (re)constructed within public discourse as moral issues that fit legitimately within

---

[1] B Wynne, 'Knowledges in Context' (1991) 16 *Science, Technology and Human Values* 111.

[2] In 2003, the circulation of Australia's *Daily Telegraph* was approximately 407,000, and the *Sydney Morning Herald* sold around 226,000 papers per day (rounded to the nearest thousand). Readership was substantially higher than circulation – estimated 2003 readership was 1.2 million for the *Daily Telegraph* and 900,000 for the *Sydney Morning Herald*. All numbers reflect Monday–Friday figures; weekend circulation and readership are higher. See Australian Press Council, *State of the News Print Media in Australia 2006* (Sydney, Australian Press Council, 2006), www.presscouncil.org.au/snpma/ch03.html#table1 (accessed 1 August 2008).

[3] DP Phillips et al, 'Importance of the Lay Press in the Transmission of Scientific Knowledge to the Medical Community' (1991) 325 *New England Journal of Medicine* 1180. Press accounts are also potentially limited by a decline in readership, although many newspapers (including the *Sydney Morning Herald* and *Daily Telegraph*) have made the conversion to electronic format as an adjunct to print publishing.

[4] RV Ericson, PM Baranek and JBL Chan, *Representing Order, Crime, Law, and Justice in the News Media* (Toronto, University of Toronto Press, 1991) 3–5.

the purview of the criminal justice system.[5] The *Folbigg* case was a major story for the Sydney newspapers. The *Sydney Morning Herald* and the *Daily Telegraph* covered the trial on a daily basis, and the guilty verdict prompted a slew of news and feature articles, including two days of front-page coverage in both newspapers. Moreover, the *Sydney Morning Herald* classified the story as the lead news story of the week in its Saturday review after Folbigg was convicted.[6] For most citizens, these press reports (together with television documentaries and televised news) comprise the total sum of their knowledge about Kathleen Folbigg and her trial.

I followed these papers' coverage of the case from the time when Folbigg was first charged until sentencing.[7] These press reports provide significant insight into how a contested trial, which included evidence in favour of both sides, came to be understood publically as a case in which the evidence for guilt was apparently overwhelming and largely uncontested. Studying the reports also makes clear which legal and medical experts, together with journalists, played an active role in reformulating recurrent infant death from a medical mystery into a criminal problem.

In this chapter, I describe the ways in which the two newspapers selectively reported some aspects of the case and excluded others. Selectivity becomes most apparent when particular articles are directly compared with the trial days they report. Overall, both newspapers focused more on the prosecution case than the defence. In section one, I provide an overview of the print reporting, considering the similarities and differences between the two newspapers in their reporting. In section two, I specifically explore the ways in which the two newspapers reported the medical evidence regarding the Folbigg children's deaths. In section three, I turn to the journalists' depiction of Folbigg's capabilities and emotional qualities as a mother. In that section, the ways in which Craig Folbigg was positioned as an authoritative, though perhaps not wholly trustworthy, source of information about Kathleen Folbigg are described and contrasted with the journalistic treatment of Kathleen's diaries.

I. News Reports of the *Folbigg* Case

The Number and Type of Print Items

Table 8.1 sets out the total number of articles published by the *Daily Telegraph* and the *Sydney Morning Herald* regarding the *Folbigg* case and also identifies the number of each type of article for each newspaper. These articles appeared

---

[5] *R v Kathleen Megan Folbigg*, trial conducted in the NSW Supreme Court, 1 April–21 May 2003, Grahame Barr J presiding. The *Folbigg* case files are held by the NSW Court of Criminal Appeal registry under file numbers 60496 of 2002, 2002/70046, 60279 of 2004 and 2004/1814.

[6] 'Monstrous Murders beyond All Reason' *Sydney Morning Herald* (24 May 2003) 44.

[7] For an outline of the *Folbigg* case, see above chs 1 and 2.

between the date on which Folbigg first appeared in the Sydney media in connection with her children's deaths (3 August 1999) and the date on which her sentence was reported by the news (25 October 2003). Most of this coverage appeared during and immediately after the trial, that is, between 1 April and 29 May 2003.

Table 8.1 Articles about the *Folbigg* Case, by Newspaper and Type

	News	Editorial	Opinion	Letter	Feature	Total
Daily Telegraph	45	2	0	1	5	52
Sydney Morning Herald	32	1	3	3	2	41

As is apparent from Table 8.1, the vast majority of print items in both newspapers were news articles. Most of these news articles reported daily court proceedings, including the trial and the preliminary hearings. Neither newspaper published any other type of article until after Kathleen Folbigg had been convicted. Presumably, this practice is designed to ensure that a newspaper does not fall foul of the stricter publication rules that apply while a case is before the courts.[8] Coincidentally, it reinforces the perception that newspapers find and report 'the facts' of a story before offering opinions about that story.

The *Folbigg* case did not seem to attract a great deal of reader comment in either newspaper. It is difficult to know why this was so. The few published letters were not particularly concerned with understanding Folbigg's motives nor with the legal issues that arose in the case. For example, the only letter published in the *Daily Telegraph* objected to the mangled English within the headline 'Monstress: The Diary of a Child Murderer'.[9] In the *Sydney Morning Herald*, one letter writer opined that Folbigg's sentence was too long,[10] while a second praised the Salvation Army Chaplain who had supported Folbigg through her trial.[11] The third letter mused on the juxtaposition between the writer's 18-month-old daughter's delighted response to the photographs of the Folbigg babies on the front page and the dismal events that the corresponding story reported.[12]

After Folbigg's sentence appeal was allowed, the *Daily Telegraph* ran a phone-in survey asking, 'Should the convicted child killer Kathleen Folbigg have had her prison sentence reduced by 10 years?' 90 per cent of the 166 callers who responded 'voted' no, seemingly endorsing a punitive criminal justice response to the case.[13] The participation rate for this survey was noticeably lower than for others in the same time period. This response rate, taken with the small number of published letters, seems to indicate a less passionately engaged public reaction to the case than

---

[8] See S Walker, *The Law of Journalism in Australia* (Sydney, Law Book Company, 1989) 40–54; and G Robertson and A Nichol, *Media Law* (London, Sweet & Maxwell, 2002) ch 7.

[9] L Wright, 'To the Point' letter, *Daily Telegraph* (Sydney, 24 May 2003) 18.

[10] D Cliff, 'A Disgraceful Sentence for Folbigg' letter, *Sydney Morning Herald* (25 October 2003) 40.

[11] M McLelland, 'Remarkable Major Harmer' letter, *Sydney Morning Herald* (26 May 2003) 12.

[12] M Wheedon, 'Bad Things Out There' letter, *Sydney Morning Herald* (24 May 2003) 36.

[13] 'Vote-line' *Daily Telegraph* (18 February 2005) 31; (19 February 2005) 20.

the volume and tone of both newspapers' coverage might suggest. It is, however, also possible that the survey (published several months after the trial coverage but immediately after Folbigg's sentence was reduced on appeal) was too distant from the trial coverage to constitute a reliable indicator of reader responses to the story.

Hints of reader ambivalence about the importance of the *Folbigg* case reinforce the need to distinguish between the information published in newspapers and the response that any given reader may have to a story. Ericson suggests that readers do not unreflexively accept what they read in the mass media. Rather, they 'negotiate control' by interpreting reported information in light of their personal social context and experiences.[14] Below, I describe and analyse the ways in which the news reporting ordered the *Folbigg* case within certain conceptions about science and gender, but this order does not necessarily represent any public consensus about the case.

Comparing Print Items with the Transcript

Ericson, Baranek and Chan have suggested that both law and media operate 'in the mode of realism' – functioning as if facts and information arise from the laws of nature rather than being filtered through an elaborate set of social and moral constructs.[15] Robert Burns has emphasised the distinction between legal truths (fact determination constrained by law's principles of materiality and relevance) and moral truths, which may be ruled legally irrelevant but must ultimately be accounted for within broader society.[16] Burns has suggested that while reliable fact-finding is important to legal actors, the incompleteness of law's fact-finding project is candidly acknowledged in the rules of evidence.[17] While this observation resonates with the ways in which lawyers and other legally trained actors often conceptualise the trial, the legal system and its actors retain a stake in maintaining a broad public perception that the trial process facilitates truth-finding:

> Law 'justifies authority and makes it appear natural' through conventions and techniques similar to those we have identified in the news. While law is politically and socially constructed, includes aspects that are fictive, and presents evaluative differences as differences in fact, its realistic functioning *in public culture* erases these aspects. It functions as if facts naturally relate to laws without human and organizational mediation. It functions as if it is in pursuit of *the* truth – as if legal truth and procedures for establishing legal truth, authenticate and guarantee 'the whole truth' rather than truth reduced to the genre capacities of the law report. It functions as if legal proof, which is largely a matter of formal procedure, and knowledge, which is largely a matter of the substance of the facts, are the same thing.[18]

[14] RV Ericson, 'Mass Media, Crime, Law and Justice: An Institutional Approach' (1991) 31 *British Journal of Criminology* 219, 221–22.

[15] Ericson, Baranek and Chan (above n 4) 8–11.

[16] RP Burns, *A Theory of the Trial* (Princeton, Princeton University Press, 1999).

[17] Ibid, 13–23 and 85–101.

[18] Ericson, Baranek and Chan (above n 4) 10 (citations omitted, emphasis added). See also KL Scheppele, 'Facing Facts in Legal Interpretation' (1990) 30 *Representations* 42.

Comparing the alternate realities constructed within the media accounts, judgments and transcripts of a trial presents a way of undermining the public claims to singular truth that are made by the legal and media accounts. To the best of my knowledge, this is the first time that trial transcripts have been directly compared with daily media reports in published research.

The quantitative aspect of my comparison between the trial transcripts and the print items of the *Folbigg* case was designed to identify disparities between the amount of court 'time' devoted respectively to the Crown and defence cases, and the amount of media coverage that each party's work in court received. I measured court time from the transcript using the proxy of number of transcript pages.[19] Each party's case included opening and closing addresses; examination in chief and re-examination of its own witnesses; cross-examination of the other party's witnesses; for the Crown, cross-examination of an unfavourable witness;[20] and legal argument. When legal argument was unreportable – for example, when it related to information ruled inadmissible – it was excluded from the pool of reportable data (although at the end of the trial, some of this information was reported by both newspapers). To summarise, the estimate of total trial time devoted to each party's case accounted for all reportable aspects of a party's work in court, including work with opposing or adverse witnesses.

Measuring the amount of coverage provided to each party's case also demanded a more nuanced count than simply distinguishing between items reporting Crown witnesses' evidence and items reporting evidence given by defence witnesses.[21] Comparing news articles with the transcript where necessary, I counted the total number of words devoted to:

- Each party's legal arguments and jury addresses; and
- Evidence elicited by each party. For example, evidence elicited by the defence in cross-examining a Crown witness was coded as a report of the defence case, whether or not it was identified as such in the relevant news item.

Some news items reported exhibits that could fairly be regarded as having the potential to assist both parties – for example, the diaries, the videotaped interview between Kathleen Folbigg and Sergeant Bernie Ryan and the emergency call Kathleen Folbigg made when Laura died. However, this evidence was adduced by the Crown and tended to advance the Crown's case. I coded this information as 'Crown exhibits' separately from 'Crown witnesses' to signal a distinction between information adduced by the Crown that pre-existed the trial and evidence that

---

[19] The trial transcript of *R v Folbigg* is contained in the *Folbigg* case files (above n 5).

[20] See s 38 of the Evidence Act (NSW) 1995, which introduces a considerably lower threshold for cross-examining an unfavourable witness than permitted by the common law concept of hostile witnesses.

[21] See SL Althaus, JA Edy and PF Phalen, 'Using Substitutes for Full-Text News Stories in Content Analysis: Which Text Is Best?' (2001) 45 *American Journal of Political Science* 707, 713–14. Compare JL McMullen, 'News, Truth, and the Recognition of Corporate Crime' (2006) *Canadian Journal of Criminology and Criminal Justice* 905, 912–13. McMullen, working with a larger sample over a longer period of time, coded each item according to a single 'news discourse' or theme.

was 'created' in the form of trial testimony. The importance of this distinction is arguable – the Crown and defence, and the journalists, tended to depict certain exhibits as more truthful and less partisan than trial testimony. I retain the distinction because I want to point to the ways in which the parties and the journalists adjudicated truth claims. Newspapers also sought information from sources who were not directly involved in the case – for example, child protection experts and community members who knew Kathleen Folbigg or her family. I coded this evidence as external (emanating from a source outside the trial), although it tended to be reported in a manner more favourable to the Crown story than the defence. In sum, when undertaking the quantitative comparative analysis, I interpreted ambiguity in a manner designed to elicit every possible gesture towards balance within the print items.

'Balance' is a central tenet of journalistic practice. Balance is a particular manifestation of the ideology of objectivity, which legitimates news media's claims to influence public opinion and government action.[22] The classic example of journalistic balance is a news item that leads with information provided by one source and draws from a second source for a counterclaim. A contested trial might seem to enable an ideal balanced news story in journalistic terms, because it provides a forum for airing alternative points of view.[23] However, contested criminal trials are not easily reduced to equivalent but opposite points of view because of the asymmetrical burden of proof – the prosecution must prove its case beyond a reasonable doubt; while the defence may choose to poke holes in the prosecution case, offer an alternative narrative or do both. Accordingly, assessing 'balance' requires careful consideration of the nature of the case itself.

Stuart Hall et al have documented how the time constraints of press reporting establish a systematic tendency to favour institutional (government and corporate) sources of print items, while Hall et al and Dorothy Chunn have separately demonstrated how claims to have achieved balance conceal the foreclosure of possible interpretations within print items.[24] The quantitative comparative analysis that follows investigates, at the most basic level, whether the *Sydney Morning Herald* or the *Daily Telegraph* achieved balance between the prosecution and defence stories when reporting the *Folbigg* case.

Table 8.2 compares the number of transcript pages devoted to each aspect of the case with the proportion of print items that covered each aspect during and immediately after trial. Because exhibits tended to be discussed as part of the testimonial evidence as well as being tendered, I have not given separate percentages for the prosecution evidence/argument and prosecution exhibits from the transcript pages. Instead, I provide a combined total proportion in the transcript

---

[22] Ericson, Baranek and Chan (above n 4) 168–72.

[23] See also DE Chunn, '"Take it Easy Girls": Feminism, Equality, and Social Change in the Media' in DE Chunn, SB Boyd, and H Lessard (eds), *Reaction and Resistance: Feminism, Law and Social Change* (Vancouver, University of British Columbia Press, 2007) 37–41.

[24] S Hall et al, *Policing the Crisis: Mugging, the State, and Law and Order* (London, MacMillan, 1978) 57–62; and JL McMullen, 'News, Truth, and the Recognition of Corporate Crime' (2006) *Canadian Journal of Criminology and Criminal Justice* 905, 907; Chunn (ibid) 49–54.

column. By contrast, the *Daily Telegraph* often devoted separate attention to the exhibits within its daily reporting, by publishing inset boxes containing the transcript of intercepted or recorded telephone conversations or separate items containing long extracts from Kathleen Folbigg's diaries. In the *Sydney Morning Herald*, the extracts tended to be less lengthy and were visually synthesised with other aspects of the daily reporting of the court proceeding, although warranting separate paragraphs within that text. The separation between exhibits and testimonial evidence reinforced the implicit assertion that journalists were reporting facts that transcended the adversarial trial process and that pre-existing information was more likely to be authentic than that elicited in testimony.[25] This tendency was particularly apparent in respect of Folbigg's diaries.

Table 8.2 Proportional Newspaper Coverage of the Various Aspects of the *Folbigg* Case in Comparison with the Trial Transcript

	Trial Transcript (1404 pages in total)	*Daily Telegraph* (23,379 words in total)	*Sydney Morning Herald* (9,976 words in total)
Prosecution Total	37%	73.3%	69.3%
Prosecution	-	(51.3%)	(57.1%)
Prosecution Exhibits	-	(22.0%)	(12.2%)
Defence	39%	13.1%	13.1%
Judicial Statements	11%	6.6%	4.4%
Unreportable	13%	-	-
External	-	7.0%	13.0%

Most importantly, table 8.2 reflects disproportionate attention given in the media reporting to the prosecution's case story and evidence. The defence witnesses accounted for approximately two days of the 22 days of evidence at trial, while the prosecution witnesses consumed 20 hearing days – a measure that reflects the ways in which the trial process tilts towards the prosecution as primary definer. However, this measure conceals the amount of work performed by defence counsel during the course of the prosecution's case. For example, the defence cross-examined Craig Folbigg at far greater length than Mark Tedeschi SC examined him in chief. John Napier Hilton, who conducted the autopsy on Sarah Folbigg, provided testimony that was favourable to the defence, although he was called by the prosecution. Much of Hilton's testimony was elicited by Peter Zahra SC representing Folbigg. Grahame Barr J was also an active participant, delivering five interim decisions regarding the admissibility of contested evidence. Accordingly, the better measure of a party's work in court is one that counts

---

[25] Sheila Jasanoff criticises a similar distinction made in US appeal courts between litigation and pre-litigation science: S Jasanoff, 'Representation and Re-presentation in Litigation Science' (2008) 116 *Environmental Health Perspectives* 123.

cross-examination of witnesses called by the other party, legal argument and jury addresses, as well as evidence elicited from that party's witness.

Table 8.2 documents the proportion of transcript pages attributable to all work performed by each party and also estimates the work performed by Barr J in regulating the trial proceeding. Legal submissions relating to information ruled inadmissible are listed as 'unreportable', although both newspapers reported some of this information before trial and after Folbigg's conviction. In all cases, the information reported in this way was prosecution evidence that had been excluded at the defence's behest. This information was invariably reported in a manner that seemed to confirm the correctness of the jury's verdict. Accordingly, where a news article reported inadmissible information favourably to the prosecution, I have coded this item as a representation of the prosecution case.

'External' reporting records instances in which a journalist obtained quotes or information about events during the trial from a source who did not testify or otherwise participate in the trial. For example, the *Sydney Morning Herald* quoted the NSW Child Death Review Team when explaining why the presence of multiple infant deaths in a single family should be treated as criminally suspicious.[26]

The imbalance between the respective lengths of the parties' cases is perhaps a common feature of criminal trials: because of the expectation that (barring exceptional circumstances) the prosecution will call all material witnesses;[27] because of the prosecution's obligation to prove its case beyond a reasonable doubt;[28] and because the prosecution possesses far greater resources with which to accumulate evidence than most accused.[29] The combination of factors that lead to this imbalance is most apparent within the taxonomy of expert witnesses called in *Folbigg*. The prosecution called a total of 19 doctors and specialists, while the defence called two. The prosecution's expert witnesses included general practitioners, specialists and pathologists who had examined the children (n=15) and specialists who had not examined the children but provided expert opinions specifically on the likelihood of various causes of death for each child (n=4). The two defence witnesses provided expert opinions on the likelihood of various causes of death, and neither had examined the children during their lives or after death. Some investigating specialists (particularly prosecution pathologists Hilton and Allan Cala) provided evidence about causes of death both in respect of a child they had examined and in respect of the other Folbigg children.

I have found it useful to maintain a working distinction between those medical specialists who were called because they had direct involvement with the Folbigg children and those retained exclusively as post-hoc expert advisors. This distinction can be overdrawn – some experts played a dual function within the trial, and

[26] A Horin, 'Gag Kept Final Death from Police' *Sydney Morning Herald* (23 May 2003) 4; and A Horin, 'How to Stop More Children from Dying' *Sydney Morning Herald* (24–25 May 2003) 37.

[27] *R v Apostolides* (1984) 154 CLR 563 (High Court of Australia); Office of the Director for Public Prosecutions for NSW, *Prosecution Guidelines*, www.odpp.nsw.gov.au/guidelines/guidelines.html (accessed 15 Oct 2008) 48; and Law Society of New South Wales, *Solicitors' Rules* (1995) A.66B(j).

[28] I am grateful to Professor Paul Roberts for making this point.

[29] See M Cooney, 'Evidence as Partisanship' (1994) 28 *Law and Society Review* 833.

individual experts within each category manifested varying allegiance to the principle of expert independence. Nonetheless, the vast majority of medical specialists called by the prosecution were called because they could provide direct information about observed events in the children's lives or about the clinical investigation of their deaths and not because they were necessarily providing strongly inculpatory evidence.

Within the news reporting, the distinction between the party calling the witness and the content of evidence given was often lost in favour of an implicit suggestion that the defence had little or no response to an overwhelming prosecution case. In fact, the defence generated an alternative case theory and elicited evidence in support of that theory, which was that each child died of natural causes; each death was thoroughly investigated at the time of each death, and nothing untoward was found on autopsy; the troubling diary entries and behavioural evidence are variously explicable as manifestations of Kathleen's grief and self-blame or attributable to Craig's anger at Kathleen's decision to leave their marriage. I investigate the subtle dimensions of the print media's portrayal of this defence case below. For now, it is enough to highlight that the media representation that the defence had virtually no response to the prosecution case was in part accomplished by chronic, albeit perhaps not entirely deliberate, inattention to defence counsel's work in court. 39 per cent of transcript pages were devoted to the defence case, while both newspapers committed only 13.1 per cent of printed words to reporting that part of the case. The prosecution case accounted for 37 per cent of transcript pages, while the *Daily Telegraph* allocated 73.3 per cent of its *Folbigg*-related reporting to the prosecution story (including exhibits), and the *Sydney Morning Herald* devoted 69.3 per cent of its *Folbigg*-related content to the prosecution (including exhibits). Even if exhibits are excluded, the numbers still favour the prosecution: the *Daily Telegraph* devoted 51.3 per cent of its printed words to the prosecution story, while the *Sydney Morning Herald* allocated 57.1 per cent of its reporting to this aspect of the case.[30]

Comparing Print Items in the Two Newspapers

The *Daily Telegraph* and *Sydney Morning Herald* used sources in a similar manner to that described by Ericson et al in their study of 'popular' and 'quality' newspapers respectively.[31] The *Daily Telegraph* relied more on police sources, its staff journalists and Craig Folbigg; the *Sydney Morning Herald* more closely reported the medical evidence and sought out institutional spokespeople to place *Folbigg* within a government systems perspective. However, overall, the two papers do not differ fundamentally in their respective representations of the trial. Figure 1

---

[30] As this is to my knowledge the first time that press coverage has been directly compared with trial transcripts, it is not possible for me to say how these figures compare with other cases. However, they bear out other research that has found an emphasis on state institutional sources within crime reporting. See, eg, Ericson, Baranek and Chan (above n 4) 342–8; and Hall et al (above n 24).

[31] Ericson, Baranek and Chan (above n 4) ch 7.

sets out the extent to which each newspaper relied on particular types of sources, expressed as a percentage of total sources reported by each newspaper. Both newspapers averaged 3.8 sources per print item.[32]

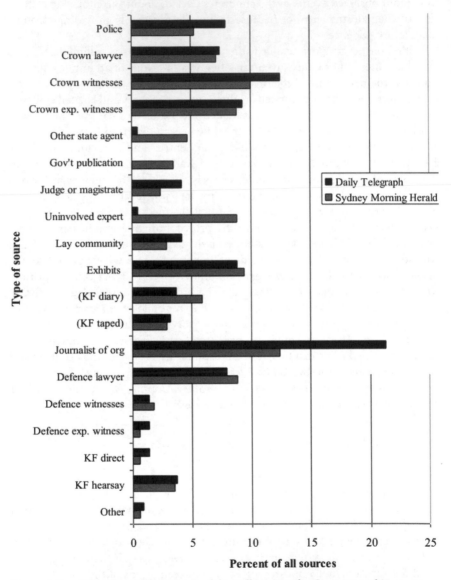

Figure 1 Use of Sources within Reports of the *Folbigg* Case, by Category and Newspaper

---

[32] As a greater number of items were published in the *Daily Telegraph* than the *Sydney Morning Herald*, comparing percentages is a more effective means of identifying differences within newspapers' use of sources than comparing absolute numbers.

For both newspapers, the most commonly used source across the life of the story was the reporting journalist, although the *Daily Telegraph* relied explicitly on this source almost twice as often (21.3 per cent) as the *Sydney Morning Herald* (12.3 per cent). Journalists reported their perception of events in court (such as an occasion on which Folbigg, apparently overwhelmed and distressed, attempted to leave the dock), as well as their visits to locations such as the site of the children's graves, and they frequently provided a history of the case based on their previous days' reporting. In each newspaper, the *Folbigg* trial was mostly reported by the same journalist (in both cases women: Lee Glendinning for the *Sydney Morning Herald*; Lorna Knowles for the *Daily Telegraph*), although occasionally another reporter stepped in.

In keeping with the journalistic precept of balance, the news items quoted prosecution and defence counsel about equally often. Once police sources are added to prosecution counsel, however, a different picture emerges: the *Daily Telegraph* reported these sources almost twice as often as defence counsel (15.3 per cent compared with 7.9 per cent), while the *Sydney Morning Herald* reported police and prosecution counsel nearly one and a half times as frequently as defence counsel (12.4 per cent versus 8.8 per cent). The newspapers did not report judicial or magistrate statements very frequently; these sources were used less than 5 per cent of the time. Journalists were not short of judicial material to draw upon, particularly in relation to pre-trial decisions and after the verdict. Their failure to report these decisions suggests a preference for reporting information received from police, prosecution and defence counsel rather than information provided by the judiciary, and it entrenched the general tendency to emphasise the prosecution story of the case.

Kathleen Folbigg's direct statements in the newspapers included only those statements she made within the hearing of a journalist, for example in the course of an application for bail. Reflecting the fact that she did not testify at her trial and would not speak to the press, Folbigg rarely constituted a direct source for newspapers. She was a direct source for the *Daily Telegraph* 1.4 per cent of the time, while the *Sydney Morning Herald* only once directly cited an in-court statement (0.6 per cent). By contrast, Folbigg's diaries and letters, her police interview and emergency services call in relation to Laura were heavily reported. Cumulatively, these sources provided 6.9 per cent of the *Daily Telegraph*'s sources and 8.8 per cent of the *Sydney Morning Herald*'s. These numbers belie the relative importance of this coverage, because both newspapers published long extracts from Folbigg's diaries and police interviews over the course of the story.[33] Another significant source of information about Kathleen Folbigg's thoughts and emotions was hearsay statements related by others, particularly Craig Folbigg when giving evidence. These statements accounted for approximately 3.5 per cent of both newspapers' sources. In total, Kathleen Folbigg's direct statements and hearsay evidence

---

[33] Eg, 'Monstress: The Diary of a Child Murderer' *Daily Telegraph* (22 May 2003) 31 (1821 words); and L Glendinning, 'Incapable of Love, Compelled to Kill: The Diaries of a Tortured Mother' *Sydney Morning Herald* (25–26 October 2003) 1 and 6 (1633 words).

accounted for 12 per cent of the *Daily Telegraph*'s sources and 12.9 per cent of the *Sydney Morning Herald*'s sources.

Differences between the Newspapers

In their study of Canadian news media, Ericson, Baranek and Chan identified the different market positioning of 'popular' and 'quality' newspapers as follows:

> 'Popular' newspapers seek acceptance through seeming to be close to reality . . . The presentation of material in an entertaining manner does not contradict the sense of being close to reality but rather underpins it. Playing on the heart and on the lower regions of the anatomy, popular newspapers are able to effect a sense of what it is 'really' like to be involved in a situation. Material that is lively also seems 'alive' and thus real.
>
> 'Quality' newspapers, by contrast, seek acceptance through more 'literary' and symbolic means . . . There is a concern with being a source of record both at the moment and historically, resulting in close attention to language and to mechanisms for correcting errors that exhume accuracy and authority.[34]

This passage provides an accurate description of the respective roles of the *Daily Telegraph* (which Ericson, Baranek and Chan would categorise as a popular newspaper) and the *Sydney Morning Herald* (which fits within the rubric of a quality newspaper). In general terms, the *Daily Telegraph* items demonstrated a great concern to present readers with the 'reality' of the *Folbigg* case, using devices such as lengthy extracts from court documents and reproductions of the children's death notices or photographs of the Folbigg children. The *Sydney Morning Herald* items were usually more synthesised and less visually striking. For example, long quotes from court documents were generally eschewed in favour of briefer summaries offered by the journalist within the narrative flow of the relevant article. Rather than publishing photographs of the Folbigg children, the *Sydney Morning Herald* most often used photographs of witnesses or Kathleen Folbigg entering or leaving the court building. Instead of focusing on the emotional dimensions of the case, the *Sydney Morning Herald* tended to place the *Folbigg* case within an institutional context of child protection and child death investigation.

The differing editorial policies were also reflected in the journalists' different use of sources external to the trial. In keeping with the findings of Ericson, Baranek and Chan,[35] Figure 1 above shows that the *Sydney Morning Herald* relied far more frequently on uninvolved experts, other state agents and government publications than the *Daily Telegraph*. Collectively, these sources accounted for 17 per cent of the *Sydney Morning Herald*'s use of sources but only 1 per cent of the *Daily Telegraph*'s sources. This margin reflects the different themes that the newspapers focused on throughout the story, particularly after Folbigg was convicted. When seeking to fit the case within the order of things,[36] the *Sydney*

---

[34] Ericson, Baranek and Chan (above n 4) 35.
[35] Ibid, 234–6.
[36] Ibid, 4.

Morning Herald suggested that regulatory failures prevented the murders from being identified sooner. Thus the post-conviction items relied heavily on institutional sources such as members of the NSW Child Death Review Team and policy reports that had called for closer scrutiny of child deaths. These items subsequently helped parliamentarians to justify changes to child protection legislation, on the premise that a weak child protection system had enabled Folbigg to continue killing her children:

> In the now well-known *Folbigg* case the Child Death Review Team was aware of a pattern of behaviour by a particular family and would have liked to have reported it to the police, possibly resulting in saving the life of the victim. It was reluctant to do so because it felt that it was constrained by the confidentiality clauses. The Government has agreed to relax the level of confidentiality to make sure that relevant reports can be made to government authorities such as the Department of Community Services, NSW Police and the Coroner.[37]

The *Daily Telegraph*, by comparison, showed little interest in the institutional mechanisms of child protection. Rather, this newspaper tried to come to terms with the personal and emotional impact of the case. The *Daily Telegraph*'s post-conviction items were particularly concerned with how it felt to participate in the case and with unearthing what aspects of Kathleen Folbigg's upbringing or character could have led her to murder her children. Therefore the *Daily Telegraph* published long interviews with Craig Folbigg; Kathleen's foster sister, Lea Bown; and investigating police officer Bernie Ryan[38] – as well as a letter written by Kathleen Folbigg to her foster sister while in prison[39] and a story about a woman who knew Kathleen Folbigg's birth parents.[40] The only time that the *Daily Telegraph* spoke to experts who were not otherwise part of the case was when a psychiatrist assessed the letter written by Kathleen Folbigg to her foster sister.[41] The *Daily Telegraph*'s proportionately greater reliance on community sources is reflected in its slightly greater use of prosecution witnesses and uninvolved lay sources. Despite these distinctions, as the more marginal differences within Figure 1 above suggest, the *Sydney Morning Herald* was also somewhat interested in understanding the emotional dimensions of the case.

The differing concerns of the two newspapers are most apparent in the editorials each newspaper published after Folbigg was convicted. In a three-part editorial headlined 'The Depths of Sadness', 'Seeds of Evil' and 'A Quiet Peace', the *Daily Telegraph* suggested that 'nature has been overturned' by Folbigg's conduct and that 'people of a normal mind will never, can never, penetrate the poisonous

---

[37] New South Wales Legislative Council, *Parliamentary Debates*, 1 July 2003, 2415. See also 2379. In this parliamentary discussion, MPs cited A Horan, 'Gag Kept Final Death from Police' *Sydney Morning Herald* (23 May 2003) 4.

[38] F O'Shea and L Knowles, 'Trio who Solved a Deadly Puzzle' *Daily Telegraph* (22 May 2003) 4 and 5.

[39] L Knowles, 'I'm the Most HATED Woman Alive' *Daily Telegraph* (9 July 2003) 1.

[40] L Knowles, 'Kathleen: Your Mum Loved You (But Your Father Was a Monster)' *Daily Telegraph* (28 May 2003) 21.

[41] L Knowles, 'Folbigg could have Repressed Memories of Baby Killings' *Daily Telegraph* (10 July 2003) 2.

depths from which such crimes arise.'[42] Rejecting the argument that Folbigg must be mad, the editorial opined that her crimes were 'the result of a latent wickedness, of an unspeakable evil that exists in the hearts – mercifully – of a depraved handful of humanity'. The editorial concluded with a call to honour Sergeant Ryan for his work 'to see justice done on behalf of the Folbigg infants'.[43] This concern to understand the emotional fallout of the case for participants other than the accused, coupled with an explicit refusal to explore whether circumstances other than inherent evil might drive a mother to murder her children, gestures towards the restoration of order through dogged police work.[44] The social threat presented by a murderous mother is thus controlled by police – not the judge or jury – and Folbigg is so profoundly ostracised as to render her outside the ken and concern of 'decent people'.[45] The editor's expressed refusal to explore Folbigg's motives is belied by the effort made within the editorial to locate her actions within the realms of evil rather than madness.

The *Sydney Morning Herald* editorial was less concerned with understanding (or refusing to understand) what might drive a mother to murder four children, although other aspects of that newspaper's reporting investigated this question. The editorial headlined 'Lessons from the Folbigg Killings' stated, 'Our institutions – and those who work in them – failed Caleb, Patrick, Sarah and Laura Folbigg. We owe it to their memory to find out why.'[46] The editorial called for a greater readiness to treat sudden infant death sceptically but also argued that '[s]uch a systemic failure should be less likely today.'[47] Like the *Daily Telegraph*, the *Sydney Morning Herald* depicted the Folbigg children as victims whose deaths demand a fitting community response. Whereas the *Daily Telegraph* located the appropriate response within punitive exclusion of the singularly evil mother, the *Sydney Morning Herald* called for more intensive institutional intervention in all infant deaths, particularly multiple infant deaths. Accordingly, the *Sydney Morning Herald* located the solution to the social problem of child homicide within properly functioning state institutions, trusting medicine's capacity to patrol the boundaries between natural infant death and murder. This was coupled with a faith in the effectiveness and expertise of properly resourced child protection agencies.

Reposing trust within medical knowledge and public institutions, the *Sydney Morning Herald* represented the changing state of knowledge about infant deaths in a somewhat strained manner. On one hand, it was 'surprising' that alarm bells were not sounded earlier about the pattern of deaths

> . . . because by the early 1990s it was well known that a small proportion of deaths attributed to SIDS were, in fact, undetected murders. Two deaths in a family should have raised suspicion.[48]

42 Editorial, 'The Depths of Sadness, Seeds of Evil, a Quiet Peace' *Daily Telegraph* (22 May 2003).
43 Ibid, 30.
44 See Ericson, Baranek and Chan (above n 4) 96–97.
45 'The Depths of Sadness, Seeds of Evil, a Quiet Peace' (above n 42) 30.
46 Editorial, 'Lessons from the Folbigg Killings' *Sydney Morning Herald* (23 May 2003) 14.
47 Ibid, 14.
48 Ibid.

On the other hand, the newspaper contended, the same failure could not recur in 2003 because

> SIDS is much better understood. . . [P]ost-mortem examinations of young children, now largely centralised in Sydney, would be less likely to wrongly attribute a death to SIDS or any other cause.[49]

This editorial ignores the expert consensus (which was reflected at trial) that it can be impossible to distinguish on post-mortem between SIDS and smothering, and it furthermore overlooks the fact that two of the Folbigg children were autopsied in Sydney under the centralised death investigation programme. The simplification seen here was typical of the newspapers' treatment of the medical evidence, as I describe below. For now, the editorial demonstrates how the *Sydney Morning Herald* managed the threat that the *Folbigg* case presented to social order through an appeal to the rationality and expertise of state and medical institutions. In Ericson, Baranek and Chan's evocative language, the *Sydney Morning Herald* editorial attempted to 'exhume accuracy and authority' as a means of restoring order to the field of infant death.[50] It sought to reassure readers that crimes like Folbigg's will not be overlooked again.

II. Reporting the Science

When science and scientists are reported in the media, the published items often reinforce the popular perceptions of science as an effective means for identifying truths about the natural world and scientists as disinterested observers of these truths.[51] One factor that helps sustain these perceptions is that expert difference, disagreement and uncertainty tend to be suppressed or omitted from news reports. In keeping with the relatively brief length and pithy style of news items, complicated or esoteric scientific debates rarely feature within media reporting of scientific knowledges. Consistently with these themes, when reporting the *Folbigg* case, newspapers depicted the paediatric pathology community's understanding of the causes of infant death as more unanimous and less controversial than the trial transcript suggests. The news items did not even begin to hint at the level of disagreement within the contemporary medical literature. This process of suppressing disagreement was not neutral – both newspapers tended to represent the medical evidence as being uniformly adverse to Folbigg. These effects were accomplished through focusing on certain experts and selected medical evidence,

---

[49] Ibid.

[50] Ericson, Baranek and Chan (above n 4) 35.

[51] See, eg, D Lupton and J McLean, 'Representing Doctors : Discourses and Images in the Australian Press' (1998) 46 *Social Science & Medicine* 947; P Washer, 'Representations of SARS in the British Press' (2004) 59 *Social Science & Medicine* 2561; J Leask and S Chapman '"The Cold Hard Facts": Immunisation and Vaccine Preventable Diseases in Australia's Newsprint Media, 1993–1998' (2002) 54 *Social Science & Medicine* 445.

while excluding alternative points of view. On occasion, a single item would cite several sources and therefore not appear overtly one-sided, but all sources provided a very incomplete perspective on the medical understanding of recurrent unexplained infant death.

In the pre-trial phase, the prosecution's medical case was largely framed through Janice Ophoven's statement that the odds of four SIDS deaths occurring within a single family were one in a trillion. I mentioned above in chapter three that Ophoven did not testify at trial, and her statistical analysis was never put into evidence before the jurors – presumably because the prosecution accepted that her opinion was inadmissible after the English Court of Appeal decision in *R v Clark*.[52] However, during an early bail application the police prosecutor referred to Ophoven's opinion as proof that the prosecution had a strong case against Folbigg. Both newspapers reported this figure in their daily reporting, but only the *Sydney Morning Herald* led with Ophoven.[53]

After Folbigg was convicted, the *Sydney Morning Herald* used Ophoven's opinion and Roy Meadow's reasoning as objective validation of the verdict:[54]

> Perhaps the inconceivable idea that a woman could murder her children had allowed Folbigg to continue to kill. This proposition surrounds a number of issues involving child death; most importantly, perhaps, the misconception of Sudden Infant Death Syndrome striking a particular family.
>
> The odds of four unexplained infant deaths happening in one family with children aged under two years was one in a trillion, Maitland Local Court heard early on.
>
> But the idea of SIDS being familial or inherited and linked to sleep apnoea had wide acceptance in the medical community because of research by Dr Alfred Steinschneider.
>
> He based his research on Waneta and Tim Hoyt, who had lost five of their children ... In 1995, Waneta Hoyt was sentenced to 75 years' jail for smothering her children ...
>
> Medical opinion on multiple SIDS is close to the observation of the British child abuse expert Sir Roy Meadow: 'Two cot deaths is suspicious, three is murder.'[55]

In this passage, the *Sydney Morning Herald* put forward the opinion that multiple infant deaths within a single family indicates murder as if it reflected consensus within the medical community. The journalist has apparently been exposed to at least some of the research underpinning that perspective.

In a similar article, Meadow's law was quoted a second time and the NSW Child Death Review Team's expertise was invoked to support the proposition that

---

[52] *R v Sally Clark (No 1)* [2000] EWCA 54; and *R v Sally Clark (No 2)* [2003] EWCA Crim 1020. Indirect support for this possibility comes from the *Folbigg* trial transcript (above n 19), eg, 1114 (defence application to exclude aspects of Susan Mitchell Beal's evidence). For discussion of *Clark*, see above ch 1, s I.

[53] E Connolly, 'Sudden Deaths of Four Siblings One-in-a-Trillion Chance, Court Told' *Sydney Morning Herald* (24 April 2001) 3. The *Daily Telegraph* led with Folbigg's desire to marry her new partner: F O'Shea, 'Accused Mother cannot Say "I Do"' *Daily Telegraph* (24 April 2001) 7.

[54] For discussion of Roy Meadow and 'Meadow's law', see above ch 4, esp s III.

[55] L Glendinning, 'Dark Secrets of the Mother who Killed Her Babies' *Sydney Morning Herald* (22 May 2003) 6.

half the deaths attributed to SIDS in the past two years in NSW have been found not to be SIDS deaths at all. . . [S]ome were due to accidental suffocation in the parents' bed. But other deaths were suspicious.[56]

As I demonstrated above in chapter four, the sceptical approach to SIDS, particularly repeat SIDS, has always been controversial and was becoming increasingly marginalised by 2003. Nonetheless, disagreement among paediatric pathologists was repressed in the *Sydney Morning Herald* reporting. Invoking the cautionary tale of Alfred Steinschneider and Waneta Hoyt, dissenting views were rendered naïve or dangerous.

In the passages quoted above, the guilty verdict was tested against a posited medical truth (recurrent infant deaths equal murder), and Folbigg's culpability was confirmed. In the process, information presented within the article blended admissible evidence with excluded information in ways that are indiscernible to readers who did not attend the courtroom or otherwise obtain access to a full record of the trial. This is important because that information was excluded, at least in part, because it had been found by other courts and eminent researchers to be unreliable. Ericson, Baranek and Chan have described how a news item 'includes elements that are fabricated and fictive, and presents evaluative differences as differences in fact'.[57] In this example, the *Sydney Morning Herald* drew from sources internal and external to the trial process, repressing controversy about the likely causes of multiple infant death within a family. Ultimately, the *Sydney Morning Herald* purported to confirm the trial outcome using highly incomplete assertions about the state of medical knowledge.[58] The fact that this journalist selectively reported certain incriminating aspects of the medical case from the competing narratives presented at trial and overlooked the even broader medical controversy about infant death was obscured by the matter-of-fact tone.

The marginalisation of alternative points of view within the *Sydney Morning Herald* post-conviction article was very like that performed by prosecution pathologist Allan Cala when testifying in voir dire about the 2001 American Academy of Pediatrics (AAP) Policy Statement.[59] This statement suggested that recurrent sibling deaths 'should indicate the possibility of intentional smothering'. Regarding the Policy Statement, Cala declared:

[T]his document would be generally accepted by all people in paediatrics and in my area of forensic pathology. I would think there might, for example, be some people, a very small minority, who may argue with parts of it, but I think that in the main the entire medical community who looks at this area would be in agreement with this document.[60]

---

[56] A Horin, 'How to Stop More Children from Dying' *Sydney Morning Herald* (24–25 May 2003) 37.

[57] Ericson, Baranek and Chan (above n 4) 10.

[58] The subsequent controversy over a juror's decision to research aspects of the case on the internet during trial demonstrates that the distinction between admissible evidence and reported information should not be too sharply drawn. See *R v Folbigg* [2007] NSWCCA 371.

[59] See above ch 5, s II.

[60] Allan David Cala, voir dire re admissibility of 2001 AAP Policy Statement, *Folbigg* trial transcript (above n 19) 724.

While Cala was not quoted in the *Sydney Morning Herald* article, he may well have been an unacknowledged source for the journalist. In any event, the medical consensus posited within the item bears a strong resemblance to his narrative of the case.

In chapter five, I suggested that Cala became the key spokesperson for the prosecution's medical case at trial. Cala was not quoted in either newspapers post-conviction coverage, and his evidence was only briefly reported during trial.[61] It is difficult to know from the textual record why the prosecution's key witness was overlooked in the post-conviction reporting. Journalists did name prosecution expert Susan Beal, paediatrician Roy Meadow and pathologist Janice Ophoven in their coverage. It may be that Cala was a less persuasive witness in person than the prosecution's strategy presumed, but this shortcoming did not translate to the written transcript. Alternatively, and more speculatively, the relative inattention to Cala may have been a journalistic response to another controversy in which Cala and his colleague Hilton had both been implicated.[62] Whatever the cause, despite Cala's absence in name from the reporting, his reasoning structured the manner in which the *Sydney Morning Herald* conveyed the state of medical knowledge to its readers. This structural effect was presumably consequent to the prosecution's medical case, which was shaped from the outset by Cala's autopsy report on Laura and reframed through Cala's subsequent expert witness statements and testimony. One can trace the institutionalisation, de-personalisation and alteration of Cala's knowledge from Laura's original autopsy report through its various incarnations until it emerges, seemingly fully objectified and entirely detached from Cala, in the *Sydney Morning Herald*'s post-conviction reporting.[63]

The only expert witness to whom both newspapers devoted news items was Susan Mitchell Beal.[64] Both newspapers focused on Beal's considerable experience and status within the community of SIDS researchers: the *Daily Telegraph* described her as a 'world renowned expert on sudden infant death syndrome',[65] while the *Sydney Morning Herald* reported that Beal 'has been involved in SIDS research for more than 30 years and was made a Member of the Order of Australia for her work in this field'.[66] Beal's firmly held view that the *Folbigg* children were murdered was reported in both newspapers, as was her evidence that she had never heard of a family suffering three or more SIDS deaths.

---

[61] 'Folbigg Baby "Healthy"' *Sydney Morning Herald* (16 April 2003) 6; and B Williamson, 'Fear and Detachment: Nurse Tells of Folbigg Parents' Attitude to Baby' *Daily Telegraph* (16 April 2003) 23.

[62] In 2001, Cala and Hilton were both implicated in a scandal in which pathologists used bodies and organs for research purposes without consent. An inquiry found that the pathologists had acted on a sincere but mistaken belief that their research was permitted by existing law. See M Robinson, 'Morgue Staff's Handling of Bodies Illegal: Inquiry' *Sydney Morning Herald* (17 August 2001) 5; and B Loff and S Cordner, 'Australian Inquiry finds Researchers Not Guilty' (2001) 358 *The Lancet* 649.

[63] For an account of the processes by which individual knowledge is institutionalised and rendered apparently objective, see DE Smith, *Texts, Facts and Femininity: Exploring the Relations of Ruling* (London, Routledge, 1990) 214.

[64] See above ch 5, s III.

[65] L Knowles, 'Case Like This Unheard of: SIDS Expert' *Daily Telegraph* (6 May 2003) 6.

[66] L Glendenning, 'Deaths "Consistent with Smothering"' *Sydney Morning Herald* (6 May 2003) 5.

After Beal testified, the *Daily Telegraph* amended the brief explanatory note it printed beside most articles reporting the case. Whereas the note had previously reported the prosecution and defence positions at trial in a few words, a third line was added: 'The evidence: Experts say three or more SIDS deaths unlikely.'[67] This note perpetuated the tendency to overlook the defence case that at least some of the Folbigg children died from identifiable causes and not from SIDS. It was drawn from Beal's evidence and, together with similarly brief statements of the prosecution and defence positions, it henceforth framed the case reporting within the *Daily Telegraph*.[68] It was also Beal who introduced Meadow's observation that two cot deaths are suspicious and three are murder 'unless shown otherwise' into the *Folbigg* case, while testifying on voir dire.[69] This observation never made it before the jury and was not reported during trial, but it may have provided journalist Glendinning with that portion of the *Sydney Morning Herald*'s post-conviction news article.[70]

Beal's colleague and co-author, the defence expert Roger Byard, received considerably less fanfare within the press coverage. Although he is as widely published and highly honoured within the SIDS research community as Beal,[71] Byard's testimony was not mentioned in the *Sydney Morning Herald* and was barely reported in the *Daily Telegraph*. In an item that focused mostly on defence evidence that Kathleen Folbigg was a good mother, the *Daily Telegraph* reported:

> The second witness called by the defence, Professor Roger Byard, told the court there was no proof the four Folbigg children were deliberately smothered.
>
> He said he could not exclude that possibility.
>
> Professor Byard, a forensic pathologist and respected SIDS expert, said after reviewing two boxes of case files on each Folbigg baby, he believed each had died from 'undetermined causes'.[72]

Byard's professed incapacity to distinguish between SIDS and unnatural causes of death was shared by all of the experts who testified in *Folbigg*, to a greater or lesser extent. I explained above in chapter four that this indeterminacy is also widely accepted within the worldwide community of SIDS experts. In this *Daily Telegraph* article, however, Byard's inability to 'exclude' unnatural causes of death is subtly cast as a reason to doubt Byard's capacity to assist the reader to decide how the Folbigg children died.

By contrast, two days earlier the *Daily Telegraph* reported Beal's evidence that various children's deaths were 'consistent' with suffocation without explaining that 'consistent' means in this context that alternative causes of death may be

---

[67] 'Folbigg had "Close Bond with Child"' *Daily Telegraph* (8 May 2003) 21.
[68] Susan Mitchell Beal, evidence in chief, *Folbigg* trial transcript (above n 19) 1143–44.
[69] Susan Mitchell Beal, voir dire, *Folbigg* trial transcript (above n 19) 986–7.
[70] Glendinning, 'Dark Secrets' (above n 55) 6.
[71] As Beal confirmed in her evidence: Susan Mitchell Beal, cross-examination, *Folbigg* trial transcript (above n 19) 1149.
[72] 'Folbigg had "Close Bond with Child"' (above n 67) 21.

equally consistent with those findings.[73] Although the two experts reached different conclusions about preferred cause of death and expressed different levels of confidence about their conclusions, both testified to similar effect about one thing – the pathological evidence was insufficient by itself to distinguish between SIDS or other natural causes of death, and smothering. The *Daily Telegraph* reported Beal's evidence as if this indeterminacy was largely irrelevant to the validity of her conclusions, while it reported Byard's evidence in a way that implies that the uncertainty rendered his opinion unhelpful at best and unreliable at worst.

Byard's preference for 'undetermined' verdicts, which was reported without the explanation Byard provided for that conclusion, reinforces the implication that Byard's evidence was at best ambivalent. In fact, decontextualised from any explanation about what constitutes an 'undetermined' verdict, Byard's opinion seems almost absurd – how can a baby 'die from' undetermined causes? Byard's testimony was also relegated to the realms of opinion rather than fact – Byard 'believed' the babies had died from undetermined causes[74] – whereas Beal 'said' and 'found' her preferred causes of death for reasons that were reproduced in the *Daily Telegraph* article.[75] The overwhelming impression given when reading this *Daily Telegraph* item without the context supplied by the transcript is that Byard was equivocating – perhaps out of squeamishness or naivety. Nonetheless, the *Daily Telegraph* did at least report that a 'renowned' expert witness would not call these deaths murder without more evidence.

The *Sydney Morning Herald*, by contrast, omitted Byard's evidence completely from its coverage, a particularly striking omission in light of that newspaper's greater emphasis on science. The item published on 8 November 2003 (the day after Byard testified) read in its entirety:

Folbigg Defence Near End

The defence case for Kathleen Folbigg, accused of murdering her four babies, is expected to finish this morning, after 1½ days of evidence, after the defence announced it would call five witnesses. The trial, originally set down for 10 weeks, may finish in under half that time.[76]

The following day's report mentioned '[t]he second expert witness, pediatric cardiologist Dr Owen Jones' without referring to Byard or his evidence.[77] Like the *Daily Telegraph* report of Byard's evidence, this item cast the defence medical case as weak and predicated on speculation rather than fact: Jones 'believed

---

[73] The Commission of Inquiry into Guy Paul Morin's wrongful conviction recommended that experts should not use the term 'consistent with' when testifying because jurors were liable to accord too much weight to that designation: F Kaufman, 'Report of the Commission on Proceedings involving Guy Paul Morin' (Ottawa 1998) 3, www.attorneygeneral.jus.gov.on.ca/english/about/pubs/morin/. This recommendation was repeated in the Goudge Report: ST Goudge, *Inquiry into Pediatric Forensic Pathology in Ontario Report* (Toronto, Queen's Printer for Ontario, 2008) 77.

[74] 'Folbigg had "Close Bond with Child"' (above n 67) 21.

[75] Knowles, 'Case Like This Unheard of' (above n 65) 6.

[76] 'Focus: Folbigg Defence Near End' *Sydney Morning Herald* (8 May 2003) 4.

[77] L Glendinning, 'Folbigg Close to Baby Laura, Gym Friends Testify' *Sydney Morning Herald* (9 May 2003) 5.

[Laura] had mild myocarditis. Under cross-examination, he said the latter almost never leads to death.'[78] The net result of these two items from the *Sydney Morning Herald* is that the defence appeared to have no answer to Beal and other prosecution experts who testified that the children were most likely murdered. The brief item published on 8 May 2003 implied that the defence had almost no case whatsoever.

As was true with the prosecution's medical case, the defence position was reported without reference to its originating source. Byard's account of the proper approach to diagnosing the cause of infant death permeates the *Sydney Morning Herald*'s reporting of the defence position at trial. The defence insistence on seeking positive indicia of smothering, which originated with Byard's expert report, was attached to the far more suspect (because self-evidently partisan) defence counsel. For example, when reporting Zahra SC's closing address, Glendinning wrote:

> [Zahra SC] said there could be explanations for all four deaths. Each of the children may have died of organic illnesses, including a lazy larynx, epilepsy, inflamed uvula and myocarditis.[79]

A reader who followed the continuing story would have been quite justified in believing that these alternative explanations were dreamt up by the defence lawyers, particularly since even the defence's expert witness seemed to doubt the possibility that Laura died of myocarditis. In fact, the submission was based on weeks of careful work establishing the possibility of these alternative causes of death with expert witnesses called by both parties. It began with Byard's original admonition to avoid imprecision when estimating the likelihood of four natural deaths in one family.[80] The effects of disconnection between source and position were quite different for the defence than for the prosecution: the defence case was made to appear unscientific and speculative, while the prosecution case was rendered objectively factual by being reconstructed as an unassailable expert consensus.

Hilton's evidence had the potential to present a significant challenge to the *Sydney Morning Herald* story of the medical case against Folbigg, not to mention the prosecution's case at trial. Hilton, who was called by the prosecution, testified strongly in favour of Folbigg. He resisted Cala's position that multiple infant deaths within a single family excluded the possibility of SIDS or other natural causes. Hilton suggested that it was improper for a pathologist to raise the spectre of a smothering death in the absence of positive evidence. He gave evidence on 14 April 2003 and was recalled to testify further on 23 April 2003. The *Sydney Morning Herald* news item on 15 April 2003 reported towards the end of the article:

> John Hilton, who carried out Sarah Folbigg's post-mortem examination, said he found two pinpoint abrasions under her lip, which he agreed were consistent with force being applied to the child's mouth. The post-mortem findings had been consistent with death by asphyxiation.

---

[78] Ibid.
[79] L Glendinning, 'Case against Folbigg Very Shaky: Defence' *Sydney Morning Herald* (15 May 2003) 5.
[80] See above chs 3 and 5.

The Crown prosecutor, Mark Tedeschi, QC: 'Does that include deliberate smothering ...'

Professor Hilton: 'Yes.'

I want to suggest ... you ought not have diagnosed Sarah Folbigg's death as SIDS, but as 'unknown causes'.

[Hilton:] – With respect, I would disagree.[81]

On 24 April 2003, the *Sydney Morning Herald* reported additional questioning about the pinpoint abrasions, noting Hilton's opinion that they were more likely to have been caused by a jewelled ring than a pillow or soft toy.[82] These two reports collectively imply that Hilton's evidence was more favourable than unfavourable to the prosecution case.

The *Sydney Morning Herald* accomplished the sense that Hilton's evidence was favourable to the prosecution in part through another unexplained use of the term 'consistent'. In addition, the use of direct quotes from the testimony, which was relatively unusual for that newspaper, entrenched the perception that the item allowed readers to see for themselves how the medical evidence was playing out. The passage from which the first part of the *Sydney Morning Herald* quote is apparently taken reads at greater length:

Q. Those findings in and around the lungs, are you able to say whether they are consistent with the child being asphyxiated to death?

A. They are consistent with an asphyxial mode of death.

Q. By 'an asphyxial mode of death', does that include a deliberate smothering of the child?

A. Yes.

Q. Does it also include other causes of asphyxiation?

A. Yes. And indeed, other things as well. There is nothing very specific about these little blood haemorrhages in that particular.

Q. It is not a specific finding for smothering; is that correct?

A. That is right.

Q. But it is a finding that is commonly found if a child has been smothered?

A. It is a finding which has been recorded in smothering. In my own experience I can only recall one case of deliberate inflicted smothering which showed these little blood spots

[81] L Glendinning, 'Inherited SIDS unlikely, court told' *Sydney Morning Herald* (15 April 2003) 6.
[82] L Glendinning, 'Tearful Memory Of Second Baby Death' *Sydney Morning Herald* (24 April 2003) 5.

on the lungs. So in a limited sense it is indicative, but
only indicative.[83]

As is apparent from this longer extract, the meaning and limits of the phrase
'consistent with' were explored by both prosecution counsel Tedeschi and the
witness. Hilton explained his view that the post-mortem findings were also consistent with other causes of death and hinted at his belief that other causes were
more likely. The second quoted passage in the news item appears almost 30 pages
later in the transcript, after the prosecution received permission to cross-examine
Hilton.[84] Hilton's intervening evidence that smothering was 'no higher than a
possibility' when there were multiple infant deaths in a family was not reported by
the *Sydney Morning Herald*.[85] Nor was his statement that 'it was my opinion then
the most likely diagnosis on the balance of probabilities was sudden infant death
syndrome.'[86] Finally, the defence cross-examination, in which Hilton provided a
much fuller explanation of his reasons for favouring SIDS over smothering in
Sarah Folbigg's case, was not mentioned in the daily report. Such selective omission of parts of the evidence within quotes was a recurrent feature of the newspaper coverage; for example, the *Sydney Morning Herald* did the same thing when
reporting Craig Folbigg's cross-examination.[87]

In addition to the selectivity apparent within the *Sydney Morning Herald* report
regarding Hilton's substantive evidence, Hilton's credentials were downplayed
within the item. Hilton's designation 'John Hilton, who carried out Sarah Folbigg's
post-mortem examination' makes no reference to his expertise in the fields of
SIDS research and forensic pathology. Hilton testified that he had been chair of the
SIDS International Pathology Committee, was the head of the NSW Forensic
Pathology Service and had conducted more than 2,000 autopsies on children.
Although the *Sydney Morning Herald* reported similar details about Beal, they
omitted this information from their news items about Hilton's evidence. The
implicit denigration of Hilton's utility to the fact-finding enterprise is compounded by the fact that his evidence was reported towards the end of an article
that led with a long discussion of the unlikelihood that SIDS has a genetic component. These narrative devices secured the *Sydney Morning Herald* story of a medical enterprise that has the capacity to distinguish between SIDS and smothering
and that possesses a consensus-based understanding of the significance of multiple
infant deaths within individual families.

The *Daily Telegraph* did not report Hilton's evidence. Like the *Sydney Morning
Herald*, it reported the evidence given by David Cooper about the unlikelihood
that there was a genetic component to SIDS deaths.[88] On 24 April 2003, the *Daily*

---

[83] John Napier Hilton, examination in chief, *Folbigg* trial transcript (above n 19) 619.
[84] Ibid, 648.
[85] Ibid, 632.
[86] Ibid, 649.
[87] L Glendinning, 'Father of Dead Babies Says He Lied to Police' *Sydney Morning Herald* (8 April
2003) 8.
[88] B Williamson, 'Unlikely for SIDS to Hit a Family Twice' *Daily Telegraph* (15 April 2003) 11.

Telegraph reported the evidence given by Craig Folbigg's sister, Carol Newitt, at some length.[89] This item focused on Kathleen Folbigg's emotional response to Patrick's death and on the accused's concerns about her capacity to be a good mother. In other words, the *Daily Telegraph* opted for exclusion rather than selective and derogatory inclusion of Hilton's evidence. The lack of attention to Hilton's evidence was in keeping with the *Daily Telegraph*'s relative indifference to the medical aspects of the case and its intense interest in the emotional ramifications of the children's deaths and Folbigg's trial.

Overall, the *Sydney Morning Herald* presented a relatively coherent story of the medical investigation into the cause of the Folbigg children's deaths as a truth-finding process that overwhelmingly established Folbigg's guilt. The *Daily Telegraph* devoted less attention to the medical aspects of the case, but the themes that emerged from this reporting were very similar to those within the *Sydney Morning Herald*. Over the life of the story, both newspapers reported admissible medical evidence in combination with inadmissible information – the occurrence of multiple infant deaths within a family was presented as proof of murder in the absence of alternative explanations.

In both newspapers, medical knowledge provided by particular experts was detached from its source and transformed into other forms of knowledge. This process operated differently for the prosecution than for the defence. Whereas Cala's opinion became the asserted unanimity of an expert community, Byard's interpretation was devalued and rendered unscientific through being recast as advocacy. Gary Edmond has suggested that this is a common tactic used by competing experts to entrench their truth claims.[90] In this particular context, the practice enabled the *Sydney Morning Herald* to report the prosecution's medical evidence as if no plausible alternative explanations for the children's deaths were presented by expert witnesses at trial.

The perception that the defence had no credible medical case was further reinforced by both newspapers' selective resort to the credentials of particular experts. Whereas Beal's illustrious career as a SIDS researcher was highlighted within the news reporting, Byard's and Hilton's similarly luminous track records were not mentioned by the *Sydney Morning Herald*, and Byard's credentials were barely referenced in the *Daily Telegraph*. When medical knowledge was attributed to particular knowers, Beal became the primary definer for both newspapers, together with Ophoven and Meadow in the *Sydney Morning Herald*. Byard's and Hilton's opinions were variously unreported or deprecated. Finally, both newspapers used technical scientific terms such as 'consistent' without providing an explanation for lay readers about their import. Again, this practice entrenched the perception that the medical evidence was uniformly negative to Kathleen Folbigg's case.

[89] L Knowles, 'The Loneliest Cry in the World . . . Mother Found Sobbing after Baby's Death' *Daily Telegraph* (24 April 2003) 9.

[90] G Edmond, 'Azaria's Accessories: The Social (Legal-Scientific) Construction of the Chamberlains' Guilt and Innocence' (1998) 22 *Melbourne University Law Review* 396.

III. Reporting Folbigg's Motherhood

Much of the emotional power of the Folbigg story comes from the allegation that she killed her children serially over the course of a decade. This behaviour does not readily fit with existing cultural narratives[91] – not the loving, protective mother, not the mentally ill postpartum mother who kills her child(ren) in a moment of psychosis, nor even the stereotypical infanticidal teen-mother who murders her newborn in an act of denial. In chapter six above, I suggested that Folbigg's refusal to admit to or express remorse for her alleged crimes magnified the threat she seemed to present.

Ericson, Baranek and Chan suggest that newspapers report crime as a means of ordering chaotic and threatening events within moral frameworks.[92] The need to find moral order within the *Folbigg* case permeated the news reporting, particularly those aspects that focused on Folbigg's status as a wife and mother. As a correlate to imposing order, both newspapers, particularly the *Daily Telegraph*, sought to comprehend what circumstances or personal characteristics produced a mother like Folbigg. The news and feature articles highlighted deviant emotions, thoughts and behaviours as a way of demonstrating that Folbigg was different from other mothers. Within this process, certain explanations and causes were proposed while others were merely hinted at or left completely unexplored. Two news sources became the primary definers of Folbigg's emotional state and mothering capacities: Kathleen Folbigg, through her personal writings and police statements; and Craig Folbigg.

The newspapers were predictably fascinated by Folbigg's diaries and letters, using them as evidence of deviant mothering in much the same way as the prosecution did.[93] The *Sydney Morning Herald* used or referred to Folbigg's diaries in almost one quarter of its published items, while the *Daily Telegraph* used the diaries slightly less frequently but at greater length. In accordance with the newspapers' differing editorial styles, the *Daily Telegraph* tended to use extensive edited extracts from the diaries, while the *Sydney Morning Herald*'s reporting was briefer and more self-consciously analytical. The *Sydney Morning Herald* occasionally framed reports with sentence-length extracts from the diary, using these snippets to shed light on reported events or testimony.[94] For both newspapers, the diaries were reported as if they presented a complete insight into Folbigg's experience of motherhood and, especially, her inadequacies as a mother. Certain entries, recurring within the reporting, enabled the journalists to categorise Folbigg as a manifestly dangerous and unnatural mother. Like the prosecution, both newspapers accepted the diaries as a relatively uncomplicated, literal record of Folbigg's actions and emotions.

---

[91] Discussed at greater length in ch six.
[92] Ericson, Baranek and Chan (above n 4) 4–11.
[93] See above chs 6 and 7.
[94] Eg, L Glendinning, 'Father Tells How the Wife He Loved Got on with Her Life after Babies Died' *Sydney Morning Herald* (3 April 2003) 9.

The diaries first appeared in the news reporting when Folbigg was charged in August 1999. The *Daily Telegraph* printed an edited version of the police information tendered to the Local Court in support of the charges. This report mentioned Folbigg's note that Caleb was 'finally asleep' on the night that he died.[95] The *Sydney Morning Herald* did not pick up on the diaries in its report, focusing instead on Ophoven's opinion about the rarity of multiple infant deaths.[96] While framed by the police version of events, the *Daily Telegraph* report evinced some sympathy for Kathleen Folbigg – for example, in the headline 'Mum's Waking Nightmare', which does not presume Folbigg's guilt but signals the distress of losing one or more children.[97]

The *Daily Telegraph* retained this sympathetic perspective for much of the time it covered the story, although by the end of the trial it also evinced the far more punitive attitude that was apparent in its post-conviction editorials. The retention of a sympathetic perspective is interesting because the tendency of popular media to focus on emotion more often works against the accused.[98] An example of the more sympathetic reporting arose when Kathleen Folbigg cried in court while watching a video of Laura playing. The *Daily Telegraph* framed its story with Folbigg's emotional response, following up with Craig's evidence.[99] In contrast, the *Sydney Morning Herald* focused on Craig's testimony and barely mentioned Folbigg's tears.[100] The *Daily Telegraph*'s ambivalence between sympathy and condemnation seemed to stem from an acknowledgement that Folbigg suffered real grief, while ultimately excluding her from the realms of empathy because the crimes of which she was convicted were unforgivable. The *Sydney Morning Herald* focused on Folbigg's anger and other seemingly probative emotions but was unwilling to recognise that Folbigg may also have suffered grief at her children's deaths.

Each newspaper's narrative of Folbigg's emotional world was in large part accomplished through the diaries. On 5 April 2003, the first Saturday after the trial began, the *Daily Telegraph* published a long article containing several of the more damning diary entries. Framed through Craig's 'aghast' reaction to Kathleen's request for a fourth child, the article maintained a gesture towards balance, mentioning the defence argument that the diaries 'reflected "the fairly normal, human reactions of grief, guilt, shame, responsibility"'.[101] The entries that

[95] F O'Shea, 'Four Babies Dead, Mother Charged with Their Murders' *Daily Telegraph* (20 April 2001) 7; and 'Mum's Waking Nightmare' *Daily Telegraph* (20 April 2001) 22.

[96] D Proudman, 'Four Children Dead in 10 years – Now a Mother Stands Accused' *Sydney Morning Herald* (20 April 2001) 1.

[97] 'Mum's Waking Nightmare' (above n 95).

[98] I am grateful to Dorothy Chunn for making this point.

[99] L Knowles, 'Mother's Tears at Home Video: The Last Day of Her Child's Life' *Daily Telegraph* (4 April 2003) 12. On two other occasions, the *Daily Telegraph* reported that Kathleen Folbigg wept or became distressed during trial: L Knowles, 'The Questions Kathleen Folbigg was Asked by Police' *Daily Telegraph* (1 May 2003); and L Knowles, 'Dead Baby and a Mother's Call' *Daily Telegraph* (2 May 2003). These items do not suggest that the journalist interpreted Folbigg's affect as mendacious.

[100] L Glendinning, 'Diary Stirred Grieving Father's Doubts' *Sydney Morning Herald* (4 April 2003) 8.

[101] Zahra SC quoted in L Knowles, 'Desperate Diary of an Anguished Mum' *Daily Telegraph* (5 April 2003) 17.

were subsequently reproduced within this item seem to belie that submission, starting with Folbigg's statement that 'stress made me do terrible things' and concluding with the observation that Laura 'saved her life by being different' from Sarah.[102]

In keeping with the popular newspaper's commitment to showing its readers the reality behind news stories, the *Daily Telegraph* journalist presented the entries without comment, and readers were left to judge for themselves whether the defence submission could succeed. The narrative presumed that readers would judge the entries against a broadly held normative standard of mothering. It was not necessary to explain the strangeness of these entries because the dominant ideology of motherhood has already constituted the terrain in which they are read. Neither the journalistic work involved in selecting certain entries nor the decontextualisation of those entries from others within the diary are apparent from the news item itself. The *Sydney Morning Herald* used a similar strategy when it first reported the diaries during trial, but in contrast to the *Daily Telegraph*, it made no reference to the defence's interpretive submission.[103]

Later in the trial, both newspapers reported some of the explanations that Folbigg gave for the diary entries in her police interview. In particular, they recorded Folbigg's assertions that her frustration was directed at herself or Craig rather than the children, and that her sense of responsibility for the children's deaths was related to her belief that she could have done more for them.[104] However, the *Daily Telegraph* item was framed by the headline 'Mother Wrote of "Losing Control"' and opening paragraph: 'A mother accused of smothering her four babies yesterday described her feelings of guilt and responsibility for their deaths.'[105] The *Sydney Morning Herald* is similarly headlined 'I Shouldn't be Writing it all Down, Folbigg Told Police'.[106] Both articles reinforce the sense that Folbigg's diary was overwhelmingly inculpatory. Neither reported Folbigg's general statements to police that the diaries should not be interpreted as literally true, nor her explanation that they did not capture the entirety of her experience of motherhood. While reporting some of the detail of Folbigg's exculpatory explanations, the two journalists screened out a broader interpretive context, which might have helped readers understand the diaries' place in Folbigg's mothering.

After Folbigg was convicted, the *Daily Telegraph* printed a long edited extract from Folbigg's diaries and correspondence.[107] The item included some extracts that suggest Folbigg felt warmly positive towards Laura. It also included some of the entries in which Folbigg complained about Craig's lack of support. Mostly,

---

[102] Kathleen Folbigg, diary entries quoted ibid. For further discussion of these particular diary entries, see above ch 7.

[103] Glendinning, 'Father Tells How the Wife He Loved Got on with Her Life' (above n 94).

[104] L Knowles, 'Mother Wrote of "Losing Control"' *Daily Telegraph* (30 April 2003) 19; and L Glendinning, 'I Shouldn't be Writing it all Down, Folbigg Told Police' *Sydney Morning Herald* (30 April 2003).

[105] Ibid.

[106] Glendinning, 'I Shouldn't be Writing it all Down' (above n 104).

[107] 'Monstress' (above n 33).

however, this item dwells on diary entries in which Folbigg confessed to feeling some ambivalence about Laura or the other children, expressed a lack of confidence in her mothering capacity or mental stability or hinted at having harmed her children. Interspersed letters from Folbigg to her foster sister presented the impression of a woman who knows how to mimic good motherhood in public but is privately incapable of living up to its standards. Reading this full-page item, which was published on the same day as the editorial in which the *Daily Telegraph* essentially denied Folbigg's humanity,[108] it is difficult to find a coherent internal logic to the newspaper's portrayal of Folbigg. While Folbigg's actions were roundly condemned, and she is ostracised by virtue of her 'poisonous depths', the diary extracts published in the *Daily Telegraph* do not disclose the unspeakable evil of which the editorial speaks.

In keeping with its openly analytical approach, the *Sydney Morning Herald*'s longest item about the diaries eschewed extensive extracts in favour of an article by Glendinning, who had 'read them all'.[109] This item began:

> Kathleen Folbigg loved the feeling of the baby moving and kicking inside her. Enjoyed the idea that her child was growing fat and healthy, and felt a happiness she never thought possible when she held her child in her arms.[110]

The fictionalised style in which this front-page Saturday item proceeds constructs the sense that Folbigg was literally unable to mother her children and similarly unable to control her desire to murder them. Drawing more explicitly than did the *Daily Telegraph* on motherhood as a performance, Glendinning described Folbigg as

> . . . living a conventional life with ordinary aspirations. It's one she never feels she fits into. Isolated, lonely, like everyone is a practised and rehearsed actor, but she doesn't belong in the play.[111]

In this passage, it is not clear whether Glendinning was quoting Folbigg's words or drawing directly from her diaries. In fact, Glendinning seems to have used her own metaphors to convey Folbigg's experience of motherhood. This is a subtle and complicated image – Folbigg's purported sense that everyone else was acting was contrasted with the 'ordinary' and 'conventional' life she was trying to lead. Folbigg's own words were conflated with Glendinning's interpretation, to the point where a reader may have trouble identifying where Folbigg's self-report leaves off and Glendinning's interpretation takes over. Within this grey area, Folbigg's (self-professed? legally proven? or simply journalistically asserted) inability to do what comes naturally to everyone else – or even to read the script that others take for granted – is what alienates her.

Glendinning did not explicitly write that the diaries contain a direct confession to murdering the children. This sense is, however, pervasive, from the statement that Folbigg 'filled her diaries with her deepest thoughts' to the observation that the

---

[108] See text to n 42 above.
[109] Glendinning, 'Incapable of Love' (above n 33).
[110] Ibid.
[111] Ibid.

'most damning' entries were 'used by the prosecution to convict her'.[112] This article mixed fact and fiction more thoroughly than many news items. Glendinning's right to speak for Folbigg's experience of motherhood is premised on the twin assumptions that the diaries provide a direct, unvarnished entry point to Folbigg's consciousness and that their meaning is self-evident to a journalist who has read the diaries and watched the trial. I criticised both of these assumptions above in chapter seven.

In co-opting Folbigg's voice and blending it with her own, Glendinning accomplished a discursive slippage that is similar to but more insidious than prosecutor Tedeschi SC's courtroom work with the diaries.[113] Unlike the jurors, the *Sydney Morning Herald* readers were not given the opportunity to compare Glendinning's interpretation with the diaries themselves. Furthermore, the fictionalised narrative presented as a news item did not simply conflate Folbigg's voice with Glendinning's interpretation, or even decontextualise that voice; it completely subsumed the diary entries. Finally, returning to the notion that newspapers provide the conduit by which a broader public becomes aware of what happens in criminal courts, the article rendered Folbigg's supposedly guilty subjectivity so obvious that few readers would question either the verdict or the correlate beliefs that Folbigg was a disturbed woman and a profoundly inadequate mother. Evidence that the children were healthy and well cared for, that they seemed comfortable and happy in their mother's presence, is screened out of this picture of a mother who was 'incapable of love'. A difficult and complicated trial thereby became a relatively straightforward morality tale about the type of mother who is likely to harm or kill her children. Implicitly, if the murderous mother is so self-evidently incapable of performing ordinary life, it is not too difficult to identify and contain her – one merely needs to take her self-doubt quite literally.[114]

The newspapers covered Craig Folbigg's testimony very closely during trial. Both newspapers interviewed Craig and published lengthy feature articles about him. The journalistic interest in Craig seems to have been prompted by two motivations. First, like the prosecution, the media used Craig as a primary definer of Kathleen Folbigg's character. Second, accepting that Kathleen was guilty of the crimes with which she was charged, both newspapers tried to understand how Craig could have remained in love and unsuspecting as Kathleen successively murdered their children. This second theme overlapped with and helped to give shape to the newspapers' depiction of Kathleen Folbigg's character, while also meditating on the defence attack on Craig's credibility. The defence argued at trial that Craig's evident love for Kathleen during their marriage and his repeated praise for her mothering qualities were more trustworthy indications of Kathleen's relationship with her children than Craig's adverse testimony.

---

[112] Ibid.

[113] Discussed above ch 7.

[114] Briar Wood has observed a similar quest to identify markers of maternal inadequacy in Lindy Chamberlain's case: B Wood, 'The Trials of Motherhood' in H Birch (ed), *Moving Targets: Women, Murder and Representation* (London, Virago Press, 1993) 69.

The notion that (even as an often absent husband) Craig possessed an authoritative understanding of Kathleen's character and particularly her mothering style was apparent both from the extent of print attention given to Craig and from the manner in which his words were reported. In the early days of the trial, the two newspapers conveyed some concerns about Craig's veracity, in particular reporting the defence case that Craig was testifying against Kathleen because he was vengeful after Kathleen left him. Nonetheless, Craig remained an important witness within these items:

> Craig Folbigg, the estranged husband of the woman accused of killing her four babies, admitted yesterday that he lied to police at his wife's demand because he was blinded by love . . .
>
> His wife's barrister, Peter Zahra, SC, asked him yesterday: '"I was in love with her" – was that why you are going to say, why you lied?'
>
> 'Yes, I guess I am,' Mr Folbigg replied. 'It wasn't for revenge, it was for concern.'[115]

The opening sentence to this item accepts Craig Folbigg's explanation for the inconsistency between his original (exculpatory) police statement and his subsequent, more damning testimony.[116] The verb 'admitted' used in this context suggests that Craig Folbigg has made some acknowledgement that reflects badly upon him. Reading on, the relevant concession seems to be that Craig was 'blinded by love', a condition that prompted him to lie to police but from which he has now emerged. A picture then developed throughout the remainder of the piece of a man who was untrustworthy in the past because he was manipulated by his wife. Implicitly, having freed himself from the constraints of an unhealthy relationship, his credibility is rehabilitated.

The moral responsibility for Craig's lies was laid at Kathleen's feet within the reporting – Craig lied 'at his wife's demand'. The article does not mention that Kathleen and Craig's telephone conversation was intercepted, and Kathleen had demanded that Craig return to the police station and 'tell them the truth'.[117] Craig argued that Kathleen meant 'her truth', that she was asking Craig to lie that she was a good and loving mother.[118] This evidence, which had the potential to cast light on Craig and Kathleen's respective sincerity, is glossed over within the first sentence. Having framed the story in this way, the news item goes on to quote Craig's out-of-court statement that he had lied to police in order to seek revenge on Kathleen for leaving him: 'I'll f--- your life, you f---ed mine. I'll go and tell some f---ing horrible things about you that the police think you did anyway.'[119] While the item signalled reason to be cautious about accepting Craig's evidence, it began and ended with Craig's narrative about the way things were with Kathleen:

---

[115] Glendinning, 'Father of Dead Babies Says He Lied' (above n 87).

[116] Craig Folbigg's testimony is reviewed above in ch 6.

[117] Craig Folbigg, cross-examination, *Folbigg* trial transcript (above n 19) 355.

[118] Ibid.

[119] Craig Folbigg, intercepted telephone conversation reported in Glendinning, 'Father of Dead Babies Says He Lied' (above n 87).

'[There are] parts of Kathy as a mum from when that little fella was born until he died that I kept to myself,' he told the court, 'I've carried stuff inside me for years.'[120]

Several days' reporting ultimately confirmed the impression that Craig held unique insights into Kathleen's capacity and failings as a mother. In particular, the *Sydney Morning Herald* framed its reports of the defence attack on Craig's credibility through Craig's evidence: that Kathleen did not seem to care about Laura's sleep monitor;[121] that Kathleen withdrew from social interactions after Sarah's death because she believed she was fat and not because she was grieving;[122] that Craig told Kathleen 'what I thought [she] would like to hear' when he praised her mothering, rather than speaking truthfully to her;[123] and that Kathleen had crudely expressed relief that she could get on with her life immediately after Laura's funeral.[124] While the defence submissions were mentioned in these items, Craig's perception defines the reports. Craig's assertion that Kathleen did not show the appropriate level of care and concern for her children during their lives or after their deaths became the dominant theme within the *Sydney Morning Herald*'s portrayal of Folbigg's mothering style.

The *Daily Telegraph* emphasised the extent to which Craig loved his children, juxtaposing a description of Craig's videotaped interactions with Laura in the family pool against Kathleen's alleged hostility towards Laura:

> Her father's voice can be heard on the video asking, 'Laura, show us how you use your kickboard, darling.'
>
> When she tries to clamber out of the pool, he advises 'Go up the step, bubby.'
>
> . . . Folbigg's estranged husband and Crown witness Craig Folbigg said he noticed that day that Laura had steered clear of her mother. When he asked his wife about it, she told him 'she's got the shits with me. . . I lost it with her.'
>
> She told him how she had screamed at Laura the day before for following her around the house causing her to fall over.
>
> The day Laura died, Mr Folbigg said his wife had pinned the toddler's hands to her highchair table, tried to force feed her and let out a 'guttural growl', screaming 'I can't handle her when she's like this.'
>
> Later that day, Mr Folbigg said he received a call to say Laura was at hospital, where she was later pronounced dead.[125]

In this passage, the story of Laura's death was told to *Daily Telegraph* readers for the first time. The loving tones in which Craig spoke confirmed his appropriate parenting skills and reinforced his capacity to provide insight into Kathleen's failings. Kathleen's reported aggression, her use of physical force and crude language seem incompatible with the unstinting warmth and patience expected of a mother, and doubly so when compared with Craig's manner. Subsequent items

---

[120] Glendinning, 'Father of Dead Babies Says He Lied' (above n 87).
[121] Glendinning, 'Diary Stirred Grieving Father's Doubts' (above n 100).
[122] L Glendinning, 'Folbigg Changed His Story, Court Told' *Sydney Morning Herald* (9 April 2003) 8.
[123] L Glendinning, 'Folbigg Great as a Mother, Letter Said' *Sydney Morning Herald* (10 April 2003) 9.
[124] L Glendinning, 'Court Hears of Folbigg's Relief after Funeral' *Sydney Morning Herald* (11 April 2003) 10.
[125] Knowles, 'Mother's Tears at Home Video' (above n 99).

reported the defence submission that Craig's evidence was exaggerated, highlighting Craig's propensity to swear in conversation.[126] These items skated over the particulars of that submission, including the suggestion that Craig had fabricated Folbigg's alleged violence to Laura at breakfast and other inculpatory behaviour. This submission was premised on the uncontested fact that Craig had related these events for the first time at trial, despite having given several detailed statements to police over the preceding two years:

> Mr Folbigg denied he had tried to portray 'normal domestic situations' as more sinister over time.
>
> He said it was 'incorrect' that he had sought to minimise his wife's grief by telling the jury she 'cried on cue' and went to the gym on the first Monday after Laura's funeral.[127]

The use of quotation marks in this extract, without direct attribution to Zahra SC, invited readers who recalled Kathleen's alleged words or actions from earlier items to judge for themselves whether Craig's evidence related to normal domestic situations. The defence submission as reported in this item seemed to minimise the seriousness of Kathleen's alleged actions, rather than questioning whether the episodes ever occurred.

The cross-examination from which this item was taken suggested that Craig had fabricated entire incidents, as well as exaggerating some events. A typical extract is:

```
Q. I put it to you that you exaggerated the tone of your
conversation.

A. That's not correct.

. . .

Q. You have attempted wrongly to suggest that she wasn't
properly caring for the child that morning?

A. That's not correct.

. . .

Q. She did not say words to the effect of, 'I've lost it with
her' as you suggested?

A. She did say those things.

. . .

Q. I put to you that she told you that she had inadvert-
ently knocked over the child and that the child had become
upset as a result of that.

A. Yes, that's true.[128]
```

---

[126] L Knowles, 'Revenge or Grief: Denial by Accused Woman's Husband' *Daily Telegraph* (8 April 2003) 11; and L Knowles, 'Father Joked: "I'm Going to Hire Harry M. Miller"' *Daily Telegraph* (9 April 2003) 23.

[127] L Knowles, 'Love Letter to Suspect Mum' *Daily Telegraph* (10 April 2003) 15.

[128] Craig Folbigg, cross-examination, *Folbigg* trial transcript (above n 19) 406–7 (9 Apr 2003).

Zahra there went on to secure Craig's agreement that he had not previously told police or the prosecution about Kathleen's alleged violence towards Laura on the morning of Laura's death, despite attending police interviews and conferences with the prosecutor.[129] Craig's evidence that Kathleen was violent towards Laura appeared unchallenged within the news reports published in the *Daily Telegraph*.

By the time that Folbigg was convicted, the *Sydney Morning Herald* had come to portray Craig as another of Kathleen's victims. His lack of suspicion was rendered understandable: 'Post-mortems had not found anything suspicious about the deaths of their babies, so why should he suspect his wife?'[130] In a long feature article that 'explores the abiding mysteries of the Folbigg marriage', the journalist described Craig's pleasure in fatherhood, his drive to find a medical explanation for the children's deaths and his transition from denial to belief that Kathleen had murdered their children. Remarkably, given how hotly Craig's veracity was contested in court, the episodes that he related for the first time at trial are cited as examples of an 'almost photographic memory':

> Craig has what he calls a 'flashbulb' memory for dates, times, clothing. It was all like a videotape in his head. He could recall every event – including everything that he came to see as not quite right.[131]

This passage rescued Craig from the defence assertions that he was lying or exaggerating when he related episodes for the first time at trial. A 'videotape' is often understood as the most reliable form of evidence because, judges and jurors presume, it cannot be manipulated or made to show what is not there.[132] If Craig was testifying from a videotape in his head, it is implicit that he was accessing an authentic, pre-existent reality rather than offering a changing and contestable interpretation of events within the Folbigg family.

The journalist also depicted the defence's criticisms of Craig as strategically motivated and therefore unfair or untruthful:

> The defence painted him as of dubious character, someone who had lied to police (to protect his wife), a car salesman who would use his children's deaths to sell cars, and who intended to hire Harry M. Miller[133] to handle the media.[134]

This is a remarkable list. Craig testified that he had lied to police to protect his wife; the defence argued that he was lying when he testified at trial. Similarly, the posited allegation that Craig 'would use his children's deaths to sell cars' came from an intercepted phone conversation in which Craig said exactly that,[135] as did the suggestion that Craig planned to hire Harry M. Miller.[136] The verb 'painted'

---

[129] Ibid.
[130] L Glendinning, 'Hear No Evil, See No Evil' *Sydney Morning Herald* (24–25 May 2003) 33.
[131] Ibid.
[132] But see JM Silbey, 'Cross-Examining Film' (2009) 8 *University of Maryland Law Journal of Race, Religion, Gender and Class* 1.
[133] A well-known celebrity publicist.
[134] Glendinning, 'Hear No Evil, See No Evil' (above n 130).
[135] Craig Folbigg, cross-examination, *Folbigg* trial transcript (above n 19) 246.
[136] Ibid, 314.

insinuates that these were baseless allegations, and the article missed the opportunity to explore the more important question whether these matters and other inconsistent statements were sufficient to discredit Craig's testimony about Kathleen's behaviour. Instead, the guilty verdict was read as a vindication of Craig's character. The concerns about Craig's conduct throughout the investigation, which were reflected in the *Sydney Morning Herald*'s earlier reporting,[137] were repudiated in favour of a saccharine rendition of the loving, concerned father who became the unwitting dupe of a manipulative, murderous mother.

Unlike the *Sydney Morning Herald*, the *Daily Telegraph* eventually conveyed some of the questions that swirled around Craig's credibility. As well as reproducing diary entries in which Kathleen expressed concerns about Craig's lack of support,[138] the *Daily Telegraph* also published an item based on an interview between Craig and journalist Knowles. This interview was conducted before the trial, but the item was printed after the guilty verdict. Printed under the headline 'Trio who Solved a Deadly Puzzle: The Husband', the item was largely positive about Craig, but it also raised questions about his motives. For example:

> Craig had also taken countless hours of videos of Laura. Realising that she was so precious after what they had lost, he was keen to capture everything about her.
>
> During the trial, Craig conducted lengthy negotiations with the media, offering to sell these images – claiming the money would form a trust fund in memory of the children.
>
> He also spoke of using the money to provide for the children he hopes to have with his new fiancée.[139]

The significance of this information was not pursued, but it resonates with the suggestion that Craig's actions throughout the police investigation and trial were partly motivated by self-interest or revenge. While Kathleen came off badly in this article (she 'demanded that the children's ashes be laid to rest properly' despite Craig's desire to keep them at home and then 'didn't attend' the ceremony), Craig was not constructed as a wholly trustworthy source. The item reported Craig's intercepted statement that he had lied to police when he inculpated Kathleen 'because I was full of hate and spite and anxiety and grief and anguish over the fact that not only had I lost my daughter, I'd lost my wife'. Although Craig did not emerge unsullied from this article, his insight into Kathleen's emotions and motivations was confirmed by the editorial decision to name him as one of the three people who 'solved a deadly puzzle' about the Folbigg children's deaths. The article ended with the observation that Craig 'now emphatically believes Kathy killed the four children'.[140]

---

[137] Including Glendinning, 'Father of Dead Babies Says He Lied' (above n 87).
[138] 'Monstress' (above n 33).
[139] F O'Shea, 'Trio who Solved a Deadly Puzzle: The Husband' *Daily Telegraph* (22 May 2003) 4.
[140] Ibid.

IV. Conclusion

Newspapers are an important public source of information about the criminal justice system and, especially, particular criminal cases. Ericson, Baranek and Chan have noted that newspapers have the capacity to produce longer and more detailed news stories than other media such as radio or television.[141] For this reason, they provide a fertile site for research into public information about criminal justice. Even so, news articles can only capture a small fraction of the events that take place in court on any given day. In light of that constraint, the fact of selectivity within news reporting is less interesting than the editorial and journalistic choices made on a daily basis about what to report and how prominently to report it.[142] When exercising selectivity, journalists also perform the task of narrativising events – ie, constructing a story about what happened. As Patricia Ewick and Susan Silbey have written, 'narrativizing is impossible without moralizing.'[143] The process of converting a day's court proceeding into a story with a beginning, middle and end is necessarily also a process of fitting the proceeding into pre-existing conceptions of moral order.[144] When a newspaper is reporting a continuing story, the narrative operates at two levels: individual news items must be intelligible to readers on a stand-alone basis; and across the life of the story, one or more meta-narratives will often emerge.

Both the *Daily Telegraph* and the *Sydney Morning Herald* systematically and chronically attended more closely to the prosecution story of the *Folbigg* case than to the defence. Within individual news items and over the life of the story, this created the impression that Folbigg had little or no answer to the allegations made against her. The selectivity that permitted this impression to persist is most apparent when one compares particular news items with the transcripts of evidence that they reported. The Australian Press Council, which self-regulates Australian print media, publishes a statement of principles against which it evaluates complaints about press reporting. These principles enshrine the journalistic value of balance. For example:

> 5. Publications are free to advocate their own views and publish the views of others on controversial topics, as long as readers are readily able to recognise what is fact and what is opinion. Relevant facts should not be misrepresented or suppressed, headlines and captions should fairly reflect the tenor of an article and readers should be advised of any manipulation of images and potential conflicts of interest . . .

---

[141] Ericson, Baranek and Chan (above n 4) 22.

[142] W Haltom and M McCann, *Distorting the Law: Politics, Media, and the Litigation Crisis* (Chicago, University of Chicago Press, 2004) 266.

[143] P Ewick and S Silbey, 'Subversive Stories and Hegemonic Tales: Towards a Sociology of Narrative' (1995) *Law & Society Review* 197, 201, citing H White, *The Content of the Form* (Baltimore, John Hopkins University Press, 1987).

[144] See also Ericson, Baranek and Chan (above n 4) introduction.

8. Where individuals or groups are singled out for criticism, the publication should ensure fairness and balance in the original article. Failing that, it should provide a reasonable and swift opportunity for a balancing response in the appropriate section of the publication.[145]

In this chapter, I have demonstrated that both major Sydney newspapers failed to strike a balance when reporting the *Folbigg* trial. Both numerically and qualitatively, content disproportionately favoured the prosecution case against Folbigg.

---

[145] Australian Press Council, 'Statement of Principles', www.presscouncil.org.au/pcsite/complaints/sop.html.

9

Conclusion

T HE LEAST SATISFYING conclusion is one that insists upon uncertainty. Uncertainty is, however, the prevailing theme of contemporary medical and legal knowledges about recurrent unexplained infant death. I began this project with a sense of unease about the confidence with which judges and journalists rejected Kathleen Folbigg's claim that she had not killed her four children. This unease was informed by the controversy that raged about the likely causes of recurrent unexplained infant death. As Folbigg's case is the only similar example in Australia or England in which a conviction still stands, I hoped to understand what distinguished Folbigg's case from others in which mothers had been given the benefit of the doubt. Accordingly, this book has traversed the territory of Kathleen Folbigg's trial, including the medical and cultural knowledges from which the legal process emerged and to which it returned.

This concluding chapter draws the strands of this book together in an effort to assess what my research has revealed about the relationship between medicine, motherhood, criminal justice and the media. In light of the findings of the previous chapters, does Folbigg's conviction remain as sound as it appeared to appeal courts and journalists? It is not possible or necessary to say how Folbigg's children died. Rather, the current state of medical knowledge raises questions about whether it is possible fairly to conclude beyond a reasonable doubt that they were murdered. In this book, I have documented how Kathleen Folbigg was wrongly convicted.

I. The *Folbigg* Case

Remarkably, as the medical community's adherence to a criminal explanation for multiple infant deaths became more uncertain, several of the prosecution experts involved in the Folbigg case became increasingly sure that these deaths must be murder. Connecting the evidence presented at trial to the broader research literature, it appears that the medical narrative that prevailed in Folbigg's trial was premised in large part on an abiding suspicion of mothers in general, and this mother in particular.

It appears from the textual record that some experts and Craig Folbigg became increasingly certain of Kathleen Folbigg's guilt as the trial progressed. Knowingly or unknowingly, their testimony at trial conveyed a confidence that did not exist in the early stages of the investigation. This growing certainty seems to have been a result of the adversarial process and perhaps of the desire to secure a conviction. It did not reflect any change in the witnesses' material knowledge about the facts of the case.[1]

A second theme that emerges from analysis of the *Folbigg* case is the preparedness of expert witnesses (including defence pathologist Roger Byard) to generalise extemporaneously – and wrongly – about the state of medical knowledge. The evidence that medical literature did not reliably report any case in which three or more infants from the same family died of natural unexplained causes was simply incorrect. Research published since Folbigg's trial has cast further doubt on the criminal explanation for recurrent unexplained infant death. The unanimous testimony that medical literature did not report natural recurrent unexplained deaths may have had a significant impact on the trial.

Third, it appears from my analysis that gendered knowledges about motherhood inform the process of allocating criminal responsibility in subtle ways. The diagnosis of likely cause of infant death is influenced by a particular expert's expectations of what constitutes adequate caregiving. Mothers who do not meet normative expectations of motherhood may become doubly vulnerable if a pathologist's diagnosis, which draws adverse conclusions in part from that failure to meet expectations, is used as independent validation of behavioural evidence against them. Folbigg did not appear to fit this category when her children were autopsied, although Allan Cala would seemingly have placed her in this category solely by virtue of the number of infant deaths in the Folbigg family. It is, however, likely that emergent information such as the diaries informed experts' trial testimony and expert reports about how her children died.[2] Similarly, Craig Folbigg's testimony regarding Kathleen's alleged violence towards Laura and Sarah may also have influenced experts who heard or became aware of that testimony before they testified. If so, the expert evidence was not independent of the behavioural evidence, contrary to the NSW Court of Criminal Appeal's apparent assumptions.

Finally, comparing daily transcripts with news items, it becomes apparent that in this case, journalists chronically and systematically ignored exculpatory narra-

---

[1] By 'material', I am alluding to information that properly fits within the sphere of that witness's testimonial capacity. Craig Folbigg gave far more incriminating testimony at trial than the statements he had given police after they found both of Kathleen Folbigg's diaries. Experts who testified about likely causes of death did not allude to the diaries, and arguably it falls outside their expertise to have regard to the diaries or to Folbigg's demeanour when she was being interviewed by police, when the question at issue is the likely cause of death based on autopsy and an associated death investigation. See ST Goudge, *Inquiry into Pediatric Forensic Pathology in Ontario Report* (Toronto, Queen's Printer for Ontario, 2008) [Goudge Report] 380–84.

[2] Based on the fact that the prosecution's expert witnesses were given copies of Folbigg's police interview and other documents when preparing their opinions. See *R v Kathleen Megan Folbigg*, (14 April 2003), New South Wales 70046/02 (NSWSC) [*Folbigg* trial transcript] 983–88.

tives. Far from providing a balanced depiction of the events in court, the news reporting perpetuated and entrenched a sense that Folbigg had no answer to the charges against her.

II. Comparing Folbigg with its Companion Cases

In his expert report for *R v Matthey*, Stephen Cordner, the chief pathologist of the Victorian Institute for Forensic Medicine, wrote, 'There is no merit in forcing certainty where uncertainty exists.'[3] In *R v Cannings*, the Court of Appeal of England and Wales observed regarding recurrent infant death that 'such deaths can and do occur naturally, even when they are unexplained.'[4] Lord Justice Judge warned:

> [G]reat care must be taken not to allow the rarity of these sad events, standing on their own, to be subsumed into an assumption or virtual assumption that the dead infants were deliberately killed, or consciously or unconsciously to regard the inability of the defendant to produce some convincing explanation for these deaths as providing a measure of support for the Prosecution's case.[5]

Similarly, in the three cases of *Phillips*, *Clark* and *Anthony*, courts held that mothers must be given the benefit of scientific uncertainty about how infants died. *Phillips*, *Clark* and *Anthony* also emphasised that it is inappropriate to rely on ambiguous behavioural evidence to supplement inadequate scientific knowledge.[6]

Nonetheless, in *Folbigg*, the trial judge concluded, 'The arguments in favour of natural explanations for the deaths and Patrick's ALTE were unimpressive in light of the whole of the evidence.'[7] The NSW Court of Appeal affirmed that it was possible for the jury to conclude that none of the four deaths was caused by an identified natural cause. The *Folbigg* appeal court also held that the possibility of each event being caused by an unidentified natural cause was 'a debating point possibility and not . . . a reasonable possibility'.[8]

Two factors seemingly differentiate *Folbigg* from its companion cases. First, the *Folbigg* trial court never learned about medical research that supports a natural explanation for recurrent unexplained infant death. This research was not put before the NSW Court of Criminal Appeal either, except to the extent that it was reflected in the decisions in *Clark* and *Cannings*. The lack of evidence about natural

---

[3] S Cordner, expert report quoted in *R v Matthey* [2007] VSC 398. For further discussion of *Matthey*, see above ch 1.

[4] *R v Cannings* [2004] EWCA Crim 1 para 138. For further discussion of *Cannings*, see above ch 1.

[5] Ibid, para 177.

[6] *R v Phillips* [1999] NSWSC 1175; *R v Clark* [2003] EWCA Crim 1020; and *R v Anthony* [2005] EWCA Crim 952. For further discussion of these cases, see above ch 1.

[7] *R v Folbigg*, 7 May 2003 (Unreported, NSWSC, Barr J) para 32. ALTE stands for acute or apparent life-threatening episode. For further discussion of this term, see above ch 1, n 19.

[8] *R v KF* (2005) 152 A Crim R 35, [2005] NSWCCA 23 (17 February 2005) para 186.

recurrent unexplained death was compounded by some positive statements by expert witnesses that any such research was non-existent or, at best, unreliable. Second, Folbigg's diaries contained troubling admissions that seemed to suggest that Folbigg believed she had caused her children's deaths. In the next section, I consider the medical evidence and suggest how the courts' approach to contentious medical evidence might be improved. In the section that follows, I turn to the diaries and behavioural evidence.

III. Approaching Contentious Medical Evidence

Doubt is managed within a criminal trial in particular ways. Evidentiary and persuasive burdens are carefully allocated, and minimum standards of reliability apply to some kinds of evidence. Medical scientists also confront uncertainty and try to circumscribe their conclusions accordingly. Despite sharing an interest in managing uncertainty, lawyers and medical experts do not always understand one another's methods or vocabularies. The difficulties of translating knowledge from one field to another are demonstrated by the wrongful convictions arising from unexplained infant deaths during the last two decades.[9] This book has explored how and when mistranslations occur at the intersection of law and medicine. These mistranslations became most apparent when evidence given in a particular case is compared with broader debates within the medical literature.

The Medical Evidence in Folbigg

When the NSW Court of Criminal Appeal reviewed the medical evidence against Folbigg it held that:

- the jury was entitled to conclude that it was not reasonably possible that any single Folbigg child died of an identified natural cause of death; and
- it was similarly possible to exclude identified natural causes of Patrick's acute life threatening episode (ALTE).

Having excluded identified causes of death and illness, the second question posed by the NSW Court of Criminal Appeal was whether it was reasonably possible that each child died of unidentified natural causes. Sully JA held that the jury could answer 'no' to this second question. He relied upon the evidence given by prosecution experts and defence pathologist Byard that the scientific literature did not reliably report any case in which a family suffered three or more SIDS deaths.[10] No evidence was presented at trial or appeal to suggest that the informa-

---

[9] Eg, *Clark* (above n 6); *Cannings* (above n 4); *Anthony* (above n 6); and the cases described in the Goudge Report (above n 1).

[10] *R v Folbigg* [2005] NSWCCA 23.

tion before the jury was incorrect. My review in chapter four of the expert knowledge regarding recurrent unexpected infant death suggests that the jury and the court were misled by the experts' answers.

Chapter four explains that medical knowledge regarding recurrent unexplained infant death lacks consensus. Individual experts' opinions are coloured by their belief about whether caregivers should receive the benefit of uncertainty about cause of death.[11] Experts also disagree about the extent of uncertainty presented by particular deaths. Peer-reviewed articles certainly report cases of multiple natural unexplained infant deaths in individual families, and the authors of these studies stand by the correctness of their conclusions. Perhaps the *Folbigg* experts who testified that no multiple unexplained infant deaths were reported within the medical literature were reinterpreting published findings according to some unstated version of Roy Meadow's controversial theory about the conclusions to be drawn from the fact of multiple infant deaths in a given family.[12] Possibly, they were simply unaware of the published studies, although there are glimpses within the transcript and in other cases that at least some experts were aware of these studies. The criminal law provides the benefit of uncertainty to an accused. If they are to be useful to the court, expert opinions that are introduced into a criminal courtroom should at a minimum identify areas of uncertainty. The evidence presented at Folbigg's trial and relied upon in the appeal judgment misrepresented the extent of uncertainty within paediatric forensic pathology about the likely cause of repeat unexpected infant death.

At Folbigg's trial, the expert witnesses were expressly prohibited from having regard to the pattern of infant deaths within the Folbigg family when ascribing the cause of death to any individual child. I explain in chapters two and five that Grahame Barr J characterised the reasoning that multiple unexplained infant deaths are more likely to be homicide as common sense, which is within the jury's exclusive preserve. Nonetheless, this reasoning seemingly emerged within the expert evidence. The expert testimony that multiple natural unexplained infant deaths were unknown within the medical literature was crucial to this re-emergence. Similarly, as I explain below, some experts may have given opinions about the causes of individual deaths that were predicated on the pattern of deaths, despite being cautioned not to do so.

A further factor, which was canvassed in *Cannings*, is also important to *Folbigg*. I explain in chapter four that some findings on autopsy, such as the presence of blood in the nose or mouth, pressure marks on the lower face or torn skin inside the mouth, are considered to be more consistent with smothering than natural infant death. These signs seem to be more likely to appear as an infant becomes older. From the court record, it appears that none of the Folbigg children had

---

[11] Sheila Jasanoff has similarly identified that scientific debate within the courtroom exposes the social commitments of individual experts more predictably than it identifies contingencies within scientific knowledge: S Jasanoff, *Science at the Bar: Law, Science and Technology in America* (Cambridge, MA, Harvard University Press, 1995) 211.

[12] For a full discussion of Meadow's law, see above ch 4, s III.

these indicia on autopsy. This is perhaps most significant in relation to Laura, who was thoroughly examined by a pathologist who suspected homicide, and who was 19 months old when she died.[13] John Napier Hilton, who autopsied Sarah, pointed at trial to an absence of positive signs when defending his decision to ascribe Sarah's death to sudden infant death syndrome (SIDS). In *Cannings*, Judge LJ observed:

> It is of course possible to smother a baby without leaving any physical signs discernible on medical examination or at post mortem. Nevertheless, given that all four children were said by the Crown to have been subjected to violence sufficient to cause death, the absence of any physical signs of injury was somewhat surprising.[14]

In contrast and despite Hilton's evidence regarding the absence of physical signs of injury, little attention was paid at trial by either party to the fact that none of the Folbigg children had positive signs of smothering when they died. Perhaps this inattentiveness reflects the extent to which the enquiry at trial came to focus on Folbigg's (in)ability to prove how her children died. This focus probably arose because the prosecution's medical evidence seemed overwhelmingly persuasive, particularly when coupled with Folbigg's diaries. Subtle objections made by the defence and some expert witnesses to the prosecution reasoning were either misunderstood or swamped by the apparent weight of prosecution evidence. Whatever the causes of this shift in focus, the adversarial flattening of a complex field of medical research ultimately and unfairly worked to Folbigg's detriment at trial.

The medical evidence against Folbigg should be reconsidered in light of the literature review contained above in chapters three and four. The evidence heard at trial was at best a partial representation of the expert community's approach to determining the causes of infant death. The evidence given about recurrent unexplained infant death was particularly flawed. Additional concerns arise from the criticism levelled by Coldrey J at *Folbigg* prosecution experts Cala, Susan Mitchell Beal and Janice Ophoven in the later *Matthey* decision;[15] the disappearance of questions about why none of the four children had any positive signs of smothering; the inadequate attention paid to the ways in which individual expert opinions shifted over the course of the case; and the subsequent changes to the American Academy of Pediatrics (AAP) Policy Statement on unexplained infant death, on which Cala relied in court.[16]

Thinking beyond the Case: Legal and Medical Knowledges

While the immediate focus of this book is Kathleen Folbigg's trial, the review contained in chapters three and four also extends Sheila Jasanoff's challenge to legal

---

[13] That is, well above the age most often quoted as the upper limit of indiscernible smothering, which is 12 months.

[14] *Cannings* (above n 4) para 160.

[15] *Matthey* (above n 3).

[16] For discussion of the AAP Policy Statements, see above ch 5, s II.

conceptualisations of scientific knowledge. My methodology allows me to provide some empirical support for Jasanoff's conceptualisation of law and science (in this case, medical science) as co-producers of hegemonic knowledge. For example, the content and limits of 'scientific knowledge' about recurrent unexplained infant death have been shown to be co-constructed with the evidence itself as the trial unfolded. Future research using transcripts and court records may reveal that these patterns repeat themselves.

Jasanoff has suggested that courts tend to 'shop' for scientific knowledge in the hope that science might provide 'facts untouched by values or social interests'.[17] Chapters three and four demonstrate that the range of problems and the answers generated within medical research are at least partly informed by cultural conceptions of what constitutes incompetent, neglectful or dangerous parenting. Lacking conclusive physical signs of smothering, child death investigators ground 'scientific' conclusions in culturally relative judgments about the caregiver's competence and trustworthiness. Different child death review teams may variously classify the cause of a given infant death as natural or unnatural. These differences correlate with the harshness of the team's judgment regarding a parent's caregiving capabilities.[18]

Jasanoff has also suggested that legal proceedings influence 'the production of new scientific knowledge and techniques'.[19] An important theme emerging from chapters three and four is the extent to which some cases, particularly those that attract public attention, affect the course of medical research. In chapter three, I describe Waneta Hoyt's 1995 conviction for murdering her children in New York State and the attention that conviction received within paediatric forensic pathology. This conviction, coupled with the inconclusive results of research predicated on Alfred Steinschneider's apnoea hypothesis,[20] enabled a more suspicious discourse to eclipse the welfarist and public health model of studying infant death. Given that paediatric forensic pathology is imbricated with social and legal knowledges about good parenting, the judicial practice of using medical knowledge to provide independent validation of social and legal reasoning begs reconsideration.

An unexpected finding of my research is that some medical scientists also invoke legal verdicts as providing independent validation of their knowledge and conclusions. The best example is Meadow's 1999 assertion that his research had been validated by the putatively rigorous judicial process of assessing expert evidence.[21] Subsequent reversals to the convictions in *Clark*, *Cannings* and *Anthony* have cast considerable doubt on Meadow's reasoning. More generally, the English cases cast doubt on the proposition that law is presently systematically capable of providing a rigorous second opinion on the causes of infant deaths.

---

[17] Jasanoff (above n 11) 207.
[18] P Fleming et al, *Sudden Unexpected Deaths in Infancy: The CESDI SUDI Studies 1993–1996* (London, The Stationery Office, 2000) 113.
[19] Jasanoff (above n 11) 50.
[20] For further discussion of Steinschneider's apnoea hypothesis, see above ch 3, s II.
[21] R Meadow, 'Unnatural Sudden Infant Death' (1999) 80 *Archives of Disease in Childhood* 7, 10.

This study has demonstrated that some knowledge emerging from paediatric forensic pathology has been decontextualised and co-opted for purposes far removed from the authors' original intent. The starkest example of this mistranslation is the ways in which work by John Emery and colleagues has been used within paediatric pathology and criminology. This work has frequently been cited to support the proposition that a significant number of parents who kill their children are either undetected or do not receive any criminal sanction in circumstances in which such sanction is warranted. This misconstruction has consistently been challenged within the scientific literature, but it has received little contest within criminology.

In chapter four, I suggest that this type of mistranslation might be avoided if criminologists and legal scholars differentiated rigorously between three categories of infant death:

1. **Category one deaths**, which are identified on autopsy alone as probable deliberately inflicted deaths (for example, through anatomical, histological or toxicological findings);
2. **Category two deaths**, which forensic pathologists, coroners or police identify as probable deliberate smothering deaths, based on the death investigation or 'psychosocial' information about the infant's family, perhaps in combination with findings on autopsy; and
3. **Category three deaths**, which are deliberately inflicted but not identified as such through autopsy, death investigation or otherwise, either because a thorough investigation is not performed or because the death is indistinguishable from a death by natural causes.

None of these categories corresponds with the criminal requirements of proof beyond a reasonable doubt. Categories one and two provide a baseline from which criminal outcomes might be studied. Such assessments should not make the simplistic assumption that every death within those categories should lead to a guilty verdict or even a criminal charge. This taxonomy avoids the tendency to conflate identifiable smothering deaths with those deaths that are unidentifiable after full autopsies and death investigations.

Chapter four also provides a survey of original empirical research into multiple unexplained infant deaths. The published studies vary enormously in methodology, size of research population and conclusions. Early recurrence studies tended to focus on estimating the likelihood of a genetic predisposition, on generating new ways to study the causes of unexplained infant death and on how best to advise parents who have suffered unexplained infant death. As the possibility that recurrent infant deaths might actually be covert homicides came to seem more real, some researchers focused on estimating the likely extent of covert homicide. Some of the published studies arguably began with an assumption that recurrent unexplained infant deaths *were* homicides and proceeded accordingly. Others, notably Robert Carpenter and colleagues, have insisted that thorough autopsy and death investigation is the best way to distinguish natural from unnatural deaths, even when a family experiences recurrent unexplained infant deaths.[22] Carpenter and colleagues have emphasised the continuing uncertainty about what causes some multiple infant deaths. I suggest in chapter four that studies such as Carpenter's are least likely to lead criminal courts into error. These studies are appropriate to criminal proceedings because they identify uncertainty rather than obscuring it and because they provide caregivers with the benefit of doubts that forensic pathology cannot presently resolve.

The Admissibility Enquiry and Trial Safeguards

Judges have sought to identify and expel rogue experts from the trial process. Those who have studied systemic failures have redesigned the admissibility enquiry to reduce the criminal justice system's vulnerability to poor-quality expert evidence.[23] These analyses are predicated on a belief that it is possible to distinguish between reliable and unreliable expert evidence with a more thorough admissibility enquiry. They seek to exclude evidence that risks misleading judges and juries. In chapters one, four and five, I suggest that these procedural safeguards have the potential to reduce the risk of wrongful convictions.

Chapter four proposes an approach to expert forensic pathological evidence that is informed by the criminal requirement of proof beyond a reasonable doubt. This approach requires a pathologist who ascribes an unnatural cause of death to describe the investigations and reasoning process that led to his or her conclusion. The expert should be capable of situating that reasoning process within the scientific literature and particularly of describing any areas of scientific doubt or uncertainty. Minimally, this requires a pathology expert to be familiar with relevant published literature, able to explain the limits of knowledge within the field and capable of delineating differences of opinion within his or her field. *Cannings* arguably also mandates an acquittal when reputable experts disagree about cause of death and there is no other cogent evidence of deliberate harm.[24] At least in this context, it is inadequate simply to allow a jury to choose which of two conflicting but reputable opinions it prefers.

[22] RG Carpenter et al, 'Repeat Sudden Unexpected and Unexplained Infant Deaths: Natural or Unnatural?' (2005) 365 *The Lancet* 29.

[23] Most relevantly, see the recommendations made in the Goudge Report (above n 1), as well as the principles that emerge from *Clark* (above n 6); *Cannings* (above n 4); *Anthony* (above n 6); and *Matthey* (above n 3). See also H Kennedy, 'Sudden Unexpected Death in Infancy: A Multi-Agency Protocol for Care and Investigation' (Royal College of Pathologists and Royal College of Paediatrics and Child Health, London, 2004).

[24] *Cannings* (above n 4) para 178. The Court of Appeal of England and Wales elaborated upon and arguably limited this principle in *R v Kai-Whitewind* [2005] EWCA Crim 1092; however, in that case there was relatively strong evidence of a pattern of physical abuse to the single child whose death was at stake. The Court of Appeal emphasised the need to consider *Cannings* in its legal and factual context and in particular the fact that, in *Cannings*, 'nothing, or virtually nothing at post-mortem revealed factual material which assisted the Crown's experts and supported their view': *Kai-Whitewind*, para 77. The physical evidence in the *Folbigg* case is far more closely analogous to *Cannings* than *Kai-Whitewind* was.

To these requirements, it may help to add a particular caution about experts who have changed their views over the course of a proceeding. When an expert shifts from expressing a tentative or probable opinion to a firmer view, it seems appropriate for counsel and trial judges to explore the reasons and justifications for this shift. A particular risk arises when an expert shifts his or her opinion from acknowledging the possibility of a natural cause of death to a stronger insistence upon an inflicted cause such as smothering. In chapter five, I describe how prosecution pathologist Cala, who autopsied Laura Folbigg, underwent such a shift over the course of the *Folbigg* case. Before trial, Cala suggested that myocarditis might have been his preferred cause of Laura's death if there had not been previous deaths in the family. At trial, Cala was prohibited from considering the other children's deaths when giving his opinion about the cause of Laura's death. Nonetheless, Cala testified before the jury that it was not reasonably possible that Laura had died of myocarditis. Cala did not provide any information that would allow the judge or parties to assess why he had changed his position. Despite Barr J's observation that Cala's testimony on cause of death surprised him, the jury never learned that Cala's opinion had changed. In chapter five, I note that the doctors who investigated Patrick's ALTE and death also testified in a way that contradicted their original findings. The shifting positions at trial seem to reflect the risk that individual experts may harden their views during the adversarial process. These shifts during *Folbigg* warranted closer scrutiny than they received at trial or upon appeal. As I next explain, the shifts that occurred while the prosecution was making its case against Folbigg are further illuminated by a gender analysis of mothers' murder trials.

IV. The Dominant Ideology of Motherhood

Many published discussions of *Clark*, *Cannings* and *Anthony* exclude a gender analysis in preference to focusing on scientific evidence. Nonetheless, a gender analysis is important – and perhaps inevitable – when a mother is accused of killing her children. Medical and legal enquiries into cause of death assume that dangerous mothers can be identified in part through their lack of compliance with a dominant ideology of motherhood. In chapters six and seven, I explore how Folbigg was constructed as a distinctively dangerous mother and explain how that construction contributed to her conviction.

The gendered domestic arrangements within the Folbigg family were reconstructed at trial as distinctive similarities between the charged incidents, which supported the inference that the four deaths and Patrick's ALTE were caused by Kathleen Folbigg. Before the trial, the prosecution relied upon a coincidence schedule that contained a number of precise similarities that were not ultimately proven. The prosecution's final coincidence schedule largely consisted of asserted 'coincidences' that were more incidental to Folbigg's primary caregiving role than compelling evidence of smothering. Examples of such factors include the facts that Folbigg found each of her children dead and that they died at home during sleep periods. The decision to rely on coincidence factors that were linked inextricably to the privatised, gendered allocation of caregiving was inappropriate because the prosecution did not demonstrate that these factors rationally affected the probability that the Folbigg children were murdered. Relatedly, *Phillips, Clark* and *Cannings* provide germane warnings against reasoning from a belief that a mother must be guilty when assessing the probative value of coincidence evidence. The coincidence reasoning should also have been undermined by a dispute about whether Caleb and Sarah, who died at night, were warm to the touch when found. However, the jury's attention was not drawn to this dispute. On the prosecution's case, Folbigg killed her children and then immediately raised the alarm. If, as some evidence suggested, Caleb and Sarah were cool to the touch, they had presumably died some time earlier.

Paying attention to the gendered allocation of caregiving responsibilities within the Folbigg family also illuminates Craig Folbigg's role at trial. By the time that the trial began, Craig had come around to the belief that Kathleen had killed their children. He was a central witness for the prosecution, who relied upon his testimony to characterise Kathleen as an abusive parent with relatively few coping skills. Craig's position as an authority on Kathleen's mothering relied on the assumption that, as Kathleen's husband and the children's father, Craig possessed an inherent understanding of the family's domestic affairs. This assumption persisted despite the fact that Craig was generally working or sleeping while Kathleen cared for the children. Craig's testimony at trial was far more damning than his previous statements had been. His preparedness to acknowledge doubt or contradictory evidence correspondingly decreased. For Craig, as for the expert witnesses, the experience of testifying at trial seems to have been one of shifting towards a more extreme position.

Prior work on motherhood and criminal law has tended to focus on understanding why a mother might harm or kill her children. This book addresses how an accused mother's failure to meet hegemonic expectations can inform the process of proving that she has murdered her children.[25] In chapters six and seven, I observe that the *Folbigg* trial enacted a narrower and less flexible ideology of motherhood than might operate within broader society. This flattening of the normative expectations of motherhood may be a common feature of the criminal trials of mothers.[26] Extending this study to similar cases would provide an opportunity to assess whether mother-defendants are subjected to more rigid standards

---

[25] See also F Raitt and MS Zeedyk, 'Mothers on Trial: Discourses of Cot Death and Munchausen's Syndrome by Proxy' (2004) 12 *Feminist Legal Studies* 257.

[26] Anecdotal support for the proposition comes from my earlier research into the Chamberlain case: E Cunliffe, 'Weeping on Cue: The Socio-legal Construction of Motherhood in the Chamberlain Case' (LLM thesis, University of British Columbia, 2003); and my as yet unpublished research into the *Matthey, Clark* and *Cannings* cases.

than their peers who are not suspected of criminal behaviour. In this trial, Folbigg's occasional resistance to mothering overshadowed indicia that she was a competent mother. Evidence that Folbigg fed and clothed her children appropriately, related well to them, and that the children seemed happy in her presence was rendered marginal. Instead, her occasionally expressed ambivalence about mothering became a personal failing and a motive to commit murder. This ambivalence was tied to action by Craig's new accounts at trial of Kathleen's physical aggression towards Sarah and Laura and by some passages in the diaries.

Chapter seven focuses particularly on Folbigg's diaries and the uses to which these diaries were put within her trial. The prosecution depicted the diaries as akin to a mind-reading machine, suggesting that they contained direct admissions that Folbigg had killed her children. Despite the troubling nature of some of the diary entries, it is difficult to untangle expressions of emotional guilt from admissions of criminal action. Words such as 'guilt', 'blame' and 'responsible' perform dual work in society's shared vocabularies of moral responsibility and factual causation.[27] Folbigg insists that when she used those words in her diary, she did not mean that she had in fact killed her children, nor that she had ever physically harmed them. Rather, she felt emotionally responsible for their deaths and second-guessed whether their deaths could have been avoided with more attentive care. She also questioned whether their lived environment might have been improved if she had exercised greater emotional self-control. It seems overly simplistic to approach Folbigg's diaries as if they provide an unvarnished account of her consciousness. As Patricia Ewick and Susan Silbey have reminded us, even the most personal narratives express 'ideological effects and hegemonic assumptions'.[28] Folbigg's diary provides many glimpses of a person who tried hard to live up to the expectations society imposes on mothers and women.

Women's personal narratives are admissible, relevant evidence in a trial such as Folbigg's, when the diarist is the accused. It is not adequate simply to hope that they will not be used unjustly. The defence was correct to point at trial to the complicated relationship between literal and emotional truth. More work needs to be done on how one might interpret women's narratives fairly within the inherently coercive environment of a criminal trial. I suggest several preliminary interpretive principles in the conclusion to chapter seven. These principles are designed to avoid the risks of pathologising women's emotional lives. They seek to respect women's capacity to define their own meanings. They also attempt to avoid assessing women's narratives according to the degree to which they comply with the normative expectations of gender performance. Above all, they insist upon a distinction between frustration or anger expressed within what Folbigg once called 'bloody books'[29] and action that

---

[27] For instance, the sense of self-blame that a parent often experiences upon a sudden infant death should be distinguished from the proposition that a parent's actions or neglect physically caused an infant's death.

[28] P Ewick and S Silbey, 'Subversive Stories and Hegemonic Tales: Towards a Sociology of Narrative' (1995) 29 *Law & Society Review* 197, 210.

[29] L Knowles, 'I'm the Most HATED Woman Alive' *Daily Telegraph* (9 July 2003) 1 and 4–5.

physically harms a child. Within Folbigg's journal, it seems that 'losing it' with her children consisted of getting frustrated and walking away. At trial, with the benefit of the new evidence provided by Craig, that phrase came to mean physically harming her children.

The NSW Court of Criminal Appeal felt that Folbigg's diaries:

> . . . gave terrible credibility and persuasion to the inference, suggested by the overwhelming weight of the medical evidence, that the five incidents had been anything but extraordinary coincidences unrelated to acts done by the appellant.[30]

This passage constructs the diary evidence as subsidiary to an overwhelming medical case. It is difficult to accept that the diaries compensate for other uncertainties within the case, given that our cultural scripts simply do not tell us how a mother might respond to losing multiple infants to natural causes. As the English Court of Appeal observed in *Cannings*, much depends on one's starting point:

> If . . . the deaths were natural, virtually anything done by the mother on discovering such shattering and repeated disasters would be readily understandable as personal manifestations of profound natural shock and grief.[31]

The common law insists that we begin from this premise. The burden remains with the prosecution to prove an unnatural cause of death from scientific or behavioural evidence, or both. In light of the discussion contained in this book, it is appropriate to revisit the question of whether the evidence for Folbigg's conviction is as conclusive as appeal courts previously believed.

V. Newspaper Reporting

The press reporting overwhelmingly represented Folbigg's guilt as certain. While I expected that the newspapers might use prosecution actors as primary definers, I was surprised by the extent to which both newspapers ignored the defence's work in court. This inattention is apparent from both numeric and qualitative comparisons between the transcripts and news items. Witnesses who testified favourably to the defence case were either not reported or represented as supporting the prosecution theory. In this case, the press reporting attended far more closely to the prosecution case than to the defence. Within individual news items and over the life of the story, this created the impression that Folbigg had little or no answer to the allegations made against her.

The *Sydney Morning Herald* did emphasise different aspects of the case from the *Daily Telegraph*, but these differences were largely stylistic. Both newspapers presented Folbigg's diaries as a window into Folbigg's experience of motherhood and especially into her inadequacies as a mother. Neither newspaper adequately

[30] *R v Folbigg* (above n 10) para 132.
[31] *Cannings* (above n 4) para 11.

explained the nature of the defence objections to the prosecution's medical reasoning. The guilty verdict was claimed as a vindication of dogged medical and police investigations. Journalists portrayed the jury's verdict as a victory of common sense over judicial compunctions about such matters as the relevance of Kathleen's family history. Although both newspapers reported some of the issues that arose at trial regarding Craig Folbigg's credibility, he was ultimately constructed as another of Kathleen's victims. A difficult and complicated trial thereby became a relatively straightforward morality tale about the kind of mother who is likely to harm or kill her children.

Press reports form an important source of knowledge about criminal trials. Perhaps most importantly, these reports are a means by which law's ideological messages are disseminated to a broader public. A methodology that compares daily transcripts with news items provides one way to measure whether press reports convey information about criminal trials neutrally and impartially. Given that most people will never learn about most cases in any other way, it matters tremendously to investigate how well the media discharges its asserted commitment to balance. In this example, balance was notably absent.

VI. Conclusion

It is not possible to understand the *Folbigg* case without appreciating the mutually constitutive, mutually reinforcing nature of the discourses conducted within and between medicine, law and the media. Tracing the multiple relationships across these fields through a detailed analysis of textual records, as this book has done, makes sense of the permeability of medical, legal and journalistic knowledge. This approach allows one to move away from stereotyped understandings of each of these fields as independent from the others. The ways in which medicine, law and the media work together to construct hegemonic accounts are more complex than previous treatments of unexplained infant death allow.

The boundaries between medical expertise, legal fact-finding and media discourses are not fixed. In a complex criminal trial, these boundaries are constantly negotiated and redrawn. A text-based methodology that looks behind judgments allows one to displace ready certainties about criminal guilt, medicine and motherhood. Comparing medical literature, transcripts and press reporting is laborious and time consuming and therefore best suited to case studies. Nonetheless, it allows researchers to explore empirically how law valorises and translates some extra-legal knowledges while decontextualising and disapproving others.

Connecting the court records and medical literature with press reporting about a case, it becomes possible to identify the messages about medicine and law that are conveyed to a broader public. Research of this kind may contribute to countering the punitive demands made within public discourses regarding unexplained infant death. The legal, medical and social enquiry should focus on the limits of current knowledge rather than compensating for uncertainties in scientific evidence with the ambiguous personal narratives or disputed behaviour of individual mothers. Any alternative approach replaces real and continuing uncertainty with a conviction that runs too great a risk of being wrong.

BIBLIOGRAPHY

Alder, C and Polk, K, *Child Victims of Homicide* (Cambridge, Cambridge University Press, 2001).

Allison, DB and Roberts, M, *Disordered Mother or Disordered Diagnosis? Munchausen by Proxy Syndrome* (London, Analytic Press, 1998).

American Academy of Pediatrics (AAP), 'Prolonged Infantile Apnoea' (1985) 76 *Pediatrics* 129.

——, 'Distinguishing Sudden Infant Death Syndrome from Child Abuse Fatalities' (2001) 107 *Pediatrics* 437.

——, 'The Changing Concept of Sudden Infant Death Syndrome: Diagnostic Coding Shifts, Controversies Regarding the Sleeping Environment, and New Variables to Consider in Reducing Risk' (2005) 116 *Pediatrics* 1245.

——, 'Distinguishing Sudden Infant Death Syndrome from Child Abuse Fatalities' (2006) 118 *Pediatrics* 421.

Anderson, T, Schum, D and Twining, W, *Analysis of Evidence*, 2nd edn (Cambridge, Cambridge University Press, 2005).

Appell, AR, 'Protecting Children or Punishing Mothers: Gender, Race, and Class in the Child Protection System' (1997) 48 *South Carolina Law Review* 577.

Arnestad, M, Vege, Å and Rognum, TO, 'Evaluation of Diagnostic Tools Applied in the Examination of Sudden Unexpected Deaths in Infancy and Early Childhood' (2002) 125 *Forensic Science International* 262.

Asch, SS, 'Crib Deaths: Their Possible Relationship to Post-partum Depression and Infanticide' (1968) 35 *Mt Sinai Hospital Journal of Medicine* 214.

Ashe, M, 'The "Bad Mother" in Law and Literature: A Problem of Representation' (1992) 43 *Hastings Law Journal* 1017.

Attarian, HP (ed), *Sleep Disorders in Woman* (New Jersey, Humana Press, 2006).

Australian Bureau of Statistics, *Causes of Infant and Child Deaths* (Canberra, Australian Government Publishing Service, 1998).

——, *Mortality and Morbidity: Infant Mortality* (Canberra, Australian Government Publishing Service, 2002), www.abs.gov.au/Ausstats.

——, *SIDS in Australia 1981–2000: A Statistical Overview* (Canberra, Australian Government Publishing Service, 2003).

Australian Law Reform Commission (ALRC) et al, 'Uniform Evidence Law', ALRC Report No 102 (Sydney, Australian Government Printing Service, 2005).

Australian Press Council, 'Statement of Principles', www.presscouncil.org.au/pcsite/complaints/sop.html.

Axford, N and Bullock, R, *Child Death and Significant Case Reviews: International Approaches* (Edinburgh, Scottish Executive, 2005).

Ayres, S, '[N]ot a Story to Pass On: Constructing Mothers Who Kill' (2004) 15 *Hastings Law Journal* 39.

Bacon, CJ, 'Standard System for Postmortem Examination and Certification Needs to be Agreed' (2000) 320 *British Medical Journal* 310.

——, 'Repeat Sudden Unexpected Deaths' (2005) 365 *The Lancet* 1137.

——, 'How Common is Repeat Sudden Infant Death Syndrome?' (2008) 93 *Archives of Disease in Childhood* 323.

——, 'Recurrence of Sudden Infant Death Syndrome' (2008) 122 *Pediatrics* 869.

Backhouse, C, *Petticoats and Prejudice: Women and Law in Nineteenth-Century Canada* (Toronto, Women's Press for the Osgoode Society, 1991).

——, *Colour Coded: A Legal History of Racism in Canada, 1900–1950* (Toronto, University of Toronto Press for the Osgoode Society, 1999).

Balfour, G and Comack, E, *Criminalizing Women* (Halifax, Fernwood Publishing, 2006).

Banaschak, S, Schmidt P and Madea, B, 'Smothering of Children Older than 1 Year of Age: Diagnostic Significance of Morphological Findings' (2003) 134 *Forensic Science International* 163.

Bass, M et al, 'Death Scene Investigation in Sudden Infant Death' (1986) 315 *New England Journal of Medicine* 100.

Baxter, J, Hewitt, B and Haynes, M, 'Life Course Transitions and Housework: Marriage, Parenthood, and Time on Housework' (2008) 70 *Journal of Marriage and Family* 259.

Baxter, J, Hewitt, B and Western, M, 'Post-Familial Families and the Domestic Division of Labor: A View From Australia' (2005) 36 *Comparative Journal of Family Studies* 583.

Beal, SM, 'Sleeping Position and Sudden Infant Death Syndrome (Letter)' (1988) 149 *Medical Journal of Australia* 562.

——, 'Sudden Infant Death Syndrome in Twins' (1989) 84 *Pediatrics* 1038.

——, 'A Scientific Review of the Association between Prone Sleeping Position and Sudden Infant Death Syndrome' (1991) 27 *Journal of Paediatrics and Child Health* 323.

Beal, SM, Baghurst, P and Antoniou, G, 'Sudden Infant Death Syndrome (SIDS) in South Australia 1968–97, Part 2: The Epidemiology of Non-Prone and Non-Covered SIDS Infants' (2000) 36 *Journal of Paediatrics and Child Health* 548.

Beal, SM and Blundell, H, 'Sudden Infant Death Syndrome Related to Position in the Cot' (1978) 2 *Medical Journal of Australia* 217.

——, 'Recurrence Incidence of Sudden Infant Death Syndrome' (1988) 63 *Archives of Disease in Childhood* 924.

Becker, H, 'Whose Side Are We On?' (1967) 14 *Social Problems* 239.

Beckwith, JB, 'Intrathoracic Petechial Hemmorhages: A Clue to the Mechanism of Death in Sudden Infant Death Syndrome?' (1988) 533 *Annals of New York Academy of Sciences* 35.

Berger, D, 'Child Abuse Simulating "Near-Miss" Sudden Infant Death Syndrome' (1979) *Journal of Pediatrics* 554.

Bergman, AB, 'Wrong Turns in Sudden Infant Death Syndrome Research' (1997) 99 *Pediatrics* 119.

Bergman, AB, Beckwith, JB and Ray, CG (eds), *Proceedings of the Second International Conference on the Causes of Sudden Death in Infants* (Seattle, University of Washington Press, 1970).

Betz, P, Hausmann, R and Eisenmenger, W, 'A Contribution to a Possible Differentiation between SIDS and Asphyxiation' (1998) 91 *Forensic Science International* 147.

Birch, H (ed), *Moving Targets: Women, Murder and Representation* (London, Virago Press, 1993).

Blair, PS and Fleming, PJ, 'Recurrence Risk of Sudden Infant Death Syndrome' (2008) 93 *Archives of Disease in Childhood* 269.

Bohnert, M, Große Perdekamp, M and Pollak, S, 'Three Subsequent Infanticides Covered up as SIDS' (2004) 119 *International Journal of Legal Medicine* 31.

Bools, CN, Neale, BA and Meadow, R, 'Co-morbidity Associated with Fabricated Illness (Munchausen Syndrome by Proxy)' (1992) 67 *Archives of Disease in Childhood* 72.

Bouchard, DF (ed), *Language, Counter-Memory, Practice* (Ithaca, Cornell University Press, 1977).

Boyd, SB, 'Some Postmodernist Challenges to Feminist Analyses of Law, Family and State: Ideology and Discourse in Child Custody Law' (1991) 10 *Canadian Journal of Family Law* 79.

——, 'Is There an Ideology of Motherhood in (Post)Modern Child Custody Law?' (1996) 5 *Social and Legal Studies* 495.

——, *Child Custody, Law, and Women's Work* (Toronto, Oxford University Press, 2003).

——, 'Demonizing Mothers: Fathers' Rights Discourses in Child Custody Law Reform Processes' (2004) 6 *Journal of the Association for Research on Mothering* 52.

Boyd White, J, 'Law as Rhetoric, Rhetoric as Law: The Arts of Cultural and Communal Life' (1985) 52 *University of Chicago Law Review* 684.

Boyle, C and MacCrimmon, M, 'To Serve the Cause of Justice: Disciplining Fact Determination' (2001) *Windsor Yearbook of Access to Justice* 55.

Boyle, C, MacCrimmon, M and Martin, D, *The Law of Evidence: Fact-Finding, Fairness and Advocacy* (Toronto, Emond Montgomery, 1999).

Boyle, C and Nyman, J, 'Finding Facts Fairly in Roberts and Zuckermann's *Criminal Evidence*' (2005) 2(2) *International Commentaries on Evidence* article no 3.

Bridges, GS and Myers, MA (eds), *Inequality, Crime and Social Control* (Boulder, Westview Press, 1994).

Brookman, F and Nolan, J, 'The Dark Figure of Infanticide in England and Wales' (2006) 21 *Journal of Interpersonal Violence* 869.

Brownley, MW and Kimmich, AB (eds), *Women and Autobiography* (Wilmington, DE, Rowman and Littlefield, 1999).

Bunkers, SL, '"Faithful Friend": Nineteenth-Century Midwestern American Women's Unpublished Diaries' (1987) 10 *Women's Studies International Forum* 7.

Burns, RP, *A Theory of the Trial* (Princeton, Princeton University Press, 1999).

Busby, K, 'Discriminatory Use of Personal Records in Sexual Violence Cases' (1997) 9 *Canadian Journal of Women and the Law* 148.

Byard, RW, 'Inaccurate Classification of Infant Deaths in Australia: A Persistent and Pervasive Problem' (2001) 175 *Medical Journal of Australia* 5.

Byard, RW and Beal, SM, 'Munchausen Syndrome by Proxy: Repetitive Infantile Apnoea and Homicide' (1993) 29 *Journal of Pediatrics and Child Health* 77.

——, 'Has Changing Diagnostic Preference Been Responsible for the Recent Fall in Incidence of Sudden Infant Death Syndrome in South Australia?' (1995) 31 *Journal of Paediatrics and Child Health* 197.

Byard, RW and Donald, TG, 'Initial Neurologic Presentation in Young Children Sustaining Inflicted and Unintentional Fatal Head Injury' (2006) 116 *Pediatrics* 1108.

Byard, RW and Krous, HF, 'Suffocation, Shaking or Sudden Infant Death Syndrome: Can We Tell the Difference?' (1999) 35 *Journal of Paediatrics and Child Health* 432.

——, *Sudden Infant Death Syndrome: Problems, Progress and Possibilities* (New York, Oxford University Press, 2001).

——, 'Pediatric Forensic Pathology in Crisis' (2004) 7 *Pediatric and Developmental Psychology* 212.

Byard RW, MacKenzie, J and Beal, SM, 'Formal Retrospective Case Review and Sudden Infant Death' (1997) 86 *Acta Paediatrics* 1011.

Cameron, JM, Johnson HRM and Camps, FE, 'The Battered Child Syndrome' (1966) 6 *Medicine, Science and the Law* 2.

Campbell, MJ et al, 'Recurrence Rates for Sudden Infant Death Syndrome (SIDS): The Importance of Risk Stratification' (2008) 93 *Archives of Disease in Childhood* 936.

Camps, FE and Carpenter, RG (eds), *Sudden and Unexpected Deaths in Infancy (Cot Deaths): Report of the Proceedings of the Sir Samuel Bedsor Symposium, Cambridge, 1970* (Bristol, Foundation for the Study of Infant Death, 1972).

Canadian Centre for Justice Statistics, 'Family Violence in Canada: A Statistical Profile' (Ottawa, Statistics Canada, 1998–2005), www.statcan.ca/english/freepub/85-224-XIE/free.htm.

Carlen, P, *Magistrates' Justice* (London, M Robinson, 1976).

Carpenter, RG et al, 'Repeat Sudden Unexpected and Unexplained Infant Deaths: Natural or Unnatural?' (2005) 365 *The Lancet* 29.

——, 'Authors' Reply' (2005) 365 *The Lancet* 1138.

Carrington, K and Hogg, R (eds), *Critical Criminology: Issues, Debates, Challenges* (Cullompton, Willan Publishing, 2002).

Chamberlain, L, *Through My Eyes: An Autobiography* (Port Melbourne, William Heinemann Australia, 1990).

Chan, W, Chunn, D and Menzies, R, *Women, Madness and the Law: A Feminist Reader* (London, Glasshouse Press, 2005).

Chunn, DE, Boyd, SB and Lessard H (eds), *Reaction and Resistance: Feminism, Law and Social Change* (Vancouver, University of British Columbia Press, 2007).

Chunn, DE and Lacombe, D (eds), *Law as a Gendering Practice* (Oxford, Oxford University Press, 2000).

Conley, J and O'Barr, W, *Just Words: Law, Language, and Power* (Chicago, University of Chicago Press, 2005).

Coghlin, AM, 'Regulating the Self: Autobiographical Performances in Outsider Scholarship' (1995) 81 *Virginia Law Review* 1231.

Collier, R '"Waiting till Father Gets Home": The Reconstruction of Fatherhood in Family Law' (1995) 4 *Social and Legal Studies* 5.

Cooney, M "Evidence as Partisanship" (1994) 28 *Law and Society Review* 833.

Craft, AW and Hall, DMB, 'Munchausen Syndrome by Proxy and Sudden Infant Death' (2004) 328 *British Medical Journal* 1309.

Creighton, SJ, 'Fatal Child Abuse: How Preventable Is It?' (1995) 4 *Child Abuse Review* 318.

Cunliffe, E, 'Weeping on Cue: The Socio-Legal Construction of Motherhood in the *Chamberlain* Case' (LLM Thesis, University of British Columbia, 2003).

——, 'Without Fear or Favour? Trends and Possibilities in the Canadian Approach to Expert Human Behaviour Evidence' (2006) 10 *International Journal of Evidence and Proof* 280.

——, '(This is Not a) Story: Using Court Records to Explore Judicial Narratives in R v Kathleen Folbigg' (2007) 27 *Australian Feminist Law Journal* 71.

Cunliffe, E and Cameron, A, 'Writing the Circle: Judicially Convened Sentencing Circles and the Textual Organisation of Criminal Justice' (2007) 19 *Canadian Journal of Women and the Law* 1.

Davies, M, *Delimiting the Law* (London, Pluto Press, 1996).

DeFrain, J, 'Learning about Grief from Normal Families: SIDS, Stillbirth, and Miscarriage' (1991) 17 *Journal of Marital and Family Therapy* 215.

de Kock L, 'New Nation Writers Conference in South Africa' (1992) 23 *Ariel: A Review of International English Literature* 29.

Derrida, J, 'Force of Law: The Mystical Foundation of Authority' (1990) 11 *Cardozo Law Review* 920.

Diamond EF, 'In Five Consecutive Siblings Sudden Infant Death' (1986) 170 *Illinois Medical Journal* 33.

DiMaio, D and DiMaio, V, *Forensic Pathology*, 1st edn (New York, Elsevier, 1989).

DiMaio, V, 'SIDS or Murder' (1988) 81 *Pediatrics* 747.

——, 'Letter' (1995) 96 *Pediatrics* 168.

——, 'Repeat Sudden Unexpected Infant Death' (2005) 365 *The Lancet* 1137.

DiMaio, VJ and DiMaio, D, *Forensic Pathology*, 2nd edn (Boca Raton, CRC Press, 2001).

Dreyfus, H and Rabinow, P (eds), *Michel Foucault: Beyond Structuralism and Hermeneutics* (Chicago, University of Chicago Press, 1982).

Duggan, L, *The Twilight of Equality? Neoliberalism, Cultural Politics, and the Attack on Equality* (Boston, Beacon Press, 2003).

Eades, D, 'I Don't Think it's an Answer to the Question: Silencing Aboriginal Witnesses in Court' (2000) 29 *Language in Society* 161.

Eagleton, T, *Ideology: An Introduction* (London, Verso, 1991).

Eaton, M, *Justice for Women? Family, Court and Social Control* (Milton Keynes, Open University Press, 1986).

Edmond, G, 'Azaria's Accessories: The Social (Legal-Scientific) Construction of the Chamberlains' Guilt and Innocence' (1998) 22 *Melbourne University Law Review* 396.

——, 'Constructing Miscarriages of Justice: Misunderstanding Scientific Evidence in High-Profile Criminal Appeals' (2002) 22 *Oxford Journal of Legal Studies* 53.

Emery, JL, 'The Deprived and Starved Child' (1978) 18 *Medicine, Science and the Law* 138.

——, 'Infanticide, Filicide, and Cot Death' (1985) 60 *Archives of Disease in Childhood* 505.

——, 'Families in which Two or More Cot Deaths have Occurred' (1986) i *The Lancet* 313.

——, 'Child Abuse, Sudden Infant Death Syndrome, and Unexpected Infant Death' (1993) 147 *American Journal of Diseases of Children* 1097.

——, 'Cot Death and Child Abuse' (1993) 1 *Bailliere's Clinical Paediatrics* 235.

Emery, JL, Gilbert, EF and Zugibe, F, 'Three Crib Deaths, a Babyminder and Probable Infanticide' (1988) 28 *Medicine Science and the Law* 205.

Emery, JL and Taylor, EM, 'Investigation of SIDS' (1986) 315 *New England Journal of Medicine* 1676.

Emery, JL and Waite, AJ, 'These Deaths Must be Prevented without Victimising Parents' (2000) 320 *British Medical Journal* 310.

Erickson, M, *Science, Culture and Society: Understanding Science in the Twenty-First Century* (Cambridge, Polity, 2005).

Ericson, RV, 'Mass Media, Crime, Law and Justice: An Institutional Approach' (1991) 31 *British Journal of Criminology* 219.

——, 'The Decline of Innocence' (1994) 24 *University of British Columbia Law Review* 367.

Ericson, R, Baranek, P and Chan, J, *Representing Order: Crime, Law, and Justice in the News Media* (Toronto, University of Toronto Press, 1991).

Ericson, R and Haggerty, KD, *Policing the Risk Society* (Toronto, University of Toronto Press, 1997).

Ewick, P and Silbey, SS, 'Subversive Stories and Hegemonic Tales: Towards a Sociology of Narrative' (1995) 29 *Law and Society Review* 197.

——, *The Common Place of Law: Stories from Everyday Life* (Chicago, University of Chicago Press, 1998).

Falagas, ME et al, 'Comparison of PubMed, Scopus, Web of Science and Google Databases' (2008) 22 *FASEB Journal* 338.

Fineman, MA and Karpin, I (eds), *Mothers in Law: Feminist Theory and the Legal Regulation of Motherhood* (New York, Columbia University Press, 1995).

Firstman, R and Talan, J, *The Death of Innocents: A True Story of Murder, Medicine, and High-Stakes Science* (New York, Bantam Books, 1997).

Fitzpatrick, P, *Modernism and the Grounds of Law* (Cambridge, Cambridge University Press, 2001).

Fitzpatrick, P (ed), *Dangerous Supplements: Resistance and Renewal in Jurisprudence* (London, Pluto Press, 1991).

Fleming, PJ et al, 'Categories of Preventable Infant Death' (1991) 66 *Archives of Disease in Childhood* 170.

——, *Sudden Unexpected Deaths in Infancy: The CESDI SUDI Studies 1993–1996* (London, The Stationery Office, 2000).

Fraser, H, 'Issues in Transcription: Factors Affecting the Reliability of Transcripts as Evidence in Legal Cases' (2003) 10 *International Journal of Speech Language and the Law* 203.

Freedman DP, Frey, O and Zauhar, FM, *The Intimate Critique: Autobiographical Literary Criticism* (Durham and London, Duke University Press, 1993).

Garland, D, *The Culture of Control: Crime and Social Order in Contemporary Society* (Oxford, Oxford University Press, 2001).

Gavigan, S, 'The Criminal Sanction as it Relates to Reproduction' (1984) 5 *Journal of Legal History* 20.

——, 'Law, Gender, and Ideology' in Bayevsky, A (ed), *Legal Theory Meets Legal Practice* (Edmonton, Academic Printing and Publishing, 1988).

——, 'Paradise Lost, Paradox Revisited: The Implications of Familial Ideology for Feminist, Lesbian and Gay Engagement to Law' (1993) 31 *Osgoode Hall Law Journal* 589.

Geertz, C, *The Interpretation of Cultures: Selected Essays* (London, Hutchinson and Co, 1973).

Gibbons, J, *Forensic Linguistics: An Introduction to Language in the Justice System* (Malden, Blackwell, 2003).

Goodrich, P, *Languages of Law: From Logics of Memory to Nomadic Masks* (London, Weidenfeld and Nicolson, 1990).

Gordon, C (ed), *Power/Knowledge: Selected Interviews and Other Writings, 1972–1977* (Brighton, Harvester Press, 1980).

Gornall, J, 'Was Message of Sudden Infant Death Study Misleading?' (2006) 333 *British Medical Journal* 1165.

Gold, AD, *Expert Evidence in Criminal Law: The Scientific Approach* (Toronto, Irwin Law, 2003).

Goldwater, PW, 'Sudden Infant Death Syndrome: A Critical Review of Approaches to Research' (2003) 88 *Archives of Disease in Childhood* 1095.

Gotell, L, 'When Privacy Is Not Enough: Sexual Assault Complainants, Sexual History Evidence, and the Disclosure of Personal Records' (2006) 43 *Alberta Law Review* 743.

Goudge, ST, *Inquiry into Pediatric Forensic Pathology in Ontario Report* (Toronto, Queen's Printer for Ontario, 2008).

Grant, I, Chunn, D and Boyle, C, *The Law of Homicide* (Scarborough, Carswell, 1994).

Green, MA, 'A Practical Approach to Suspicious Death in Infancy: A Personal View' (1999) 51 *Journal of Clinical Pathology* 561.

Gregory, GJ, 'Citation Study of a Scientific Revolution: Sudden Infant Death Syndrome' (1983) 5 *Scientometrics* 313.

—— , 'Influence of the Public on a Scientific Revolution: The Case of Sudden Infant Death Syndrome' (1990) 11 *Science Communication* 248.

Gunteroth, WG, Lohmann, R and Spiers, PS, 'Risk of Sudden Infant Death Syndrome in Subsequent Siblings' (1990) 116 *Journal of Pediatrics* 520.

Haack, S, *Defending Science within Reason: Between Scientism and Cynicism* (Amherst, Prometheus Books, 2003).

Hacking, I, *The Social Construction of What?* (Cambridge, MA, Harvard University Press, 1999).

Hall, S et al, *Policing the Crisis: Mugging, The State, and Law and Order* (London, Macmillan, 1978).

Haltom, W and McCann, M, *Distorting the Law: Politics, Media, and the Litigation Crisis* (Chicago, University of Chicago Press, 2004).

Hamer, D, 'Similar Fact Reasoning in *Phillips*: Artificial, Disjointed and Pernicious' (2007) 30 *University of New South Wales Law Journal* 609.

Hans, V et al, 'Science in the Jury Box: Jurors' Views and Understanding of Mitochondrial DNA Evidence', Cornell Law School Research Paper 07-021 (SSRN).

Havill, A, *While Innocents Slept: A Story of Revenge, Murder, and SIDS* (New York, St Martins True Crime, 2002).

Hennessy, R and Ingraham, C (eds), *Materialist Feminism: A Reader in Class, Difference, and Women's Lives* (New York, Routledge, 1997).

Hick, JF, 'Sudden Infant Death Syndrome and Child Abuse' (1973) 52 *Pediatrics* 147.

—— , 'Very Important Erratum? Twenty Years Later' (1994) 93 *Pediatrics* 944.

Hill, R, 'Multiple Sudden Infant Deaths: Coincidence or Beyond Coincidence?' (2004) 18 *Paediatric and Perinatal Epidemiology* 320.

Hilton, JMN, 'Smothering and Sudden Infant Death Syndrome' (1989) 299 *British Medical Journal* 178.

Ho, HL, 'What Does a Verdict Do? A Speech Act Analysis of Giving a Verdict' (2006) 4 *International Commentary on Evidence.*

Hunt, A, 'Marxism, Law, Legal Theory and Jurisprudence' in P Fitzpatrick (ed), *Dangerous Supplements: Resistance and Renewal in Jurisprudence* (Durham, NC, Duke University Press, 1991) 102.

Hunt, A and Purvis, T, 'Discourse, Ideology, Discourse, Ideology, Discourse, Ideology . . .' (1993) 44 *British Journal of Sociology* 473.

Hunt, A and Wickham, G, *Foucault and the Law: Towards a New Sociology of Governance* (London, Pluto Press, 1994).

Hunt, CE and Brouilette, RT, 'Sudden Infant Death Syndrome: 1987 Perspective' (1987) 110 *Journal of Pediatrics* 669.

—— , 'Methylxanthine Treatment in Infants at Risk for Sudden Infant Death Syndrome' (1988) 533 *Annals of the New York Academy of Science* 119.

Hymel, KP and American Academy of Pediatrics (AAP), 'Distinguishing Sudden Infant Death Syndrome from Child Abuse Fatalities' (2006) 118 *Pediatrics* 421.

Irenyi, M, Kovacs, K and Richardson, N, *Fatal Child Abuse* (Melbourne, Australian Institute of Family Studies, 2008).

Irgens, LM, Skjaerven, R and Peterson, DR, 'Prospective Assessment of Recurrence Risk in Sudden Infant Death Syndrome Siblings' (1984) *Journal of Pediatrics* 349.

Jackson, M (ed), *Infanticide: Historical Perspectives on Child Murder and Concealment, 1550–2000* (Aldershot, Ashgate, 2002).

Jasanoff, S, *Science at the Bar: Law, Science and Technology in America* (Cambridge, MA, Harvard University Press, 1995).

——, *States of Knowledge: The Co-Production of Science and Social Order* (London, Routledge, 2004).

——, 'Representation and Re-presentation in Litigation Science' (2008) 116 *Environmental Health Perspectives* 123.

Johnson, MP and Hufbauer, K, 'Sudden Infant Death Syndrome as a Medical Research Problem since 1945' (1982) 30 *Social Problems* 65.

Johnson, R, *Taxing Choices: The Intersection of Class, Gender, Parenthood and the Law* (Vancouver, University of British Columbia Press, 2003).

Jonge, JG and Engelberts, AC, 'Cot Deaths and Sleeping Position (Letter)' (1989) ii *The Lancet* 1149.

Josselson, R and Lieblich, A, *The Narrative Study of Lives* (London, Sage, 1993).

Katz, J, 'What Makes Crime "News"'? (1987) 9 *Media, Culture and Society* 47.

Kaufman, F, 'Report of the Commission on Proceedings involving Guy Paul Morin' (Ottawa, 1998), www.attorneygeneral.jus.gov.on.ca/english/about/pubs/morin/.

Kelly, D, 'SIDS or Murder? Reply to Vincent DiMaio' (1988) 81 *Pediatrics* 747.

Kelly, KD, '"You Must Be Crazy if You Think You were Raped": Reflections on the Use of Complainants' Personal and Therapy Records in Sexual Assault Trials' (1997) 9 *Canadian Journal of Women and the Law* 178.

Kempe, CH et al, 'The Battered-Child Syndrome' (1962) 181 *Journal of the American Medical Association* 105.

Kennedy, H, *Sudden Unexpected Death in Infancy: A Multi-Agency Protocol for Care and Investigation* (London, Royal College of Pathologists and Royal College of Paediatrics and Child Health, 2004).

de Kock, L, 'New Nation Writers Conference in South Africa' (1992) 23 *Ariel: A Review of International English Literature* 29.

Kramar, KJ, *Unwilling Mothers, Unwanted Babies: Infanticide in Canada* (Vancouver, University of British Columbia Press, 2005).

Krongrad, E, 'Infants at High Risk for Sudden Infant Death Syndrome??? Have They been Identified??? A Commentary' (1991) 88 *Pediatrics* 1274.

Krous, HJ et al, 'Sudden Infant Death Syndrome and Unclassified Sudden Infant Deaths: A Definitional and Diagnostic Approach' (2004) 114 *Pediatrics* 234.

Krous, HF, Byard, RW and Rognum, TO, 'Pathology Research into Sudden Infant Death Syndrome: Where Do We Go From Here?' (2004) 114 *Pediatrics* 492.

Krugman, RD, 'Landmarks in Child Abuse and Neglect: Three Flowers in the Desert' (1998) 102 *Pediatrics* 254.

Kuhn, TS, *The Structure of Scientific Revolutions*, 3rd edn (Chicago, University of Chicago Press, 1996).

Kukull, WA and Peterson, DR, 'Sudden Infant Death and Infanticide' (1977) 106 *American Journal of Epidemiology* 485.

L, JF, 'A Housewife is Convicted of Murdering Her Five Children' (1995) 95 *Pediatrics* A32.

——, 'Mothers Who Murder Their Children' (1996) 98 *Pediatrics* A38.

Landry, D and Maclean, G (eds), *The Spivak Reader* (New York and London, Routledge, 1995).

Lansdowne, R, 'Infanticide: Psychiatrists in the Plea Bargaining Process' (1990) 16 *Monash Law Review* 41.

Lawrence, R, 'Understanding Fatal Assault of Children: A Typology and Explanatory Theory' (2004) 26 *Children and Youth Services Review* 837.

Leadbetter, S and Knight, B, 'SIDS and Suffocation' (1989) 299 *British Medical Journal* 455.

Leask J and Chapman, S, '"The Cold Hard Facts": Immunisation and Vaccine Preventable Diseases in Australia's Newsprint Media, 1993–1998' (2002) 54 *Social Science and Medicine* 445.

Ledwon, L, 'Diaries and Hearsay: Gender, Selfhood and the Trustworthiness of Narrative Structures' (2000) 73 *Temple Law Review* 1185.

Lempert, R, 'Telling Tales in Court: Trial Procedure and the Story Model' (1991) 13 *Cardozo Law Review* 559.

Leo, RA, 'Rethinking the Study of Miscarriages of Justice: Developing a Criminology of Wrongful Conviction' (2005) 21 *Journal of Contemporary Criminal Justice* 201.

Levene, S and Bacon, CJ, 'Sudden Unexpected Death and Covert Homicide in Infancy' (2004) 89 *Archives of Disease in Childhood* 443.

Levi, JN and Walker, AG (eds), *Language in the Judicial Process* (New York, Plenum Press, 1990).

Little, GA and Brooks, JG, 'Accepting the Unthinkable' (1994) 94 *Pediatrics* 748.

——, 'Reply to DiMaio and Samuels and Southall' (1995) 96 *Pediatrics* 168.

Lothian, LA, 'Mapping Contesting Terrain: The Doctrine of Failure to Protect in Canadian Criminal Law' (LLM Thesis, University of British Columbia, 2002).

Lupton, D and McLean, J, 'Representing Doctors: Discourses and Images in the Australian Press' (1998) 46 *Social Science and Medicine* 947.

MacCrimmon, MT, 'Fact Determination: Common Sense Knowledge, Judicial Notice, and Social Science Evidence', International Commentary on Evidence (1998), www.bepress.com/ice/vol1/iss1/art2/.

Malloy, MH and MacDorman, M, 'Changes in the Classification of Sudden Unexplained Infant Deaths: United States, 1992–2001' (2005) 115 *Pediatrics* 1247.

McClain, PW et al, 'Estimates of Fatal Child Abuse and Neglect, United States, 1979–1988' (1993) 91 *Pediatrics* 338.

Meadow, R, 'Munchausen Syndrome by Proxy: The Hinterland of Child Abuse' (1977) 2 *The Lancet* 343.

——, 'Munchausen Syndrome by Proxy' (1982) 57 *Archives of Disease in Childhood* 92.

——, 'Fictitious Epilepsy' (1984) ii *The Lancet* 25.

——, 'ABC of Child Abuse: Suffocation' (1989) 298 *British Medical Journal* 1572.

——, 'Recurrent Cot Death and Suffocation' (1989) 64 *Archives of Disease in Childhood* 179.

——, 'SIDS and Suffocation: Author's Reply' (1989) 299 *British Medical Journal* 455.

——, 'Suffocation, Recurrent Apnea and Sudden Infant Death' (1990) 117 *Journal of Pediatrics* 351.

——, 'Unnatural Sudden Infant Death' (1999) 80 *Archives of Disease in Childhood* 7.

——, 'Different Interpretations of Munchausen Syndrome by Proxy' (2002) 26 *Child Abuse and Neglect* 501.

Menashe, D and Shamash, ME, 'The Narrative Fallacy' (2008) 3 *International Commentary on Evidence* 1.

Bibliography

Miller, WJ and Hill, GB, 'Prevalence of and Risk Factors for Sudden Infant Death Syndrome in Canada' (1993) 149 *Canadian Medical Association Journal* 629.

Minford, AMB, 'Child Abuse Presenting as Apparent "Near-Miss" Sudden Death Syndrome' (1981) 282 *British Medical Journal* 521.

Minow, M, 'Interpreting Rights: An Essay for Robert Cover' (1987) 96 *Yale Law Journal* 1860.

Mitchell, EA et al, 'Definition of Sudden Infant Death Syndrome: Keep Current Definition' (1994) 309 *British Medical Journal* 607.

Murdocca, C, 'The Racial Profile: Governing Race through Knowledge Production' (2004) 19 *Canadian Journal of Law and Society* 153.

Murphy, JC, 'Legal Images of Motherhood: Conflicting Definitions from Welfare "Reform", Family and the Criminal Law' (1998) 83 *Cornell Law Review* 688.

Nobles, R and Schiff, D, 'Misleading Statistics within Criminal Trials: The Sally Clark Case' (2005) 2 *Significance* 17.

Nolan, T, 'Depiction of the "CSI Effect" in Popular Culture: Portrait in Domination and Effective Affectation' (2007) 41 *New England Law Review* 575.

NSW Child Death Review Team (CDRT), *Fatal Assault of Children and Young People* (Sydney, NSW Commission for Children and Young People, 2002).

Nyman, J and Boyle, C, 'Finding Facts Fairly in Roberts and Zuckerman's Criminal Evidence' (2004) 2 *International Commentary on Evidence*, www.bepress.com/ice/vol2/iss2/art3/.

O'Halloran, RL et al, 'Child Abuse Reports in Families with Sudden Infant Death Syndrome' (1998) 19 *American Journal of Forensic Medicine and Pathology* 57.

Oren, J, Kelly, DH and Shannon, DC, 'Familial Occurrence of Sudden Infant Death Syndrome' (1987) 80 *Pediatrics* 355.

Panel on Justice and the Media, 'Report to the Ministry of the Attorney General for Ontario' (Toronto, August 2006).

Pearson, P, *When She was Bad: How and Why Women Get Away with Murder* (Toronto, Vintage Canada, 1998).

Pennington, N and Hastie, R, 'A Cognitive Theory of Juror Decision Making: The Story Model' (1991) 13 *Cardozo Law Review* 519.

Peterson, DR, Chinn, NM and Fisher, LD, 'The Sudden Infant Death Syndrome: Repetitions in Families' (1980) 97 *Journal of Pediatrics* 265.

Peterson, DR, Sabotta, EE and Daling, JR, 'Infant Mortality among Subseqent Siblings of Infants who Died of Sudden Infant Death Syndrome' (1986) 108 *Journal of Pediatrics* 911.

Phillips, DP et al, 'Importance of the Lay Press in the Transmission of Scientific Knowledge to the Medical Community' (1991) 325 *New England Journal of Medicine* 1180.

Pinholster, G, 'SIDS Paper Triggers a Murder Charge' (1994) 264 *Science* 197.

——, 'Multiple "SIDS" Case Ruled Murder' (1995) 268 *Science* 494.

Pollack, HA, 'Changes in the Timing of SIDS deaths in 1989 and 1999: Indirect Evidence of Low Homicide Prevalence among Reported Cases' (2006) 20 *Pediatric and Perinatal Epidemiology* 2.

Prentice, MA, 'Prosecuting Mothers who Maim and Kill: The Profile of Munchausen Syndrome by Proxy Litigation in the Late 1990's' (2001) 28(3) *American Journal of Criminal Law* 373.

Pue, WW, 'In Pursuit of Better Myth: Lawyers' Histories and Histories of Lawyers' (1995) 33 *Alberta Law Review* 730.

Pue, WW, 'The War on Terror: Constitutional Governance in an Age of Perpetual Warfare?' (2003) 41 *Osgoode Hall Law Journal* 267.

Raitt, F and Zeedyck, MS, 'Mothers on Trial: Discourses of Cot Death and Munchausen's Syndrome by Proxy' (2004) 12 *Feminist Legal Studies* 257.

Rambaud, C, Guilleminault, C and Campbell, P, 'Definition of Sudden Infant Death Syndrome' (1994) 308 *British Medical Journal* 1439.

Raring, RS, *Crib Death: Scourge of Infants, Shame of Society* (Hicksville, NY, Exposition Press, 1975).

Reece, H (ed), *Law and Science: Current Legal Issues, 1998* (Oxford, Oxford University Press, 1998).

Rich, A, *Of Woman Born: Motherhood as Experience and Institution* (New York, WW Norton and Co, 1986).

Roberts, D, 'Motherhood and Crime' (1993) 79 *Iowa Law Review* 95.

—— , 'Welfare Reform and Economic Freedom: Low-Income Mothers' Decisions about Work at Home and in the Market' (2004) 44 *Santa Clara Law Review* 1029.

Roberts, J et al, 'Is There a Link between Cot Death and Child Abuse?' (1984) 289 *British Medical Journal* 789.

Roberts, P, 'Science in the Criminal Process' (1994) 14 *Oxford Journal of Legal Studies* 469.

Roberts, RF, Innes, KC and Walker, SM, 'Introducing ICD-10-AM in Australian Hospitals' (1998) 169 *Medical Journal of Australia* S32.

Robertson, G and Nichol, A, *Media Law* (London, Sweet and Maxwell, 2002).

Robertson, S, 'What's Law Got to Do with It? Legal Records and Sexual Historys' (1995) 14 *Journal of the History of Sexuality* 161.

Rosen, CL et al, 'Two Siblings with Recurrent Cardiorespiratory Arrest: Munchausen Syndrome by Proxy or Child Abuse?' (1983) 71 *Pediatrics* 715.

Rosen, CL, Frost, JD and Glaze, DG, 'Child Abuse and Recurrent Infant Apnea' (1986) 109 *Journal of Pediatrics* 1065.

Rosenberg, DA, 'Web of Deceit: A Literature Review of Munchausen Syndrome by Proxy' (1987) 11 *International Journal of Child Abuse and Neglect* 547.

Samuels, MP et al, 'Fourteen Cases of Imposed Upper Airway Obstruction' (1992) 67 *Archives of Disease in Childhood* 162.

Samuels, MP and Southall, DA, 'Child Abuse and Apparent Life-Threatening Events' (1995) 96 *Pediatrics* 167.

Sanders, J, 'Kumho and How We Know' (2001) 64 *Law and Contemporary Problems* 373.

Sarat, A, 'Rhetoric and Remembrance: Trials, Transcription, and the Politics of Critical Reading' (1999) 23 *Legal Studies Forum* 355.

Sarat, A and Kearns, T (eds), *History, Memory and the Law* (Ann Arbor, University of Michigan Press, 1999).

Sarnikar, S, Sorenson, T and Oaxaca, RL, 'Do You Receive a Lighter Prison Sentence because You Are a Woman? An Economic Analysis of Federal Criminal Sentencing Guidelines', Institute for the Study of Labor Discussion Paper No 2870 (Bonn, June 2007).

Savage, R, 'The Sudden Death of a Child' (2004) 328 *British Medical Journal* 7435.

Scheppele, KL, 'Facing Facts in Legal Interpretation' (1990) 30 *Representations* 42.

Schklar, J and Seidman Diamond, S, 'Juror Reactions to DNA Evidence: Errors and Expectancies' (1999) 23 *Law and Human Behavior* 159.

Schwarz, LL and Isser, NK, *Child Homicide: Parents who Kill* (Boca Raton, Taylor and Francis, 2007).

Schwarz, PJ, Southall, DP and Valdes-Dapena, M (eds), special issue of *Annals of the New York Academy of Science* entitled 'The Sudden Infant Death Syndrome: Cardiac and Respiratory Mechanisms and Interventions' (1988) 533 *Annals of the New York Academy of Science.*

Seglan, PO, 'Why the Impact Factors of Journals should Not be Used for Evaluating Research' (1997) 314 *British Medical Journal* 497.

Sesardic, N, 'Sudden Infant Death or Murder? A Royal Confusion about Probabilities' (2007) 58 *British Journal for the Philosophy of Science* 299.

Shannon, DC and Kelly, DH, 'SIDS and Near-SIDS' (1982) 306 *New England Journal of Medicine* 1022.

Silbey, JM, 'Cross-Examining Film' (2009) 8 *University of Maryland Law Journal of Race, Religion, Gender and Class* 101.

Silbey, SS (ed), *Law and Science Volume I: Epistemological, Evidentiary and Relational Engagements* (Aldershot, Ashgate, 2008).

Silbey, SS (ed), *Law and Science Volume II: Regulation of Property, Practices and Products* (Aldershot, Ashgate, 2008).

Simon, J, 'Crime, Community, and Criminal Justice' (2002) 90 *Californian Law Review* 1415.

—— , 'Governing through Crime Metaphors' (2002) 67 *Brooklyn Law Review* 1035.

Smart, C, 'Woman of Legal Discourse' (1992) 1 *Social and Legal Studies* 29.

Smart, C and Brophy, J (eds), *Regulating Womanhood: Historical Essays on Marriage, Motherhood and Sexuality* (London, Routledge, 1992).

Smith, DE, *The Conceptual Practices of Power: A Feminist Sociology of Knowledge* (Toronto, University of Toronto Press, 1990).

—— , *Texts, Facts and Femininity: Exploring the Relations of Ruling* (London, Routledge, 1990).

—— , *Writing the Social: Critique, Theory and Investigations* (Toronto, University of Toronto Press, 1999).

—— , *Institutional Ethnography: A Sociology for People* (Lanham, MD, AltaMira Press, 2005).

—— (ed), *Institutional Ethnography as Practice* (Lanham, Rowman and Littlefield, 2006).

Southall, DP, 'Two-Year Study of the Causes of Postperinatal Deaths Classified in Terms of Preventability' (1983) 58 *Archives of Disease in Childhood* 75.

—— , 'Role of Apnea in the Sudden Infant Death Syndrome: A Personal View' (1988) 81 *Pediatrics* 73.

Southall, DP et al, 'Apnoeic Episodes Induced by Smothering: Two Cases Identified by Covert Video Surveillance' (1987) 294 *British Medical Journal* 1637.

—— , 'Covert Video Recordings of Life-Threatening Child Abuse: Lessons for Child Protection' (1997) 100 *Pediatrics* 735.

Southall, DP, Samuels, MP and Stebbens, VA, 'Smothering and Sudden Infant Death Syndrome' (1989) 299 *British Medical Journal* 178.

Spender, D, 'Journal on a Journal' (1987) 10 *Women's Studies International Forum* 1.

Spinelli, MG, *Infanticide: Psychosocial and Legal Perspectives on Mothers who Kill* (Washington, DC, American Psychiatric Publishing, 2003).

—— , 'Infanticide: Contrasting Views' (2005) 8 *Archives of Women's Health* 15.

Spivak, GC, 'Can the Subaltern Speak?' in Nelson, C and Grossberg L (eds), *Marxism and the Interpretation of Culture* (Urbana, University of Illinois Press, 1988) 271.

Stanley, FJ and Byard, RW, 'The Association Between Prone Sleeping Position and Sudden Infant Death Syndrome (SIDS): An Editorial Overview' (1991) 27 *Journal of Paediatric and Child Health* 325.

Stanton, AN, 'Sudden Unexpected Death in Infancy Associated with Maltreatment: Evidence from Long-Term Follow-Up of Siblings' (2003) 88 *Archives of Disease in Childhood* 699.

Stanton, J and Simpson, A, 'Murder Misdiagnosed as SIDS: A Perpetrator's Perspective' (2001) 85 *Archives of Disease in Childhood* 454.

—— , 'Filicide: A Review' (2002) 25 *International Journal of Law and Psychiatry* 1.

Steinschneider, A, 'Prolonged Apnea and the Sudden Infant Death Syndrome: Clinical and Laboratory Observations' (1972) 50 *Pediatrics* 646.

—— , 'Reply to John F Hick' (1973) 52 *Pediatrics* 147.

Stenson, K and Sullivan, RR (eds), *Crime, Risk and Justice: The Politics of Crime Control in Liberal Democracies* (Cullompton Devon, Willan Publishing, 2001)

Strang, H, *Children as Victims of Homicide* (Canberra, Australian Institute of Criminology, 1996).

Supreme Court of New South Wales, 'Annual Review 2002', www.lawlink.nsw.gov.au/lawlink/supreme_court/ll_sc.nsf/pages/SCO_annual_review_2002.

—— , 'Annual Review 2005', www.lawlink.nsw.gov.au/lawlink/Supreme_Court/ll_sc.nsf/pages/SCO_annual_review_2005.

Swift, KJ, *Manufacturing 'Bad Mothers': A Critical Perspective on Child Neglect* (Toronto, University of Toronto Press, 1995).

Taylor, EM and Emery, JL, 'Two-Year Study of the Causes of Postperinatal Deaths Classified in Terms of Preventability' (1982) 57 *Archives of Disease in Childhood* 668.

—— , 'Categories of Preventable Infant Deaths' (1990) 65 *Archives of Disease in Childhood* 535.

Thearle, MJ and Gregory, H, 'Evolution of Bereavement Counselling in Sudden Infant Death Syndrome, Neonatal Death, and Stillbirth' (1992) 28 *Journal of Paediatrics and Child Health* 204.

Valdes-Dapena, M, 'Sudden Infant Death Syndrome: A Review of the Medical Literature, 1974–1979' (1980) 66 *Pediatrics* 597.

—— , 'The Pathologist and the Sudden Infant Death Syndrome' (1982) 106 *American Journal of Pathology* 118.

—— , 'The Sudden Infant Death Syndrome: Pathologic Findings' (1992) 19 *Clinics in Perinatolology* 701.

Valverde, M, *Law's Dream of a Common Knowledge* (Princeton, Princeton University Press, 2003).

Waite, A et al, 'Report on 5000 Babies Using the CONI (Care of Next Infant) Programme' (University of Sheffield, 1998).

Walker, S, *The Law of Journalism in Australia* (Sydney, Law Book Company, 1989).

Ward, CA, *Attitudes toward Rape: Feminist and Social Psychological Perspectives* (London, Sage, 1995).

Washer, P, 'Representations of SARS in the British Press' (2004) 59 *Social Science and Medicine* 2561.

Watkins, SJ, 'Conviction by Mathematical Error?' (2000) 320 *British Medical Journal* 2.

Wearing, B, *Ideology of Motherhood: A Study of Sydney Suburban Mothers* (Sydney, Allen and Unwin, 1984).

Weisman, R, 'Showing Remorse: Reflections on the Gap between Expression and Attribution in Cases of Wrongful Conviction' (2004) 46 *Canadian Journal of Criminology and Criminal Justice* 121.

—— , 'Showing Remorse at the TRC: Towards a Constitutive Approach to Reparative Discourse' (2006) 24 *Windsor Yearbook of Access to Justice* 221.

Wetlaufer, GB, 'Rhetoric and its Denial in Legal Discourse' (1990) 76 *Virginia Law Review* 1545.

White, H, *The Content of the Form* (Baltimore, John Hopkins University Press, 1987).

Wilczynski, A, *Child Homicide* (London, Greenwich Medical Media, 1997).

Willinger, M, James, LS and Catz, C, 'Defining the Sudden Infant Death Syndrome (SIDS): Deliberations of an Expert Panel Convened by the National Institute of Child Health and Human Development' (1991) 11 *Pediatric Pathology* 677.

Willinger, M, Hoffman, HJ and Hartford, RB, 'Infant Sleep Position and Risk for Sudden Infant Death Syndrome: Report of Meeting Held January 13 and 14 1994, National Institute of Health, Bethesda, MD' (1994) 93 *Pediatrics* 814.

Wishart, D, 'The Selectivity of Historical Representation' (1997) 23 *Journal of Historical Geography* 111.

Wittgenstein L, *Philosophical Investigations* (Oxford, Blackwell, 1958).

Wolkind, S et al, 'Recurrence of Unexpected Infant Death' (1993) 82 *Acta Paediatrics* 873.

Wrennall, L, 'Munchausen Syndrome by Proxy/Fabricated and Induced Illness: Does the Diagnosis Serve Economic Vested Interests, Rather Than the Interests of Children?' (2007) 68 *Medical Hypotheses* 960.

Wigglesworth, JS, 'Pathological Investigations in Cases of Sudden Infant Death' (1987) *Journal of Clinical Pathology* 1481.

Wynne, B, 'Knowledges in Context' (1991) 16 *Science, Technology and Human Values* 111.

Young NH, *Innocence Regained: The Fight to Free Lindy Chamberlain* (Sydney, Federation Press, 1989).

APPENDIX
CHRONOLOGY OF FOLBIGG
CHILDREN'S LIVES AND DEATHS

The following chronology of the Folbigg children's lives, deaths and ascribed causes of death is drawn from autopsy reports and death certificates contained in the case files of *R v Kathleen Megan Folbigg*, New South Wales Supreme Court, 1 Apr–21 May 2003, Barr J presiding. The *Folbigg* case files are held by the NSW Court of Criminal Appeal registry under file numbers 60496 of 2002, 2002/70046, 60279 of 2004 and 2004/1814.

Name	Date of Birth	Date of ALTE*	Date of Death (Age at Death)	Ascribed Cause of Death
Caleb Folbigg	1 February 1989	–	20 February 1989 (19 days)	Sudden infant death syndrome (SIDS)
Patrick Folbigg	3 June 1990	18 October 1990	13 February 1991 (Eight months)	On death certificate: Asphyxia due to airway obstruction; epileptic fits On autopsy report: Encephalopathic disorder leading to seizures; underlying cause of encephalopathy not determined on autopsy; asystolic cardiac arrest at home leading to death
Sarah Folbigg	14 October 1992	–	30 August 1993 (10½ months)	Sudden infant death syndrome (SIDS)
Laura Folbigg	7 August 1997	–	1 March 1999 (19 months)	Undetermined

* 'ALTE' stands for 'acute life-threatening episode'. For discussion of the term, see above ch 1, n 19.

INDEX